*This book is dedicated to the memory of Fred Wostbrock,
the best friend that TV game shows ever had.*

ACKNOWLEDGMENTS

Thank you to David Baber, Emory and Henry College librarian and a fellow author (*Television Game Show Hosts: Biographies of 32 Stars*, published by McFarland) for unlimited generosity and enthusiasm for this project, including access to numerous newspaper and magazine clippings as well as academic research papers.

Thank you also to my parents: my father, Roger Nedeff, a historian and research wizard in his own right, for helping me with access to the bulk of the newspaper articles used in the making of this book, and my mother, Linda Nedeff, who checked for clarity and aptness of thought.

Rosanne Ullman and Robben Barquist did the proofreading, and were both good sports about it.

Thank you also to quiz bowl historian Tom Michael, who oversees the Facebook page *College Bowl Valhalla,* for his valuable contributions regarding the early history of *College Quiz Bowl* and *G.E. College Bowl.*

Thank you to Mary Alice Moore at Mineral Point Library for the time and effort she gave in supplying samples of Allen Ludden's personal papers. Mineral Point Library is the home of the Allen Ludden Archive, an impressive treasure trove of photos, clippings, scripts, and other artifacts from Allen's life, donated by Betty White, all available to the public for viewing. Please pay them a visit if the opportunity ever presents itself.

Thank you to Brendan McLaughlin for his impressive collections of data regarding Allen's shows and guest appearances.

A special tip of the hat to Chris Lambert, who came up with the title.

And thank you most of all to Fred Wostbrock for his generosity and his enthusiasm in helping me salute this wonderful performer.

FRED WOSTBROCK COLLECTION

INTRODUCTION

Betty White is a pop culture institution, there's no arguing that. Generations have watched her on television, on *Life with Elizabeth*, *Date with the Angels*, *The Betty White Show*, *The Mary Tyler Moore Show*, hundreds of commercials, and virtually every talk show, variety show, and game show spanning the first 70 years of television.

From the 1980s onward, though, there was a consistent element of the characters she depicted: On *The Golden Girls* and *The Golden Palace*, she was Rose Nylund from St. Olaf, who spoke lovingly of her departed husband Charlie. On *Mama's Family*, she was Ellen Jackson, divorcee. In the film *Lake Placid* (1999), she was the crocodile advocate whose husband died under mysterious circumstances. On *Hot in Cleveland*, she was Elka Ostrovsky, a feisty widow.

And her public image isn't that much different. She's posed in a variety of tongue-in-cheek publicity stills surrounded by buff young studs. And when she walks a red carpet, she walks it alone. Two generations of TV lovers can't picture Betty White walking arm-in-arm with anybody. She's on her own.

But once upon a time, it was impossible to imagine Betty White without somebody. In public, she was always arm-in-arm with a special man. They did talk show interviews together. They competed together — and sometimes against each other — on TV game shows. They crisscrossed the country, appearing on stage after stage in the lead roles of one play or another. The man in Betty White's life was Allen Ludden.

For nearly twenty years, "Allen Ludden and Betty White," or "Betty White and Allen Ludden," either way, their names were almost always spoken together, as if they formed a single long word. As far as star power was concerned, they were equals, with credentials that complemented each other nicely. She was a primetime star; he dominated daytime and weekends. She acted on television; he appeared on television almost exclusively as himself. The general public saw her as a funny lady; they saw him as a professorial type. They were the most perfect yin and yang that television ever brought together.

Allen Ludden died in 1981, and Betty picked up the pieces and moved on with her career. Despite the projects they had pursued as a couple, their entertainment industry legacies were distinctive, even contrasting. She co-starred on a handful of acclaimed primetime shows that enjoyed decades of extended life in reruns, while he thrived largely on game shows which, by and large, didn't earn that kind of adulation. Ultimately, Betty, through no extraordinary effort other than continuing to perform decades after her husband's death, eclipsed her husband professionally.

Fans of Betty White, therefore, may know little to nothing about the husband she so adored — the educator and pioneer broadcaster who starred in one of the most popular daytime programs in history and was co-creator of an iconic competition measuring academic achievement. For fans of TV game shows, though, Allen Ludden is an old friend that you remember — or may have forgotten until now. His life was cut short, but his story is long with insight into the workings of both mid-20th century television and the rare commodity of a happy Hollywood marriage.

Allen, age five (circled), and a number of other kids in Mineral Point dressed up and staged an informal parade to promote a neighborhood entrepreneur's new soft drink. PHOTO PROPERTY OF THE MINERAL POINT HISTORICAL SOCIETY — MINERALPOINTHISTORY.ORG

CHAPTER ONE

"NAME"

The Ellsworths and the Luddens lived in two very different worlds.

Reuben and Charlotte Coker Ellsworth were farmers in Cobb, Wisconsin. Reuben's parents had been early settlers in southwest Wisconsin, arriving in 1846. Charlotte's grandparents, Pierre and Sarah Calame, were there even earlier, putting up a log cabin in Clifton in 1836. Pierre, an immigrant born in Bordeaux, France, was described in a magazine article as a "colorful Frenchman of the early days who possessed such remarkable strength that he once carried a wood beam fourteen-inch stubble plow, weighing about 150 pounds, home from Galena, forty miles, on his shoulder, making the journey both ways afoot."

In 1889, Reuben and Charlotte Ellsworth, along with their four daughters, uprooted to Nebraska. In 1892 the Ellsworths welcomed a son, Elmer. By 1900, when Reuben and Charlotte were awaiting the arrival of their tenth child, the whole clan returned to Iowa County, Wisconsin, and moved into a piece of property called Spensley Farm. Young Elmer loved the farm and quite literally left his mark on it. Decades later, the family living in the house pointed out numerous spots in the barn with "EE" carved into the wood work, and the attic still boasted a large "ELMER ELLSWORTH" painted on one wall.

Whatever you could say about the Ellsworths' life on the farm, you couldn't call it boring. Broken arms and legs were a stunningly common occurrence every winter, as the ten children enjoyed riding toboggans down the steep hill behind the farm and could not be discouraged from the activity, no matter how many fractures they accumulated. Most of the boys lost fingers during woodworking accidents, too. While Elmer managed to keep all of his fingers, keeping him in shoes was another matter. Elmer wore out his leather shoes faster than his parents could afford to replace them. A nearby farmer cut up his copper washboiler — a machine that boiled laundry — and used the strips to patch up Elmer's shoes.

After Elmer finished high school in 1912, he settled into a job as an ice dealer, carving his blocks from a pond near the family farm. In June of 1915, Elmer married his high school sweetheart, a farmer's daughter named Leila M. Allen, and together they brought a son into the world, Allen Packard Ellsworth, on October 5, 1917. The family prepared for the quiet, normal life of an ice dealer and his wife raising an infant son.

The Ludden family, on the other hand, never needed copper strips attached to their shoes. They were prosperous and prominent. The name "Ludden" carried a lot of weight in Wisconsin.

Homer Ludden was born in Chicago in 1872. He received an M.D. from the University of Chicago and interned at St. Mary's Hospital in Milwaukee before moving in 1906 to Mineral Point, Wisconsin, where he became a general practitioner. While maintaining his general practice, he found time to serve as a member of the school board, a member of the park board, president of the Farmers Savings Bank, president of the Iowa County Medical Society, trustee of the Iowa County Hospital and Home, member of the American Medical Association, lifetime member of the Wisconsin State Medical Society, chief of staff at St. Joseph's Hospital in Dodgeville (where the medical library is now named for him) and, for two terms, mayor of Mineral Point. He was so revered that, when he attempted to retire from medicine in 1947, the town rejected the retirement. Patients kept calling his office to make appointments, and Dr. Homer Ludden continued practicing for eight more years after the "retirement."

Homer's nephew, Homer J. Ludden, became an electrical engineer in the early 20th century, at a time when "electrical engineer" was a newly designated line of work. He entered into a business partnership with a renowned Wisconsin businessman and politician, W.A. Jones, and together they essentially bought electricity, acquiring the distribution rights from the Mineral Point Zinc Works and turning Mineral Point into an electric city. Before long, Ludden and Jones had seen to it that every home had electric lights, electric appliances, electric heating and even air conditioning. Record books from the period indicate that Homer J. Ludden was probably making $300 a month from the partnership (adjusted for inflation, about $8,000 a month today). By 1907, Jones had sold his share of the business to Ludden, who enjoyed several years of being the sole purveyor of electricity for Mineral Point.

In 1919, Elmer Ellsworth died in the influenza epidemic. After Elmer's death, newly widowed Leila moved in with her parents at 307 South Iowa Street, bringing her young son Allen into a bulging household that also included Leila's parents Charles and Clara Allen, Leila's sister Bessie, and a pair of boarders — two women who taught at the neighborhood school. Two-and-a-half-year-old Allen was tended to, and pampered by, this team of five women and one man.

Homer J. Ludden had seen action in World War II and just finished his military assignment in France when he returned to Mineral Point and moved in down the street from the Allen house to 201 South Iowa Street. He'd attended the same high school with Elmer and Leila, and considered Elmer his best friend. When Leila moved into the neighborhood, Homer courted her and won her over. In October 1920, Homer J. Ludden and Leila M. Allen Ellsworth were married in Janesville. After they were wed, Homer legally adopted Leila's son, whose name was changed to Allen Ellsworth Ludden.

Allen rarely talked about his own childhood, but his mother was eager to tell people what kind of little boy she had raised.

"[His] imagination was always rather keen," Leila remembered in a 1948 interview. "He's been directing somebody…all his life."

That trait was on display one weekend during her courtship with Homer, when Leila brought four-year-old Allen along on a visit she made to Chicago, about a one-day drive at the time. Together, mother and son saw a play, *Lightnin'*. Character actor Frank Bacon played the role of Lightnin' Bill Jones, a swift-footed, lovable liar who got himself into a series of predicaments. It was a tremendously popular show in its time, setting a Broadway record for longevity with 1,291 performances at Gaiety Theatre. The play left an impression on Allen. Whereas most children enamored of a play would want to be one of the performers onstage, little Allen grasped that somebody, unseen to him, had told the actors what to say and where to stand, and he wanted that job. He told his mother he wanted to be a director in the theater.

Allen was also fearless around strangers from an early age, always enthusiastic about getting to know them. Leila said, "Allen…always liked to be with people, to hear them talk."

After Homer and Leila were married and added Allen's half-brother Franklin a year later, the family moved around quite a bit, briefly living in the Wisconsin towns of Janesville, Elkhorn, Antigo, and Waupaca before moving south to Corpus Christi, Texas, where they remained from the time that Allen turned fifteen. Throughout his teenage years, though, Allen continued to spend his summer vacations in Janesville, Wisconsin.

Homer found a job as an engineer for the Central Power & Light Company, while Leila settled into making a new home for her family.

Allen attended Corpus Christi High School where, before long, he found a girlfriend, Margaret Frances McGloin. In a way, Allen had fallen for a girl like his mother; Margaret's family had deep roots in the state. Her great-great-great grandfather had co-founded the McMullen/McGloin Colony. And, much like the Ludden family that Leila and Allen were now part of, Margaret's family had an upper-class pedigree. As a teenager, Margaret attended, and sometimes organized, lavish parties and luncheons that got write-ups in the society section of the local newspaper. It was her knack for putting together social engagements that won Allen's heart. Margaret and her mother gave Allen a surprise party for his fifteenth birthday.

Allen fit in, with a stepfather and step-granduncle who were educated, prominent, and respected. They were innovators, pioneers, renaissance men.

In later years Allen would recall that, throughout elementary school and junior high school, he was a quiet loner. It wasn't until he moved to Corpus Christi and entered high school that he came out of his shell and blossomed. Showing a knack for performing, Allen joined the Presbyterian Church Dramatic Club and starred in a production called *Hell Bent for Heaven*. In his senior year, he performed in a school production of *Drums of Death*. When Corpus Christi High School staged a variety show for fundraising, Allen took to the stage, the sole tenor performing with a group of ten girls, to sing "Darkness on the Delta" and "Sweetheart Darling." He also sang for First Presbyterian Church; his singing talents were so appreciated that instead of the customary "Here Comes the Bride" on the organ, brides at the church would walk down the aisle as Allen performed a solo. He eventually worked his way up to the position of director for the church choir and, at school, of business manager for the school newspaper. Allen liked being in charge.

That's why he was so crushed by the only significant setback he experienced in high school. The nearby Edison High School had a group called The Congress Society; as Allen recalled later, it was similar to a fraternity for high school students, and it blackballed him when he applied for membership. This disappointment remained a sore spot for Allen for years afterward. For all the recognition and accolades that he received as a singer and actor, when Allen looked back on his high school years he could never shake the sting he felt when he was rejected by The Congress Society.

Allen finished high school in 1934 but, at his father's insistence, he waited a while before enrolling in college.

Allen later explained, "My father believed, and so do I now, that most people shouldn't go to college right after they leave high school...Too many people go too young."

Homer Ludden passed down the opinion that a high school graduate who went straight to college after summer vacation didn't give college the serious consideration that it deserved, because it felt like just beginning another school year. The student would treat the first two years like high school and buckle down and get serious during junior year, but the student could never get back those first two years. Homer felt that high school graduates should take a year off altogether from education and spend it exploring the real world — what's referred to today as a "gap year."

Allen spent his gap year exploring what he might want to do with his life. He knew that making a career of acting was a long shot and considered other lines of work. He gave thought to becoming a lawyer, a teacher, or a salesman. It gradually dawned on him that all of those professions involved acting anyway, and he thought he'd be happy in any of them.

College would wait a second year as Allen sold office supplies for the Jack Bonner Company, and then went to work selling clothes at a couple of department stores. By 1936, he and his father agreed that it was time for higher education, and Allen enrolled at Sul Ross State Teachers College in Alpine, Texas.

He quickly assembled a full schedule of classes and extracurricular activities. Shortly before making the move from Corpus Christi to Alpine, Allen joined Le Cercle Francais, a small club conducted exclusively in French and formed for members to exchange stories. At Sul Ross, he pledged Alpha Psi Omega. Meanwhile, his high school sweetheart Margaret remained in Corpus Christi and was named Duchess (most popular) at Corpus Christi Junior College.

Allen got busier during his sophomore year at Sul Ross. He was named president of the Alpine Pioneer Club, a group devoted to preserving customs, costumes, and native dances from the early history of the southwest U.S. He was president of the school's Glee Club, on staff at the school's yearbook *The Brand*, and a member of the school's Mask and Slipper Dramatic Club, where he starred in *Romeo and Juliet*. But Allen's greatest performance at the school was as a student. He made honor roll again and again, with grades that put him in the top ten percent for the entire school.

After his sophomore year, Allen transferred to the University of Texas in Austin, enrolling in the School of Arts and Sciences with a major in English.

"I don't believe in drama majors," he later explained. "I don't believe in giving a college degree for make-up and set design...I found that the drama curriculum, at that time, allowed for no electives. That's a mistake."

Allen recalled later that he was profoundly influenced by one professor, Dr. Harry Ransom, who Allen said taught him the importance of sincerity.

"[Ransom] was one of the great influences in my life," Allen later told the school's alumni magazine. "Nobody exemplified excellence more than he did. I took Browning and Tennyson just because he taught them."

In Austin, Allen continued his heavy schedule of extracurricular activities. He joined the school's Curtain Club, not only as an actor but also taking the initiative to oversee publicity for each of the club's productions. He played Private Webster, the third corpse, in Irwin Shaw's *Bury the Dead*. Set during war time — which war is never expressly stated, but World War I is implied — the expressionist play presents six dead soldiers who resist their impending burials, rising from their graves one at a time to express their frustration at the futility of war and the thought that the women in their lives will move on without them. Private Webster confronts his wife, who complains that he never let her in on what he was thinking when they were married. Their conversation reveals that they tried to have children, but Webster was unable to make his wife pregnant. They commiserate about the friends and neighbors who were able to have children, and Webster finds himself sharing aspirations and frustrations with his wife that he could never bring himself to discuss while he was alive. The play was so well received that, after its initial run, the school revived it as part of an Armistice Day celebration the following November. Allen also played the role of Donald Navadel in another anti-war play, Robert E. Sherwood's *Idiot's Delight*.

The school's production of *Fashion* marked another highlight of Allen's collegiate acting career. Written by Anna Cora Mowatt and originally performed in 1845, *Fashion* was the first major American comedy written by a woman. The play chronicled the life of Elizabeth Tiffany, a shallow woman obsessed with the latest fashions and trends despite her minimal knowledge of the subject. (A running joke in the play is that she can't pronounce French terms.) Allen performed in the role of Colonel Howard, one of the only honorable and respected characters.

In between his performances, Allen tried his hand at directing shows for Austin's Little Theater, a community group of performers. As much as he appreciated the kind remarks for his acting abilities, it really wasn't what he wanted to do. The Little Theater gave him a chance to pursue his real ambition.

He later said, "I never wanted to be a performer. I wanted to be a producer-director."

The busier Allen got, the more he thrived as a student, and by his senior year he qualified for the elite Phi Beta Kappa scholastic fraternity, originated at the College of William and Mary in 1776 as America's first scholastic honor society. Liberal arts and sciences students were admitted if they consistently ranked in the top ten percent of their class. Recipients have gone onto renown as inventors (Eli Whitney, Samuel Morse), authors (Nathaniel Hawthorne, Henry Wadsworth Longfellow), politicians (John Calhoun, William Seward), and activists (W.E.B. DuBois, Gloria Steinem). Its members have included seventeen presidents, thirty-eight Supreme Court justices, 136 Nobel laureates...and one game show host.

On June 3, 1940, Allen received his diploma, one of 185 to graduate with honors in a class of 1,260. With World War II already underway in Europe, commencement address speaker Dr. Daniel Samper Ortega pondered that the fate of the entire world might be decided by a single, minute episode of conflict thousands of miles away. Dr. Ortega also implored the class to live and think rationally, urging them balance their sense of idealism with facts. He implored the graduates to use common sense and show "more faith in yourselves than in your arms."

Faith in himself wouldn't be a problem for Allen. By the time he graduated, he had made his name as a student, a singer, and an actor. He made living up to the family name look easy.

Just 165 miles southeast of Mineral Point, Wisconsin — so close and yet so far away — is a town near Chicago called Oak Park, Illinois. It's the birthplace of Edgar Rice Burroughs, Ernest Hemingway, and Frank Lloyd Wright. And it's where Horace White, an executive at Kraus Heinz Electrical Company, and his homemaker wife, Tess, welcomed a daughter into the world on January 17, 1922. You can learn a little something about Horace and Tess from the name they gave their daughter: Betty. Not Elizabeth. Her legal first name was a nickname. Horace and Tess liked the sound of "Betty" and decided to avoid the options inherent in the name "Elizabeth." Their daughter would never be "Liz," or "Ellie," or "Beth," but always "Betty." That's the way they liked it.

When the girl was barely two, Horace's bosses transferred their star employee (Horace specialized in outdoor lighting; among his career accomplishments, the Mormon temple in Salt Lake City), and the White family packed up and moved to California. Betty had a happy childhood. She was an only child and was on the receiving end of all of the love that Horace and Tess would have given to a larger family. Her mother in particular helped nurture a vivid imagination. Together, they played a game they called "Whatif" (they always said it as if it were a single word), in which they conjured up wild scenarios. They also would ask each other, "What would (famous person) do on his day off?" and try to come up with answers.

The Whites made frequent extended trips to the Sierra Mountains, where they would venture through the mountains as part of a pack train, riding horses or mules until they settled down on a prepared campground. They would remain there, living out of a tent, for about three weeks every year.

Horace and Tess had a sincere love for animals that they happily shared with Betty. Together, they helped Betty raise an imaginary horse that they called Bill Promise. On frequent long car trips to Carmel, a beautiful area of California about 320 miles north of Los Angeles, Horace would pretend to load Bill Promise in the car and make sure to

Betty as a child in Oak Park, Illinois.
PINTEREST

tie him to the bumper when they came to an extended stop. Betty was responsible for feeding the horse every night.

In many ways, Betty's parents were every child's dream come true. As she told Lifetime in 2000, "I was the luckiest little kid in the world... every once in a while, they would come home with [an animal] and say, 'He followed me home; can we keep him, Betty?'"

Homer, in particular, loved animals so much that he began a side business to care for pets abandoned during the Great Depression. Homer would build radios from scratch and trade it for a pet that a family couldn't afford to continue to support.

"The radios didn't eat, but the animals did," Betty remarked in 2000. "It wasn't the best business deal he ever made."

Despite their playful approach to parenting, Homer and Tess were serious about the lessons they tried to instill in Betty — mainly honesty. Tess once told her daughter, "Bets, you can lie to anyone in the world and even get away with it perhaps, but when you are alone and look into your own eyes in the mirror, you can't sidestep the truth. Always be sure you can meet those eyes directly. Otherwise, it's big trouble, my girl."

Growing up, Betty always had self-confidence, but she never really saw herself as pretty. The key offense, as she saw it, was a pair of annoying dimples, inconveniently placed directly next to her mouth.

During an interview with Kathy Whyde, she later ruminated about her dimples, "Isn't that always the way it goes? People who have them don't like them. People who don't wish they did…Maybe it's because when you're little, grown-ups make a great point of telling you how cute they are."

Betty received all of her formal education in Beverly Hills and initially envisioned a career as a writer. That plan changed her senior year of high school, when she wrote herself into the lead role of an original play for the school and became hooked on acting. She was also in a production of *Pride and Prejudice* and later cited that as the experience that made up her mind for good. She also sang, much like a fellow down in Texas did during his high school years. She sang at her high school graduation ceremony and briefly considered pursuing a career as an opera singer before admitting to herself that her voice wasn't quite good enough for that. However, just a month after her 1939 graduation, her voice earned her an invitation to sing for an experimental television broadcast.

For her performance, Betty climbed the stairs to the appointed building's sixth floor, proudly wearing the same dress that she had donned for graduation. She sang a song from *The Merry Widow* and did a waltz, while on the street level below her a screen was simultaneously showing her performance to entertain a crowd that had gathered for an auto show. The technology was new at the time, and the crowd expressed understandable excitement at the "miracle" of viewing something that was happening six stories above them.

Betty skipped college, enrolling instead in the Bliss-Hayden Little Theater Group, a local community group of performers.

FRED WOSTBROCK COLLECTION

CHAPTER TWO

"THEATERS"

After finishing up his work in the classroom, Allen got to work in the…well, in the classroom. Allen decided to earn his Master's Degrees at the University of Texas. With Dr. Harry Ransom's help, he received a fellowship and was given a fast-track to the degree in exchange for teaching. Allen quickly secured a job at Austin High School and spent a year teaching English and dramatics classes.

Although he had taken the job primarily as a means to an end, he admitted later that a classroom was a good fit for him. "I think I made a good teacher," he said. "It takes ham."

His teaching evolved. In 1972, when Allen looked back a few decades later at the way he had handled a classroom in the late 1930s, he said, "If, according to the new ideas, my teaching was different, we did a lot of innovating. I was doing it intuitively rather than with a lot of science."

Once the assignment was completed in 1941, Allen left Austin High School and the University of Texas with his Master's Degree. He headed back to Corpus Christi, where he took a job as an announcer and commercial salesman for a local radio station, KEYS-AM. By December, the world events that Dr. Ortega had predicted in his graduation address were erupting. Reeling from the Japanese attack on Pearl Harbor, the United States entered World War II. KEYS held a scrap rubber drive at a landmark on the Corpus Christi Marina called the "Peoples Street T-Head." Every day for a week, Allen was supposed to say, "Peoples Street T-Head," but, every day, Allen would say, "Teople Treat P-Head."

Within months, Allen's involvement in the war effort went beyond a scrap rubber drive, and he found himself in a theater that, a few years earlier, he probably hadn't planned on seeing: the Pacific theater of operations.

In California, Betty had amassed a bit of experience and praise for her emerging talents as an actress in the Bliss-Hayden Little Theater Group.

She tried to parlay it into a film career, making her way from studio to studio in Hollywood in search of a contract, an audition, anything. But she was bluntly told that she was too plain-looking to be a film star. Betty took the rejection in stride and decided that if film didn't want her, she would look for work in radio.

Radio welcomed her. She didn't make a lot of money — radio gigs paid as little as five dollars — but she was relentlessly enthusiastic, bouncing from station to station for any paying job she could grab, sometimes making announcements and delivering commercials, and other times providing something as minor as background noise for a scene set in a crowded room. She enjoyed the work and, although she wasn't being paid much, steady work in such an unsteady business gave her enough encouragement to stick with it. Nothing could pull her away from her goals. Except for World War II.

Allen enlisted in the Army at the end of 1941 and was assigned to a military base in Fargo, North Dakota. He hopped in his car and made the drive from Corpus Christi, Texas, to his new assignment. He almost didn't make it. As he was passing through Oklahoma, his car collided with a truck. Allen needed seventeen stitches on the side of his face and spent five days in an area hospital recuperating. Years after, he would occasionally tell the story while slowly running his hand down that side of his face, amazed that the incident left no permanent scarring.

Allen's half-brother Frank would enlist in the Army too; he would earn a Purple Heart for wounds received in Luxemburg, making him the only second-generation Purple Heart recipient in chapter 1919. He would set a record for achieving the rank of Master Sergeant faster than any other enlistee.

Allen eventually made it to Fargo to complete training. He returned to Corpus Christi just long enough to marry Margaret on October 11, 1943, shortly before reporting to his assignment in the Central Pacific Base Command — the Hawaiian Islands, and later the Marshall and Gilbert Islands. But he never saw the front lines of battle. The Army got to know Allen's background, his education, his directing experience with theater and music, and concluded that Allen was of more use as a morale officer.

Special Services, which the Army had initiated the previous year, was and still is something of a diversion department, organizing shows, sporting events, and social gatherings for soldiers. Allen was put in charge of staging and directing plays. His official title in the Army was

Officer-in-Charge of the Entertainment Section of the Pacific Ocean Areas. Allen later remembered it as the best job he ever had.

For the endeavor, Allen paired up with Maurice Evans. Born in England in 1901, Evans was a second generation actor who amassed an impressive list of credits in Shakespeare plays. He had played Romeo, Richard II, Hamlet, Falstaff, MacBeth, Iago, and Malvolio.

For the Army, Evans took pen in hand and wrote *GI Hamlet*, collaborating with Allen in hopes of making Shakespeare more appealing to the modern, young, mostly male audiences who made up the troops. Instead of setting it on a plain in Denmark, Evans set his version in a seaport where soldiers gathered before being shipped off to battle. The fencing scene takes place in a gym; Ophelia thumbs through a book of flower prints instead of holding a garland of posies. Evans added a brief waltz by the king after the murder of Hamlet's father to illustrate the king's callousness, and deleted the famous graveyard scene ("Alas, poor Yorick....") altogether because the scene contained jokes that he felt would have come across as "too corny" if he had tried to modernize them.

GI Hamlet was such a success that Evans made plans to bring it to Broadway as soon as the war ended. He and Allen decided to keep their partnership going for the rest of the war. Together, they produced and directed more than forty shows.

For the role of Laertes in *GI Hamlet*, Allen and Maurice cast a young writer from radio named Howard Morris who, at 120 pounds, cleared the Army's minimum weight requirement only because he drank an excessive amount of water on the day he enlisted. Morris' writing partner from New York City, Carl Reiner, had also enlisted and was on his way to an assignment. Before he left, Reiner went to see *GI Hamlet* in Hawaii to support his friend.

After the show, Morris told Reiner, "You have to audition for our unit."

"I can't," replied Reiner. "I'm shipping out." Reiner insisted that the audition was a waste of time when he didn't know where he would be stationed. He knew only that he could never join Special Services.

When Reiner mentioned the situation to another serviceman, Sol Pomerantz (who would be the namesake of a character on *The Dick Van Dyke Show*), Pomerantz convinced him to audition anyway.

"At least you'll know how good you are," Pomerantz reasoned.

Finally Reiner agreed to meet with Allen. He performed some jokes he had written, and he knew he had given a good audition.

Allen told Reiner, "We need you."

Reiner again said, "I can't. I'm leaving tomorrow."

Allen assured him, "We'll take care of it."

Reiner was going to be assigned to signal corps and was indeed ready to go, but Allen personally got on the phone and made a call to General Robert C. Richardson. In Reiner's words during an interview with TV historian Stu Shostak, Allen "traded him like a ballplayer" so Reiner could help the Special Services unit write shows for a full year. Reiner's unit, on the other hand, was assigned to Iwo Jima.

Allen and Maurice Evans were so pleased with the material that Reiner whipped up for his assignments that Evans agreed to show it to a producer, helping to kick-start the soldier's postwar career in comedy writing.

Decades later, Carl Reiner remembered, "I wouldn't have a career without Captain Ludden."

By the end of the war, Allen had made it to lieutenant, and then major. Maurice Evans left the military at the end of the war, leaving Allen to solely oversee Special Services during the following year. One year after the war ended, Major Allen Ludden returned to civilian life, bringing a Bronze Star with him as a souvenir. And with virtually all of Allen's prospects and experience laser-focused on theater, Allen and Margaret didn't move back to Texas after Allen's discharge; they moved to New York City.

Betty spent most of World War II in the American Women's Voluntary Services, delivering supplies to the soldiers in training in Los Angeles County. The assignment came with plenty of rec hall get-togethers, dances, and other social gatherings at night. During the day, Betty and the other AWVS volunteers would take care of alterations and sewing for the uniforms.

Within a year, Betty was engaged to a soldier named Paul who had won her over. After he shipped off to Italy, they wrote each other almost daily for two years until Betty, suddenly stricken by a bad case of cold feet, sent him a final letter, including her engagement ring with it. (Paul did have a happy ending — he married a woman whom he met while stationed in Italy, and the marriage lasted the rest of his life.)

In 1945, a few weeks after V-E Day, Betty married a P-38 pilot named Dick Barker. A few weeks after V-J Day, Barker left the military, and the newlyweds packed up and moved to Bell Center, Ohio, population 835. After spending nearly her entire life in the bustling metropolises of southern California, interspersed with vacations in the sprawling mountains up north, a tiny village in Ohio was a culture shock for Betty. Within a few months, the couple moved back to California together, but it didn't help. Dick and Betty divorced after six months.

Maurice Evans knew a good thing when he saw it, and the end of the war wasn't the end of his relationship with Allen Ludden. Evans hired Allen to manage his career, overseeing all of Evans' theatrical productions for the ensuing few years, including a national touring production of *GI Hamlet*. Allen also handled his friend's emerging career as a much sought-after guest lecturer at colleges. He worked as an "advance man," traveling ahead to the towns where Evans was booked to appear and generating publicity.

Allen in his natural habitat after the war. Whether preparing a lecture or a radio script, he'd get very well acquainted with his typewriter in the coming years. FRED WOSTBROCK COLLECTION

As in high school and college, Allen filled up every minute of free time. He made himself available as a freelance director for local productions of plays, sometimes traveling to do so. For several weeks, he resided in Middletown, New York, about seventy-five miles north of New York City, to direct a production of *Goodbye Again*. And he found some work as a performer, starring in summer stock productions in Princeton, New Jersey and Westport, Connecticut. He also traveled the country to raise funds for assorted causes by putting together variety shows presented at high schools and colleges and featuring area students, Army enlistees, and special guests from out of town.

It was Evans' guest lecturing gigs at colleges that sent Allen's career in a fateful direction. Evans fell ill one night, and since Allen was so knowledgeable about the subject matter himself, he delivered the lecture in Evans' place. The first time he did so, Allen felt that he needed to impress the audience right away and assure them that he was a smart fellow. He walked onstage clutching his Phi Beta Kappa key and feeling, by his own admission, somewhat superior.

And then he opened the floor to questions. As he recalled in 1962, "I didn't feel superior after those kids started asking questions! They were sharper than any adult group I had ever addressed."

Allen enjoyed the experience so much that he and Evans agreed to make the understudy duty a permanent arrangement. Whenever illness or inclement weather precluded Evans from making an engagement, Allen, in the area anyway because of his duties as the advance man, would deliver the lecture in his place. The plan worked so well that Evans stopped delivering the lectures altogether and focused on the stage performance. Allen would always deliver the lecture before the arrival of *GI Hamlet*. Allen, by his own estimation, would deliver his lecture a total of five hundred times, and later identified this as the most memorable experience of his pre-show business years.

Allen came into the lectures with confidence. He had unlocked the secret, he said, to delivering a good lecture, and it was a surprisingly straightforward one. "In my Shakespeare lectures, I'd get away from the lectern and walk slowly across the stage," he later explained. "If all those heads out there turned with me, then I knew I had them hooked."

Having studied the works of Shakespeare thoroughly and directed a few productions, Allen was eminently qualified to lecture on the topic, but he would always open the floor to questions after every one of those five hundred lectures, and every time, he was astounded by the amount of knowledge demonstrated by some of the high school and college students who attended. He remembered later that he had to rewrite some of his presentation to keep up with the audience's level of sophistication.

Allen said, "I thought the kids would be bored, but I found them to be the most alert, hungry-for-knowledge, receptive audience possible...I was amazed and delighted."

After a lecture in Hartford, Connecticut, one night, a local radio station, WTIC, offered Allen a job on the spot. It was a hard offer to ignore. It would allow Allen to settle down and establish roots somewhere and keep him close to summer stock opportunities. It was a stable, secure job offering a salary of $100 a week, which was a healthy sum of money at the time. And that was especially important because a few weeks before that particular lecture, Allen and Margaret received some news about what 1947 had in store for them: they were adding a baby to the family.

Betty had seemingly yelled out "Do-over!" and reset her life. She was single again. She was in Los Angeles again. She was pursuing an acting career again. She began attending a school/theater in Beverly Hills, paying $50 a month in tuition and acting in two shows before the head of the theater waived the tuition in return for her promise to continue to perform.

Betty did more radio shows, too. When she got hired to deliver a single line in a commercial on *The Great Gildersleeve,* she was told that

the show required its actors to join the union. She borrowed the induction money from her parents who, as usual, had no reservations about helping their daughter chase her goals. Her father playfully told her, "If you don't work too often, we can almost afford it!"

It was by accident that Betty received a role on *Blondie,* a radio show based on the comic strip. She walked in for the audition and was greeted by a roomful of confused faces because they were expecting another Betty White, who was also acting in southern California at the time. The "wrong" Betty won everybody over

Betty got a fresh start in California; newly single and pursuing a new career in radio. AUTHOR'S COLLECTION

and got the part. She also did a few small roles on *This Is Your FBI,* a program that offered her nothing more significant than passing lines like "Good morning!" or "Merry Christmas." But work was work, and radio kept offering it to Betty.

Her theater appearances included the plays *Spring Dance* and *Dear Ruth.* The money was still miniscule, but she kept at it, and it was a good thing, because *Dear Ruth* was about to bring a critical person into her life: a manager.

Most of the talent agencies in Los Angeles would send representatives to small theaters once in a while to see whether any potential stars were emerging from these tiny productions. One night during the run of *Dear Ruth,* agent Lane Allan liked what he saw in the woman playing

Ruth. After the production, he showed up backstage and invited Betty for a drink to talk business. Betty accepted, although she suspected that he had other "business" on his mind.

She was right, and before long, Homer and Tess White got the news about what 1947 had in store for them: they were adding a son-in-law to the family.

FRED WOSTBROCK COLLECTION

CHAPTER THREE

"MIND"

Allen Ludden and Maurice Evans amicably went their separate ways in 1947. Evans continued acting, remaining in theater but ultimately making his way into television (Samantha's father on *Bewitched*) and films (Dr. Zaius in the 1968 version of *Planet of the Apes*). Allen settled into Hartford with Margaret and got right to work at WTIC with a side job as a press agent for the Summer Theatre in nearby Ivoryton because, after all, Allen couldn't stand the thought of having one job.

Allen climbed the ladder quickly at WTIC, first becoming continuity director — the person in charge of messages and announcements between songs or between shows — and then program executive.

He would later credit his rapid rise to one executive in particular, Program Director Leonard "Pat" Patricelli, whose own employment had a colorful story. Straight out of college in 1929, Patricelli had gone to WTIC hoping to get hired as a scriptwriter. A vice president of the company that owned the station conducted the job interview and, seeing the resume and realizing that Patricelli had just finished college, jokingly asked, "Young man, did Hamlet feign insanity in his relationship with Ophelia?" Patricelli, a Shakespeare buff, surprised him by giving an off-the-cuff answer that took fifteen minutes. He was hired on the spot and made his way to the program director position fourteen years later.

Allen took his turn at hosting some of the shows that he developed. He synergized both of his jobs by creating a talk show, *Backstage*, on which all of his guests were performers at the Summer Theatre.

But in the nascent years of Allen's broadcasting career, one trait that served him extremely well was his strong, abiding respect for young people, particularly teenagers. He appreciated their intelligence and their sensibilities. Leonard Patricelli had an idea for a program that would challenge teenagers to solve other teens' problems. His theory was that young people rebelled because so much of what they were told to do was handed down by authority figures, and this rebellion could be curbed if the suggestions came from other youths. As Patricelli himself put it, the idea was to talk *with* youth, instead of talking *to* them or talking *at* them. Allen eagerly stepped forward to help shape the program.

With Allen's help developing the concept, Patricelli launched *Mind Your Manners*, named to reflect the intent of "combating juvenile delin-

A big break that Allen never really sought out, his popular radio show *Mind Your Manners*. Early in his career, Allen ditched the spectacles for publicity photos. FRED WOSTBROCK COLLECTION

quency by presenting positive means of instruction to the uninformed youngster." Each weekday at 4:30 p.m., Allen hosted the program, overseeing a panel of seven youngsters: six teenagers split evenly between boys and girls plus one pre-teen. Allen would suggest hypothetical situations, and the panel would discuss the proper way to handle it.

On the surface, it sounded exactly like a program that a group of adults in the 1940s would have developed for children. The show opened with the sound of a young voice proclaiming, "By golly, it's FUN to mind your manners!" And the show's boisterous announcer introduced Allen as "the man who makes manners fun!" In the beginning, that's what the people behind the show were probably expecting. Allen expected the teenagers' problems to be manageable issues like how to behave on a date. Like Patricelli, he hoped that the common sense solutions coming directly from other teenagers would be highly regarded.

As he told *The New York Times*, "If the idea that it is smart to mind your manners becomes the popular idea…good manners can become the normal behavior pattern for young people everywhere."

Allen encouraged listeners to send in questions, many of which were the type that Allen and Patricelli had predicted. But from the get-go, a check of the mail revealed that teenagers faced much more complicated and serious dilemmas than the adults had assumed. Rather than steer clear of the heavy topics, Allen and *Mind Your Manners* tackled them head-on. The "little things" and the big head-scratchers were given equal consideration each week.

In one episode, a fourteen-year-old girl wrote in to complain that, when walking together on a sidewalk, her boyfriend would walk on her wrong side. One of the girls on the panel dismissively answered, "Well, there's nothing a girl can do. She just has to let him stay there. It would be impolite to say to get on the other."

In the same episode, a young teen girl asked for advice about how to react to a gift of lingerie from her boyfriend, and a boy wanted to know whether kids could help to curtail racially driven unrest. Allen came to enjoy grilling the teens about current events to see how they viewed the problems of the world.

The panelists could be extremely blunt when they felt that a letter writer was misguided. Allen once read a letter from a lonely girl who said, "I'm not popular because I don't smoke like the others."

One of the panelists immediately jumped in and said, "I don't think smoking or not smoking has anything to do with it. That girl better find the real reason why she's not popular!"

They had a sense of humor, too. One fretful girl wrote in advance of a double date, concerned that the other couple might be planning to park and make out. The letter writer wasn't ready to take her own relationship that far yet and wanted to know how to handle that scenario should it arise.

A boy on the panel advised her to tell her date, "Let's sit back and watch!"

Once in a while, Allen would be so touched by a listener's letter that he'd reply with a personal letter or even a gift. He once sent an encouraging letter and a record player to a boy who was afraid of being called a sissy if he took his school's homemaking courses.

Mind Your Manners was meticulously cast. Allen had a picture in mind of exactly what type of teens he wanted to join the panel. A press release described them this way: "They are six typical teen-agers with varying social background, but with one thing in common. They are the popular boy and girl…the 'hero' and 'heroine' with the personality to lead their contemporaries. They are not 'Quiz Kids.' *Mind Your Manners* panel members are genuine…normal…happy…and bright enough to speak up and say what they think. They're the sort of youngsters that grown-ups like, too…the kind of teen-agers you'd want your youngsters to turn to for counsel…the kind of teen-agers you want your youngsters to be!" Allen's rather ingenious casting blurred the boundaries between high school cliques, giving more awkward teens, writing in anonymously, access to popular kids, who were sympathetic and eager to offer help.

Mind Your Manners was a fast success for Allen. Only three months after its premiere, word of mouth alone was strong enough for NBC's program department to take notice. In early March, NBC reviewed a presentation of the program made specifically for the network's consideration and, less than two weeks later, *Mind Your Manners* expanded from its Connecticut teenager base to become a national show broadcasting on NBC Radio from Hartford, Connecticut every Saturday at 9:30 a.m. The first NBC nationwide broadcast, on March 13, 1948, wouldn't be the most noteworthy part of that day for Allen; a few hours after the broadcast, Margaret gave birth to David Ellsworth Ludden. In the next few years, David would be joined by two sisters, Martha, and Sarah.

The national version of *Mind Your Manners* added two regular features that awarded prizes, an omen of things to come for Allen. "Letter of the Month" awarded a prize not for a problem but for a response. Listeners were encouraged to write in with feedback to any on-air remarks made by Allen or the panel. Each month, the writer of the letter deemed "the most stimulating comment" received a complete thirty-volume set of the Encyclopedia Americana.

The other new prize feature, "Top Teener of the Month," encouraged listeners to nominate worthy teenagers. Nominees were never told they were in contention, so that the big winner could be surprised. One month's big winner, seventeen-year-old James Moses, was recognized for rescuing his nine friends who had become stranded on an ice floe in Lake Erie. At a special ceremony, Moses was presented with the Top Teener of the Month Award as well as a camera with leather case and a gold watch. The watch wasn't a prize from the show; the parents of the rescued kids had pooled their money together to buy it for him.

Critics raved about the program, praising the opportunity for young people to talk anonymously to impartial, helpful peers without the fear of being laughed at or talked down to. The show was fearless in the nature of the problems addressed. One observer raved that the show was "always as frank as possible…about sex." This was just as true for alcoholism and drug addiction.

It wasn't solely columnists who had kind words. A high school teacher spoke emphatically about the program, saying, "The teenager…has found

Allen sorts through this week's mail on *Mind Your Manners,* in search of a worthy Letter of the Month or Top Teener candidate. FRED WOSTBROCK COLLECTION

a source of information which is youth-oriented. The *Mind Your Manners* panel gives advice in moralistic terms, but is entertaining also. It is rather like a quiz show, where the adolescent who writes takes a chance that he is right. And the panel decides if he really is."

A professor at Columbia University added that the show gave teenage listeners "psychic rewards," explaining that teenagers' self-esteem improved merely from hearing members of the panel acknowledge that they had been through similar experiences. Other experts colorfully called the program "a safety valve for social tensions."

There were material incentives as well for kids at home to share their problem with the radio audience. Teens whose letters were read on the air received five dollars' worth of trading stamps, with one letter selected to receive a savings bond worth twenty-five dollars. Allen also played a true-false quiz about etiquette with young members of the live audience in the studio and encouraged the kids to try for a higher score than the previous audience.

Before long a steady stream of trophies was pouring into WTIC's offices. In 1949, the show received a special citation by the Parents'

Allen is all smiles. At only 33 years of age, he already has a George Foster Peabody Award, one of broadcasting's highest honors.
FRED WOSTBROCK COLLECTION

Institute. *Variety* magazine gave WTIC a special award for outstanding youth programming for *Mind Your Manners*, among other shows, and the program received an honorable mention in the Ohio State Exhibition of Educational Radio Programs. The following year, 1950, *Mind Your Manners* received an Ohio State Broadcasting Award for the most outstanding youth-oriented program in America.

In that same year, the station received the most prestigious honor in broadcasting, the George Foster Peabody Award. The Peabody Award was specifically created to honor quality rather than mass popularity or critical acclaim. The Peabody Award is not broken down into fields or categories.

Each year, approximately twenty-five to thirty-five awards are given based entirely on the individual merits of the shows being honored. The other winners in 1950 were comedian Jimmy Durante, the Metropolitan Opera (which aired its productions on ABC Radio), Radio Free Europe, "for contribution to international understanding," and CBS Radio, for *Hear It Now*, Edward R. Murrow's series of documentaries. *Mind Your Manners* was in very good company.

The show became so popular that Allen took it on the road to broadcast from high school auditoriums, always to enthusiastic audiences. In October 1950, *Mind Your Manners* did a special broadcast from United Nations Headquarters, with a panel of teenagers representing different countries And, for the show's third anniversary in 1951, Allen and his regular panelists gave an interview to nationally syndicated newspaper writer Kay Sullivan.

By that point, the show had received more than half a million letters from teenagers. Although a lot of the problems were unique, Allen and his panelists identified a number of common themes among the questions and prepared a series of generic responses to the most frequently asked questions:

How can I be popular? "Stop thinking about yourself! Try to 'bring out' the other person and FIND something you can enjoy talking about — sports, art, movies, books. Don't criticize other friends...behind their backs. Other friends may agree with you at the time. But later, they are apt to think of you as treacherous."

Must I neck/drink/smoke to be popular? "Set your standards high and keep them high. You'd be amazed to know how many of your friends already have high standards and will be secretly glad to find them in you. Girls with low standards lose self-respect and the respect of boyfriends — and the word quickly spreads among boys."

My parents will not let me have dates. What can I do? "First, you must prove to your parents you are reliable. Sit down with them; talk the situation over. Point to your reliability in other matters. Promise to honor their objections to late hours. The girl who is 'kept under wraps' is often the one who fails to learn how to conduct herself with boys and may even get into trouble. For younger kids, [we] suggest [that you] start with afternoon dates and double dates; don't start by dating boys several years older than yourself, and don't date boys known to be wolves. Boys are advised not to date girls much older than themselves."

I have a license but my dad won't let me drive. "Again, you have to PROVE your reliability. Some teeners have earned a reputation for reckless driving, which is now hurting others. Try a 50-50 deal with your parents: if you can be trusted driving the car on small errands, you may be trusted to use it on occasional dates. Always tell your father or mother where you are going; how many will be along; when you expect to return. (Stick to your promise!) Keep the family car washed and polished in return for its use."

Should I go steady? "Letters indicate that girls like the idea; boys don't...It's better in every way to 'date around' when you're in high school. You make more friends, develop more personality. You're not tied down, you join in more activities. Girls start this steady business...They think it means security for them; actually, it's bad because if the boy breaks off, the girl often has trouble getting other dates."

A panel of typical everyday teenagers helping their peers through problems on *Mind Your Manners.* Seated at bottom right, future Supreme Court Justice Antonin Scalia. FRED WOSTBROCK COLLECTION

So prized was the kids' advice that, as *Mind Your Manners* grew more popular, the show frequently received mail from parents asking for help with problems they were having with their teenagers. Some tried to hand down direct orders or punishments through the show, saying in their letters that their kids never listen to Mom and Dad but trusted every word that Allen Ludden and the kids on *Mind Your Manners* had to say. In response, Allen introduced a regular segment on the show called "The Adult Problem," in which the kids answered a single letter concerning a disagreement between a teenager and the adult who had written the letter.

Allen took the responsibility of trusted advisor seriously and tried to make it clear that the show should not be relied upon as a definitive resource. He told Professor Raymond Forer of the University of Connecticut, "[We do not] tell them the final answer, particularly in a complicated social problem. In procedural problems, yes, we do say what is and what is not accepted as the right way to do things; but, for the most part, in our problems dealing with the relationships of boys and girls and adults, we try to thrash out a problem and think it out loud without setting ourselves up as the final authority. If from a discussion of a problem, a listener gets new ideas that he can use in solving his own problem, then that is all we can possibly ask. Often we suggest that the writer of the problem turn to an immediate agency close at hand. I think it is safe to say that fifty percent of the complicated problems we discuss on the program are never actually answered."

Despite that caveat, teenagers continued to trust and revere *Mind Your Manners*, so much so that Allen was able to cobble together a side job as an advice columnist for teen magazines. He answered readers' letters for *Fashion and Fiction*, *Varsity*, *Compact*, *Senior Prom*, and *Movie Stars Parade*.

ALLEN LUDDEN'S COLUMN IN MOVIE STARS PARADE
(undated)

Reading your problems over with Peter Lawford this month, I found that you M.S.P. readers have presented very interesting and intelligent problems...and picking the ones to talk about was not easy. But...we had to choose...so, here they are. Number one came from M.S.F. in Barnesville, Georgia...and she writes...

I like a boy very much and he seems to like me because he pays a lot of attention to me at parties. We always have a lot of fun together, but he just won't ask me for a date. He was jilted by another girl last year and ever since he hasn't dated anybody. I know he likes me, and I just can't understand why he won't ask for a date. Would you please explain it?

When I talked this one over with Pete Lawford, I asked him what he thought of girls who seem too anxious to get a boy to date them, and he said the same thing lots of other men have said on the subject: "Men do not like to be chased; they like to be the pursuer."

So taking that as a theme, let's look at this problem. The boy likes M.S.F.; he has a good time with her at parties. She likes him, and it's very possible she shows it. He has been jilted before, and is just a little bitter about it. He doesn't quite trust women in general. So…it seems obvious that it is up to M.S.F. to stimulate his interest, to make him feel that he will have to work at getting a date with her. As it stands, he knows she's dying to have a date with him, and for that very reason, he doesn't ask her. Maybe this answer is too simple, but it's certainly a likely one. And we recommend that M.S.F. continue to be friendly, but not too friendly. Don't be too receptive when this boy pays so much attention to you at a party. Bide your time, and let him get the idea. It may take time, and it may not work…but the chances are that it will, and you stand only to gain by trying it.

Mind Your Manners balanced spontaneity with preparedness. The research process began with Allen himself, who would canvas area schools and talk with dozens of kids in search of typical teenagers, many of whom had been suggested by principals and teachers. The kids chosen for the panel tended to have above-average academic records along with experience with average kid problems.

No scripts were written; no rehearsals were held. A few hours prior to each broadcast, the kids and Allen came into the studio and opened the mail themselves. They would select the problems they felt worthy of discussing on the air, and briefly preview their thoughts before heading into the studio to have the thorough conversation live on the air. In each episode, the panel would discuss six letters from youngsters in depth, plus a single letter from an adult before ending the program with "The Answer Box," a segment of rapid-fire solutions to problems that could be answered easily.

When drugs began showing up in letters in the spring of 1951, Allen found his panel unprepared for the topic. The *Mind Your Manners* youths claimed to have neither dealt with narcotics themselves nor known any kids involved with drugs. With encouragement from Leonard Patricelli, Allen took a microphone and recording equipment to a Connecticut correctional facility and met with a teenage girl who had been convicted of narcotics use. She discussed her life and her addiction. After Allen aired the interview, he conducted a panel discussion, with his panel-

Allen looks on as Governor John Lodge enacts a law inspired by *Mind Your Manners.* PHOTO ORIGINALLY APPEARED IN BROADCASTING MAGAZINE

ists agreeing that the dealers selling the substances were the ones who bore responsibility.

In reaction to high interest expressed in the audience feedback, WTIC's general manager, Paul Morency, began studying state and federal laws regarding narcotics. He concluded that Connecticut's laws were "woefully inadequate." On May 20, 1951, WTIC and Connecticut Governor John Lodge drafted a bill that would enforce harsher sentences on drug dealers who sold to minors — fifteen to thirty years for a first-time offense. However, the bill was drafted only seventeen days before the state legislature would adjourn, and the docket was full. WTIC encouraged listeners to write state representatives and ask them to make sure the bill made it through before the adjournment. With two days to spare, the bill was approved, and Governor Lodge signed it into law, with Allen Ludden standing behind him and a WTIC microphone on the desk in front of him.

America's entertainment habits were changing, however, and *Mind Your Manners'* move to TV was inevitable. A *New York Times* article in 1951 made note that many of the new television shows premiering that year were actually adaptations of radio shows. Commencing on June 24, 1951,

Allen hosts the TV version of *Mind Your Manners* in 1951. The set of books on Allen's desk was actually a hollow frame concealing a monitor. AUTHOR'S COLLECTION

a national television version of *Mind Your Manners* aired every Sunday afternoon on NBC. The TV version emanated from the studios of WNBT (now WNBC), NBC's flagship station in New York City. Allen commuted every weekend to host the show, with a new panel of teenagers from the New York area.

Although the kids were arguably the stars, Allen's image shone through. An early critic, Bernard Kalb, referred to him as "a crew-cut, horn-rimmed man of thirty-three with a display of manners that would leave Emily Post agog."

Allen's television efforts in the early days of the medium could practically be considered a public service. WNBT in New York was, at that time, enjoying a reputation for being strongly committed to educating viewers and serving the needs of young people. The station received tremendous acclaim for an unusual children's program that taught children art by playing a variety of sounds and music and encouraging young viewers to paint whatever they imagined they were hearing. WNBT further developed its niche as the socially conscious station with the addition of *Mind Your Manners* and entered into women's issues when it picked up a new show, *It's a Problem*, created by wealthy young socialite Phyllis Adams. Tired of what she labeled "typically mindless" programming aimed at women, Adams hosted groups of women discussing topics like segregation, the psychological effects of divorce on children, and birth control. Reviews were enthusiastic, with one well-meaning critic praising Adams for possessing "the vigor, perseverance, and understanding of a man."

Shortly after *It's a Problem* scored a national slot on the NBC network, a group representing *Life* Magazine and the New York Board of Education asked Adams to produce a documentary miniseries. Allen joined Adams as a co-producer. The resulting seventy-episode miniseries, *Inside Our Schools*, was described as "an effort to better acquaint the public with what goes on in the city schools."

Inside Our Schools aired installments on WNBT-TV and WNBC radio, some running as short as fifteen minutes while others were three hours long. Most episodes contained an extended report about a specific public school in the New York area, with information gathered from that school's administrators, parents, students, and teachers, along with municipal officials.

Episodes included airing an open forum conducted by the school board to look into a school board member's mismanagement of funds, the site selection for a new school, and the process for hiring teachers. Students became the focus in installments that followed a non-English-speaking girl as she adapted to the school system, explored the issue of drug addiction, and interviewed adults who were attending night school.

An extended portion of each program merely planted the cameras in a school and watched a typical day. On one episode, viewers saw a 5th grade class in Harlem walking through the school library and doing research for an upcoming Pan American Day Celebration; another exposed viewers to special schools offering large-print textbooks and a slower pace for students suffering from eye and heart conditions.

Allen hosted two installments of *Inside Our Schools*, titled "Teen-Age Congress," that had a familiar premise: he sat down with a group of five high school students to discuss a variety of issues. Topics ranged from homework and cliques to cheating on tests and dropping out of school just short of graduation at age eighteen to enlist in the military.

In an effort to make the conversation as natural as possible, Allen eliminated much of the pretense of the television format, sitting with the kids at a camera-unfriendly roundtable to force their focus on each other. A TV critic reviewing the show noted that it had a voyeuristic touch, making viewers feel they were eavesdropping on a real conversation between a group of kids and a trusted authority figure. The critic noted

Allen's preferred elements for good television, real kids and real conversations. FRED WOSTBROCK COLLECTION

how jarring it was when Allen broke the illusion by glancing at the camera late in the show. This was Allen Ludden's early TV trademark: delivering real kids and real conversations.

Advertising *Inside Our Schools* followed the same "real life" strategy. Full-page ads in New York's major newspapers mimicked editorial pages, with columns and brief articles revolving around the subject matter of upcoming programs. *Life* printed up one million copies of a four-page checklist, inserted into issues of the magazine sold in the New York area, that encouraged parents to score each program's profiled school for various attributes and also give a score for their own child's school. The campaign earned WNBT an award from *Billboard* Magazine for television program promotion.

Unlike the varying lengths for installments of the radio version, all TV episodes of *Inside Our Schools* ran two hours on Thursdays. Eventually, this daunting length was split up with a one-hour episode in the morning and another in the afternoon. It was received well enough by critics and local stations that an attempt at syndicating the show placed shorter versions of the show in a few cities throughout New York State, but the syndication never extended beyond that handful of stations.

Nonetheless, *Inside Our Schools* was considered an extremely successful and productive project. On its fifty-fifth and final episode, the series wrapped up with a follow-up report from community and school leaders about the changes and improvements in their schools since their feature spot on *Inside Our Schools*.

Not long afterward, the House of Representatives Subcommittee on Interstate and Foreign Commerce held hearings about television. These hearings came about not in reaction to any particular controversy, but rather as part of a timely House evaluation of possible offensive or corrupt television programming. NBC Vice President Charles Denny testified at the hearings, citing *Inside Our Schools* as an example of television's potential benefits. He noted that "an important civic issue was brought directly to the people and they were given an understanding of the problem that will help them deal with it intelligently and effectively."

At the same time, *Mind Your Manners* was touted as an example of what was right with radio. At a 1952 convention of radio broadcasters, the future of the business was on everybody's mind. Some station managers were concerned that radio wouldn't survive in a TV-dominated world while others urged the approach of considering television like any other competitor — the same way that you'd think of a new radio station moving into town.

A special broadcast of *Mind Your Manners*, hosted by Allen Ludden, was among presentations delivered at the convention to provide a reminder of the good that radio could do. The television version had fizzled after only nine months, and the national radio version ended with it, torpedoing Allen's plans for a syndicated newspaper feature based on the series. But the local WTIC version survived in Connecticut and, as evidenced by its role at the convention, *Mind Your Manners* was still held in high regard nationwide, continuing to pocket awards after leaving NBC. The local version on WTIC was voted "Outstanding Teenagers' Program of the Year" by *Scholastic Teacher Magazine* and the National Association for Better Radio and TV, while the American Federation of Women's Clubs named *Mind Your Manners* "Best Program for Young People."

At another point in the convention, the conversation moved to sagging ratings and possible solutions. A program director from Washington, DC, offered ways that faltering radio stations could stay in business. Among his suggestions: game shows.

Betty's career was on the rise when she married Lane Allan. By the time they wed, she had done commercials, radio programs, and even, at long last, a co-starring role in a low-budget film. Lane's career hit an unexpected bump in the road, however. His agency closed its doors, and he found a job selling furniture to stay above water.

Betty pounded the pavement, looking for more acting gigs and recycling glass bottles to scrounge up extra money. Then one day, out of nowhere, she received an offer to appear on television. At the time, Los Angeles had only three television stations and just under a thousand home TVs in the entire city. But a few ambitious radio personalities wanted to explore the new territory and were producing a one-time program.

After a successful audition for the host, disc jockey Dick Haynes, Betty performed two songs on the television special, and Haynes personally recommended her for a regular series, *Tom, Dick and Harry*. She got the part, but *Tom, Dick, and Harry* lasted only a few weeks. Betty landed on her feet, getting hired

Betty White with Al Jarvis, who turned her into a television star. AUTHOR'S COLLECTION

immediately for the game show *Grab Your Phone*. Emcee Wes Battersea would ask trivia questions to the home audience, while Betty and three other women sat at a desk ready to answer telephones. Viewers could win five dollars by calling the studio and supplying a correct answer. While the other women at the phones received ten dollars a week for the gig, Betty earned twenty because she was able to chat and ad-lib with Wes Battersea during slower moments.

That easy banter on *Grab Your Phone* caught the attention of longtime Los Angeles disc jockey Al Jarvis, who himself was making the leap to television with a daily five-hour program, *Hollywood on Television*, on station KLAC. The format had Jarvis chatting with a regular cast member, spinning records, answering viewer mail, interviewing guests and occasionally talking to passersby on the street. At some points the camera would focus on a fish tank so the audience could watch the fish for a while. Betty agreed to be the other person in the chat segment.

"We were on the street, and there was a door nearby," Betty recalled in a 1985 interview. "Anybody who would stick their head through the door, we'd interview them. We were the only game in town, so anybody

Betty (seated at far left) with her co-stars on *Hollywood on Television*; the dailyfive-and-a-halfhourshowwasquiteacrashcourseinad-libbing,which would serve Betty well in her future endeavors. AUTHOR'S COLLECTION

who was coming through town would do our show. We gave race results. We had Dr. Ernest Wilson, who'd come on with a religious message. And he was so thrilled that we'd put him on after the race results, because the bars were watching for that and he could get his message out to the people in the bars."

After only three weeks, the show added a half hour and a sixth weekly episode, giving Betty thirty-three hours a week on television. Jarvis determined that Betty was so instrumental to the show's success that he bumped her weekly salary from fifty dollars to $300.

With now a full-blown show business career, Betty gradually became aware that her marriage to Lane Allan seemed to be cooling off. She avoided any confrontation or unpleasantness for as long as she could but eventually, Lane admitted what he had been holding back: he wanted to have a family, and he had never envisioned being married to a woman with a career. What Betty wanted and what Lane wanted were two paths that would never intersect.

"If I did have a baby, that baby would have to be the whole thing for me," Betty said in 2000. "And that's not my field of expertise."

Betty, along with new co-star Eddie Albert, on *Hollywood on Television.*
AUTHOR'S COLLECTION

There was another source of tension in the marriage. Betty, who saw her career on the rise in a medium that, it was quickly becoming apparent, was the next big thing, candidly admitted, "There was a little jealousy."

Betty and Lane divorced in 1949. It was a crushing blow for Betty. The letdown of her first marriage was something that she was able to think of as a learning experience but, this time around, she felt she had truly failed. She hadn't met Lane's expectations, despite entering the marriage with the mindset that she could deliver on that. Dejected, Betty moved back in with her parents.

The 1950s brought growth in the television industry. Los Angeles now had seven television stations and nearly 600,000 homes with TVs. Although *Hollywood on Television* was still cranking out hours of live programming every day, Betty accepted an offer to do another show on KLAC. Between her strong work ethic and her love of the business, she cherished a busy schedule with multiple gigs. Also, this gave her the opportunity to have her own series, *The Betty White Show*, airing on Sundays. Viewers wrote in seeking advice, and Betty would talk through the problem and try to settle on a solution.

The Betty White Show evolved into an amateur hour, which Betty co-hosted with Al Jarvis. That show ended when Jarvis gave his notice to the

Budding mogul Betty White was the star in front of the camera, and the boss behind the camera, for the sitcom *Life with Elizabeth*. AUTHOR'S COLLECTION

station and departed from *Hollywood on Television*, which continued with Betty and her new co-host, Eddie Albert (later of *Green Acres*).

During its short life, the amateur hour that Betty and Jarvis helmed featured a series of recurring comedy skits between the acts, and in the most popular the co-hosts played a married couple, Elizabeth and Alvin. Several months after Jarvis left KLAC, Betty collaborated with KLAC station manager Don Fedderson and a joke writer from the amateur show to turn the "Alvin and Elizabeth" skits into a full series with a new actor, Del Moore, in the role of Alvin. Betty wrote some of the episodes and formed a production company to oversee the new venture, which was syndicated to stations across the country. *Life with Elizabeth* made Betty the first woman to write, produce, and be the owner of her own sitcom.

Each thirty-minute episode of *Life with Elizabeth* comprised three one-act "incidents," typically seven or eight minutes apiece. Announcer Jack Narz provided the narration as Elizabeth got into a variety of predicaments that exasperated Alvin, and most adventures concluded with his storming out of the room and threatening to leave her.

"Elizabeth," the deep baritone of Jack Narz would implore at the incident's conclusion, "aren't you ashamed?"

Elizabeth would look at the camera, smile devilishly, and shake her head "no."

Newspaper columnist Terry Vernon raved, "It is good clean domestic comedy about little things that are plausible enough to have happened to nearly anyone. The show isn't lavish in cost and settings but it does have the exceptional talents of Betty White and her co-star, Del Moore. If you have never seen *Life with Elizabeth*, we suggest that you tune in… and we believe you'll find a new favorite."

Among the perks of Betty's newfound success in show business was a chauffeur-driven convertible. AUTHOR'S COLLECTION

AUTHOR'S COLLECTION

CHAPTER FOUR

"BOWL"

Grant Tinker was a former executive for NBC Radio who had since moved to the other side of the table and, by the spring of 1953, he was a producer in search of ideas for new shows. One day, a business associate named John Moses handed him a thin idea for a quiz show that had been suggested six years earlier by Don Reid, a former member of the basketball team at McGill University in Montreal. Reid's idea pit students from two different colleges against each other.

The idea of thrusting schools into direct competition wasn't totally new. In 1946, a high school competition called *Campus Quiz* premiered in Philadelphia and lasted about a year. Living in Canada, Don Reid probably wasn't aware of *Campus Quiz*, and he organized team trivia competitions for the USO during World War II, so more than likely, he based his idea on that experience. He named his quiz show *College Bowl* but never fully fleshed out the idea. Both the name and the proposal collected dust for six years.

Tinker wasn't enthusiastic about the proposal, but he needed a show and knew somebody he thought was capable of working with this *College Bowl* concept. Grant Tinker knew Allen Ludden.

Tinker went to the Ludden household in Hartford and asked Allen to have a look at the brief pitch for *College Bowl*. Ludden immediately pulled out a yellow writing tablet and a pen and within a few minutes had effortlessly outlined a viable format along with rules of the game. Then he sketched out the logistics and technical aspects needed to execute the idea.

Tinker was stunned by Allen's enthusiasm for an idea dropped into his lap with no prior discussion. Allen not only committed to it but by the end of that week had resigned his executive position at WTIC in Hartford, although he continued hosting WTIC's *Mind Your Manners*, which remained on the air long after it had disappeared from NBC's network radio schedule. The Ludden family moved from Hartford to Dobbs Ferry, New York, about an hour north of Allen's new location at Tinker's Manhattan office.

Tinker and Allen sold the idea to radio which, by this time, was an easier sell than the more dominant TV. Jack Cleary, an executive at NBC Radio, gave the proposal scant attention before agreeing to put the show

Even as new opportunities presented themselves elsewhere, Allen faithfully continued hosting *Mind Your Manners* for WITC. FRED WOSTBROCK COLLECTION

on the schedule with the minimal change of renaming it *College Quiz Bowl* to clarify that it was not a sports program.

There was a more pressing issue for Tinker and Allen to tend to. Radio's diminished importance meant diminished paychecks for the people working in it. *College Quiz Bowl* wasn't going to premiere for several months — NBC Radio was saving it for the fall line-up — and the new, untested series lacked sponsors. With a family and a new home, Allen was rapidly draining his bank account. Facing the same problem for the same reason, Tinker whipped up a solution called *New Talent USA*.

Tinker pitched *New Talent USA* as a fourteen-week summer series with the specific goal of having NBC Radio air it in the weeks leading up to the premiere of *College Quiz Bowl* so that he and Allen could begin collecting paychecks immediately.

New Talent USA was an easy pitch for the network because, as Tinker recalled, the idea would cost NBC almost nothing. Every week, the network would air a two-hour broadcast divided into thirty-minute segments, each programmed by a different NBC affiliate that would present local amateur performers. A panel of judges in New York, joined by Allen as master of ceremonies, would pick a winner at the end of the night and for the final episode, the thirteen winners were flown to New York to compete for a grand prize.

Tinker's strategy worked. *New Talent USA* kept him and Allen above water during the summer of 1953 while they prepared *College Quiz Bowl* for the fall. That summer, Allen needed to devote only one day each week to *New Talent USA* and *Mind Your Manners*. He spent the rest of his time on the road promoting *College Quiz Bowl*, visiting college campuses to convince school administrators to participate. Allen followed up as liaison between the school and the show, answering all correspondence and phone calls from the schools participating in the first season. Despite all this effort, Allen would never receive producer credit; he was identified only as host of *College Quiz Bowl*. Creator credit was shared by Don Reid and John Moses.

Billed as "the varsity sport of the mind," *College Quiz Bowl* debuted in the fall of 1953 and each week matched up two four-member teams from different schools. No traveling was required; Allen hosted the show from a studio in New York City, while each team competed from a stage on its own campus, joined onstage by a "referee" — an announcer from the local NBC affiliate. Allen would read a question, the referee would determine, by calling out the name, which player was the first to raise a hand to answer, and Allen, in the studio, would give that player the chance to answer. In execution, the game proved too confusing for the audience to follow, so the following week everybody was hooked into the game via a complex telephone set-up that Allen and a team of NBC engineers designed. Each referee had lockout buttons and would press it when they saw a player raise a hand. Each lockout button would activate both a unique sound effect and a unique light in the New York studio, while also shutting off the opposing team's button. This technologically advanced arrangement allowed the players and referees to function as if all the parties were in the same room.

Allen began each round by reading a toss-up question (originally called a kick-off), worth ten points. The team that answered the toss-up was given a bonus question worth anywhere from ten to thirty additional points. The game was divided into two eight-minute halves and, at the end of the game, the higher scoring team received $500 in scholarship funds for the school plus the right to face a new school the following week. This "reigning champion" component was the only element that deviated from Allen's proposal. He had wanted every game to be a contest between two new schools, with the entire season structured as a tournament and building to a final championship game every May.

The series got off to a relatively smooth start, with Northwestern defeating Columbia with a final score of 135-60. Among the Northwestern players was Ruth Duskin Feldman, one of the "child geniuses" featured on the previous decade's *Quiz Kids*, an immensely popular radio program that invited home listeners to mail in postcards with trivia questions that might stump a panel of bright children.

Allen reminds you to tune in for *College Quiz Bowl.* FRED WOSTBROCK COLLECTION

Because *College Quiz Bowl* aired on radio, the home audience never saw how primitive the program was, despite the lavish telephone system. There were no fancy set pieces keeping track of the game's progress. Grant Tinker stood to Allen's side and kept score on a chalkboard and, by his own admission, made numerous math mistakes that somebody would catch, leading to occasional pauses in the game when Allen would vamp while Tinker calculated and adjusted the score. Another unanticipated outcome was that the teams were so darn smart that, frequently, Allen would barely start a question when a player would ring in with the answer.

The show was debugged very quickly, and not only with regard to technical issues. Elements of the game that didn't work were identified and phased out after the first handful of programs. The show dropped "expository bonus questions" that awarded a team twenty points for speaking off the cuff about a topic suggested by Allen, such as "Why are blondes more fun than brunettes?"

And a solution was found to the problem of the early interruptions by contestants. If Allen read the full question and a contestant gave a wrong answer, there was no penalty. If a player interrupted Allen's reading and gave a wrong answer, there was now a five-point penalty. Most contestants now waited until they were <u>positive</u> of the answer, giving the listening audience more of a chance to play along.

Overall, though, the game worked well. The rules were clear-cut, the teams evenly matched and the games close and exciting. The audience that was tuning in was dazzled by how smart America's college students truly were.

"According to Dr. Benjamin Spock, an eminent authority on baby care, a mother bathing her baby should hold him carefully under the armpit with her forearm supporting the baby's head. For ten points, why would Dr. Spock have been horrified at the way a Greek mother named Thetis held her baby to bathe him?"[1]

"For a twenty-five point bonus, Hervey Allen wrote *Anthony Adverse*. Kenneth Roberts wrote *Captain Caution*. For five points apiece, name a book with an alliterative title written by each of the following authors: Herman Melville, Charles Dickens, Booth Tarkington, Tobias Smollett, Sir Walter Scott."[2]

"If an 'aesthete' is one who cultivates an unusually high sensitivity to beauty, and an 'aesthetician' is one versed in the theory of beauty and artistic expression, explain the difference between 'gourmet' and 'gourmand.'"[3]

Both the toss-up and bonus questions were written by Nancy Fobes, a Sarah Lawrence College graduate who studied further at the University of London on a Fulbright scholarship. Fobes was a reporter and *Life* Magazine editor before getting hired to write the questions for *College Quiz Bowl*. For each week's single episode, Fobes would write five full games' worth of material and send all of the questions to an advisory board at the World Book Encyclopedia for an accuracy check. One pile of questions was for the actual show, but she also prepared four practice games so that the teams could warm up before going on the air.

1. Thetis' son was Achilles. Thetis bathed him by holding his heel and dipping him in the River Styx.
2. Melville: *Billy Bud*. Dickens: *Nicholas Nickleby* or *A Christmas Carol*. Tarkington: *Alice Adams*. Smollett: *Roderick Random*. Scott: *Rob Roy*.
3. A gourmet is a connoisseur of food & drink. A gourmand is a glutton, someone who loves food indiscriminately.

Fobes later explained to an interviewer the delicate science of making a challenging quiz show interesting for a radio audience: "To make up a good show you need some tough academic questions that might leave viewing audiences cold, but impresses them. They want to see what the kids can do. Then you put in some facet of common things everybody

Allen began adopting a more scholarly look when he hosted *College Quiz Bowl,* **and it suited both he and the show very well.** FRED WOSTBROCK COLLECTION

knows, such as American history. Then there are fun questions, which describe things terribly scientifically and have simple answers."

It quickly became apparent that Allen had to be careful not to accidentally read two toss-up questions in a row rather than following up the toss-up with a bonus question and not to blurt out a multi-part bonus question instead of a single-answer toss-up. A system of color-coding the questions was implemented to help him. The questions were typed onto index cards, with yellow cards used for the toss-ups and white for the bonuses.

But nobody could find yellow index cards! Either they hadn't been invented yet or weren't sold in New York City. Someone on staff bought up yellow poster board instead and hand-cut a stack of cards about the right size. As a courtesy, after each broadcast, *College Quiz Bowl* would mail a stack of used cards to a school that was preparing to send a team to the show so that the team could practice.

College Quiz Bowl continued Allen's pattern of high regard for women. Every *Mind Your Manners* panel featured three girls and three boys, with girls' problems and boys' problems given equal play, and Allen made sure that girls were represented on *Inside Our Schools* as well. On *College Quiz Bowl*, not only did a woman write the intellectual questions, but it was the show's policy that any all-male school that was affiliated with a nearby all-female school had to combine forces and send a mixed team.

Soon colleges were soliciting the show rather than the other way around. In the early weeks of *College Quiz Bowl*, the New York-based series used mainly schools in the northeast, but as time went on it became a truly national competition.

There were two particularly noteworthy hold-outs, though. Harvard and Yale were repeatedly asked to send teams to compete on the show, and both schools routinely declined, viewing *College Quiz Bowl* as an everything-to-lose, nothing-to-gain prospect. A team from Harvard or Yale would be expected to win, and nobody would bat an eye if it did. But if a Harvard or Yale team lost, it would be front page news.

The notion that a loss would reflect so poorly on a school had not occurred to anyone at *College Quiz Bowl* when the program was developed. Allen would periodically address that fear by reciting a disclaimer at the opening of a game: "Before Jack Costello explains our *Quiz Bowl* rules, may I point out that we recognize full well that in putting the emphasis here in the *College Quiz Bowl* on a quick recall of specific facts, we are finding out only one of the objectives of college education. We are likewise trying to give you an opportunity to meet a few of the many remarkable, well-rounded personalities to be found on every American campus. Now how about those rules, Jack?"

Allen and *College Quiz Bowl* were a perfect fit. Like *Mind Your Manners*, it was a series that celebrated the good in America's younger population, and Allen enjoyed sharing the stage with them. Moreover, Allen — partially because of his background in education and partially because it was his nature — exuded an authoritative tone as he spoke to the players and read the questions, sounding not unlike an instructor teaching a course and expecting the class to participate.

The show routinely received favorable feedback from listeners and good critical reviews. The show got plenty of press, as local newspaper reporters were as excited about covering the campus quiz team's victories as they were about covering the football games. Students everywhere were eager to root, root, root for the home team each week. When Washington & Lee University's team won for three consecutive weeks, the school auditorium filled to capacity almost two hours before showtime for the fourth game.

Allen's ability to relate to the younger set caught the attention of WCBS, the flagship television station for CBS in New York City. The station was collaborating with the New York City Board of Education to develop an educational program for children based on *Garroway at Large*, a popular series hosted by Dave Garroway around the time that he became the first host of *Today*. On *Garroway at Large*, Dave wandered through the studio, occasionally walking off the set and weaving through technicians and equipment, as he presented a wide variety of features under a very loose format. WCBS recruited Allen Ludden to host a children's version titled *On the Carousel*.

Each week, Allen met a different child in the studio and walked him or her through a series of stops for each segment of that week's show. On the premiere broadcast, Allen and the youngster watched a magic show, visited with children from the Philippines about their lives, learned how to handle animals brought by a woman from the Bronx Zoo and enjoyed a brief concert by a 300-member orchestra from a school in the Bronx. The show ended with a tour of the studio and a demonstration of the equipment conducted by a child actress.

In its review of the premiere, *Variety* fawned, "Allen Ludden, who for most of his show biz career has been associated with radio, makes his first major plunge into video here, and comes up as a winning personality. He's gentle and informal with the kiddies, he doesn't push them or talk down to them, and if the series maintains the standards set by the first show, they'll soon be calling him Uncle Allen."

To his own surprise, Allen became in such high demand that he hired a talent agent, Carl Eastman, to oversee his on-air career. He outlined his earnings in a letter to Eastman in early 1954:

Dear Carl:

As of this date, I receive the following income as a performer on radio and television:

MIND YOUR MANNERS (WTIC) $40.00 *(per week)*
YOUNG AMERICA (WTIC-NBC) $35.00 *(per week)*
COLLEGE QUIZ BOWL (MOSES NBC) $300.00 *(per week)*
ON THE CAROUSEL (WCBS-TV) $175.00 *(per week)*

Adjusted for inflation, Allen's income was equivalent to about $250,000 a year in 2010 dollars.

AUTHOR'S COLLECTION

CHAPTER FIVE

"PLAIN"

Allen appreciated the critical encouragement and the suggestion that television was a good fit for him, because for the moment, his radio gig didn't look long for this world. *College Quiz Bowl* was a "sustaining show," which meant that it was on the air without a sponsor; the network was airing it at a loss in hopes of attracting a sponsor who'd be willing to sign on for the show and make it profitable. Potential sponsors were unfortunately now viewing network radio shows the same way that the network itself regarded network radio shows. *College Quiz Bowl* aired without a sponsor for six straight months, which meant that NBC lost money with every broadcast.

So one night, Allen strolled up to the microphone for the non-sports show with the sports-like title, and, to borrow another term from sports, he threw a Hail Mary pass. On the March 14, 1954 broadcast of *College Quiz Bowl*, Allen told the audience exactly what was happening behind the scenes. The show had no sponsor, and NBC was losing money each week by keeping it on the air. If nothing changed, he said, the show would air its last episode on April 4. He gave NBC's mailing address at Radio City and implored students and parents to write the network and tell them how much they liked *College Quiz Bowl*.

The campaign worked! NBC received a stream of letters from listeners across the country. It also didn't hurt that the team from Washington & Lee University had enjoyed a five-week winning streak that gave the show a sudden burst of publicity. One of the teams that Washington & Lee defeated was Princeton. Princeton experienced the worst fears of Harvard and Yale; their loss did get quite a bit of attention in newspapers across the country. The losing Princeton team reacted to the loss with a hilarious written statement rife with winking and nudging poor sportsmanship. Princeton complained that all four Washington & Lee players were Phi Beta Kappas, which Princeton called "cheating" because they had kept it to a gentlemanly <u>one</u> Phi Beta Kappa on their own team, and trying to save face by stating that Washington & Lee probably couldn't beat them in a beer drinking contest.

The letter-writing campaign and the publicity from the Washington & Lee games grabbed the attention of NBC and of a potential source for funds. NBC kept *College Quiz Bowl* on the air and finally acquired a sponsor, *Good Housekeeping* Magazine, to bankroll it. It was a nice bit of news for Allen because up until that sponsorship was obtained, his fortunes with television had seemingly turned. WCBS released him, replacing him on *On the Carousel* with Paul Tripp (formerly TV's "Mr. I. Magination") and putting more of an emphasis on music.

Betty is on top of television, figuratively and literally, in the 1950s. AUTHOR'S COLLECTION

On February 8, 1954, Betty White, having conquered local television and syndication, arrived on network television. NBC President Sylvester "Pat" Weaver was in search of programming to beef up the daytime lineup and sent an associate, Fred Wile Jr., to Hollywood to seek out local personalities who might be what they were looking for.

Wile later said, "I met a tidal wave of enthusiasm for a young lady named Betty White. I held auditions and joined her long list of supporters."

Meetings were held at NBC where Betty and the executives discussed her potential future with the network. One concern of theirs amused her. She explained in 2000, "They said, 'Do you think you can do a half-hour every day, five days a week?' I thought, 'A half hour? What will we do with the rest of the time? I've been doing five and a half hours for six days a week!'"

Instead, Betty held her tongue and told NBC, "I'll try."

Betty was signed to an incentive-filled five-year contract with NBC that gave her the potential to collect up to a million dollars. She hosted a talk show, *The Betty White Show*, in daytime on NBC television. Betty welcomed a broad array of guests, including celebrity guests but mostly "ordinary people" who had something extraordinary to talk about. Betty welcomed a man who claimed to have been abducted by a UFO and a woman who was trying to establish a speed record for flying around the world.

Betty occasionally sang, but for the most part, the show was driven by pleasant chat and demonstrations of various activities, all intentionally slow-paced. She didn't want to ambush her viewers and knew that most housewives who were tuning in were doing chores anyway, and she helpfully designed the show to be more of a companion than a distraction.

Betty seemed to have all the right traits for success: she was bright, outgoing, and pretty without being off-putting. As one critic described her, "Betty is one of TV's unsophisticated beauties…who shuns plunging necklines but whose high-necked sweaters still attract admiring male attention."

Columnist Bob Foster raved, "This young lady…is not only good looking, but can act. She sings, and she can dance…She's got personality and gives to television something that few others have accomplished. That is, being intimate. Miss White is one of those girls who gain a name as big as Liberace and will climb high in the television world to be the first real 'Miss Television.'"

Another writer chimed in, "It is one of the strongest daytime shows that NBC has come up with in a long time. Miss White is easy to look at and has an easy-going manner about her that immediately makes every viewer feel at home. This gal is going places and we'll join the group that claims she is headed for stardom…"

Broadcasting Magazine said, "*The Betty White Show*…is as unpretentious as its name and as charming as its young star…She appears to be a TV natural, a pretty girl with innate stage presence and talent besides. Miss White handles a song nicely. She has a small voice but uses it well."

Betty didn't work alone. She was joined by a live band, led by Frank DeVol, who had attained national prominence with his slow and eerie arrangement of Nat King Cole's "Nature Boy." DeVol had a few running gags that she played with Betty on the program. He would set up segments by passing Betty a note with some important information on it, opening the note by assuring Betty that he was addressing the note to her and then a long list of other singers and talk show hosts that he promised not to be writing to. He also had a vast collection of toupees and made thorough use of them, amusing Betty and the audience by wearing a different toupee on every episode.

Despite all the praise for her natural, unassuming demeanor, Betty was quite nervous about the new effort, very aware of her previous status as a big fish in a small pond, and now realizing that network television was thrusting her right into the Pacific Ocean. Betty tried to calm herself by playing heavily to the audience at home. There was an audience in the studio for each program, but Betty kept her eyes fixed right on the camera and tried to perform the show as if she was alone.

NBC showed remarkable faith, keeping *The Betty White Show* on the air as a sustaining show for some time, although at least one major affiliate, KRON in San Francisco, dumped it in favor of airing old movies and collecting all of the profits from local commercials. But the network's faith paid off. Ratings picked up, the show acquired a sponsor, Geritol, and Betty looked like she had a solid future on NBC. On the East Coast, where viewers saw it at noon, Betty White was a daily lunchtime companion for millions of viewers.

At the time that *The Betty White Show* debuted, *Life with Elizabeth* was still in production, giving Betty a work schedule that left some people speechless. She was usually at NBC's studios in California by 6 a.m. for make-up, and after going through the appropriate preparations and rehearsals, *The Betty White Show* went on the air live at 9 a.m., although oddly enough, many NBC stations on the West Coast aired a film of the program later in the day because they didn't sign on the air that early. Betty left the studio as soon as she signed off and headed across town to work on that week's episode of *Life with Elizabeth*, with writing, rehearsals, and filming giving her a full work day all through the week. She usually didn't finish work at *Elizabeth* until midnight, and then she headed home to do it all again at 6 a.m. It was work ethic not typically seen in show business, except for another employee of NBC over in New York City.

This being the 1950s, many newspaper writers looked at this single woman who threw herself into her work and all wanted to ask the same question: Why didn't she have a man in her life?

Betty was quick to answer, "There's no time to meet anybody." Despite her financial comfort, she was completely happy sharing a home with her parents and three dogs, and at that point, she wasn't interested in settling down. She said she wasn't opposed to marriage at all, as a few people suspected. She just hadn't found the right man yet.

The truth was, after two failed marriages, the term "old maid" had crossed her mind a few times, and quite honestly, Betty had learned to accept the notion.

But still, being a single woman in the public eye meant that eventually some interviewer was going to ask what she was looking for. Grace Fischler, of *TV Stage Magazine*, and Betty began contemplating her Dream Man.

"I hope he'll have a lot of sweetness and tenderness," she ruminated. "I hope he's very romantic — a dreamer. I want to be able to talk to this

Betty serenades the nation on *The Betty White Show*. AUTHOR'S COLLECTION

man, to discuss our dreams together. The so-called practical man isn't like that; on the other hand, a husbands should be practical, I suppose. You can see it's not going to be easy. But of course when I fall in love I'll be the first to compromise.

"…And about this I'm adamant: a man who isn't as daft about animals as I am just has nothing in common with me. My fella should be decidedly taller than I. I'd hate to have to check store windows to see if I had on the right heels. I hope he's an outdoor man and not too intellectual, 'cause I'm not."

She added one other stipulation, one apparently borne more of necessity than desire: her ideal mate had to be somebody in show business. It was the only career she had ever known, nearly all of her friends were in show business too, and she was working constantly. As long as she was pursuing television, Betty White expected that her Prince Charming was in television too.

If Allen Ludden wanted to stay in television, there was always going to be at least one person in his corner: Grant Tinker. Although the

Who wouldn't fall in love with her? Betty White, still a bachelorette in the mid-1950s. AUTHOR'S COLLECTION

connection was never made official, Tinker said in later years that he took it upon himself to be something of a career manager for Allen. For a time, Tinker saw to it that Allen was involved in absolutely anything that he put on the air. As a result, the summer of 1954 saw Allen at the helm of three regular series.

Two new shows both premiered on the same day, July 5. WABC Channel 7, ABC's flagship station in New York, was looking to take a bite out of *Today*, which had premiered two years earlier and was enjoying big ratings with almost literally no competition. Tinker sold WABC on doing their own version of *Today*, called *Good Morning*. It was alien territory for all involved. The folks at *Today* were the only ones who had experience doing a show like it, so the staff of *Good Morning* had to learn by doing. ABC was off to the slowest start of all the major networks in television at that point and didn't know how to deal with selling advertising spots. The vast majority of radio and television shows to that point were bankrolled by a single sponsor, who wielded heavy power with regards to the shows' content and presentation. NBC head honcho Sylvester "Pat" Weaver, who had created *Today*, came up with the revolutionary concept of selling that show's advertising as a series of individual thirty- and sixty-second spots, all sold with the understanding that the network would retain total control over the show and its content.

Good Morning would do the same thing, without a firm grasp on how to sell the advertising. Tinker recalled in his memoirs that he wasn't sure if they way they did it was legal, in hindsight. He and the ad salesmen at the station divvied up the open spots in each episode, sold them to local businesses, kept a percentage of whatever the sponsor paid for themselves, and forked over the rest of the cash to the station. Despite being a local program, the show also tried to entice major corporations to advertise on the show with an interesting sales pitch, offering up *Good Morning* as a testing ground for new ad campaigns. If a company had a new idea for a commercial that they weren't sure about, they could buy the ad time and air it on *Good Morning* once to measure the feedback from that single airing on a single local program.

Each morning's episode of *Good Morning* began with a low-frills opening that rather creatively reflected the title. Since the studio was on the ground level of the building, one camera would be stationed outdoors, aiming down 66th Street near Central Park. The camera would stay pointed on whatever hustle and bustle was happening on that sidewalk for a few moments until Allen, responding to a cue, would emerge from behind a nearby corner and walk toward the camera, as if he had just arrived. He would greet the home audience, open the door, and walk in the studio with the camera following him. He would take off his trench coat, pour a cup of coffee for himself, stick some bread in a toaster, and get things rolling from there.

On one disastrous morning, there was a communication gap and Allen missed his cue to turn the corner. There was really no way to begin the show proper without Allen on camera, so the camera stayed fixed on that continuous shot of 66th Street while somebody tried to get Allen's attention. As the camera remained in place, a stray dog walked right in front of the camera, squatted down, and moved its bowels as the show's pleasant theme song continued playing.

Good Morning was an extremely slow-paced program, consisting of news from Allen, weather reports from a pretty blonde woman named Scotty Scott (her forecast consisted of actually looking out the window and describing how it looked), and pre-recorded music; Allen would spin the record while a camera slowly panned back and forth across the set.

The show searched in vain to find some sort of gimmick to give the show an identity. *Today* had state-of-the-art technical facilities, allowing them to check in with reporters in different cities at a moment's notice, and their weather reports were assembled on the air as phone calls were placed to different correspondents around the country, with the various oncoming fronts being drawn on a blackboard for the viewers. CBS had recently attempted their first go at a similar program, simply called *The Morning Show*, forgoing technical wizardry and placing more of an emphasis on music-driven segments. But the one thing those shows had in common was that a viewer didn't have to sit through the whole thing. That was intentional; *Today* had been developed — and the idea borrowed by CBS — with the notion that viewers could drift in and out of the broadcast without feeling as though they missed anything.

Good Morning, in search of a hook, went the opposite extreme, with each broadcast featuring some element that spanned the entire broadcast. For one broadcast, a camera on the street fixed itself on the image of a man pasting pictures to a lamppost to create a design. On another episode, a woodcutter etched and carved away for the entire broadcast and ended the program by showing her finished product. The problem was, as talented as artists were, watching the actual process of creating a piece of art isn't always particularly engaging.

The perturbed critic for *The New York Times* explained, "Watching the show…is a frustrating experience. No matter how much one gets the feeling that something is going to happen, it never does. A viewer may wind up with the unhappy thought of having been neither informed nor entertained."

The other Allen Ludden show that debuted on July 5 was *Dance Time*, another "borrowed" idea. In 1953, Philadelphia TV station WFIL had introduced what proved to be a wildly successful afternoon TV show called

Some *Mind Your Manners* listeners were growing up and moving into the real world, and Allen was still there to help them with the *Plain Talk* book series.

Bandstand, in which local disc jockey Bob Horn played current top 40 hits, and area teens were invited to come to the studio and dance on camera throughout the show. The show cost almost nothing (the set was sparse because so much space was needed for the dancing, and the kids came in for free to be seen on TV) and the emergence of rock music, the appeal of teens doing the latest dance moves, and a time slot right after school led to big ratings for WFIL. All of a sudden, it seemed as though every local TV station that could afford to pay a disc jockey was unveiling its own version of *Bandstand*. So WPIX in New York put *Dance Time* on the air.

A newspaper columnist, H.I. Phillips, casually mentioned stumbling upon the show by accident one day, and prophetically raved, "[A] youthful master of ceremonies, Allen Ludden…seems a sure-fire bet for a big-time TV career."

And when Allen wasn't helping early morning viewers wake up, or spinning records for a daily dance party, what was he doing? Relaxing? Come on. By this point, you know better. Allen got another job to occupy his time. He wrote books.

Allen was justifiably proud of *Mind Your Manners*. He had helped countless people with no-nonsense solutions, not from textbooks or advanced education or data from peer-reviewed studies. He had solved so many problems with plain talk, leveling with the kids on his panel and the kids in his audience. Allen couldn't help thinking he had a lot to offer, so he wrote a series of books called *Plain Talk*, offering more advice. He wasn't reaching out to teens, exactly. The books seemingly reached out to the kids who had listened to *Mind Your Manners* from the beginning and had now grown into adults, and the books offered a guide for those former listeners who were now taking their first steps in the real world, with titles like *Plain Talk for Men Under 21, Plain Talk for Women Under 21, Plain Talk for Young Marrieds,* and *Plain Talk About College.*

EXCERPT FROM PLAIN TALK FOR MEN UNDER 21: *Being alone with a girl is really something. What's more, until you've parked, you've never been alone with a girl. Maybe you've walked with her many times…held her hand in the soda shop when no one else happened to be around…even been invited over to somebody's house when she was babysitting…been with her many times and in many places when you thought you were alone. But when you sit in a parked car together for the first time, you'll notice a big difference. Don't be surprised if it catches you off balance and even frightens you a little. There's something about the doors and windows of a car that seems to force the two of you closer together than you've ever been before. The rest of the world is entirely closed out. You're absolutely and irrevocably isolated. If you've been foolish enough to choose some lonely remote spot, you may impulsively turn on the car radio (if it isn't playing already) just to drown out the sound of your breathing. That brings us to the most obvious hazard of parking. That feeling of isolation and loneliness you'll experience when you stop the car and kill the ignition may well touch off a biological chain reaction that you wouldn't have dreamed possible. With absolutely no malice aforethought, young couples who park often find themselves battling purely physical impulses that can be overpowering. Make no mistake about it, my friend, the so-called "sex drive" is the most potent force active in a healthy young man. If you're normal, physically, it's a force to be reckoned with. Both you and your date are extremely vulnerable to situations that suggest sex. And a parked car does. As I said, this is your problem. My only point of view is that you should have your own moral point of view established before you find yourself in such a situation.*

EXCERPT FROM PLAIN TALK FOR WOMEN UNDER 21: *Sociologists will have a great time in a few years explaining the phenomenon of this "going steady" fad which has so taken over since the end of World War II. They may find out it is all part of that generation's search for security. Wanting to mature early, that generation jumped ahead of itself and adopted the attitude of marriage during high school years through the custom of going steady. So history has been written. You can't change that. But you can do something about the next generation's record. It's possible for you and your friends to turn over to a new page...Act your age and have some fun. At no other time in your life is it possible to know so many people so well, mix so often with people of your age, and have so many contacts with members of the opposite sex. Shop around. You're supposed to at your age. Later, it's wrong. Now, it's RIGHT. You're sure to do it sometime; so do it when nature planned that you should.*

EXCERPT FROM PLAIN TALK FOR YOUNG MARRIEDS: *"To top it all off, you're a lousy lover!"...Trouble with most husband-wife brawls is that often things do come out that are better left unsaid. In this fight, though, I think the blow that appears to have done the most damage may prove to be the kindest one anybody ever threw at you...When the lifetime partner you have chosen issues a scathing indictment of your sexual prowess, OF COURSE it's going to hurt! But sulking isn't the option I'd recommend...Once you get accustomed to that idea and can turn it around in your mind without flying into a towering rage or sinking into profound despondency, get practical. Approach the matter like almost any other problem in marriage — trying to avoid emotion, trying to be rational, trying to find a solution. I'm not passing up the possibility that you may eventually have to consign the problem to a doctor...Try to answer questions like this: Did you unconsciously wrap up most of the romance after the wedding and stow it up in the attic somewhere? Did you unwittingly abandon all the art of loving — and we may call it that — and retain nothing but the physical license you applied for with your marriage license? Do you still tell your wife you love her...often? Do you make a sincere effort to show her you do?"*

EXCERPT FROM PLAIN TALK ABOUT COLLEGE: *There is a kind of "College Fever" spreading through our country today and from the way it sounds to me, as I talk to people, it is not very healthy. I have sensed in many conversations with students and their parents an attitude that bothers me, because it indicates a set of phony values. Time after time, I hear these people talk about the crowded colleges and the competition for college admission, and much too often I realize as they*

*are talking that their primary concern is simply to get in. Staying in or
learning something while in college do not occupy their attention nearly
so much as the major achievement of getting in…It is a result of the same
"keeping-up-with-the-Joneses" idea that has sold so many automobiles,
dishwashers, and fur coats. But when it is applied to education, this
attitude seems even more foolhardy and much more wasteful. Just because
everybody in your class is trying to do it or because everybody else's son
and daughter are "going away to school" is not enough reason to think
that you, too, must get into a college.*

Allen got almost entirely favorable reviews for the books, receiving
praise for his "slangy conversational style" and "straight from the shoulder"
tone. Many critics made note of his approach when it came to laying
down the law. Rather than telling his readers what do to, he went to the
roots and explained why certain rules existed. "Do-not-do" passages were
explained in the tone of discussion, not criticism. He successfully spoke
his audience's language and seemed to succeed in getting through to
them. Several years after the *Plain Talk* books were released, the United
States Marine Corps commissioned Allen for a radio show aimed at
teenage listeners. Originally to be titled *Teen Talk*, the show would con-
sist of Allen's brand of no-nonsense advice and counsel for the youth of
America. Before the program premiered, the title was logically changed
to *Plain Talk*.

ALLEN: *Hi, this is Allen Ludden, with some Plain Talk on STUDIES.*

(Intro)

ALLEN: *Remember when the teacher first asked you to write a "composition" about your favorite pet, or your summer's vacation, or the story
of your life?*

Remember your first spelling test?

Or the first time a teacher returned a paper to you with a grade on it?

*That's when you began your preparation for college. It's all logical, too,
when you realize that the brain is a muscle. Like any other muscle in
the body, it must be exercised if it is to increase its working capacity. To
lift a three-hundred-pound weight, to do a complicated ballet leap or to*

throw a baseball, you must get your muscles in shape for it. You certainly cannot expect to accomplish it the first time you try.

During your years in elementary and junior high school, your brain has been put through a systematic set of exercises. Each year, your courses have been designed to build on the learning of the preceding years. When you put up a tower, you start with the foundation. The taller the tower, the deeper the foundation. No one would consider trying to put the top trim on a building until the base of it is solid.

Yet, high school juniors and seniors try to do it. When the pressure gets tough during the last two years of high school, they "see the light." They make an attempt to change their whole attitude toward school work. With the shaky base of indifferent work during ten grades of foundation studies, they expect to launch into the last two years of high school and to understand what it's all about.

I'll be back with more Plain Talk on Studies, but first, here are some words from Dick Stark:

(Commercial)

ALLEN: *Just willingness to work at studies will sometimes improve grades. But the unfortunate fact of the matter is that poor groundwork in mathematics and English composition shows up and slows up any junior or senior who is trying to make up for it with increased effort brought about by his new attitude toward his work. The best way to make up for a lack of understanding of the basics is to go back to the basics and learn them. If the foundation's shaky, fill in the weak spots and make it solid enough to build on.*

For the high school junior or senior who has "seen the light" and wants to do better work during his last years than he has done during the earlier times, I have one firm recommendation: talk to your teachers. Ask them to give you achievement tests that will show up your specific weaknesses.

Then, with their help, take reviews courses, work with a tutor. Use your initiative. Go to summer school. Look around; maybe there's a good fourth-grade teacher who will run you through some of the material you never mastered. You'd be surprised how much they teach in the fourth, fifth, and sixth grades — surprised, that is, if you didn't make an effort to get it at the time it was available for you.

Face the logical, simple truth: a willingness to do better is not enough. Most often, the junior or senior who wants to make up for past negligence in his studies simply does not know how. He needs encouragement and instruction to keep him on a constructive path. To sit for hours with homework that makes no sense can do more harm than good. He must learn to walk before he can run, and at all times during his learning, he must experience the pleasure and profit of knowing that his effort is getting him somewhere. Even if it's slow, a student who is trying must sense some progress. I repeat: to avoid spinning your wheels, get help. TALK TO YOUR TEACHERS.

Wheel-spinning is a waste. Neither you, as an individual, nor your nation, as a whole, can afford such waste.

Allen had one minor setback. *Good Morning* was a flop and it was canceled at the end of the summer. However, there were a couple of reasons Allen didn't grieve the end of the show too much. For one, *Good Morning* required him to leave the house at 6 a.m., and because of the work schedule required of the other programs he had on the air, he was not seeing his wife and children while *Good Morning* was on the air. The other reason Allen wasn't saddened was because he already had another gig lined up.

Good Morning aired its final episode on Friday, August 27. The following Monday, August 30, Allen was hosting a new series. *Sentimental You* featured Allen and co-host Toni Southern interviewing guests about events in their past, with a soundtrack of popular songs from the time period of the stories told. For example, one program was "A Tribute to the Radio Pioneers." Allen welcomed guests H.V. Kaltenborn ("the Dean of Commentators"), announcer Norman Brokenshire, and singer Joe White (a.k.a. "The Silver Masked Tenor"). Together, they talked about the radio shows they worked on, sharing their favorite warm and fuzzy memories of the good old days, while Allen occasionally paused the proceedings to play some songs that figured prominently into his guests' memories.

A short time after the premiere of *Sentimental You*, the fall rolled around, and like a lot of younger folks in the fall, Allen went back to *College*. NBC had actually canceled *College Quiz Bowl* in the spring of 1955 after its second season, but reluctantly so. They had Allen and the staff shoot a pilot for a television version, with the hope of shopping it around to prospective sponsors and getting one of them to sign up. When no sponsor expressed any interest in a TV version, NBC gave *College Quiz Bowl* a reprieve for the 1955-56 season. *College Quiz Bowl* had been attracting a lot of press in the past two years. Cities were so proud of their local schools being invited to participate that with every episode, *College Quiz Bowl* was guaranteed to get at least two newspaper articles somewhere in America. The thinking from NBC was that they could get an additional sponsor to latch on if *College Quiz Bowl* kept getting attention from the press. For added help, the third season of *College Quiz Bowl* consisted entirely of returning winners from the first two seasons, in the hopes that they would have exciting, close, high-scoring battles that would win over sponsors.

FRED WOSTBROCK COLLECTION

CHAPTER SIX

"SURVIVE"

Allen's early forays into television, like *Good Morning* and *Sentimental You* had not caught on quite the way he probably hoped, but Allen was doubtlessly successful in a realm that, funnily enough, was on its way out: traditional radio programs. *Mind Your Manners* was still chugging along at WTIC, and the national version, at the time of its cancelation, had been one of the longest-running radio shows in the history of NBC. As more and more of the decision makers and stars of the golden age of radio were giving up on it, it appeared that Allen Ludden was one of the last remaining figures in the business who could make it work. And what separated Allen from most personalities is that most air talents who reached that level of success would declare themselves to be strictly air talents, and that they were done with behind the scenes work. Allen, on the other hand, took yet another job on his off-days from his radio shows. He co-produced a newscast for NBC.

The program was called *Weekend,* touted by NBC as "The Sunday newspaper of the air." Airing on Sunday afternoons, the program was divided into sections, like a newspaper. The first segment consisted of a rundown of the top news stories, followed by a "column" from syndicated news writer Earl Wilson discussing current show biz gossip and a review of a new Broadway play. Jinx Falkenburg hosted "The Women's Page," with fashion reports and news about notable women. Each program also featured a segment called "Young America." In the premiere broadcast of *Weekend*, the "Young America" segment consisted of a panel of kids debating the pros and cons of necking, the establishment of designated smoking rooms in some high schools, and the use of lipstick. The "Young America" segment was hosted and produced each week by you-know-who.

STRAIGHTEN UP AND DRIVE RIGHT!
An Editorial for Young Drivers
by Allen Ludden
For Weekend, *Sunday, July 4*

It's possible, you know, that this weekend there are more cars on the American road than at any other time in our history. The statistics are not in yet, of course, but there have been some dire predictions by the experts.

Anybody who has listened to the radio these past few days has been told time and time again to drive carefully. We hope it's done some good. But, being an optimist, I still believe there's time to talk some drivers out of accidents that are yet to happen. All we've got to do is make those drivers stop and THINK. And with that in mind, I'd like to talk to YOUNG drivers…drivers under 25.

I've got some facts here before me that ought to interest you. Did you know that drivers under 25 constitute only about 15% of all licensed drivers…and yet they are involved in…if not actually responsible for… almost TWENTY-FIVE PERCENT of all fatal accidents…and TWENTY PERCENT of all non-fatal accidents?

Know what that means? That's a factual indictment against young drivers that's mighty hard to argue. I've spent a lot of time defending young people, because I believe they are very often misjudged. But here I've come face-to-face with a fact that is frightening. The fact that you young drivers have more accidents than their share is conclusive proof that, as a group, you have not learned the fundamentals of safe driving, caution, and courtesy.[1]

There are those who say that this means we must have more and better driver training programs in schools and closer supervision of new drivers. I agree. The more carefully you are taught to drive, the more you'll know about it. And the closer supervision, the less likely you'll be to go crazy behind the wheel. But parents and police officers cannot ride with you ALL the time; so let's be practical; the burden of the whole problem lies with YOU!

1. Allen rewrote this script just before going on the air with it. This sentence originally read, "Not only do young drivers have more accidents than their share, but they have more FATAL accidents than NON-FATAL accidents. That's conclusive proof…"

It's high time every young driver in this country straighten up and drive right!

Remember that old gag about the gay young blade who announced slyly "…You're the first girl I ever kissed"…as he shifted gears with his knee! Well, back in the days when automatic transmissions were just drafting board dreams, manipulating that gear shift without taking your right arm off the girl's shoulder was a neat trick…but it never was very funny. The young lovers with the one-arm routines went to the hospital faster than to church. And the story's the same today.

Automobile manufacturers have worked wonders, but they've yet to come up with a car that can be handled properly with just one arm. They may some day, but that day's not even on the drafting boards yet. Chances are we'll NEVER see the day when a driver can manage a car with anything less than ONE HUNDRED PERCENT of his attention.

As a matter of fact, in spite of technical advances, driving an automobile calls for more skill and more coordination today than it ever did before. Our roads have not kept pace with the speed and capability of modern cars, and the human machine is being hopelessly outclassed. That's why thousands of lives are lost or ruined on the highways each year.

Now I'm not suggesting that we start a "back-to-the-horse-and-buggy" campaign. I'm just saying to all drivers…and particularly to young drivers, that driving a car is a serious challenge. It's a "give it all you've got" business.

If you're just starting to drive…start right now to cultivate the habit of being alert…(And I mean being just as alert as you would be if you were driving on a winding one-lane mountain road in the Swiss Alps!) You've got YOUTH on your side. Your reflexes are quicker. Your coordination is better. You are potentially the safest driver on the road. You are…until you get cocky. Then you lose sight of the fact that you hold, not just your own life, but MANY lives in your hands whenever you drive.

If you fail to take your driving seriously, if you take unnecessary chances, if you drive too fast, drive when you're drowsy, drive a car that's not mechanically safe, drive after drinking, drive as if you're immune to traffic laws…if you commit any of these crimes, or any others you might know about...you're an IDIOT! Frankly, I believe any jerk can be a daredevil. It takes real guts to be careful!

Now, maybe you're taking all this with a grain of salt. Okay! That's your business, my friend...and maybe your funeral, too. But whatever you're thinking, I want to sound off and say that I sincerely believe that young people with the proper attitude toward driving can help reduce the carnage on American roads.

All you've got to do is THINK about it. Once you'll do, you'll see that it makes SENSE to drive a car with care! Give it some thought...today!

Despite an awful initiation — the premiere broadcast aired in direct competition with game five of the 1953 World Series between the Yankees and the Brooklyn Dodgers, which meant that nobody, particularly in New York City, was listening to *Weekend* — the show ultimately attracted a respectable audience and good reviews from critics. *Broadcasting* magazine praised the rather ingenious structure of the show; like a newspaper, it had something for everybody but it was unlikely that everybody would be interested in every single element...but this also meant that listeners had to listen to the whole show to hear the parts that they wanted; a nice ploy to entice advertisers that this show would be a success.

And succeed it did! One season later, Allen went into the fall of 1954 still with three radio shows on the air. But though Allen Ludden felt secure in radio, he was part of a shrinking minority in that regard. NBC's vice president in charge of the radio network resigned, giving no explanation other than "personal reasons." A week later, operating Vice President Red Cott submitted his resignation, giving no explanation other than "personal reasons." NBC Executive Vice President Robert W. Sarnoff (son of network founder "General" David Sarnoff) announced that neither man would be replaced.

Early in 1955, NBC's radio affiliates received this message from Robert Sarnoff: "Our radio operation today is geared to one fundamental belief: That we can bring new money into radio and make old money return by providing new services which will hold and build our audiences."

One week after delivering that statement, NBC's radio division announced a drastic change in its radio programming strategy. Effective June, every weekend on the network would be filled by a single, forty-hour-long program. The new show would last for twenty years. Titled *Monitor*, it was and is widely hailed as the last great radio show. Emanating from a new high-tech facility called Radio Central, *Monitor* consisted of absolutely everything that could possibly fill a forty-hour show. There were news reports, in-depth magazine stories, live coverage from events taking place around the world, celebrity interviews, mail from listeners, commentaries, and sketch comedy. Holding each broadcast together would be the "communicators," a who's-who of broadcasting, who took turns hosting three or four hours at a time. The original communicators included Hugh Downs, David Brinkley, Dave Garroway, Clifton Fadiman, and Ben Grauer. Allen never served as a communicator, but instead picked up where he left off. *Weekend* had been sacrificed to make way for *Monitor*, and Allen was diligently working behind the scenes as a producer on the new endeavor, whipping up ideas, coordinating all the necessary pieces, and getting the segments on the air every weekend.

As all that was going on, so too was *Mind Your Manners*. After eight years, a national radio version and a national TV version had come and gone, but the local version on WTIC was still chugging along. The University of Connecticut found it amazing that a radio show could have so much influence even when its original target audience had outgrown it and conducted a study of high school students throughout the state of Connecticut to gauge the influence of *Mind Your Manners* on teenagers. The study found that fifty-seven percent of teenagers said they had heard the show at some point. Of the group that said they had heard the show, more than half listened to the show regularly. Nearly half said they had been regularly listening for a year or more. Over one-third identified themselves as "intensive" listeners. Three-quarters of the kids had watched the television version and nearly half of them watched the TV version regularly. Fifty-five percent said they didn't listen to radio shows anymore but that they liked *Mind Your Manners* enough that they'd watch it regularly if another TV version was introduced.

And they weren't just listening, they were taking it to heart. Forty-nine percent of kids say they were more prone to take the advice given by the show than the advice given by teenagers that they knew. When quizzed about multiple alternate sources of media, such as books, magazines, and newspapers, the majority of teenagers, in every case, said that *Mind Your Manners* gave better advice. Eighty-two percent of the teens said that the advice given on the show was "usually very good," and nearly sixty-nine percent said that they made an effort to follow the advice given.

Back at NBC, the revolutionary *Monitor* concept had worked so well that by summer's end, NBC was already overhauling its Monday-Friday radio schedule to look a little more like their breakout hit. Allen was removed from his producing post at *Monitor* to instead go to work as producer on the new endeavor, titled *Weekday*.

Seemingly blending equal parts *Today* and *Monitor*, NBC's *Weekday* was a five-and-a-half hour offering co-hosted by Mike Wallace and Margaret Truman. The show aired from 10:00 a.m. to 3:30 p.m. each day, and in a remarkable display of courtesy to the show's staff, *Weekday* actually had a built-in lunch break, with NBC offering space in each program for local stations to plug in their own content while the show's staff got something to eat.

Wallace was at an interesting crossroads in his career. He was a veteran radio broadcaster who had narrated a number of shows and starred in a crime drama. He moved to television, where he briefly provided commentary for professional wrestling and hosted a number of early TV game shows. He wanted to pursue journalism and began making a name for himself with a controversial local talk show in New York titled *Night Beat*. The show gained a reputation instantly for hard-hitting questions and guests that most other talk shows would never touch. Truman was likewise at a crossroads. The only daughter of President Harry S Truman, she had spent several years as a professional singer with some degree of success — she made the cover of *Time* Magazine, but generally speaking, critics tended to agree that she was good, not great. She would later emerge as an extremely prolific author of non-fiction and murder mysteries. But in between those two pursuits, she co-hosted *Weekday*.

So how did NBC fill a massive chunk of airtime like *Weekday*? A typical episode, reviewed by the critic for *Broadcasting*, included a cooking segment, shopping tips, composer/playwright Meredith Willson playing some samples of "long-hair music" and explaining its emerging popularity, Audrey Hepburn and Mel Ferrer promoting their new film with an interview, music from Eddie Fisher and Debbie Reynolds, a French record explaining painless childbirth, a regular feature in which a portion of a novel was read to the home audience each day until the entire novel had been read on air, a segment on interior decorating, and reports from correspondents in Hollywood and Washington.

Now imagine doing five of those broadcasts every week and you'll probably gain tremendous respect for the staff of eleven, including Wallace and Truman, who put it together. And Allen, as usual, was tireless in his efforts to make it easier on everybody else. To save Wallace and Truman the late hours that would have come with preparing the segments for the next day's show, Allen would conduct some interviews himself, then take Wallace and Truman into a studio and record their voices asking the questions that he had asked, and then splice that audio into the interview while simultaneously removing his own voice from the tape. The home audience heard an extremely well-informed and well-conducted interview, and the truth was the interviewers didn't have to do a bit of research or writing to get it done.

Before long, Allen's voice did make it onto *Weekday*. The show instituted a regular pair of features called "Teenage Forum" and "Family

Betty and Gloria DeHaven give Gene Rayburn a good luck kiss as he prepares to take over *Make the Connection;* Betty had originally been considered to host the show herself, but had to settle for being a panelist.

AUTHOR'S COLLECTION

Forum." "Teenage Forum" was substantially the same as *Mind Your Manners,* while "Family Forum" was geared toward resolving family disputes. Allen was asked to moderate the discussions for both segments. It was, after all, familiar territory for him.

In 1954, Betty White seemed to be in good shape, with two hit shows on the air, but for reasons that she couldn't control, both shows abruptly ended before their time. *The Betty White Show* was uprooted from its successful noon timeslot to 4:30 in the afternoon, and the ratings slid. Betty and her producers flew from Los Angeles to New York in an attempt to convince NBC executives to put the show back in its original spot, but to no avail. *The Betty White Show* aired its last episode on New Year's Eve, 1954.

Life with Elizabeth had proven successful, airing sixty-five episodes during two seasons to favorable reactions, but it met a premature demise for an odd reason. The company that distributed the show to local stations felt that the show had produced too many new episodes in only two seasons, and that would make it an undesirable property when the time came to try to sell reruns. The series ended early in 1955, and Betty looked for new ideas for her next career move. Among the suggestions: panel shows.

NBC was collaborating with producers Mark Goodson and Bill Todman, the undisputed kingpins of TV game shows, on a summer replacement series for 1955. Goodson-Todman had a hit on CBS with a panel show called *I've Got a Secret*, in which a celebrity panel tried to guess some secret about a contestant. Now, for NBC, Goodson and Todman were preparing to introduce a new series that was almost exactly the same show.

On *Make the Connection*, a panel of four celebrities would face a pair of contestants who had connected secrets. For example, a student and teacher appeared with their secret being that the student had given her teacher measles. A man and a baby appeared; the baby had fallen out of the window of a high-rise apartment building and the man caught him. Each panelist had a turn asking yes-or-no questions, trying to make the connection. The turn ended when a bell sounded, awarding the contestants twenty-five dollars, and the game ended when the connection was guessed or the bell sounded a total of six times.

NBC and Goodson-Todman originally asked Betty to audition for host. She had already proven herself an adept television hostess with *Hollywood on Television* and *The Betty White Show*. On New Year's Day 1955, she was the host of NBC's coverage of the Tournament of Roses Parade in Pasadena. It was the beginning of a long, successful run of providing commentary for television coverage of parades. She would host, by her own count, twenty Rose Parades, six Grand Floral Parades in Portland, Oregon, and ten Macy's Thanksgiving Day Parades in New York City. Since Betty had hosted everything else, NBC and Goodson-Todman figured, why not a game show?

She enthusiastically said yes, did an audition, and hosted a series of run-through games while the show was in development. But then, the very people who had asked Betty to audition were now telling her "No thanks."

There had been a female game show host previously. Arlene Francis had been at the helm of a game called *Blind Date* on both radio and television, but she was the exception. The prevailing wisdom was that since the master of ceremonies on a game show had to enforce rules, they should have some air of authority. Even if they were witty, smiled a lot, shook hands, and told corny jokes, there still had to be some sense of being in charge. And the thinking was that men were naturally more authoritative than women, so game show hosts were strictly a boys' club.

As a consolation, Betty was asked to join the panel, sitting alongside actress Gloria DeHaven, disc jockey Gene Klavan, and actor Eddie

Bracken. Each week featured a celebrity guest, including famous names of the time like Victor Borge, Buster Keaton, Eartha Kitt, and J. Fred Muggs. The first few weeks were hosted by sportscaster Jim McKay, who was replaced very quickly by Steve Allen's sidekick and announcer from *The Tonight Show*, Gene Rayburn.

Columnist Jack O'Brian was less than kind to the show, but explained in his review that there was nothing wrong with the program in and of itself. It's that the production seemed to be creatively bankrupt.

O'Brian wrote, "[W]e would suggest [Goodson and Todman] call a conference among themselves and stop killing their golden goose, *What's My Line?*...[P]erhaps they should have studied their own methods of lifting their very own panel design and placing it all over the channels under other names which, boiled down, turn out to be just copies of *What's My Line? I've Got a Secret*, the Goodson-Todman quizcast which passed *What's My Line?* in the ratings recently, is just another pale switch on the John Daly-moderated original. Now they have tried again with something called *Make the Connection*. This also is a fuzzy carbon of *What's My Line?*"

And it appeared that O'Brian was right. *Make the Connection* never returned after its initial summer commitment. But Betty enjoyed the experience of playing a game, and she decided it was something she was up for in the future of any game shows were to invite her.

FRED WOSTBROCK COLLECTION

CHAPTER SEVEN

"REVIVE"

As much as Allen Ludden had managed to hang on in an ever-changing medium that was squeezing out a lot of personnel, he couldn't fight change forever. In 1956, after nearly a decade, WTIC finally ended *Mind Your Manners*, and NBC pulled the plug on *College Quiz Bowl* at the end of its third season. Anticipating the changing fortunes of radio, the *College Quiz Bowl* staff had, a year earlier, filmed a game to serve as a pilot for a television version as a means of surviving, but no networks or sponsors took the bait. There would be no TV version of *College Quiz Bowl* — at least not yet — and the radio version was now history.

Weekday survived and Allen remained at his post as producer, although he still looked for ways to keep himself occupied. He continued writing books and returned to Corpus Christi for a Southwest Writers Conference, in which he spoke at a session concerning writing for television and radio.

At the end of the summer, NBC's radio division, still trying to find its way while keeping costs low, gave Allen new responsibilities behind the scenes. He helped sell commercial time for a while before being reassigned to programming development.

Betty was having an uneventful 1956. She gave her name and face to several products for advertising while her business partner, Don Fedderson, tried to sell networks and packagers another Betty White sitcom. By the fall, he had succeeded, selling ABC Network and MGM on a new sitcom called *Date with the Angels*. It was a series about a newlywed couple, conveniently with the last name Angel, who got themselves into a series of uncomfortable and unfortunate circumstances. The wife, Vicki — Betty's character — had a vivid imagination, and the show frequently cut away to fantasy sequences showing Vicki imagining how things could have worked out.

Vicki's husband, Bill, was played by Bill Williams (best known to western fans as "Kit Carson") — Betty really wanted to work with Del Moore again, but everybody agreed it would make the show look like a "warmed-over" revival of *Life with Elizabeth*. *Date with the Angels* did retain one indirect link with *Life with Elizabeth*. *Life with Elizabeth* had been narrated by announcer Jack Narz. *Date with the Angels* would have its

voiceovers provided by Jack's younger brother, up-and-coming announcer Jim Narz. To avoid professional confusion with his brother, Jim would eventually change his name to Tom Kennedy and emerge as one of the great game show hosts of the next thirty years.

The nerves that Betty felt when she got called up to the big leagues for *The Betty White Show* on NBC had disappeared. She was far more relaxed about *Date with the Angels*, reasoning that she had such a secure contract that she had no reason to be afraid.

She told a reporter, "I have a contract for seventy-five

Betty keeps herself occupied, with help from a friend, while waiting to see what opportunities television would bring her next. AUTHOR'S COLLECTION

weekly shows — and it's non-cancellable. Naturally we're thrilled not to be wondering every week whether our options will be picked up. But it works to mutual advantage. Knowing that our sponsors have so much confidence in us makes it difficult for us to let them down. And from their point of view, they don't have to worry about revising the characters. We're all stuck with each other."

Date with the Angels survived only seven months on ABC. The show actually had a unique premise and a tremendous amount of talent putting together each week's episodes, but the sight of a flighty woman and her husband getting into wacky predicaments caused a number of thumbs-down reviews from critics who casually dismissed it as an *I Love Lucy* clone. Oddly, the show's sponsor, Plymouth, responded to the criticism to reinforcing it. Insisting that television audience didn't like fantasies, Plymouth told the writers to eliminate the portions of each program revolving around Vicki's daydreams. Since sponsors wielded enormous power behind the scenes in that era, the writers complied. And without the fantasy sequences, the show was one more domestic sitcom, with no identity to make it stand out in the crowd.

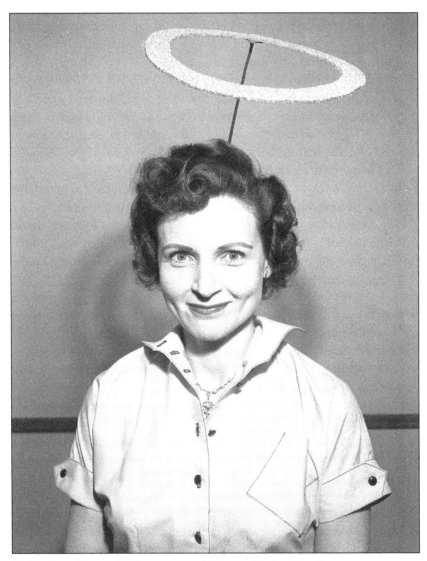

Halo, there! Betty White stars on *A Date with the Angels.*
AUTHOR'S COLLECTION

Everyone grew so frustrated that after thirty-three episodes, Betty and everyone else involved agreed to throw away the *Date with the Angels* concept. That still left Betty, ABC, and Plymouth with forty-two episodes on their contract, and Betty delivered a new series, reviving the title *The Betty White Show*. She teamed up once again with Del Moore and a new cast of supporting actors, and returned to the *Life with Elizabeth* concept of three stories in every episode, the twist being that although the show had a regular cast, it would have no regular characters. Betty and her co-stars were telling entirely new stories with entirely new personalities every time.

Don Fedderson had a little more success in 1956 and 1957 with a quiz show he had mounted called *Do You Trust Your Wife?*, hosted by ventriloquist Edgar Bergen. Quiz shows were in vogue in 1956. The previous year, *The $64,000 Question* had exploded on CBS, and before long, quiz shows were all over the network airwaves: *The Big Surprise, Break the $250,000 Bank, Twenty One, TicTacDough, Giant Step*, among others.

The problem was that many of these quiz shows were fixed. Contestants were coached on which categories to pick and what answers to give. Ratings were carefully watched and specific contestants' fortunes would rise and fall with the ratings. The more an audience loved the returning champion, the more he won. If the audience's interest seemed to be waning even slightly, it was time to crown a new champion.

In 1958, the quiz shows collapsed. Bitter contestants stepped forward with evidence that their games were rigged. Producers and network executives pointed fingers and passed bucks as much as they could. People committed perjury in congressional hearings. Quiz shows were almost entirely wiped off the schedules. Game shows, which emphasized skill more than straight knowledge (*The Price is Right, Concentration*, and *Beat the Clock* for example) thrived, but the overwhelmingly bad publicity and other consequences from the big money quiz shows scared the major networks away from questions and answers. More importantly, the Congressional hearings led to the passage of new laws implementing fines and prison sentences for anyone who rigged game and quiz programs.

One of the big problems with most of the rigged quiz shows was that they wouldn't work otherwise. *The $64,000 Question* was a perfect example. The money doubled with every correct answer, and the contestants couldn't play for a higher amount without first agreeing to forfeit the money already won. No contestant would sacrifice $32,000 for a slim chance at $64,000 without knowing there was some sort of guarantee. Another notorious quiz, *Twenty One*, had attempted to play its premiere episode legitimately, and the game played out so badly that the audience in the studio was actually laughing at the contestants.

Those fixed quiz shows had delivered wonderful results, though. Audiences devoured them, and sponsors experienced big increases in business by supporting them. Was there a way to get a legitimate show on the air that involved hard questions and people who actually were smart enough to answer them? Somewhere along the way, a television executive looked at shows from the recent past and realized that if the television audience wanted hard questions and answers, then the network already had a perfect show ready and waiting.

Announcer Tom Kennedy chats with Betty on *A Date with the Angels*; game shows would lead the two of them to cross paths time and again over the next thirty years. AUTHOR'S COLLECTION

Allen once told a reporter, "I'm one of those people who enjoys everything he does, whatever it is. I'm not sure whether that's good or bad. All I know is that as long as I can keep working and keep the kids fed, I'm happy."

It was a good thing he had that attitude because new opportunities presented themselves and Allen fearlessly approached unfamiliar territory whenever he dealt with it in his career. Early in 1957, Allen was put to work as a producer for another NBC radio show, *Pocketbook News*. Wilma Soss, founder and president of the Federation of Women Shareholders in American Business hosted the program, in which she broke down, in unsophisticated terms, why she expected various stocks to rise or fall in the coming months based on the companies' recent business decisions. She also offered commentary targeting the companies themselves, in which she laid into corporations that she felt weren't doing enough to appease their stockholders. NBC plugged the show into a not-particularly desirable time slot, Sunday night at 11:15 p.m.

Back home, the Ludden family was in crisis. Margaret was diagnosed with lung cancer. The medical bills began piling up quickly, and Allen's job at NBC wasn't going to be enough. *Weekday* had gone off the air, and the de-emphasis on radio's importance meant that Allen's executive position in programming development didn't entail very much. Allen felt that, for his family's sake, it was time to move on.

In May, he turned in his resignation and moved across town to WCBS Radio for a position as program director and got to work rebuilding his career. It might have seemed like a strange career move for somebody who had enjoyed so much success as a program host up to this point and almost certainly stood to find work as an on-air talent, but television was a different beast from radio, and he told one reporter that he'd rather be a program executive than a television performer. Besides, the jobs off the air carried far more security than the jobs on the air. If Allen tried hosting a show, it could be gone in a matter of weeks and he'd be right back to square one. For Margaret's sake, he needed a dependable job.

Allen's first order of business at WCBS: switching the station to stereo. American Airlines was the catalyst. They were the sponsors of a national program called *Music 'Til Dawn* and begin pushing and pushing quite hard for the local stations that carried the show to make the switch to stereo. Allen was one of the program directors who eagerly complied, broadcasting stereo recordings from two separate radio transmitters. This method wasn't very practical — depending on where the listener was, it meant one channel or the other would be in better quality — but it worked well enough, and with radio putting stronger emphasis on music programming, making the change generated some publicity and got some people to swivel their dials to WCBS.

But Allen had some dark days as WCBS program director, too. John Henry Faulk, a popular humorist on the station, left for a one-month vacation during the summer of 1957, and Allen was instructed by those above him at CBS to fire Faulk. Allen had to carry out the orders while Faulk was gone, thousands of miles away and unable to take any real action about what had happened to him. Faulk was a victim of the ominous Blacklist. Senator Joseph McCarthy, who spearheaded the anti-communist movement in America, had by this point, been censured and left office in disgrace, but his movement had inspired the creation of AWARE, a for-profit anti-communist group. Faulk, as a member of the American Federation of Radio and Television Artists (AFTRA), had successfully wrestled control of the union away from AWARE-supported officers. It left Faulk with a target on his back.

When Faulk returned from his vacation, he initially suspected that ratings had declined (he admitted he never really paid attention to his own ratings data), but things turned suspicious when it became clear that Allen had been given a different reason for firing him. Allen said he had been told that Faulk had to go because the station was preparing to change formats and Faulk wasn't a good fit for their future plans.

A distraught Allen told Faulk that he couldn't imagine AWARE had been involved. Allen told him, "I can't believe that WCBS would do anything that underhanded."

But they had. The big bosses had gone over Allen's head, and with AWARE's encouragement, Faulk was out of a job. Allen apologetically told Faulk that as suspicious as everything was, he had to take full responsibility for the decision. Faulk understood Allen's grace under fire, and deep down, he didn't blame Allen. With the help of Edward R. Murrow, Faulk would eventually file a multimillion-dollar lawsuit against AWARE and ultimately received a $3.5 million judgment from the jury, and the era of the Blacklist essentially ended.

Allen, an employee of a CBS affiliate, was in exactly the right place at the right time when word came out that a show from his past was on its way back. Network executives liked the big rating that came with hard quiz shows like *The $64,000 Question* and *Dotto*, but not the consequences they had to deal with from those shows, and finally decided that *College Quiz Bowl* was perfect. They negotiated a deal with Don Reid and John Moses to put a television version on the air. Allen, despite his misgivings about remaining in television as a performer, had loved hosting the radio version, and as Reid and Moses told him, the radio audience had identified him so closely in the role of host that if they watched the television and heard the voice of any other host, they'd reject it. Allen, they said, had to host it. Allen eventually agreed.

As Allen explained at the time, hosting *College Quiz Bowl* offered him many more reasons to say yes. One reason that he kept to himself was Margaret. She was still battling lung cancer and Allen still had to keep up with the hospital bills. But Allen was eager to talk to the press about the other reasons that *College Quiz Bowl* was a good career move. The show was airing on Sunday afternoons, which meant that it would never interfere with his work week at WCBS. More importantly, because he had done so much to get the original idea off the ground, it was clear that the show's staff would defer to him most of the time (although, ultimately, Allen still didn't get the tournament format that he wanted for each season).

Allen told a reporter at the time, "I think it's safe to say this is the only show I'll do…and I'm doing it only because I'm being allowed to do it the way I want and I like working with young people. I was a performer…a long time ago, and while I made more money than I've ever made in my life, I'm a program director and that's my field! Doing more than this one show would interfere with my work."

Judging from the old clock on the wall, it's time to start a new television version of *College Bowl*. FRED WOSTBROCK COLLECTION

Jack Cleary, the former NBC radio executive who had greenlit the show in 1953, would now be serving as co-executive producer along with Don Reid and John Moses. All they needed was a sponsor. And that turned out to be an easier task than anybody could have expected.

Allen told a reporter, "All of us connected with the show thought it was great...but we couldn't sell it to TV. I guess it was just never shown

G.E. brought good things to life in 1959 when they agreed to sponsor *College Bowl.* FRED WOSTBROCK COLLECTION

properly. This time it took about four hours from the time it was first shown to G.E. until it was finally accepted."

Jack Cleary left the office early one afternoon and took a train to the Maxon, Inc. advertising agency. There he met with the executives who oversaw the account for General Electric, and told them of the format of the radio quiz that he was now adapting for television. The advertising agency liked what they heard so much that they made a phone call to General Electric's housewares and radio receiver division in Bridgeport, Connecticut, and suggested they take a meeting. General Electric agreed, but they didn't want to wait for the meeting. Cleary took another train out of New York to Bridgeport. By 5 p.m., he had closed the deal.

The program was accordingly renamed *G.E. College Bowl.* General Electric supplied commercials, many of which were brief animated spots that the show's staff privately felt were condescending in tone and beneath the style of the program that they were appearing on. Allen himself redeemed things somewhat by ending each episode with a very sincere delivery of G.E.'s slogan: "Progress is our most important product."

The announcer for *G.E. College Bowl* was a voiceover artist named Don Morrow. Morrow remembers, "I came to the attention of a vice president at Maxon. His name was William Lewis. As I recall, we went to a bar to confirm the deal. He and I became very close friends and being a redhead, he became known to all of us as Red Dawg. I shortened it to Dawg soon after. Next I met John Cleary, Jon Moses, and Don Reid. After that, I met Allen and his wife Margaret, whom we all called Maggie.

"My first impression of Allen was that he was a very likable guy. My second impression of him was that he was afraid of flying. Dawg and I found that out on our first weekend flight, when we did the premiere from Brown University. He seemed to be the only crew member that was, and I'm almost ashamed to tell you that Dawg and I took full advantage of that. We'd say 'Luddy, buddy, don't look out on the wing.' He'd ALWAYS respond, 'Why?!' and we'd give the obvious 'Cuz it's on fire.' Or variations on the same. It was a continual party and Allen really took it good-naturedly."

Maggie would sometimes tag along for some of the programs too. Morrow remembers, "Maggie told Dawg and me about her lung cancer during a flight to San Francisco, when we were doing an episode from Stanford University. She was just the greatest. I remember she'd say things like 'Let's us three go to a bar someplace and talk dirty.' God, we loved that girl."

CBS had faith in the show despite the scandals of the previous year. The network hoped that the television audience that was so repelled by the quiz show scandals would keep enough of an open mind to give them a chance. This wasn't a show that gave away life-changing amounts of money to contestants who would become minor celebrities as a result of their success. Only $2,000 would be awarded each week. $1,500 for the winners and $500 for the losers (although Allen preferred the term "runners-up"). And the contestants themselves wouldn't see the money. The payoffs were going straight into scholarship funds for their schools.

Actually, there was one effect that the scandals had on *G.E. College Bowl*. Nobody associated with the program knew how to classify it. "Quiz show" had become a dirty word for network executives and the press, and at least one reporter who interviewed Allen for a story about the new program noted that Allen absolutely refused to call it a quiz show, even when the reporter himself had used the term first during their conversation.

"It's a game," Allen told the reporter. "It's more like a basketball game than a quiz. There's plenty of action and the participants are all under constant pressure."

Allen wasn't alone in using the basketball metaphor. Don Reid, for years, maintained that he had been the actual creator of the *College Bowl* format, despite Grant Tinker's account of watching Allen formulate the game out of thin air and onto a writing tablet. Reid said that while he was attending college and playing for the basketball team, he got to thinking of an idea for a quiz show that would be a "mental basketball game." The way he described it, the jump ball at the outset of the game became the ten-point toss-up question. The run down court for the team that got the ball became the bonus question for the team that answered the toss-up.

There may have been some truth to this story. Reid undoubtedly had the basic idea for the competition between two colleges, and he may have had it in his head that the framework of a basketball game may have been a good basis for a quiz, but it was Allen Ludden who actually put the meat between the bread and turned Don Reid's idea into *College Quiz Bowl* and *G.E. College Bowl*.

One of the curiosities about the show is how readily America latched onto it as if it was a sport. Player biographies and team statistics would appear in local newspapers leading up to the next game ("The Notre Dame team has two mathematics majors and two English majors, one of whom is on the debate team…"). And there was at least one report of an opposing coach being hanged in effigy after a losing effort. When the University of Notre Dame returned home after a victorious effort over Georgetown, one writer, probably to the delight of Allen Ludden and Don Reid, recapped a game by referring to the five-point penalty for interrupting a toss-up with a wrong answer as a "foul" and calling the bonus questions "free throws."

The new television version eliminated the complicated inter-campus telephone hook-ups of the radio version. But there was one technological breakthrough developed for the television *College Bowl*, and once again, it was Allen's idea.

Television screens weren't very big in the late 1950s, and with eight players and Allen onscreen, there was a real danger that the home viewers were going to be stuck watching nine tiny specks on the screen. Allen's suggestion for fixing this was to keep one camera fixed on him between questions and at the start of the next question. Then the director would cut to shots of the two teams; one camera on each team at the same time, and the audience at home would see both camera shots at the same time by way of Allen's idea: a horizontal split in the middle of the screen. A viewer today wouldn't bat an eye at a camera shot composed that way, but before 1959, it had never been done. Allen insisted it would work and asked the CBS technical crew to at least try it.

The reason it worked so well was because the cameramen and director Lamar Caselli maximized the dramatic effect. The cameramen would

Who will win? It's a toss-up...followed by a twenty-point bonus, on *G.E. College Bowl.* FRED WOSTBROCK COLLECTION

keep a watchful eye on the players and were ready to zoom at a moment's notice. As soon as a player rang in, the appropriate cameraman did a fast zoom, and at the same time, Caselli would wipe away one half of the split screen by using the other half to fill the picture, so in a split second, the camera shot went from eight faces to a single face filling the screen. In a close game, it was a very effective trick.

G.E. College Bowl also found that the television screen allowed them to do something imaginative that they couldn't do on radio. They could actually have silent questions. On one episode, Allen announced that a ten-point toss-up was forthcoming. Then he put down his question cards and picked up, in order, a pair of high heel shoes, a pair of toy boats, a jar of wax, a cabbage, and a poker hand showing four of a kind.

A contestant from Barnhart University rang in and supplied the correct answer: The objects made reference to the line "Of shoes and ships and ceiling wax, of cabbages and kings" from the poem *The Walrus and the Carpenter* by Lewis Carroll.

G.E. College Bowl initially traveled to college campuses all over the country instead of remaining confined to a studio. For the series pre-

The entire nation was Allen's classroom as he asked the questions on *G.E. College Bowl.* FRED WOSTBROCK COLLECTION

miere, they were live on the campus of Brown University, with Brown and Pembroke sending a team into battle against Northwestern University. Northwestern won, which meant that the following week's show would emanate from Evanston, Illinois. This was a clever extra incentive that the show added for winners. The championship team always had the home field advantage. If the game ended in a tie, there was no tiebreaker. Both teams returned the following week and competed on the same campus.

College Bowl historian Tom Michael notes a rather bold display made on the premiere broadcast. "…[W]hile public school desegregation was moving with a slow, deliberate speed, and universities, interstate transportation, movie theaters, and water fountains were still rigidly segregated throughout large parts of the U.S., the Northwestern team was comprised of three white men and Fred Browne, an African American from Atlanta, Georgia."

G.E. College Bowl didn't get any significant backlash over the Northwestern team. In fact, they didn't get backlash over anything. Audiences gravitated toward the show despite the previous year's repercussions from the quiz shows; fifteen million people made the show a Sunday afternoon habit. And critics, who generally tended to dislike quiz and game programs, adored *G.E. College Bowl*.

Critic Charles Mercer raved, "Although I never thought it would happen, I've found myself thoroughly enjoying a television quiz show… There's no hokum about the program. Panel moderator Allen Ludden runs a forthright show…What I enjoy most about the program is watching the faces and reactions of the kids. I also enjoy observing how much purely academic information I've forgotten since I was in college twenty years ago.

"Probably closer to the basic point of the program than my own remarks was that of a high school senior who is glued to it every Sunday. A husky type inclined to spurn books in favor of athletics — to his own regret as he seeks admission to college — he said: 'There ought to be more of this sort of thing. It makes you see the book boys aren't squares at all.'"

John P. Shandley of *The New York Times* wrote, "One of the most refreshing things about *College Bowl* is its policy of respecting the intelligence of its panelists. Unlike some of the dreary quizzes on TV, which make the questions absurdly simple, *College Bowl* proceeds on the assumption that the contestants are unusually well-informed and bright."

There was another reason that the show worked, and it was almost an accident. But positive reviews of the show almost always said something to the effect of "Allen Ludden is well-suited to serve as moderator; he has a Phi Beta Kappa key and graduated with a master's degree in English…"

Allen Ludden was well-educated, and he carried himself as such. You could hear it in the way he talked and see it in the way he walked. He was very straightforward; pleasant but not in-your-face, witty but not funny. And there was something about the way he presented himself — he dressed without flash, always in a conservative, timelessly-styled suit and a bowtie. He wore an inconspicuous pair of tortoiseshell glasses, and his hair was developing some flecks of silver. Poised behind a lectern and surrounded by students, he looked uncannily like a professor — one of the tough graders, too. Allen and *G.E. College Bowl* were a perfect fit, to such a degree that it was hard not to notice.

CBS took notice, too. At the same time that *G.E. College Bowl* began to catch on, another CBS game, *What's My Line?* from Goodson-Todman Productions, was having personnel issues. Host John Daly routinely clashed with the show's producers (one of whom, Gil Fates, felt that the show suffered from "hardening of the creative arteries") and would stonewall any attempt to try something different on a show that was

Allen greets the team from Smith College. In the years before Women's Liberation or the E.R.A. movement emerged, *G.E. College Bowl* portrayed women as equals, and often superiors, in the weekly battle of brains. AUTHOR'S COLLECTION

very, very set in a routine. As Daly's issues with the *What's My Line?* staff became harder to ignore, CBS took matters into their own hands and offered Allen the job of hosting *What's My Line?* in addition to *G.E. College Bowl*.

Don Morrow remembers, "Allen often called me for career advice, which I found humorous being that he was several years older than me. Whenever he was worried that anything would disrupt his executive position, I'd always say 'Keep the day job'. He asked me to come to his office when he got the offer for *What's My Line?* This time, I told him 'Are you kidding? Take it.' He probably would have, anyway. I never felt he had a problem with his day job, but he certainly did love being a celebrity."

Allen called CBS and said that if John Daly walked out, he was ready to take over *What's My Line?* Word spread to Daly that CBS had found a suitable replacement, and Daly, surprised by that development, quietly worked things out with his bosses and kept his job.

Allen was uncomfortable with the pedestal that he was placed on sometimes as a high-brow television moderator. He insisted to one interviewer, "I'm no intellectual. Without those answer cards on *College Bowl*, I'd be lost."

Don Morrow disagreed. "He was quite intellectual, I'd say, but Dawg and I wouldn't let ourselves be exposed to that side of him."

But even true authorities in education took him seriously in that role. The University of Texas invited him to return for several days in late 1959 to assist in the planning of a closed-circuit television network to be shared by the major schools in central Texas and the San Antonio area. The hope was that the best professors that the state had to offer could teach classes to the highest possible number of students through the new system. His

Allen Ludden just had the right look for a smart, urbane show, whether it was *G.E. College Bowl* or *What's My Line?* But he had the right mind, too. FRED WOSTBROCK COLLECTION

input proved to be so valuable that he was invited back to the University of Texas the following week for a private meeting with the president of the school.

Allen was quite outspoken about education and the youth of America, and far more often than not, he sided with youth. He felt that far too many adults in power were committing themselves to merely worrying about juvenile delinquency and punishing it, and that not enough energy was put into preventative measures. He felt that schools didn't do enough to keep curricula up to date, critical of schools that invested in modernizing their facilities instead of investing in the actual learning process.

Despite a full work week, Allen still remained committed to his calling to help younger people. He wrote another book meant to advise the younger generation, and this one was a little different from the rest because he disguised it as a novel. *Roger Thomas, Actor!* was a mostly fictional tale (although more than once, it was rumored that Allen had written it as a thinly veiled autobiography) about an aspiring actor who decides to attend drama school.

Part novel and part self-help, Allen's clever book *Roger Thomas, Actor!*

COURTESY OF MATT OTTINGER

Allen deliberately filled the book's narrative with do's and don'ts and cautionary tales, in hopes that the book would let a youngster with theatrical aspirations know exactly what was in store for them.

Page 7: That night, Roger watched television. There was a dramatic show on, and it was one of those stories about a young man on the waterfront in New York. The hero was a boy just Roger's age, seventeen. As Roger watched the performance, he decided that the actor playing this role must not be much older than he was. And there this young fellow was, an established actor in New York, playing a big part on a TV show. He was very good, too. It all looked so easy.

Yet, Roger knew that it wasn't easy. It must take plenty of work to learn all those lines and create a character so believable that the viewers would actually forget they were watching an actor. Suddenly, Roger found himself trying to analyze exactly what all of the actors in the show did: how they walked and how they spoke their lines and how they got from scene to scene. This business of acting was much more than just getting up on a stage. A fellow couldn't any more just get up and act than he could go out on a football field and play a good game. There were an awful lot of "tricks of the trade" that had to be learned before you could even begin to act so that anybody would even believe you.

"By golly," Roger thought, "if I get this part, I'm going to work at it just as hard as I've been working at football training. I'm going to find out what it takes to train an actor so he can really act."

For his *Plain Talk* books, Allen had received critical acclaim for not just delving into what was right and what was wrong, but for exploring the "why" of rules, to assure his audience of suspicious readers that proper behavior wasn't arbitrary. There was reason for it. And as a novelist, Allen followed that same rule in *Roger Thomas, Actor!*, making sure that they knew the reasons for anything that frustrated them about their new pursuit.

Page 10: As Roger sat out in the empty auditorium, watching the progress of the "blocking out," he was completely bewildered by all of this "upstage left" and "downstage right" talk.

Roger came over to center stage and faced Perry, who was sitting in his usual position at the footlights, with his back to the auditorium. Roger was facing the empty rows of seats.

"Now Rog, this upstage and downstage business is very simple. A long time ago, in the theater, they were not able to build the auditorium floors so that the back part of the audience could sit a bit higher than the front part. In most of the theaters, the audience was just sitting on benches, and the floor was bare ground. They had to do something that would make the action on the stage visible to the entire audience, and the easiest thing to do was to tilt the stage. So the back part of the stage was built a little higher than the front part. This meant that when an actor turned his back on the audience and walked away from them, he would actually be walking up a little incline. And to this day, we refer to the part of stage away from the audience as upstage and that part closest to the audience as downstage."

Allen did an impressive job with balancing family, freelance writing, and his broadcasting career. He had a strong, happy bond with his wife and children, his books were well-received, he was getting a promotion — advancing from WCBS to the CBS Network for a position as director of program services for the CBS owned and operated stations, and his TV show was a hit. Viewers loved *G.E. College Bowl*. General Electric loved it too. Allen's face began popping up in General Electric's newspaper advertising.

Part of the reason the show worked so well was because it toed the line between a precision drill team and being a big happy family, and the end result was a very well-run program staffed by people who enjoyed putting it together.

As Don Morrow explains, "The show was very easy to do because it was handled like a military operation with everyone involved knowing exactly what their job was. It was so easy for us that Dawg and I started thinking of ways to rattle Allen on air. One classic happened, I think when

Once Allen was onstage, it was all business, but he and the *College Bowl* staff had a lot of fun putting the show together every week. FRED WOSTBROCK COLLECTION

we were doing the University of Minnesota, Dawg knew the mayor of the town and just as we were going on the network, LIVE, I handed Allen a little gift wrapped box, supposedly a memento from said mayor. He opened it as we hit the air explaining at the same time it was a gift from the Mayor of Minneapolis and inside was one of those plastic doggie doos. Allen cracked up on air, and I could swear he looked at us and mouthed 'You sons a'bitches'...God did we have fun on that show...that went on like that for a couple of years but I don't think we ever topped the doggie doo. But Allen would always laugh it off and then over drinks after any show, Dawg and I would start thinking of a new one to pull on him. Most emcees would not be that resilient to recover on air. Those were still the days of a lot of live television. There's nothing LIVE anymore, even the news is taped."

The only negative words that *G.E. College Bowl* was hearing came straight from CBS. Going to a new venue every time the show's championship changed hands was a strain on the show's crew, who had to work out logistics for the set and technical equipment week after week after week. The May 17, 1959 game between Goucher College and Wayne State University was so particularly rife with technical difficulties that CBS handed down

the orders immediately that going forward, the show was to be permanently based in a studio in New York City.

Betty White was going through a career slump in 1958. Part of it had to do with her resistance to leave California for New York City. Despite Hollywood's obvious status as an epicenter for showbiz, many of Betty's own friends and associates felt New York was a better fit because of the type of work she preferred doing. Betty left many friends and business associates speechless when NBC virtually handed her the job of co-hosting

Betty packs her bags for another trip to New York City. AUTHOR'S COLLECTION

Today. Betty gave it some thought, particularly after NBC tried to ice the cake by offering to put her up in a hotel suite five days a week and cover her airfare so she could come back home to California every weekend. But Betty had no interest in being permanently based in a studio in New York City.

She did feel, however, that New York City was a nice place to visit. She had delighted *Tonight Show* host Jack Paar with such a funny appearance that he had instructed his staff to extend an open invitation to Betty. Any time she was returning to New York City, all she had to do was call Jack Paar's staff, tell them which days she'd be in town, and they'd respond by telling her which of those days she was going to appear as a guest.

With no new acting jobs coming her way for the moment, and with some people in New York who were solidly in her corner, Betty established a nice routine for herself. Every few weeks, she'd book herself a round-trip flight to New York and make some hotel reservations. She'd call Jack Paar's office and the Goodson-Todman office to tell them she was coming to town, and by the end of each conversation, her schedule was set. She'd come in for one day for an interview with Jack Paar and then appear on whatever game show she was needed for. Paar paid his guests $450 and Goodson-Todman paid theirs $500, which meant Betty made back enough money to cover the plane ticket and the hotel, with a couple of bucks to spare, and then she headed back to Los Angeles. As an added bonus, she could go on a date while she was in town. Jack Paar took such a shine to Betty that he took it upon himself to play matchmaker for her.

Betty began seeing Phil Cochran, a friend of Jack's who, as a commando in North Africa and Burma during World War II, had such amazing exploits that his war record actually served as the inspiration for two comic strips, *Terry and the Pirates* and *Steve Canyon*. Betty and Phil's dates became a little more frequent when a *To Tell the Truth* regular panelist, Polly Bergen, took an extended leave from the show and Goodson-Todman asked Betty to replace her. The decision kept Betty in New York City for three full months, and she and Phil grew more serious in that time. And the public took notice, too, at least the part of the public that watched late night TV. Many of Betty's appearances with Jack Paar usually included a mention of Phil, and Jack liked hearing stories about their lives together. Phil wasn't a celebrity, but he was becoming more widely known just for being Betty White's favorite guy.

FRED WOSTBROCK COLLECTION

CHAPTER EIGHT

"PASSWORD"

In 1960, television, which Betty White had dominated early on, was still proving to be a little lean. She still managed to keep herself in the public eye with her appearances on game shows and on *The Tonight Show* (she was such a frequent guest that some articles referred to her as Jack Paar's co-star). And while television offered slim pickings for the moment, Betty found that she could pick up by going back to her old stomping grounds on the stage.

Starting in that same year, Betty explored summer stock, theaters that only presented productions during the summer time. Many took advantage of the warm weather by holding the shows outdoors or in a large tent. Because the season for this type of theater complemented the work schedule for television, many television stars began making an annual habit of leaving New York and Los Angeles to appear in summer stock productions in cities all over the country. Betty White was now one of those stars.

Betty headed to Massachusetts for a starring role in *The Boy Friend*, a quirky British musical about a school for girls. It felt good to get back into the theater. She was well-received, she had a good time, and it was guaranteed good money for a few months every year. She decided to stick with it in the summer months to come.

Also in 1960, the George Foster Peabody Awards were once again handed out, recognizing meritorious television and radio programs. Edward R. Murrow's penetrating documentary, *Harvest of Shame*, chronicling the plight of migrant farm workers, received the honor. NBC's acclaimed *White Paper* documentary series won an award, too. NBC's nightly newscast, *The Huntley-Brinkley Report*, was also singled out for the honor, and so was whimsical TV puppeteer Shari Lewis. CBS won an award for their coverage of the Olympics that year. Also taking home a George Foster Peabody Award: *G.E. College Bowl*.

The official citation for the award read: "Through contests between two teams of students, *G.E. College Bowl* helps to focus the nation's attention on the intellectual abilities and achievements of our college students. The competitions emphasize quick recall of specific facts, and therein lies its appeal, which is illuminating, educational, entertaining, and exciting. The program provides weekly scholarship grants to colleges and universities.

Betty sets sail for a new professional adventure, acting in summer stock. AUTHOR'S COLLECTION

Allen Ludden as the moderator deserves a special mention for his excellent work as *G.E. College Bowl* is given the Peabody Award for Television Youth Programs for 1960."

Allen didn't always get credit for taking the ball and running with it when the idea of teaching kids manners via a radio show was handed to him. He made *Mind Your Manners* something greater than anyone had ever envisioned. And he never got credit in the press or from his employers for being the one who had actually conjured up the *G.E. College Bowl* format. But when Allen Ludden looked in the mirror every morning, he saw the face of a man who was an integral part of two different Peabody Award-winning series. And very, very few people, even today, could say that.

Quiz bowl historian Tom Michael says, "The biggest impact of *G.E. College Bowl* was that it saved the entire quiz show genre. *G.E. College Bowl*…showed there were legitimately bright young people who used their smarts to win money for their schools, not themselves. The show… helped end calls in Congress to outlaw quiz shows outright. And the show came at a time when the US was perceived to be losing the space race, and behind the Soviets in nuclear missile technology. The show helped reassure Americans that are colleges really were turning out smart people."

But for the genuine concern he had in shaping the future of America's youth, there was a much greater accolade that he received. During a stroll down Fifth Avenue one day, a total stranger approached Allen, smiled broadly, and put his hands firmly, but warmly, on Allen's shoulders.

"Young man," the stranger said. "I want to tell you that your program is the only program that is a must in our family."

The stranger told Allen about his son, a high school senior who was bright but had never really applied himself and came to realize that his grades might not cut it if he wanted to go to college.

The stranger continued, "We started looking at your program by accident, and in three or four weeks, his mother and I noticed a distinct change in his studying. He realized he wouldn't be a grind, or unsocial, if he paid attention to his studies. And he made it into the college of his choice."

Not widely publicized was that the show went through meticulous efforts to make sure that brains were well represented on *G.E. College Bowl*. Schools were encouraged to hold tryouts leading up to their games. Potential contestants were invited to go to a local TV station in the area for an audition and the college would build its team from the most outstanding members. And on the air, so many of them proved to be outgoing, self-confident, relaxed, and talkative…a far cry from the bookish, reserved, quiet "nerd" stereotype. *College Bowl* made it okay to be smart.

And Allen was equally gratified at the mail he got from ex-contestants who just wanted to let the show know what they were up to now. With every passing year, more and more ex-contestants had become teachers. Allen was seeing first-hand that his show was being used as a stepping

G.E. College Bowl moved into a new home for its second season, Studio 59. FRED WOSTBROCK COLLECTION

stone for the great minds who would create the great minds of the future.

One of the reasons that the show worked so well and accomplished so many positive results was that the people running it believed in it so strongly. After the show stopped traveling from campus to campus and settled down in a studio, G.E. and CBS didn't treat it as money back in their pockets. They instead built an eye-catching set. Instead of the unpretentious curtains and pennants that were set up for that first year, when the show traveled, they had gone all out to make the show a sight to behold. *G.E. College Bowl* was now permanently based in New York's Brooks Atkinson Theatre,[1] which was designed to look like a stadium on game day, with Allen's lectern situated next to an elaborate game clock

1. aka CBS Studio 59; it was also the home of *What's My Line?* and *I've Got a Secret.*

and scoreboard display. The show paid the full costs of having the teams and their coaches fly to New York for every game — very unusual for TV game shows — and treated each team to the Broadway show of their choice the night before their game. They expanded the crew working behind the scenes. By 1960, Nancy Fobes had a team of five researchers helping her write the questions.

The show and the sponsor both came to think of the work they were doing as a public service. For a special pair of programs in early 1961, G.E. agreed to air *College Bowl* without commercials. The extra time was instead devoted to a panel discussion with Allen and three college professors discussing problems in the college admission process and admission requirements. In an effort to make sure that those few minutes were used to maximum effect, Allen's questions for the panel were selected by mailing a survey to high school guidance counselors, wondering what questions they'd ask. Allen, in turn, asked the questions seen most often in the returned surveys.

Allen himself remained amazingly hands-on with preparing for each program. Every Sunday morning at eleven o'clock, Allen greeted the teams in the theater, briefed them in the rules until he was sure that they knew them inside and out, pulled out the practice games that Nancy Fobes and her staff had written, and got to work. One of the reasons the contestants were so confident and comfortable when the show went on the air was because by the time the tape was rolling, they had already played the game for over two hours.

He told the press it was his favorite part of the job. On the air, he only spent about a minute talking to the contestants and introducing them to the home audience. During the warm-up sessions, he really engaged in conversations with each of them and got to know them.

Allen beamed proudly whenever he talked about the show with the press. He maintained that someday, after his career in broadcasting had ended, he wanted to return to teaching. He elaborated, "I enjoy this better than anything — working with kids like these. The kids have a ball even the losers. The essence of the motive of this show is that we are putting the spotlight on college brains rather than muscles, making campus heroes of the kids who have accomplished something academically."

As far as Allen knew, there was only one bit of negative feedback that anybody had about *G.E. College Bowl*, and it was a criticism for which he had no intention of taking action. Players only had three seconds to ring in once Allen finished reading, and once a player signaled, Allen expected an answer instantly and would call "time" if he sensed a contestant was stalling or bluffing once they pressed the button. As time went by, Allen began moving through questions faster and faster, not allowing for a breather between the completion of a bonus and the next toss-up question.

But as Allen told *The New York Times*, "Some people have criticized me for playing the game too fast, but they always seem to be the older persons…the teenagers approve of speed. They don't want us to pander."

Allen presents a silver cup to Rensselaer Polytechnic Institute, whose team retired undefeated after accumulating five victories and $7,500 in scholarship funds. FRED WOSTBROCK COLLECTION

And for all the older viewers who complained that Allen moved the game too fast for them to play along, there were just as many older viewers who watched the speed of the game and shook their heads in admiration at how smart these kids were and how impossibly quickly they knew the correct answers to such challenging questions.

G.E. College Bowl had grown so popular that Don Reid, John Moses, and Jack Cleary took an unusual, and very successful, next step with it. They began licensing the show's format for use by local TV stations. The station would pay a fee, build their own sets, hire their hosts, and in exchange, they had full permission to do their own version of the show, usually with teams of students from high schools in the viewing area. The staff of *College Bowl* would furnish the questions for them. It got good ratings for the station at a low cost, and most stations had no problem finding local schools to participate because of the most significant effect of the national show's success. Schools nationwide now had quiz teams among its extracurricular activities. They first appeared shortly after the radio version bowed in 1953. With the popularity of the television versions, the activity grew. Electronics companies began manufacturing low-main-

A professional in time of crisis. Allen put on his game face each week, even as his home life was taking a frightening turn. FRED WOSTBROCK COLLECTION

tenance, easily portable sets of buzzers for the games.

In April 1961, Allen was set for a homecoming for part of Texas' statewide Industrial week. He had been asked to come back to Corpus Christi to serve as master of ceremonies for a special night of *College Bowl* games in the city's Del Mar Auditorium, featuring players from local high schools. The game would be broadcast live on local television under the title *Allen Ludden's TV Bowl*. The Ludden family would then be guests of honor at a reception dinner after the show.

But on show night, it was Allen's brother, Frank, a resident in the Corpus Christi area, who hosted the game. Allen stayed in New York City because Margaret had gone into the hospital. She needed emergency surgery on one of her lungs. She spent a week in Roosevelt Hospital before being discharged. That was good news for the short term, but the problem was that as much as Margaret had put up a fight for the past four years, she wasn't winning. Allen was losing his wife, his children were losing their mother, and the Ludden family needed help.

Allen could take some comfort in knowing that *G.E. College Bowl* had been picked up for the 1961-62 season, and combined with a promotion at CBS — he was now consulted for creative services at CBS News, acting as a speech coach for newsmen like Charles Kuralt and Harry

Reasoner — Allen could count on a steady income to help Margaret keep fighting. The problem was that the past four years had been a costly battle and it wasn't just eating into Allen's paychecks, it was chipping away at the money that the family had saved in the bank. Allen had just bought a new home in Briarcliff Manor, New York, in the hopes that the worst was behind for his wife. But her condition was deteriorating, and Allen needed money, fast….

Backtrack about six years. When Allen had helped NBC construct their massive radio endeavor, *Monitor*, in 1955, one of the on-air talents hired was a thirty-four-year-old Canadian named Monty Hall, who, despite his age, had come to NBC with enough credentials in radio and television to be deemed a veteran broadcaster. He was hired as a pinch-hitter, filling in as needed for whichever communicator couldn't host his three-hour shift. By 1956, he was given a permanent spot on the schedule, co-hosting the Saturday 8:00 pm-midnight shift with Morgan Beatty. He'd stay there for four years.

Monty began making a name for himself in New York radio and television, accumulating credits like *Twenty One*, *Keep Talking*, and *Bingo at Home* at the same time that he was doing *Monitor*, and he made a lot of contacts along the way.

One of them was a man named Nat Ligerman, who was attempting to generate a television production company out of his laundromat. One day, as Hall recounted in his autobiography, *Emcee Monty Hall*, Ligerman pitched an idea that Hall didn't particularly like, but before Monty could walk away, Ligerman suddenly threw another idea his way.

"What's the first thing you'd say if I said the word 'black'?" Ligerman asked.

Hall answered, "White."

Ligerman said, "Yes, but maybe someone else could say 'cat' or 'dark' or 'night.' I wanted to try that on you because maybe there is a show in free association."

Ligerman didn't really have an idea fleshed out, but Hall, over the next few weeks, came up with a game. In the first half of the game, the audience would be shown the key words while contestants tried to guess the words based on clues they were given. In the second part of the show, members of a married couple would respond separately to a word association test, and score points any time that they had given the same response to a word.

Hall produced an audio tape of a demonstration game, but CBS wasn't interested in what they heard, so he went to a friend, Bob Stewart, a former radio writer who had earned a job producing shows for Goodson-Todman

Productions. By the end of his first year with the company, he had created *To Tell the Truth* and *The Price is Right*. He was exactly the guy that Monty wanted in his corner if he was going to keep trying to get a game show on the air.

Bob Stewart took the audiotape to Goodson-Todman. Goodson wasn't totally pleased with what he heard, but he liked it enough to suggest

Borrowing a page from college football, *G.E. College Bowl* presented an annual Army vs. Navy game. Here, Allen presents the trophy to the winning Navy team of Grant Richard Garritson, Al H. Morales, Robert E. McAfee, and James Henry Jr. AUTHOR'S COLLECTION

refinements, and a game of ping-pong ensued, where Monty Hall would deliver his new idea to Bob Stewart, Stewart relayed it to Mark Goodson (who wouldn't meet directly with Monty Hall for some reason), then relay the feedback to Monty Hall, who would change the format of the game accordingly. This continued for so long that it made Stewart and Hall antsy. Stewart even made arrangements with his Goodson-Todman co-workers to do a segment of *I've Got a Secret* in which host Garry Moore played a word association game with the panelists, hoping it would prod Goodson, but to no avail. Monty gave up and moved onto other things. By 1960, he got word that Goodson suddenly wanted to revisit his idea, but Goodson-Todman was still based exclusively in New York City and Monty had just given his notice to NBC and was preparing to move to Los Angeles to host a CBS game, *Video Village*.

Mark Goodson handed the idea over to Bob Stewart, and Stewart reworked and refined it. In a 1998 interview, Stewart detailed to interviewer Fred Wostbrock the creative process that followed: "I thought of an idea in which the two of us are opponents. Above your head is a word unseen by you. Let's say the word is NURSE. Above my head might be the word HOSPITAL. Now, by looking at your word, my job is to figure out what's above my head, and you're trying to do the same thing.

"So I look at the word NURSE and I say 'Doctor.' Now you know you're looking at HOSPITAL and I've just said 'Doctor.' You know where the realm of material is. So you say 'operation.' Now I go, and we take turns saying words. And this process continued until one of us got what was behind our head. I worked on that for a while and it had a terrible flaw... What if you, looking at the word DOCTOR, said to me, 'yo-yo'? There's no rule that says you can't do that. How do I make a rule that makes you say certain things within the context? You can't judge that. So that idea fell apart.

"And I kept messing around with it and I realized that if we can't do it as opponents, maybe we can do it as partners. And that sort of broke the problem we had. Because then if you're looking at the word DOCTOR, you just say to me, 'Nurse.' And I say 'Patient.' And the other guy goes and he says 'HOSPITAL.' Well, that fixed the problem because now you can still say any clue you like, but you're not going to say anything outrageous because you're trying to help your partner, rather than defeat your opponent. So it all came together. As soon as that happened, the show took form.

"We were sitting in a room doing run-throughs with four civilians, and I realized that if you saw it through a camera's eye, you would never see these four people together because you don't want to see them, you want to see the two people who are, at the moment, trying to get the password. But as you cut to the next team, them all being civilians, who knows what team you're looking at? The best way to define which team you're on and what's happening is to get two celebrities, and the instant you see them, you know where the camera is and why. And that's what caused us to bring in celebrities; it was only to define the two teams. It turned out to be a bonanza."

At the time, Bob Stewart's solution was a breakthrough innovation. Celebrities and game shows had gone together plenty of times before, but prior to 1961, celebrities always served the same capacity on every game show: they competed against contestants. The contestant had a secret, or the contestant had a line of work that had to be guessed, or three people were claiming to be the same person, but the celebrities were always trying to solve those human puzzles and setting out to win the game at the expense of the contestant. Bob Stewart's idea meant that, for the first time ever on a game show, celebrities and contestants would be working together for a common goal.

That common goal didn't just repair the flaw in Bob Stewart's original idea. It totally altered the tone of the game. The original, flawed game would have had a sense of purposeful unkindness to it in the deliberate effort to trip up your opponent with bad clues. Giving every player a teammate now gave the game a very altruistic sensibility.

The finished product was called *Password*. News finally began trickling out through trade publications that Goodson-Todman was readying a new game based on word association. Hall saw the reports and confronted Bob Stewart, who gave him a very frank explanation of what happened after he moved to Los Angeles. Goodson learned that Hall was no longer going to be involved in the project and told Bob Stewart to develop the word association game to completion. Stewart asked Goodson to give Hall a percentage of the profits from the new show, but Goodson declined, with the logic that word association games had been invented by Sigmund Freud long before Monty Hall had suggested one. Hall was upset, but not really at Stewart. Television was an ugly business and Bob Stewart had a good thing going with his position in Goodson-Todman and didn't want to risk that. Hall understood and let it be, although for years afterwards, he insisted that he had been the true creator of *Password*.

One of the Goodson-Todman staffers involved in the development of the show was Mike Gargiulo, a friend of Stewart's who had recently returned from several months in the Soviet Union to help demonstrate and develop color television. He got hired at Goodson-Todman when the company learned that one of his projects in the USSR had been a game show called *The Ruble is Right*.

Gargiulo says, "To give you some sense of the state of the business when *Password* started, ninety-five percent of the television business at the time was the three major networks, NBC, ABC, and CBS. Also, the quiz show scandals had only happened two or three years earlier, and Goodson-Todman was the only game show office that wasn't implicated in that scandal, so in 1961, that company was doing incredible business. In 1961, Goodson-Todman had something like 300 employees. It's a miracle to have a television production company grow that large.

"But of that 300, there was only a small core group that developed new games: Bob Stewart, Bud Austin, Chester Feldman, sometimes Frank Wayne, Mark Goodson, and me. We would get together after hours and have creative meetings where new ideas would be discussed and work-shopped. And the reason it was such a small group was because Mark Goodson didn't want yes-men to ruin his ideas. He knew who those people were in the company, and he kept them there because they had their place, but he did not want a yes-man anywhere near creative meetings. He only wanted people who could, and would, look him in the face and tell him things he didn't want to hear. He valued employees who had enough guts to say 'This is a bad idea you have, Mark.' And we'd sit there and play practice games just to see if the idea worked. Mark was always master of ceremonies for those practice games. I'd always be the celebrity guest star.

"What I remember about the development of *Password* is that it had a special quality about it that I never felt with any other show. It was the only time where we did the run-throughs and development already knowing the show would be a hit. This was a good game. You could see it, and you could feel it. There was no attitude of 'Let's wait and see, don't get our hopes up, we don't know.' Absolutely the opposite — we knew that we were developing a big success."

There were some final details that needed to be worked out. The first was whether or not the home audience should be able to see the passwords that the contestants were trying to guess. After a lot of discussion, the staff concluded that there would be a lot of laughs derived from contestants giving wildly wrong guesses or strange clues for seemingly straightforward words. So, the passwords would be visible on screen throughout every game.

And while Bob Stewart was at it, he felt compelled to add a personal touch to that on-screen display. His mother was an immigrant who could speak English but had never learned how to read it. Wanting his mother to be able to follow along with the new game, he decided that not only would the word be shown on screen, but that each word would be introduced by the show's announcer, who would whisper, "The password is…"

The second detail was a concern that Mark Goodson voiced: "If you can only give one-word clues, it won't work, because what are you going to do if somebody says 'mother-in-law'? Who is going to know if it's one word or two?"

The job of "judge" on a game show traditionally goes to one of the show's producers or writers. Gil Fates, another trusted producer and idea man within the Goodson-Todman company, suggested outsourcing the job of judging the game to a professional word expert.

Bob Stewart went to a bookshelf, pulled out a copy of the *World Book Encyclopedia* and saw that their staff etymologist was a man named Reason A. Goodwin, a name that immediately delighted Stewart. Stewart called World Book and found out that Goodwin was part of the large editing staff that assembled one of the group's other major projects, the *World Book Dictionary*. Stewart spoke to Goodwin and his bosses and immediately worked out a deal. Goodwin would get a fee for serving as the show's judge, and as a show of thanks to World Book for loaning out a valuable employee as needed for this job, the show would plug the *World Book Dictionary* on every episode and offer it as a gift for all contestants.

The third detail was a meeting that completely exasperated Bob Stewart, in which the staff debated whether the host should walk to the contestants to distribute the small envelopes that contained the passwords, or if the host could outstretch his arms to distribute them. The meeting lasted three hours.

Mike Gargiulo says, "Yes, it's true, we had a three-hour meeting about that. But to be clear, we obsessed over every detail of the show because, again, we already knew this would be a big hit. Up to that point, the most successful show Goodson-Todman ever did was *What's My Line?*, and while *Password* was in development, more than a few people predicted that this show was going to be our next *What's My Line?* So we would think about details, rethink them, and overthink them because we felt that this show deserved as much extra attention as we could give it. Nothing was unimportant. We wanted it to be perfect from day one. Could it be frustrating? Absolutely. But it was worth it."

The fourth detail was kind of a big one: the host himself, whoever it would be. Goodson-Todman initially wanted Gene Rayburn (formerly of *Make the Connection*), but Stewart felt that Gene was a bit too much of a ham and tended to draw attention to himself. Gene was out. Goodson-Todman was also considering acid-tongued comedian Henry Morgan (a regular panelist on *I've Got a Secret*) but Morgan was notoriously difficult to work with, and Stewart dug in his heels and absolutely would not hear any arguments in favor of him. Henry Morgan was out.

And then, out of the clear blue sky came word that Allen Ludden was making himself available. Allen was content to work behind the scenes in radio, but with the bad turn that his family's fortunes were taking, he reluctantly realized that he could probably get a high asking price if he offered himself as a master of ceremonies for hire. He had been getting the word out around town about his availability, and his name immediately got Goodson-Todman's attention. He had name recognition. He was famously low-key in his presentation, which meant that the game would be the star, as Bob Stewart wanted. He was erudite and well-educated, which made him perfectly suited to a game that revolved around words and their meanings. The more the Goodson-Todman staff thought about it, the more they realized that they didn't have to think about it. Allen Ludden was their guy.

Allen told *TV-Radio Mirror*, "We were vacationing on Fire Island when Goodson-Todman Productions summoned me to audition for a new game show. When I went into town, I took David with me. He's an astute critic — in fact, his viewpoint is so professional it's almost frightening."

Sometimes you just get a feeling. Goodson-Todman Productions thought Allen might be right for the job as soon as they learned he was interested. FRED WOSTBROCK COLLECTION

Allen went in to the audition. David joined him and quietly observed the proceedings, not offering his own input to anybody.

The Ludden men headed back to the train station and Allen asked his son what he thought of this *Password* thing that the production staff had shown them. David admitted he was impressed. "It's got more to it than any other daytime show I've seen."

"How did I do?" Allen asked.

David chose his words very carefully before finally, slowly saying them. "You were great, but…"

Allen noticed his son was hesitating. "But what?"

David replied, "You're no Bud Collyer."

With two shows on the air for Goodson-Todman, *To Tell the Truth* on CBS and *Beat the Clock* on ABC, Bud Collyer was probably a reasonable measuring stick for what Goodson-Todman was seeking in a master of ceremonies. But for *Password*, Allen Ludden was exactly what the firm was looking for.

Mark Goodson told *TV Guide*, "[Allen Ludden] is the very antithesis of what I call the 'West Coast emcee.' You know the type — the breezy, over-dressed, rather flashy guy. You wouldn't believe for a minute that someone like that even understood half the words he'd be passing out to the contestant. Allen projects an East Coast image. With the crew cut and glasses, he looks like a young Ivy League professor, popular with his students."

In 1998, Bob Stewart talked about the process of finding the right person to host a TV game show. He said, "It's pretty much like a marriage. And when you think about the fact that fifty percent of marriages don't work out, you can imagine what happens in television. But some hosts blend with the content. And that match…you can't get an instinct for it but you really can't predict it. Allen Ludden and *Password*, for example… He had exactly the right look. He looked like a guy who should be doing that. And so that worked."

Mike Gargiulo remembers, "We knew it would require a different kind of emcee. We didn't want an emcee like Bert Parks. We wanted somebody who was culturally and socially advanced. The game was word association and celebrities could talk freely before the round and after the round, and could only say one word during the game. The red flag there is only saying one word during the game. When you're dealing with celebrities, even the ones who are easier to get along with aren't going to like the idea that they can only say one word at a time. So they're going to try to get away with doing something extra. We needed a host who presented an air of authority and who could police the game.

"The other reason the host was so important was because we were planning on a low-frills game with no gimmicks. We knew the set wasn't going to have swinging doors or flashing lights. We weren't going to have a stage filled with spectacular prizes. We weren't going to have a spinning wheel or a big board that the game was going to be played on. It was such a simple, elemental game that the host was going to be one of the only aspects that would appeal to home viewers and get them watching regularly.

"We auditioned twenty people, not so much for the benefit of CBS but more for Goodson-Todman. I didn't have a vote but Allen really was the best out of all the prospective hosts. Here's the thing — and I don't want this to take anything away from Allen's talent when I say this, but as a rule, anybody who's good enough to be hosting a show already has one on the air, so out of those twenty people, Allen <u>had</u> to be the best."

Allen didn't say yes right away, though. *Mind Your Manners* and *College Bowl* had given him a certain reputation that he didn't want to betray. And given the reputation that game shows had in recent years, he had promised himself that as much as he needed the money, he would exercise extreme caution about what kind of shows he'd be willing to sign a contract for. His family understood and they were completely on his side. When Allen decided to go job-hunting to help the family's finances, he promised that whatever job offers he received in the near future would be subject to a family discussion before he made his decision. The game already secured David's stamp of approval at the audition. Now it was time for the rest of the Luddens to weigh in.

Allen later remembered, "The family didn't really want me to be an emcee…They didn't want me to do anything undignified or anything to spoil that *College Bowl* image. I took the game home and my wife and the three children played it at dinner. They liked it so I went ahead."

With his family's blessing secured, Allen returned to the Goodson-Todman office. The company made Allen an irresistible offer. He was free to continue hosting *G.E. College Bowl*. For *Password*, they would pay him double his combined salary for CBS Radio and *G.E. College Bowl*.

As Margaret's condition worsened, one of the few things that helped ease Allen's mind was how well his three children were adjusting to the move they had made into a new community. He told the story to *TV-Radio Mirror*: "We settled in just before school started, and they had little time to get acquainted. Margaret and I regarded it as a good adjustment to their new community when Sarah was elected president of her Brownie troop and Martha was chosen an alternate delegate to the student council. But it was David who really floored us. He'd been class president at [his former school], and to his complete surprise, someone nominated 'David Looden' for president at Briarcliff. He declined with thanks. It must have been quite a speech — he pointed out that he had been in the school only five days, that the person who nominated him knew so little about him he even mispronounced his name, and that he

Even at the very start, the combination just looked right. Allen Ludden was the right man to host *Password*. FRED WOSTBROCK COLLECTION

thought the interests of the class could better be served by someone more familiar with the school. I think that young man is going to take after his mother's family and be a politician!"

Margaret didn't have much time left, and soon, Allen's children were going to need him more than ever. Allen would be able to quit his creative services position at CBS and provide for his family with a new job that

A CBS promotional slide, used during station breaks to tout the upcoming new addition to the daytime line-up. FRED WOSTBROCK COLLECTION

had a drastically shorter work schedule — two episodes would tape on Wednesday, and then three episodes on Thursday. He could spend more time with Margaret, and he could be with his children when the time came that she no longer could.

Allen very reluctantly went to CBS News and requested permission to take a six month leave of absence to try his hand at hosting a game show. The leave of absence was granted, but Allen had no way of knowing that he would never be back. Allen went to the Seagram Building in midtown New York and signed his name on the dotted line for Goodson-Todman. The week before the show premiered, Margaret went back into the hospital.

Reporter Don Royal talked to Allen around the time of *Password's* premiere, asking him about giving up the behind-the-scenes executive positions he had clung to for the past several years, and embracing the job of being a television performer.

Allen, addressing his adherence to the office jobs, apologetically answered, "I suppose it was my effort to cling to respectability."

Game show hosts have a harder job than they get credit for, but historically they have not been a respected line of work in television. Allen liked the respect that he got as an executive and realized that, despite all the acclaim he had received for *Mind Your Manners* and *G.E. College Bowl*, he was now fully vulnerable to the slings and arrows of critics and some unforgiving members of the general public, and he was sensitive to that.

He also recognized that he was losing his privacy for good. He could never walk down the street without hearing his name again. It's hard to call Allen's lot in life tragic, but in a realm filled with thousands of stories of talented people who wanted a chance and never got one, and thousands more who got a chance and never should have, it is strange to reflect that Allen Ludden, a man so poised for success as a television performer and endowed with so many natural gifts for the job, absolutely never wanted to appear on television. It was a job that he kept backing into.

Reluctant as he had been to sign on, Allen admitted that he felt more reassured about his choice when he got to know his new bosses. He told United Press International, "This experience of working with Goodson and Todman is a revelation with me...They approach every show as if it was the first one they ever did. They are perfectionists; they make it a sort of science...taught me a great deal — and also restored my faith that the secret to success is professionalism and enthusiasm. They don't get the credit they deserve; the public doesn't know how good they are. They worked on this show for six months before they tried to sell it to anybody. They're phenomenal."

Mike Gargiulo says, "There was never a pilot shot for CBS. They bought the show after we played a run-through game for a few executives, but there was never a pilot shot. Bill Bohnert designed the set. And when the set was built, Mark Goodson paid $2,000 out of his own pocket for a session at CBS Studio 52. By the way, quick story about CBS Studio 52. It was called Studio 52 even though it was actually on 53th Street on Broadway, and to make things really confusing, even though the address was 53rd Street, the entrance was on 54th Street, and eventually the name was changed to Studio 54 to end the confusion. Yes, that Studio 54. That infamous disco was where we taped *Password* in the 1960s."

In addition to Bill Bohnert, the show utilized the talents of Ted Cooper, a talented production designer who conceived some of the more intricate details of the way the game would be presented. He came up with two small slide projector displays for keeping track of score. Instead of envelopes, he hid the passwords in small brown vinyl wallets that could

Day One of *Password*, with guest stars Kitty Carlisle and Tom Poston. Both were veteran game panelists veering into uncharted waters; for the first time, they were trying to help the contestants win. FRED WOSTBROCK COLLECTION

be reused again and again, and added a slightly elegant look to the game. Each wallet had a number attached to it, which allowed the staff to refer to passwords without actually revealing the answers if contestants happened to be within earshot.

Cooper also designed a chute that Allen would often refer to on the air, even though Cooper had specifically designed it to be out of the viewers' sight. Rather than having the passwords at Allen's lectern, the password wallets were kept backstage. When it was time for a new password, a stagehand would feed the wallets through a hole in the wall to slide down the chute and land right behind Allen, who would take one step back to grab them. Cooper designed this with the intention that a producer could adjust the game's progress for timing purposes; if, for example, it was almost but not quite time for a commercial, an easy password would be fed into the chute so it would be guessed quickly and the commercial would happen at the right time.

At the same time that the wallets were going down the chute, a black card with the white-lettered password would be fixed in front of a Vidicon camera, a small, unmanned, stationary camera fixed in front of the space where the black card would be inserted. The viewers at home would then see the password superimposed at the bottom of the screen as the players worked on it.

For the Lightning Round that would come at the end of each game, Cooper designed a set piece that the show's staff took to calling "the toaster": an elaborate device comprised of five pneumatic cylinders mounted beneath the desktop which used compressed air to cause the passwords to pop up out of the desktop as if by magic.

Once the set was built, Mike Gargiulo explains, an unusual practice session was held. "Mark Goodson paid $2,000 to bring in some cameramen, and bring in a stage crew to put up the set in Studio 52, and he had people come in and sit on the set for two hours just to see what it looked like. They didn't even play the game, we literally just paid people to sit in the chairs and stand behind Allen's lectern. And I sat in the control room and just had the cameramen do different shots so we could see what it looked like. The full set, a shot of five, a shot of each team, close-up of the host, a shot of the host and a celebrity, a shot of the host and a team. We all just got together and did this to see what it actually looked like."

Password went on the air on October 2, 1961, as part of a new CBS daytime line-up that included a lighter-fare newscast, *Calendar* with Harry Reasoner.

Password pitted two teams against each other: a celebrity guest and contestant versus a celebrity guest and contestant. Allen would give a member of each team the password, and those players alternated giving one-word clues to prompt their partners to say the password. A correct guess on the first clue was worth ten points, on the second clue was worth nine points, then eight points, etc. Twenty-five points won the game, $100,

The meticulous Goodson-Todman staff still felt there was room for improvement once *Password* premiered. Before the end of the show's first week, the technical crew had moved the scoreboard. FRED WOSTBROCK COLLECTION

and the right to play the Lightning Round, a bonus round played against a sixty-second clock, with five passwords worth fifty dollars each, for a possible grand total of $250 (for about a dozen years after the scandals, TV game shows were played for very low stakes).

Allen later remembered, "After the first show, I wanted to telephone home and see how my wife and the kids thought the program had gone…I was dashing down a hall toward the office of a buddy when a very important executive — who had always ignored me before — told me to use his office. I'd never been in his office before. When I finished the call, I found he was waiting for me in the hall. I'd been working for CBS for some time, so I asked him about the change in attitude. 'Oh,' he said. 'Now you're talent.'"

The games mostly went without a hitch. *Password* was already rock-solid before it ever made it out of the office, and audiences quickly grew enamored with a game that was so difficult to master and provoked so much thought as it played out, yet it was effortlessly understandable to grasp the premise and play along with it.

The only trouble the show ran into was during one of the first episodes of the series. As Mark Goodson anticipated, one of the players onstage gave a clue that was clearly unacceptable. Everyone watching from the side of the stage instantly recognized the illegal clue when they heard it, but the job of judge belonged solely to Dr. Reason A. Goodwin. Everybody turned around and looked at Goodwin, waiting for him to sound the buzzer that he had at his desk. Goodwin instead pulled out a dictionary and thumbed through it page by page until he got to the word in question. Bob Stewart couldn't believe it, saying later that the show could have brought in any staffer to do that job and do it twice as fast.

The show got a good running start, in part because Goodson-Todman was smart about its celebrity bookings for the first few weeks. They had a Rolodex filled with stars who could be depended on to master any game that they were asked to play. For the premiere week, the guests were Tom Poston and Kitty Carlisle, who had proven to be impeccable game players over the past five years on *To Tell the Truth*. For the third week, Don Ameche and Betty White were invited to play.

Betty White later wrote about that first appearance in her autobiography, *Here We Go Again*. As she remembered it: *"G.E. College Bowl*…earned [Allen] something of an egghead image. It was a pleasant surprise to see the sense of humor that surfaced on *Password*. He was the perfect host in every sense of the word, off camera as well as on, making his guests feel welcome when they arrived and never too busy to say a warm good-bye after the last show finished."

Much later, Betty would learn of Allen's family crisis. "I remembered the warm, smiling man I had met that day. Incredible how we can insulate ourselves for short periods when it is absolutely necessary to get the job done."

Mike Gargiulo says, "I had no idea his wife was sick. A lot of us didn't know. Allen didn't spend a lot of time around the coffee urn or the water cooler. Nice man but not gregarious."

Allen would remember that he worked hard to pull himself together and do the job in those final, difficult days of Maggie's illness. The stress and sorrow left him in a total fog, however. Thus, he admitted years later, Allen had absolutely no memory of the first time he met Betty White.

The early reviews trickled in for *Password*, and they revealed that the show was achieving the same impossible feat that *G.E. College Bowl* had achieved: television critics were enjoying a game show.

"Proof that day shows needn't be as flashy and noisy as a carnival midway on Saturday night: *Calendar* and *Password*, two new, plain, civilized CBS TV daytime programs...*Password*, with Allen Ludden as emcee, is an enjoyable word association game that involves degrees of telepathy, psychology, concentration, and luck. The opener was fast, lots of fun to watch, and informal." — *United Press International*

"...[T]he firm of Mark Goodson and Bill Todman has developed a game that is highly enjoyable and should prove diverting for the housewife suffering from cabin fever...For the viewer there is a high degree of personal participation...Allen Ludden, whose Sunday afternoon game, *G.E. College Bowl*, is so consistently interesting, does a fine job of keeping the game moving." — *The New York Times*

"Amusing to watch, particularly if the players are bright and perceptive." — *Cynthia Lowry, Associated Press*

The feedback was a relief to Allen, although behind-the-scenes, he was quietly concerned by some discussions he had with CBS executives in which Allen felt pressured by the network. The gist of their dialogs was this: the executives felt that Allen should choose either *G.E. College Bowl* or *Password* and depart from the other show. CBS had been fully aware of the negotiations when Goodson-Todman had initially approached Allen, and there wasn't anything in Allen's contract that stopped him from hosting *Password*. But once it was apparent that the show was going to be a success, Allen was worried that the day was coming when he'd have to make a tough decision.

Anticipating such a choice, Allen groomed Don Morrow, the announcer for *G.E. College Bowl*, to take over as host. Don had guest-hosted for Allen a few times in the past during Allen's vacations, so he had experience plus, for the audience's sake, a familiar voice. Allen was making sure there was a plan in place. He was just hoping he would never actually have to carry out that plan.

Allen's customary conclusion of each episode, telling home viewers "the password of the day," was a fixture from the start. FRED WOSTBROCK COLLECTION

With every passing day of October 1961, Margaret's conditioned worsened, and Allen virtually moved into the hospital. Because *G.E. College Bowl* was a live show, he was keeping the staff there briefed about her condition just in case an emergency arose on a Sunday, when the program aired.

By the week leading up to the Sunday, October 29 broadcast, the news had become so bad that everyone involved in the preparation was planning for Don Morrow to be the guest host that day.

Morrow recalls, "During the week leading up to that show, I received three phone calls: Cleary, Dawg, and Allen himself. All three of them told me I was going to be hosting that night. Allen wasn't coming in."

Don showed up at the theater early that day and carried out the same pre-game procedure that Allen normally carried out. He had met with the teams in the conference room, they had discussed all of the rules to everybody's satisfaction, and they all played a few hours' worth of practice games. Everybody broke for lunch breaks. The next part of the itinerary would be that the teams would get their hair and make-up done, and then gather on the stage to play two more practice games with the actual equipment used on the show.

Allen hosting *GE College Bowl*, just as Margaret wanted.
FRED WOSTBROCK COLLECTION

After lunch ended, Don walked to the stage and was shocked at who he saw: Allen. Allen had already spoken to the show's producers — he was such a stickler for manners that he wouldn't enter the studio without speaking to them first — and approached Don to explain why he was there.

As Allen explained it, "Maggie said she wanted to see me host the show one more time."

Don Morrow stood speechlessly as Allen asked his permission to host the show that night. Don agreed with no hesitation and took his usual post in the announcer's booth.

Maggie Ludden got her wish. As reluctant as Allen had been about becoming a television star, she had never felt anything but pride in everything that her husband had accomplished, and Maggie watched Allen do what he did best just one more time. The following day, October 30, 1961, just nineteen days after their eighteenth wedding anniversary, Margaret McGloin Ludden, wife and mother, died at age forty-three.

CHAPTER NINE

"FATE"

Allen gave himself time to grieve. He took a week off from *Password* while announcer Jack Clark stood in as guest-host. As he grew accustomed to life without Margaret, he realized that losing her had left its mark in a few ways. Allen used to be a voracious reader, poring through three or four books a week. But he didn't read a book for an entire year after Margaret died because, he noticed, after he lost her, he couldn't sit still for very long. In his professional life, as usual, Allen couldn't sit still either. Allen, who had always been so committed to work, was looking for more and more to do. It wasn't in his nature to stay away from anything, so one week after Margaret's death, Allen did what came natural. He went back to work.

It didn't hurt that he loved the work that he did. *G.E. College Bowl* still made him proud and happy, and he continued acclaiming the good hands that the future of the world seemed to be in.

He told a reporter, "There's nothing so stimulating as working with this group…These kids are so curious intellectually and so informed that it's dazzling. They aren't confined to their special fields either. You find a physicist quoting modern poetry, and an arts major who knows math formulas."

And the best part was, not only was he seeing those students, but a national television audience was seeing them…and glamorizing them. Allen beamed, "It's putting the spotlight on what is really the colleges' proudest product — their students…Suddenly the four most important kids on campus are the top students."

Allen enjoyed working and talking with kids so much that he was willing to provide counseling for them. He came to a high school in Rhode Island for Career Day to speak to the juniors and seniors about how to proceed with their education and finding a suitable line of work. That same day, he went to the local Kiwanis Club and addressed one hundred members on the subject of education and the youth of America. His message was one not often expressed: Don't rush the kids.

He said in his speech, "Our young people are our future...careers and career guidance are very important for young people, although I sometimes think it is better for them not to make up their minds too early in life. Sometimes they can be a richer, broader person if they look around first. I hope I can help you by talking to them, and the keynote of my address will be that nothing is so important as enthusiasm — the enthusiasm of their youth. If they can maintain this throughout life, then there is a future for us and for them...through them."

And Allen adamantly told kids themselves that they needed to slow down. "Oh, sure, the college student is conservative today and he wants to work for IBM, but when he really worries me is when he starts talking about retirement plans."

G.E. College Bowl was paying another dividend that Allen never anticipated. School scholarship funds were growing. Yes, the show paid out $1,500 in funds for the winning school and $500 for the runners-up every week, but they were growing for another reason. *G.E. College Bowl* made people want to contribute to education themselves. Schools that appeared on the show regularly reported getting a big boost in donations after their broadcast. One college, following its appearance, received an envelope with no return address, stuffed with a wad of cash that added up to $10,000.

And for all of his reservations he had about going full-speed ahead with a television career and accepting his gig at *Password*, it was amazing to Allen how quickly his misgivings dissipated. The ratings for the new series rocketed upward so fast that it didn't just make CBS executives happy. These ratings were high enough that it really made them think. Goodson-Todman had cleverly turned an episode of their prime-time panel game, *I've Got a Secret*, into virtually an infomercial for *Password* one night in early November 1961. Host Garry Moore and celebrity guest Vivian Vance instructed the show's panelists — Bill Cullen, Betsy Palmer, Henry Morgan, and Bess Myerson — to split up into teams, and they played a nice long game of *Password*. Viewer feedback for the segment was positive, and the mail in general had been overwhelmingly supportive.

Allen was particularly surprised by a consistent point being made in the letters that he saw. "I have never seen such immediate response from a viewing audience to a show. They tell us they play the game at home — that they make up their own games and play in cars and at parties."

In mere weeks, the show had gone from a new, unknown game to something that friends taught each other to play. As a bonus, the game was so uncomplicated that preparing a game for a party amounted to daydreaming and just jotting down words that came to mind for a few minutes. And as "play in cars" indicated, you didn't need to go to THAT much trouble to play. Just thinking of a word was good enough.

Allen said, "I'm not a gamester and I never have been. But *Password* is a fast-moving, catchy thing, the sort of game you can play in your own living room. The people who watch it all the time take over where the program leaves off and go on with it all evening."

The always adorable Betsy Palmer amuses Allen with a clue on *Password*. As a regular panelist on *I've Got a Secret*, Palmer had participated in a "secret" so well-received that it helped lead to a prime time slot for *Password*.

FRED WOSTBROCK COLLECTION

CBS was also noticing a steady stream of letters from viewers saying they wished it was on later in the day. Before the end of November, CBS had carved out some space on their schedule and made the announcement that, effective January 2, 1962, *Password* would air in daytime and nighttime. The primetime version would air Tuesday evenings at 8:00 p.m.

Meanwhile, Allen, who had resisted television for so long, had quickly found himself becoming one of its staunchest defenders. He told one reporter, "People who criticize TV as all blood and thunder and no brains couldn't be more wrong. The evidence is vividly to the contrary. There are more good information shows on the air now than there ever have been. And the only reason is that the audience wants them. So the sponsors are buying them. The industry recognizes it can get an audience and serve the country at the same time."

There were still people who detested bells and whistles of any kind, adamant that if a show catered to a viewer's desire to be entertained, it couldn't possibly contain any real substance. But those viewers, Allen said, were missing the point of the bells and whistles.

"To impart information correctly, you have to stimulate the entertainment that is in it — otherwise, you can't hold onto your audience, and you haven't imparted anything. [Viewers can] discover the fun of learning…And that's the only way we'll become a better educated nation."

Allen willingly admitted, when he was asked, that *Password*, in which a player said one word, another player said one word, repeat for thirty minutes, was "not the big intellectual revival of daytime TV," but he did point out that you couldn't really watch *Password* without being instinctively inclined to exercise your mind a little bit by thinking about the clues and shouting your idea of the perfect clue to the TV.

Allen very nearly didn't host the prime-time *Password*. CBS went in search of a company to serve as the nighttime version's primary sponsor and attempted to negotiate a deal with an appliance company, a competitor of General Electric. This would have made the people who bankrolled *College Bowl* unhappy, and General Electric made it clear that if the competitor signed on for the nighttime *Password*, Allen Ludden would not be appearing. Fortunately for Allen, the negotiations fell through. CBS searched elsewhere for a sponsor while Allen was in the clear to sign his contract for the nighttime show.

Prime-time *Password* premiered on January 2 with a pair of heavyweights playing — Garry Moore and his co-star on *The Garry Moore Show*, Carol Burnett. The duo was specifically chosen because they had competed against each other in November on the daytime version and played the game so well that it threw off the pace of the show. On a whim, they played the game for speed and fired off their clues so fast that the director got confused about whose turn it was, and the cameras were shooting the wrong teams at the wrong times.

Password was never a runaway smash in prime-time — it never cracked the top thirty shows in the Nielsen ratings for any season — but CBS picked its spot on the schedule wisely and used it to great effect as a counter-programming strategy. Viewers who didn't care for westerns or medical dramas watched *Password* instead. In that sense, *Password* was a success in nighttime as well as daytime, which floored the few critics who had anything bad to say about the show. A newspaper writer chastised CBS for thinking that the game was worthy of six time slots in a week of programs. Gilbert Seldes of *TV Guide* grumbled, "In *Password* they are as near to perfection as any human beings can hope to get — it is 99.9 percent nothing…[T]he whole thing is so dull it almost makes you long for the good old days of the scandal."

But the barebones game worked, because Bob Stewart and the staff worked diligently to make the game balanced. There were passwords played for laughs (like TINKLE or BLUBBER) and words played for sobriety (FUNERAL). They mixed levels of difficulty (the teams would knock off an easy word like UP, and then contend with the word BEDRAGGLED).

Pass the word! *Password* is on in prime time. Two of the daytime version's strongest players, Carol Burnett and Garry Moore, helped christen the after-dark version. FRED WOSTBROCK COLLECTION

Mike Gargiulo says "Your average viewer probably just thought we flipped through a dictionary and picked out words. We really put a lot more thought into it than that. *Password* was a hit because people talked to their television sets. That above all else makes a game show successful. *Password* made the viewers yell at their sets. And we'd sit there and come up with words and we would literally say to each other, 'Will people talk to the set?'"

The show coordinated the celebrities with care. Celebrities who frequently appeared on game shows, like Peggy Cass and Orson Bean, were generally matched against each other because they were expert players, while weaker players or newcomers were matched against each other, which meant that the show rarely had runaway games. Every day was a tight contest.

Stewart and the staff began holding auditions for every celebrity that they wanted to appear on the show. Most celebrities would have scoffed at being expected to audition for the role of game show guest, but Stewart would always lay out his logic to them when he made the phone call asking them to come in.

As Stewart would tell them, "We would like to audition you. Not because we're concerned about you, but because we don't want you to come out looking foolish."

No matter how big the star was, no game show viewer will sit through thirty minutes of a game being played poorly, so what was the point of inviting an A-lister if it meant bad games? The Goodson-Todman staff would work with every celebrity, playing practice game after practice game until the celebrity was comfortable and ready to go on the air.

One of the other reasons it worked was because only so much information could be conveyed one word at a time. The show generated so much natural humor because of the frequent confusions and misunderstandings that happened because the contestants had so little context to work with while they played.

Allen said, "The game is so fast, you get some slips of the tongue, as you almost always will in word association. One afternoon, the celebrity guest fed the word 'mean' as a clue to his partner, and the man immediately came out with 'father.' We all just gulped and moved on."

The audience had more fun with watching the celebrities try to deal with the tight parameters of the game. Anne Bancroft got so flustered with the password COZY that she spelled it in sign language as she gave her clue (Allen caught her, but nobody else realized what she doing). Bobby Morse kept breaking the show's rules by using hand gestures throughout his games. After three episodes of Allen reprimanding him and rebuking him, the show, as a one-time gag, made Morse play one game while wearing handcuffs, and then another with a straightjacket.

Better still for *Password* was the way that the show unintentionally developed a secret code of its own for giving clues. Pronouncing a word with an upward inflection implied that the password was an antonym. Dragging out the last syllable of the word for an extra second or two meant that your clue was the first word of a common phrase and the password was the second. Hand gestures were prohibited, but players could inject emotion into their delivery, implying fear, anger, amusement, or any other feeling that conveyed the essence of the word. The show had few detractors, but what the downward-thumbs out there didn't appreciate was that the game was so ingenious that playing it well was actually somewhat complicated.

Jane Fonda and James Mason join Allen for *Password.* FRED WOSTBROCK COLLECTION

Goodson-Todman knew they had put together a good, smart game. But everybody was in for a surprise. People speaking one word at a time doesn't look particularly amusing on paper, but in execution, the biggest surprise of all about *Password* was that the game was funny.

Publisher and noted punster Bennett Cerf, struggling with the password SALMON, gave his partner the clue "Schuster." Peter Lawford was faced with DONKEY and struggled before finally cracking and giving the clue "Ass." Alan King bugged his eyes and gave his partner a hilariously creepy gaze as he worked on the password STARE. In a more conservative time, Jimmy Stewart faced the word DEVIL and bemused his partner by repeating the word "Hell" over and over again. A military officer, faced with APPETITE, stunned Peggy Cass with the clue "Sexual..." Peggy's opponent, Tom Poston, walked off the stage, looking stunned. When everyone collected themselves, the game played out, APPETITE had been guessed, and Allen put his head in the palm of his hand in disbelief when he looked at the next password: LINGERIE.

And for some reason, a word as direct as "me" seemed to get more laughs out of the show than any other. Jack Benny, who drew decades of laughs on radio and television with shtick about how tight he was with a buck, saw the password MISER and got laughs and applause by offering "Me" as a clue.

Actress/consumer advocate Betty Furness and comedian Jack Carter were two of the hundreds of stars in the *Password* galaxy. FRED WOSTBROCK COLLECTION

Comedian Alan King saw the password COMIC and gave his partner the clue "Me." The contestant reflexively blurted out "Ham!" King replied, "How would you like a rap in the mouth, lady?!"

One night, the password was ME. Jack Paar, stumped for a good clue, gave up and decided to go for a laugh instead. He just looked at his partner and gave the clue "Marvelous." It got a laugh from the audience, and the contestant, stuck for an answer, said "If he can be a comedian, so can I. ME!" The contestant ended up winning the game by going for a joke.

Sometimes, the players derived entirely the wrong meaning from a clue. Betsy Palmer heard the clue "Pigeon" and froze. Unable to stop thinking about what tended to happen to the shoulders of statues upon which pigeons perched, Palmer only replied "I won't say it! I know it but I won't say it!"

Mike Gargiulo says, "It's good to have a laugh and have a fun moment, but by the same token, it's no fun to have something go so wildly wrong that it stops the game. Allen had a very, very good sense for when the game wasn't going anywhere, and he would prompt and prod the players to give their clues and guesses a little faster just to get it over with.

"I'll give you an example. We had a game between Elizabeth Montgomery and Martin Landau. Now, in *Password*, there are words you can get in two clues. Some take more. Some you can get in one clue. TOWER is a good example of a one-clue password. If you see TOWER either give the clue 'Leaning...' or you give the clue 'Eiffel...' and either one gives it to you in one clue. On the other hand, ELBOW is a two-clue password. You have to say 'arm' and you have to say 'middle'. There's no way to get ELBOW in one clue. And as a rule of thumb on our show, if it took four clues and nobody guessed it yet, that password wasn't going to be guessed. Sometimes, we'd be surprised, but by and large, a password that took more than four clues didn't get guessed at all.

"So Elizabeth Montgomery and Martin Landau are playing, Elizabeth was an outstanding player, always was. Martin Landau was frustrating to watch because there was a basic element of the game that he could not grasp. Martin Landau did not understand that you should use your clue to build on your opponent's clue. Martin would always give a clue that was totally disconnected from what his opponent just said. So Elizabeth and Martin are giving the clues. The password is BUNK and there's no way to get that in one clue. Elizabeth gives the clue 'Army.' Her partner guesses 'Navy.' We go to Martin. Now, the right way to play this would be to give the clue 'bed.' Martin gives the clue 'crap,' which would be a fine clue for that word if Elizabeth hadn't already said 'Army.' So this contestant hears the clue 'crap' after hearing 'Army' and you can see Martin's partner is just lost. It's Elizabeth's turn to give the next clue, and this time around, Elizabeth gives the clue 'bed.' Well, Elizabeth's partner's eyes just pop out because now we've had the clues 'crap' and 'bed.' And now both of the contestants are completely lost. And Allen begins nudging everyone to move the game faster, and I remember he gave a cue to Reason A. Goodwin, and Goodwin began sounding the time's-up signal a little faster in that round because everyone saw that the game was going over a cliff. But that was part of what Allen brought to the game. That round was shaping up to be a dud and he sped it up as much as he could to get it over with and get the game back to something that was more exciting."

The incoming mail from viewers gave the *Password* staff a sure sense that they were doing something right. It wasn't just mail asking for tickets or a chance to be a contestant. It wasn't fan mail gushing about Allen or the celebrity guests. *Password* was getting stacks of letters from viewers suggesting what clues they would have given for a particularly difficult word on a recent episode, or wondering why the contestants hadn't given what they considered a fairly obvious clue for a word, or defending a way-out-there clue that got a reaction from Allen and the audience and explaining why the clue actually made perfect sense. *Password* was getting mail from people who just wanted to talk about the game. You couldn't ask for better feedback than that.

Again, *Password* was lucky. Overwhelmingly positive response was rare for a game show. But even the handful of negative words for the show left Allen dumbfounded. Basically, all criticism boiled down to the notion that if the show was entertaining, it must not have any actual substance to it. That was a mindset that Allen saw permeating television more and more. He eventually wrote a nationally syndicated newspaper column about it *(see Appendix B)*.

In time, some detractors came around. One anonymous actress told *TV Guide* that she was initially appalled by Allen's "phony little-boy-getting-up-to-recite-at-Sunday-School manner. His terribly corny little bow and cute smile at the camera smacked of amateur theatricals…When he would turn to the guest stars, call them by their first names and start talking as though he was one of the gang, it used to infuriate me. 'How dare you, you hokey amateur,' I used to say to myself. But I liked the show so I kept watching it and, do you know, I've become a real fan of Allen's. I can see now that all his earnestness and friendliness and shyness are real. He comes across as a real nice man."

Mike Gargiulo says, "It's tough to explain what Allen brought to that show, but I'll try. There's a limitation to how much you can interrupt a game in progress. There's a wide shot of the set, and then a two-shot of the team, shot of Allen, shot of the other team, and the game had rhythm to it. You can't interrupt a game of word association in progress because the audience will feel that he is disrupting the flow of the thought process. Allen's talent was that he understood his role, and he stayed out of the way. He let the game take its natural course and he didn't disrupt the rhythm. He said very, very little when the game was in progress and that was important. The host is not the star, the game is the star and Allen got that. People watch a show because they want to see the game. You might like the host, you might like the celebrities, but the game is what you want to see. No matter how much you like Alex Trebek, you're watching *Jeopardy!* to read the clues on that board."

Allen also arguably gave *Password* its atmosphere. The game already had some sense of intimacy. The four players and Allen were together at a single, large desk, and their surroundings were so tiny that when you saw all five people in a single shot, you were also seeing virtually the whole

Polly Bergen and Raymond Burr play *Password*. Perry Mason almost never lost a case, and Burr's record as a *Password* player was just as strong. FRED WOSTBROCK COLLECTION

set. But everything about Allen himself gave the show an image. Every day, he walked onstage sporting a perfectly tailored jacket and pants with a crease so sharp it could probably cut paper. He had the most expressive hands on television, but his gestures were smooth and graceful. His arm would flow outward as he handed the *Password* wallets to the contestants, and then inward toward the center as he opened his hand and told the home audience, "As they look at it, we'd like you to see it."

He raised his voice only when amused, and even then, it would be only a slight elevation. There was an audible smile in his voice at all times. He enforced the rules — "Watch the hand gestures!" — but never with sternness, more with a gentle firmness, pardon the contradiction. Just the slightest choice of words from Allen affected the tone. The camera or other goody awarded to the loser of the game was never a consolation prize…in Allen's words, it was "a fine gift," as though a few pieces of luggage were the show's token of gratitude to the contestant for deciding to join that day's party. The money awarded to the winners was never a big deal; it was practically an afterthought.

The result of this atmosphere was that *Password* transcended its genre.

Rhonda Fleming and William Bendix do battle from Television City in Hollywood. *Password* began attracting so many stars that the show made regular trips to the West Coast to accommodate their schedules.
FRED WOSTBROCK COLLECTION

It was a game show that drew huge audiences because it attracted people who typically didn't like game shows. It was relatively quiet, sedate, and pleasant, with no emphasis on money or status symbols to be awarded. It was just a fun show with a game that required some intelligence and mental agility.

TV Guide itself, which initially had dismissed the game as "99.9% nothing," dramatically changed its tune only a few months after their first review. The magazine raved, "While in the Simon-pure form the game might provide some mild delight for a five-year-old, Goodson and Todman have jazzed it up ingeniously…One need only watch this show once to understand its phenomenal success. Viewer participation is built into it as into no other show on TV. It is flatly impossible to avoid playing the game along with the contestants while one watches — even knowing the password — for the simple reason that if one does not, one cannot understand what is happening."

As the weeks wore on and celebrity guests made their way in and out of the studio, Goodson-Todman Productions began keeping track of how well the celebrities were playing, in preparation for future weeks.

Allen made his own assessments to *TV Guide*: "Carol Burnett is one of the best game players — facile, very fast. But you have to watch her. She can communicate a word of meaning with just one word. When she says 'Me-e-e-ssy,' it's the messiest mess. Betsy Palmer? She's enthusiastic. But she does use her hands. Darren McGavin is excellent. He plays with great precision and drive. Zachary Scott is consistent, plays with great logic. Abe Burrows has a vivid vocabulary that he uses readily."

In time, Goodson-Todman began extending invitations for second appearances to the stars who had played the game so well in its nascent months. Unsurprisingly, Betty White was one of them. Allen, concerned about how unsociable he felt he had been the first time he met her, decided to join Bob Stewart backstage before Betty's January appearance to greet her. He just wanted to make a second first impression, that was all.

Once upon a time, a boy and a girl grew up less than two hundred miles apart, in two very different parts of the world; one on the edge of Chicago's hustle and bustle, and one in a small Wisconsin town where his family had helped the townsfolk discover electricity. They both dreamed of show business, and were blessed with parents who supported them. They sang and acted in high school, and found their way into community theater troupes. They drifted into radio. They made the choice to interrupt their lives for their country and provided service through morale. When they chased their dreams again, she was on the West Coast and he was on the East Coast. She was a star when television was just finding itself. When television succeeded, he had worked to help radio find itself. Both of them had worn wedding rings. Both of them knew what broken hearts felt like.

Maybe their life experiences shaped their personalities and their behavior came across so strongly that they could sense something right away. Or maybe Allen Ludden just had good instincts about Betty White. But they exchanged pleasantries and chatted briefly before Betty went back to her dressing room before the program. And when Betty was out of sight, Allen turned to Bob Stewart and made a declaration.

"I'm going to marry that woman."

He said it as if he was telling Bob Stewart that the sky was blue. Stewart's immediate reaction was one of pity. Allen had only lost his wife three months ago, and he was left alone to raise three children.

Stewart tried to bring Allen back to Earth. "Allen, you're just reacting to the situation. This is a tough time for you. You've lost your wife and you're in turmoil."

Allen didn't think about that assessment for a moment. He turned to Bob Stewart and repeated, "I'm going to marry that woman."

PASSWORD

Allen's serious facial expression in this CBS promotional slide may be a little out of place for a fun show like *Password,* but he wasn't kidding around after meeting Betty White. FRED WOSTBROCK COLLECTION

FRED WOSTBROCK COLLECTION

CHAPTER TEN

"CHOICE"

As Bob Stewart remembered, "He began to <u>pursue</u> her. That's the only word for it."

Allen was subtle at first. He secured a temporary job guest-hosting for Arthur Godfrey's radio show, and just politely suggested to Betty that she might make a good guest. Betty happily joined Allen for the show, considering it the same as any other guest-star spot on a TV or radio show. Allen seemed nice but that was as much thought as Betty had given him; she hadn't taken the time to speak to him outside of the confines of a studio complex, and she just figured he was a married man.

Allen stepped up his efforts. Being a workaholic, he had a different approach than most men would have had to getting the girl. He didn't ask her out on a date. He went to work with her.

Early in the year, Allen was already thinking ahead to the summer months. He knew he was going to want a vacation. He had already spent a two-week spring break traveling Europe, which mostly relaxed him, although he was a little surprised by how many of the other tourists recognized him and took time out to compliment him.

"It makes me very self-conscious," Allen said of his new-found fame. "I like it when people talk to me, and I think being asked for my autograph is the greatest compliment I can get. But when I see people just staring, I never know whether to smile at them or say 'Yes, that's who I am.'"

But that two weeks of vacation wasn't enough. Game show hosting was a deceptively difficult job.

As he explained it, "I have to watch the points in the game and I have to watch lights built into the podium that tell me where to start a new part of the game. I watch the card boy with the lead-ins to the commercials, and the teleprompter for the commercials. I have to watch the clock for the Lighting Rounds. There's a producer on one side signaling to speed up or slow down, and a stage manager on the other side giving me cues.

And meantime, you have to pay close attention to what the contestants are doing — and I mean really listen. And you have to appear easy and relaxed all the time. Sometimes I'm pretty tired after a show."

But there was a bigger reason that he wanted time off during summer. His kids would be out of school for three months, and for the first time in their lives, their mother wouldn't be there. He had considered the idea of sending them to summer camp, but given the circumstances, it didn't feel right. Life without Margaret was just as tough an adjustment for him as it was for them; he thought that a good solution might be getting everybody out of the house and getting them engaged in something they had never done before. He began pursuing summer stock productions.

It was a good career option for him. Admittedly, as much as he resisted television stardom, it was going to give him plenty of opportunities to choose from. It didn't hurt that he had such a distinctive look that he was instantly recognizable, despite the struggle that many writers had with characterizing him in print. Newspaper writers referred to his physical appearance with a broad stretch of terms, including "a tall George Gobel" and "a Scandinavian delegate at the U.N." Some just kept it strictly literal: "A Texan with piercing eyes, a crisp, carrying voice, a most likeable personality, and no illusions."

He had name value that would allow him to get by and land roles because he could sell tickets. In the early 1960s, a report in *The New York Times* on summer stock productions made the fairly obvious observation that summer theaters tried to hire celebrities to draw attention and sell tickets to the shows they were starring in, but there was one surprising detail mentioned in the report. According to many theaters that dealt in summer stock, the most lucrative celebrities were game show hosts. All over the country, audiences came in droves to watch plays starring Bert Parks, Merv Griffin, and Gene Rayburn.

The reasoning, it seemed, was that since game show hosts always appeared on television under their real names and performed as their real selves — or at least the most TV-friendly version of their real selves — the audience felt a sense of friendship. As one theater manager explained to the paper, "[Audiences] feel they know them as people, but they are curious to see if they can act and they are curious to see what they look like from the waist down."

Allen understood it and expressed his enthusiasm for summer stock for much the same reasons. He said, "We go out to make friends. It means a great deal to us to meet the people who write us and say 'hello' as if they really were our friends. It's a good feeling."

And any production that hired Allen Ludden for a lead role just because his name was going to sell some extra tickets was going to be in for a pleasant surprise: Allen Ludden could walk onto a stage and deliver.

He was cast in the lead role of a play called *Critic's Choice*. Allen would play the role of Parker Ballantine, a theater critic who, in a fit of exasperation at the shows he's seeing, tells his wife, "It's not new stories the theatre needs. It's new insight."

Parker's wife, Angela, writes a play based on her experience leaving home as a teenager, and to Parker's dismay, it's a terrible show. Parker tells her so, but Angela manages to find a producer who actually wants to support it, and the play makes it to Broadway. Everything comes to a head when Parker stays home and gets drunk on opening night, instead of attending the play and forcing himself to write an honest review. Henry Fonda had originated the role of Parker on Broadway, so Allen had a tough act to follow. In the play, Parker and Angela Ballantine had a twelve-year-old son. David Ludden was perfect for that part.

Allen studies up on his script for *Critic's Choice*. It may have just seemed like a nice career option, but it was the most important thing he would ever do for his personal life. FRED WOSTBROCK COLLECTION

The kids had never seen their dad's work in the theater, and they had certainly never worked in the theater themselves. The upcoming summer would be full of first-time experiences.

David had never shown any inclination toward show business. He had inherited his father's love of education. He was a fan of Dylan Thomas' poetry (Allen himself never cared for Thomas though, considering him "too fey") and read *The Catcher in the Rye* while he was home sick from school for a few days. While Allen was negotiating with the backers of

Critic's Choice, fourteen-year-old David was receiving acceptance letters from Phillips Exeter Academy, The Taft School, and Phillips Academy Andover, trying to figure out which of the preparatory boarding schools he'd want to attend that fall. But he thought acting was worth giving a shot and agreed to spend his summer working on *Critic's Choice*. It would be his only acting role. He instead graduated from Andover and Yale and became a professor.

In March, Betty got a call from her agent offering a summer stock gig: one week in Dennis, Massachusetts on Cape Cod, followed by a week in Skowhegan, Maine. She would be playing the role of Angela Ballantine, Parker Ballantine's wife, in *Critic's Choice*. She accepted.

Two months passed and Betty got a phone call from Allen, saying that *Password* was getting ready to do a special taping in Hollywood and that he just found out that there was a production of *Critic's Choice* happening in the same week at a small theater in Los Angeles. Allen feigned nervousness about his upcoming acting gig, telling Betty that he had never performed onstage. That wasn't exactly true, but he was definitely a few years out of practice. He suggested that it would be helpful if he and Betty saw *Critic's Choice* together before rehearsals for their own production. Betty thought that made sense, so she agreed to join him.

And while they were at it, Allen suggested, why not meet up with some friends and go to dinner together?

Allen arrived in Los Angeles and arrived at the Whites' house to pick up his companion for the evening. In his mid-forties, Allen was now faced with a situation he hadn't dealt with in more than twenty-five years. His date's parents answered the door. Luckily for Allen, he had an edge that he didn't have when he was a teenager: Horace and Tess White loved *G.E. College Bowl* and *Password*. He also made a good first impression on Betty's dogs; they were eager to greet him too.

On the way to the dinner, Allen and Betty got to know each other. Allen began talking about David, Martha, and Sarah and regaling Betty with funny stories about the things that he and the kids did together.

Betty reacted to one of the stories by chuckling and saying, "I'll bet your wife loves that."

Silence.

And then Allen answered, "I don't have a wife. She died last October."

Betty, feeling foolish, answered, "I'm sorry."

Allen recovered and quite fearlessly told her the whole story. And as the night went on, Allen kept talking. Betty sensed that Allen was sharing some feelings that he hadn't shared with anybody in the past few months.

She had been concerned that she had made things problematic with her foot-in-mouth moment earlier. Instead, Allen closed out the night by apologizing to her for talking too much.

Betty liked Allen, and so did Horace and Tess. Tess, in particular, was a loyal *Password* viewer, and her daughter thought she'd get a big kick out of having Allen over for dinner. The *Password* tapings would keep him

Meet the parents. Allen didn't have anything to worry about the first time he met **Horace and Tess White.** FRED WOSTBROCK COLLECTION

in Los Angeles for a few more days, so he'd probably appreciate a home-cooked meal. Horace and Tess responded emphatically to the suggestion, and Allen returned to the White household for supper with the family.

At the end of dinner, Allen casually mentioned that he hadn't called his children back in Briarcliff Manor, New York yet (Allen's housekeeper, Lessie, looked after the kids; David and Martha were teenagers by this

The chance to work and being near the waters of Cape Cod was enough of an incentive for Betty to take a role in *Critic's Choice*, but she had no idea what was really in store for her. AUTHOR'S COLLECTION

point, too, so they were self-sufficient enough that Allen didn't give any concern to leaving them alone for a few days while he was on business).

Horace and Tess directed him to a telephone in the next room, and Allen had a conversation with the kids. He returned to the dining room with a broad grin crossing his face.

He told the Whites, "I just told my son David that I had a lovely dinner with Betty White, and he said 'Bring her with you, Dad!'"

Betty let out a laugh and faux-flirtily replied, "Well, that's flattering! How old is David?"

Allen pretended to be insulted and responded with an exaggerated frown. "David meant to bring you back for me, not for him!"

Betty continued seeing her boyfriend Phil when she returned to New York. He was supportive of her impending two-week engagement with *Critic's Choice*. But Phil was a little put off that Allen was treating Betty to another evening at the theater. Together, she and Allen saw *Mary, Mary* and Allen explained why he needed to see Betty again. During his visit to Los Angeles, it seemed that Allen bought two puppies, and, gee whiz, in his excitement, he hadn't considered what to do with them during the weeks that he and the family would be traveling with *Critic's Choice*. He knew that Betty liked dogs a lot, so, he wondered, did Betty have any advice about what he should do with those puppies?

Betty was a little surprised by a problem that she felt had an obvious solution. She answered, "Why, bring them along, of course!"

Allen unsurprisingly agreed that it sounded like a smart idea.

As it turned out, Allen would have another reason to re-focus his energies during the summer months. He was going to need a professional morale booster after finally being forced to make the decision he was dreading. CBS was arranging its schedule for the 1962-63 season and decided to switch the prime-time *Password* from Tuesday nights to Sunday nights at 8:00 p.m. The problem was that *G.E. College Bowl* was slotted for Sunday afternoon at 5:30 p.m. And G.E. immediately voiced an objection to having a master of ceremonies hosting two different shows only two hours apart. The ultimatum was firmly laid down. Allen had to choose between *G.E. College Bowl* and *Password*.

Goodson-Todman, for their part, anticipated that it might not be an easy decision and began considering possible replacements for nighttime *Password*. One report said that the lead candidate was actor Peter Lind Hayes. (Funnily enough, Hayes would later sign with Don Reid and host a *College Bowl* spin-off.)

On May 8, Allen officially gave his notice to *G.E. College Bowl*. He put on a cheerful face for the press, trying not to let on how hard the decision had actually been. He told reporter Cynthia Lowry, "*Password* offers scope and a challenge. It has turned me into a full-time performer. Besides, I'd done the other show for a long time, so it wouldn't prove anything much to me if I did another season of it."

If Allen didn't sound particularly sad about leaving *G.E. College Bowl*, it was because it was a decision that he had been preparing for over the past year.

He told *TV Guide*, "I'm sure I surprised and disappointed a lot of people by deciding to leave *College Bowl*…but the real choice was made last summer when I decided to take the *Password* job. When I did that, I threw in my lot with being a performer full-time."

And behind the scenes, Allen found that his bosses at *College Bowl* had made the decision easier for him, for reasons that didn't really make him very happy.

No other television packager in the world could offer a master of ceremonies the paycheck that Goodson-Todman, the game show kings, could offer theirs…but other television packagers could certainly offer an ownership stake. Allen approached the co-executive producers of *College Bowl* — Don Reid, Jack Cleary, and John Moses — and told them he would stay with their show if he was made a profit participant. He wanted to own the show and the format as much as they did. In Allen's eyes, this was completely reasonable. He was the one that sketched out that format in his backyard. He was the one who figured out the logistics. He was the one who traveled from coast to coast talking schools into signing up. He was the one who gave the show an identity. He was the one who got the show to a third season on NBC Radio. For all he had given, and now for all that the format was giving the three show runners, it was perfectly logical to give Allen a stake in the program.

Reid, Cleary, and Moses, however, did not see things that way. Allen gave his notice.

Newspaper columnist Dave Felt summed up *College Bowl*'s loss nicely. "Too bad that Allen Ludden will leave *College Bowl*…In every television appearance, Allen Ludden demonstrates his background of varied learning that extends beyond the necessary notes provided in advance to ensure smooth production of the show."

Producer Jack Cleary, who had given Allen and partner Grant Tinker the go-ahead to mount the radio show nearly a decade earlier, told the press that they didn't have a new host in mind, but stated for the record that the host didn't have to be all brain. He pledged that the new host could study questions in advance and that the big words in the questions could be spelled phonetically for them.

"Any intelligent guy can do it," Cleary casually said.

Password was a smash and Allen was identified with it strongly. He was being paid too well to leave. Allen reluctantly announced that he would depart from *G.E. College Bowl* in June, at the end of its fourth television season, its seventh season overall. The worst part was that he was leaving it totally behind. He wouldn't see any of the money from the *G.E. College Bowl* home game, or the impending spin-off series, *Alumni Fun* (featuring famous graduates in place of students), or the British version, *University Challenge*, which premiered the following year, or the official *College Bowl* question books, or the licensing fees from giving the format to local stations across the country. High schools, colleges, and some elementary schools, kept adding quiz bowl teams to their extracurricular activities offered to students in response to the popularity of the show. Granted, somebody else had planted the seed. But Allen Ludden was the man who gave it water and sunlight. And in the end, he didn't get to reap any of the fruit.

Allen keeps smiling for the camera, although there were hard feelings all around when he departed *G.E. College Bowl.* FRED WOSTBROCK COLLECTION

Allen got one consolation, though. The Horatio Alger Association of Distinguished Americans was introduced in 1947 to honor Americans who persevered in spite of adversity and to honor those who made significant contributions to the cause of education. In 1962, the year that he departed from *G.E. College Bowl*, Allen was honored with a Horatio Alger Award. Previous winners had included Dwight Eisenhower, Bernard Baruch, Conrad Hilton, Dr. Ralph Bunche, J.C. Penney, Herbert Hoover, and Eddie Rickenbacker. It was the first time that the award had ever been given to somebody in the performing arts.

Allen modestly said of the award, "I can't figure out why they picked me. I was neither that poor nor am I that successful. The only explanation I've been able to give myself is that I was on *College Bowl* for so long that my name was the only one that most of the college people who did the voting ever heard of."

A Goodson-Todman staffer saw more in the award than Allen did, telling *TV Guide*, "The Horatio Alger Award was most fitting...Allen is like the good son — the one who works hard and always has a happy smile. He does his homework, keeps his shoes shined and his room neat and never has to have Mom bail him out with the school principal or an irate neighbor whose window was broken. He's a real sweet guy."

Allen's expectation that Don Morrow would replace him didn't come to fruition. The job instead went to Robert Earle, an Ithaca-based broadcaster who read in the newspaper that Allen Ludden was leaving *G.E. College Bowl*. He immediately gathered some tapes that he had of his broadcasting work, got in the car, and drove straight to New York City to drop them off at Don Reid's office.

Earle had talent, yes, but there was a cynical suspicion that there were other motives for his hiring. Robert Earle was roughly Allen's age, same height, same weight, and had a head of blonde hair that was starting to gray. And after NBC and G.E. agreed with Don Reid that he was the best man for the job, NBC had an optometrist fit Earle with an identical pair or distinctive tortoiseshell glasses.

A few writers noticed the strange resemblance between old host and new. So, too, did a perceptive viewer, who saw Allen Ludden walking outside Radio City Music Hall one night, approached him, and asked, "Who is this new man they've poured into your glasses?"

Robert Earle, the new host of *G.E. College Bowl*, sported a look that struck Allen as awfully familiar. Though Earle was a talented broadcaster and a worthy candidate for the job, Allen's suspicions about why he got hired would remain a sore spot for years after.

TOM MICHAEL, *COLLEGE BOWL VALHALLA*

Don Morrow said, "I was involved with every phase of the show in the event that anything ever happened to Allen. I knew the show backwards and forwards and was told by all the principals that if Allen ever left the show, I would take over as host. Allen definitely wanted to pass the show to me, as I thought did all the other principals concerned. Through the courtesy of Dawg, I had also been the voice on most of the G.E. commercials used on the show. In a fit of stupidity, I went to Dawg and quit. Thank God, he and I remained as pals in spite of the whole debacle."

It's worth noting that Ludden never bore any personal animosity toward Earle. The first time they ever met, Allen greeted Earle by approaching him carefully, staring at him for a long moment, and muttering, "I don't see a resemblance." Part of him found it quite funny, and maybe even flattering, that somebody — be it a CBS executive or a *College Bowl* producer, insisted on having Earle wear tortoiseshell glasses that he didn't need. The same night that Allen met his replacement for the first time, they went out for a very pleasant conversation over dinner. Whatever resentful feelings Allen may have had about *College Bowl*, he never bore those feelings toward Earle, and certainly didn't have a reason to.

To be fair to Robert Earle, he was deserving of the opportunity. Like Allen, he had a background in broadcasting and education. He had been an announcer for a number of local stations in upstate New York, as well as working as a commercial pitchman and a fashion show commentator. He had been a communications specialist in the Advanced Electronic Center at Cornell University before going to Ithaca College to head the Radio and Television Department.

Earle next reached out to Jack Cleary and won the job with the ingenious way that he went about making an audition tape for the job. He recorded the audio from an episode of *G.E. College Bowl*, and then carefully edited it to remove all traces of Allen's voice. He put the audio recording on a tape deck operated by a foot brake. He made a film of himself hosting a simulated game of *College Bowl*, reading each question and then taking his foot off the brake to play the audio of the players giving their answers. The recording earned him an audition in Cleary's office, and he won the job. *College Bowl* lasted the rest of the decade with Robert Earle at the helm on CBS and NBC. In 1963, the Primetime Emmy Awards included, for the final time, a category for game shows. That final award went to *G.E. College Bowl* with Robert Earle.

Allen's feelings were hurt by walking away from *G.E. College Bowl*, but he was hardly mourning, knowing what the summer had in store for him. In August, Betty met a pair of poodles named Willie and Emma, a chocolate-colored brother and sister. She also met David, Martha, and Sarah Ludden, and they all hit it off immediately. Sarah turned ten and Martha turned thirteen during the run of *Critic's Choice*, and a pair of birthday celebrations set just the right mood for everybody to get to know each other. Sarah, the youngest, was the first to become attached to Betty, although her brother and sister didn't take very long to catch up. Allen and the kids were going to have a picnic one day; the kids invited Betty to join them. The family was having a bull session back at their temporary home; Betty was asked to shoot the bull with them. The Luddens were going for a swim; Betty didn't swim, so she was more surprised than anybody to find herself swinging from a rope and letting herself drop into the lake. The Luddens were all encouraging Betty to take the plunge, which seemed to be a metaphor for what was to come.

Betty felt like she had her head in the clouds during the summer of 1962; she was acting and making a lot of new friends in the Ludden family. AUTHOR'S COLLECTION

During the run of *Critic's Choice*, the Luddens stayed in a lakeside cottage, while Betty had her own place down the road. Every morning, the Luddens showed up at her house, walked through the living room, and went straight to her designated section of the beach. Betty faced an onslaught of Luddens wherever she dared to go, or dared to stay for that matter, but she wouldn't have it any other way. She was growing fond of the whole gang.

On the final night of the week in Cape Cod, Phil came to give Betty a ride to Maine for the next leg of the production. He agreed to join the Luddens for dinner, and then he'd stick around for that night's performance of *Critic's Choice*.

Phil sat in the third row. The show had a very standard ending: a kissing scene, with husband and wife patching up their differences. Allen, knowing that Phil was in the audience, threw down the gauntlet that night. He held the kiss longer than he was supposed to. Betty noticed. Phil noticed too. From the stage, Betty could hear Phil clearing his throat loudly as Allen kept his arms wrapped around her.

The next day, Phil bluntly told Betty what was on his mind. "I don't like Allen Ludden."

Betty was stunned. "Everyone likes Allen Ludden!"

Phil answered, "Not somebody who loves you."

Betty snapped back, "Don't be ridiculous! This is a man with three children and two poodle puppies, and it's nothing at all."

Phil glared. And in a moment of stunning perceptiveness about how Allen had presented himself to Betty, Phil confessed, "It's the poodle puppies I'm worried about."

He knew exactly why Allen had brought them along.

The following week, Betty was in Maine and spent more time with the Ludden family. And at some point in that week, there was an abrupt change in Allen's vocabulary. He stopped saying "Hello" when he greeted Betty.

Instead, he greeted her by saying "Will you marry me?"

Betty laughed it off. Allen was playful about it and remained so. He kept saying it every time he greeted Betty during that week in Maine. Allen's kids were noticing too. They began making check-marks in the air with their index fingers every time their father said it.

On the final night in Skowhegan, Maine, Betty threw a goodbye party in her cottage for the entire cast. Allen brought along his children — of course he did. Betty looked at all of them and had a series of epiphanies; she knew the names of all of David's friends, even though she had never

met them. She knew how excited Sarah had been about the birthday that
came and went. She thought back to the night when thirteen-year-old
Martha opened up to her about a few issues that she had on her mind,
and Betty had a woman-to-woman talk with the budding young lady.

When the party went late into the evening and young Sarah showed
signs of fading away, Betty carried Sarah into her bedroom, tucked her
in, and said goodnight.

The party went on and the cast continued chatting while David decided
to step into the bedroom and say goodnight to his sister. When he came
back out, he gently nudged Betty and whispered, "You'd better go in again
and say goodbye to Sarah."

Betty walked into the bedroom and saw Sarah crying and tightly
clutching the big teddy bear she had received her for birthday. Betty
asked what was wrong and Sarah whimpered. "We'll never see you again."

Betty wiped the tears streaking Sarah's crimson cheeks and held her
close. "Darling, of course I'll see you again! You know that I come back
to New York often. I promise to come and see you."

"No you won't!" Sarah persisted. "You'll be too far away!"

"Yes I will!" Betty replied, becoming more insistent. "I promise!"

Betty went back to Los Angeles, struck by how difficult it had been
for her to say goodbye to the Luddens before going to the airport. She
went back to her normal life, living with her parents and their pets. Betty's
living arrangements, by her own admission, were a little peculiar for
somebody making such a comfortable living in show business. She had
periodically moved into apartments in Los Angeles but every time, she
found herself getting bored after a few months and moving back in with
her parents. In a way, she felt that living with her parents was a good way
to keep her ego in check. Show business is a field that requires one to
think about herself quite a bit, and she found that when she lived alone,
she was thinking only of herself. Living with her parents gave her other
people and other subjects to occupy her mind.

Allen began calling Betty regularly, just to "touch base" with her, the
way that friends do. That was enough for Betty's boyfriend Phil to voice
his objections more strongly. He'd had enough. He told Betty that for the
moment, they were still friends, but he couldn't continue being with her
unless she made up her mind about her feelings for Allen. She kept deny-
ing that she felt anything, although she came to admit that she missed
the dogs and the kids that she had spent her summer with.

The next time Betty was in New York, Allen suggested that they go
to dinner with two friends of his, Grant Tinker and Grant's new wife,

actress Mary Tyler Moore. Betty didn't let on, but as an actress herself, she was somewhat aware that this evening was a tryout. And Tinker and Moore were the ones keeping an eye on her.

Mary Tyler Moore remembered in 2000, "Grant and I were auditioning her on behalf of Allen Ludden. Allen said, 'I want you to meet her, and I really hope you like her, because I really like her.' We were as

Betty tried to keep herself occupied back in Los Angeles, but suddenly she had a lot on her mind. AUTHOR'S COLLECTION

charming and polite as we could possibly be, but we were making mental notes. *Observed: Holding Allen's hand.* That's good. *Observed: Laughing a little too hard at Allen's joke.* Perhaps she heard it before and didn't cover it up as well as she might have...But we loved her immediately. How could you not?"

A few weeks later, Betty made another one of her routine working trips to New York City and decided to treat Tess to a free trip joining her. Allen and Phil both learned that Betty's mother was in town, and it triggered the next battle in their war, with Tess very happily caught in the middle. Both of them bought Tess tickets for Broadway shows. Both of them kept tabs on the seats she had tickets for and tried to buy better tickets for the next night. Tess ate at the finest restaurants in New York during her stay. They both treated her to day trips in nice spots just outside of town.

But Allen had one slight edge. He was on television every day. Tess had been a fan of *Password* from the beginning, before she ever met Allen Ludden. She never missed it. Betty mentioned to Allen that whenever she and Tess watched *Password* together, and Allen strolled onstage at the opening of the show, Tess would playfully say "Hi, Doll!" at the television. Allen was charmed by the story.

And one day, after Betty and Tess returned to Los Angeles, they turned on the TV and watched *Password*. Announcer Jack Clark introduced Allen, Allen walked onstage, looked right at the camera, beamed, and said, "Hi, Doll!"

The Battle for Tess had been a decisive victory for Allen Ludden.

A sketch of Allen used for CBS print advertising, artist unknown. FRED
WOSTBROCK COLLECTION

"Hi, Doll." FRED WOSTBROCK COLLECTION

CHAPTER ELEVEN

"RINGS"

Despite Allen's overt on-air efforts, he and Betty actually made an effort to be somewhat discreet about their relationship. They weren't trying to keep it a secret, but they weren't exactly shouting it from every mountain, either. When Betty was invited to be a guest on *The Mike Douglas Show*, she politely declined a suggestion from the show's staff that she and Allen appear as guests together. And though Allen was opening *Password* fairly often by saying "Hi, Doll," he was coy about the meaning. When *TV Guide* asked him, he only said he was greeting the mother of "a friend."

In the fall of 1962, *Password* celebrated its first anniversary. It was still winning its time slot every day on CBS. Not just winning — dominating. *Password* owned the 2:00 p.m. time slot and CBS had no intention of moving it. NBC had thrown in the towel on the competing program *The Jan Murray Show* when *Password* began regularly tripling its audience. ABC had given up on the game show *Number Please* (funnily, also a Goodson-Todman Production) and then waited six months to plug in a replacement series, *Day in Court*, which wasn't faring much better.

Password rapidly emerged as a popular party game across the country. *TV Guide* printed a full explanation of the game's rules so readers could assemble their own games for get-togethers. Even though a home game really wasn't necessary — you could easily pull words out of the dictionary and keep score on a piece of scratch paper — Milton Bradley released a *Password* home game in 1962 and had an instant hit with it. The game attractively packaged bowling-style scoresheets, a scorekeeping dial, long perforated cards with passwords printed on them, and leatherette word holders that made it an irresistible addition to living room shelves across America.

One of the most readily visible indicators of success was the way that the show's star power was rising. A Goodson-Todman creation of the 1950s, *What's My Line?*, had emerged into such a big hit that stars who normally wouldn't touch game shows eagerly appeared on that one. Now, in the 1960s, Goodson-Todman's *Password* was accomplishing the same thing. Olivia de Havilland, Douglas Fairbanks Jr., Jimmy Stewart, Raymond Burr, Anne Bancroft, Robert Goulet, Anthony Perkins, Ginger Rogers, Woody Allen, and Lucille Ball eagerly lined up for their turns. Lucille Ball loved *Password* so much that when she was working on her own TV shows, she kept a copy of the home game in her dressing room and rounded people up to play during rehearsal breaks.

Her daughter, Lucie Arnaz, later said, "Honestly, I think it would have hurt her feelings if [*Password*] didn't call her every few months to invite her."

Many of the stars grew just as addicted to the game as the audience had. Carol Burnett compared it to eating a bag of peanuts. Ginger Rogers appeared as a guest and then kept her husband awake the entire night playing more games. Chuck Connors had such a good time that he stunned Goodson-Todman by calling the office and offering to pay his own airfare if they'd invite him back for another turn. Peter Lawford was known to throw *Password* parties at his home, while Jimmy and Gloria Stewart would frequently take their copy of the home game to social engagements.

It was interesting that so many celebrities were so enthusiastic about playing the game because there was one readily noticeable effect of playing five straight episodes at a time. Any illusions or images a star had built up for themselves in the public eye came crumbling down.

Allen said, "Anyone who is celebrated by reason of accomplishment can play it, usually very well…The only people who can't are the paper creations of Hollywood and television. It isn't that the game is so difficult. But it places a celebrity in a position calling for spontaneity, a certain amount of intellectual depth, and the ability to achieve a rapport with a stranger not of the show business world, his partner. If the celebrity has substance, is genuine and honest, it shows immediately. If not…." Allen finished the thought with an unsympathetic shrug.

He continued, "For real people, it's the greatest showcase of all the quiz shows, and we have no trouble at all getting genuine celebrities to appear. But there is, and should be, trouble involved in getting the phony celebrities because when they appear, it's the kind of disaster I don't care to be associated with."

And some stars were aware that disaster was a possibility. Allen was gracious enough to avoid naming a name, but became fond of telling a tale about a time that he appeared as a guest on a talk show, and backstage, he was greeted by a top film actress.

As Allen told it, the actress said, "I would give simply anything to play *Password*."

Allen cheerfully replied, "Well, isn't this a coincidence! We've always wanted you on the show, and I know for a fact that at least a half a dozen

Password gives new meaning to "family game night." Lucille Ball and her daughter Lucie Arnaz do battle against Lucy's husband, Gary Morton, and Desi Arnaz Jr. FRED WOSTBROCK COLLECTION

offers have been made to your agent. So why haven't you been on *Password?*"

The actress replied, "Darling, I didn't say I hadn't been invited to play *Password*. I have! It's just that I wouldn't dare!"

Sometimes, a star's ability could be a pleasant surprise. Allen personally invited Joey Bishop to be a guest on the nighttime show early in its run. Joey accepted, but with an unusual request; he suggested actress Abby Dalton for his opponent. The truth was that Bishop suspected that Abby Dalton was a dumb blonde, and he knew she had never done a game show before, so she'd be nervous to boot. Dalton, instead, mopped the floor with Bishop and was invited back to *Password* repeatedly.

And some other stars handled the game so well that nothing could shake them. Florence Henderson was nine months pregnant when she

appeared on *Password*. During a break in the game, Florence turned to
Allen and calmly told him that she was going into labor. Allen immediately became nervous and notified a few staffers, but Florence considered
herself a pregnancy veteran — this was her third — and told the staff
that it wasn't an emergency. She was having such a good time playing *Password* that she was going to finish the taping because she knew

Florence and Skitch Henderson do battle; Florence would be
responsible for one of the more unnerving episodes that Allen ever
hosted, insisting that she play the game even though she was in labor.
FRED WOSTBROCK COLLECTION

from experience that she still had enough time. To Allen's astonishment,
Florence played the game without any trace of distress or distraction,
finished the taping, then calmly exited the studio, went straight to a
hospital, and gave birth.

Goodson-Todman staffer Frank Wayne scoffed at any stars whose fear
held them back from accepting an invitation. Failing at word association
was quite a bit different than failing at any other game.

Wayne said, "The game is challenging enough to make them want to
try their hand at it while at the same time, they never come off looking
stupid. There are a number of perfectly logical synonyms for each word
used on the show. So, if a star doesn't light on the exact word called for,
it makes little difference. It's not as though we were asking questions of

fact, which can make any contestant look a little backward. You ask a man for the capital of Wisconsin, for instance, and in most cases, he's either going to look blank or come up with the wrong answer. In either case, he comes off looking like a loser."

The mental struggle to find a perfect clue, the stress of deciphering the clues you were hearing…On panel games, you merely had to ask yes-or-no questions, and if you could get one or two laughs while doing that, you were golden. On *Password*, you were working in tandem with a total stranger trying to earn money. The pressure was enough that the stars couldn't be preoccupied with maintaining a façade. For anyone wondering "What's so-and-so really like?" all they had to do to find the answer was watch so-and-so play *Password*.

One thing that made Allen proud about *Password* was that it really did place a strong emphasis on smarts for its celebrity guests. One of the reasons that some stars were so eager to be on the show was that they were hoping to shake away the public's perception of them as empty-headed or vapid.

Allen boasted, "We're getting away from the Hollywood dumb blonde image. These are honest, cultivated, bright people. Arlene Francis is a prime example. She's no phony, but a solid, quick, bright person. She's curious and she listens. I have a theory that TV has bred a whole new type of entertainer — a genuine, bright, talented person. The phonies can't appear on a show like ours which is unrehearsed. The game would show them up."

Allen told another reporter, "It gives them a chance to be themselves as they play the game with non-professionals. Under the x-ray of tele-visions, the phonies in the business show up very quickly. The stars are usually very nervous at the outset of the show because, after all, they are playing themselves instead of a role. But once they get started, they relax and enjoy themselves."

But despite how relaxed they were, they were playing for blood. The stars got a flat rate for agreeing to appear on the show, but day after day, Allen watched stars behave as if the contestant's cash prizes were their very own. "And that," Allen said, "is the beauty of it. That's the great intangible you can't buy and that has made the show the success that it is."

The people who worked on game shows for a living were susceptible to the *Password* addiction, too. Allen and his kids played it frequently at home. Bob Stewart admitted playing games that lasted as long as four hours at a time, attributing the long games to the belief that the next word would be the one that, for sure, you would have a perfect clue for. The crew of *The Price is Right* on NBC would play the game in host Bill Cullen's dressing room, with stakes of ten cents per point.

Allen had now fully severed himself from *G.E. College Bowl* but hadn't been gone very long. And he was firmly entrenched in the role of TV game show host with *Password*. And it was funny how his extracurricular

Allen has his tuxedo and the car is ready to take him to the airport; he's on his way to Texas for the Miss Teenage America Pageant. FRED WOSTBROCK COLLECTION

activities now reflected a dual reputation. During the month of October, 1962, he was master of ceremonies for a banquet honoring distinguished alumni at The University of Texas. That same month, he went to Dallas and co-hosted the Miss Teenage America Pageant on CBS.

Part of the appeal of the Miss Teenage America Pageant that year probably had to do with the unusual duty that Allen was charged with for the pageant. The contestants were being judged on personality, talent, self-confidence, and awareness of current events. The pageant, this year, decided to test their self-confidence under pressure. The finalists acted with Allen and two other performers in a series of brief improvised skits to demonstrate their poise in a situation they weren't prepared for. (Example: "You want a new party dress. Your father, played by Allen Ludden, says you have too many dresses already.")

At the University of Texas banquet, Allen quipped that he was offended that the pageant had included a performance by the Texas A&M Glee Club. Each of the alumni honored at the banquet had a chance to speak about the pursuits that they were most dedicated to. Allen, as emcee, was extended the same opportunity, and continued his crusade to cajole people to stop thinking of "entertainment" and "information" as mutually exclusive.

He said in his speech, "My theory on the subject — and it's not a very profound one — is something I began framing and vocalizing when I was in the news division. I'm tired of people equaling entertainment only with those shows in the variety, comedy, or dramatic fields. The classic definition of entertainment is something which takes one's mind off one-self, something which diverts one's mind. Well, I insist that if a man is a football nut and if he listens to the football scores with his total attention for a few minutes on a Saturday afternoon, that man is diverted, ergo, he is entertained. Network executives are saddled with the erroneous idea that something must be either entertaining or informational. Phooey! Newsmen generally shy away from the devices of the theater to make presentations exciting and interesting. And the entertainment people are equally guilty. They feel if something is egghead, it must be dull, and who needs it?"

After the speech, Allen returned to New York, soon to be joined by Betty. Allen had invited her to Briarcliff Manor for Thanksgiving dinner. It was the first time that the Luddens' housekeeper had ever met Betty, and after spending a few hours with her, Allen's housekeeper Lessie told Allen that they should get a silver tea service, since he was going to be getting married soon.

That was the last time that the subject was mentioned that Thanksgiving, but Betty's next order of business was a necessary one. After returning to Los Angeles and ringing in 1963, she met up with Phil, who proved to be not-exactly surprised when Betty admitted that she had fallen in love with Allen. She and Phil broke it off for good. Betty went straight back to New York. Allen went to the airport to get her.

Allen didn't know that Betty had broken up with Phil until Betty met up with him at the airport. Allen smiled and told her that he had already planned a full two days of activities, and promptly treated Betty do a countryside drive and lunch at an old mill converted into a restaurant, situated next to a frozen waterfall.

When they returned to New York City, they went out to dinner and Allen handed her a wedding ring. Not an engagement ring, a wedding ring.

"You might as well keep it," he told her, "because one of these days you'll put it on for keeps."

Betty had always lived very much on her own terms, as Lane Allan had already learned. And the idea of moving all the way across the country and giving up the familiarity and the comfort of the city where she had spent most of her life didn't appeal to her. She had also starred in a few TV shows and was worried about the risk attached to leaving the city where her career had taken shape — although, at the time, New York still was still a thriving hub for national television programming. In fact, Betty's own agent had been gently nudging her for the past few years about moving there. There was also the issue of David, Martha, and Sarah. Betty loved those kids and had spent the past year getting acquainted with them; they had been three good pals for her. Pals. And at first, the thought of making the switch from being a buddy to being a stepmother rubbed her the wrong way.

Betty remembered, "…[T]he kids courted me right along with their father, and I fell in love with the whole gang."

Betty also had to weigh in on how much of herself she wanted to give. Marriage meant giving everything she had. That's how you made a marriage work. Arguably, her first two marriages ended partly because of a reluctance to give more than she was offering.

As Betty explained it in later years while being interviewed by McLean Stevenson, "It looks bad for the poodles if you just have light housekeeping. You really have to make it serious and get married."

As much as she loved Allen, as much as she had enjoyed getting to know him over the past year…the proposal made her angry. She handed the ring right back to him without taking it out of the box.

Allen's reaction to the rejection surprised Betty more than the proposal. He very quietly put the ring in his pocket, waited for her to calm down, and continued with dinner; business as usual.

The next time Betty saw Allen, he was wearing that wedding ring himself, on a gold chain around his neck. He never drew attention to it, never brought up the subject of marriage again. He just made it a point to always have it on whenever Betty was around.

Mark Goodson noticed the ring too. Mark took a personal interest in Allen, more than his other hosts. When Margaret died, Mark's heart went out to him. He began taking Allen to dinner at Toots Shor's Restaurant in New York somewhat frequently. At first it was to help Allen deal with his heartbreak over Margaret. But in time, the dinners were happening just because Allen and Mark enjoyed each other's company.

One night, as Allen sat down, he undid the top button of his shirt, and Mark asked him about the ring on the chain. Allen answered, "I'm going to wear this ring — I don't care how long it takes. I'm going to wear it until Betty White says yes to me."

Allen took that rejection in stride. He also had a professional disappointment to contend with. In February 1963, he went back to work for Don Reid, John Moses, and Jack Cleary for one night only, appearing not as host, but as a contestant on their new game show. *Alumni Fun* pitted colleges against each other, not with students representing the schools but with famous alumni. For the premiere telecast, Allen played on the University of Texas team for the premiere broadcast. *Alumni Fun* structured its series as a season-long tournament, the idea for *College Bowl* that Allen could never get anybody to go along with. But the disappointment for Allen was that, the following month, CBS announced it was moving *Password* from Sunday night to Monday night to counterprogram it against the medical drama *Ben Casey*, totally negating the reason given to Allen for why he could no longer host two game shows. Allen also vocally objected to CBS putting the show in a 10:00 p.m. timeslot. So many of the incoming letters since the inception of the nighttime version had come from teachers who said that they were using *Password* as a learning tool in their classes. Putting the show at 10:00 p.m. meant that most children wouldn't be allowed to watch it.

Despite the reluctant departure from *College Bowl*, Allen continued his crusade for education, complaining to one writer, "The science of education has not progressed like the other sciences."

Allen told the reporter that he was eager to continue pursuing the cause and wanted to make himself available to schools to discuss the issue. He felt that it would be putting his status from *Password* to good use. People might not listen to the average teacher's ideas for improving education, but for some reason, they always put stock into what celebrities said. So Allen, figuring that he was a celebrity now, thought he could make some contributions to education.

A few years after having to bow out of his Corpus Christi *College Bowl* presentation to tend to Margaret, Allen finally did return to the city to stage a night of *Password*, live on stage at the Del Mar Auditorium featuring the mayor and other prominent townspeople as the players, with autographed copies of the *Plain Talk* books available as souvenirs in the lobby. The local boy who made good and returned home, and the fact that the number one show on daytime TV was coming live to Corpus Christi, made it the social event of the spring. All of the money raked in that night was used to expand the Corpus Christi Museum of Science and History.

Allen paid another visit to Los Angeles in March 1963, not for work, but just to visit Betty, leaving Jack Clark to run *Password* for a week. He went to NBC Studios in Burbank and stood on the sidelines while he watched Betty play a new game show taping its first week of programs for the network. *You Don't Say!*, produced by Ralph Andrews and Bill Yagemann, was a word association game in which celebrity-contestant teams tried to convey the names of famous people and places by giving clues to common words that sounded like those famous names. (For example, if the answer was "Betty White," you might try to give clues that would lead to the words "bet," "tea," and "wine", and your partner, figuring out "bet," "tea," "wine," would guess that the name was Betty White.) The show's host was Betty's former announcer from *A Date with the Angels*, Tom Kennedy.

Tom remembers, "That was the first time I met Allen, and he was there courting Betty. He came over to NBC and he was in the studio just to watch Betty. I remember being told not to acknowledge Allen because Mark Goodson had got word that NBC was starting a new word association game called *You Don't Say!*, and he considered it a rip-off of *Password*. He discouraged the stars who did his shows from appearing on *You Don't Say!*, and he was all pissed off because there was nothing he could do to stop it. And I had been a fan of *Password* from the beginning; I greeted Allen and we talked, and then I remember he went straight to Betty, hugged her, kissed her, and off to dinner they went.

"We had heard the stories. We knew that Allen was pursuing her heavily, and that Betty didn't feel ready for marriage, but I was pulling for her. And for him."

Allen and Betty went to dinner that night. Allen revisited the subject of marriage, and he seemed to change his tack somewhat. He was making a sales pitch to Betty.

"Don't be afraid of marriage. It has so much that makes life wonderful," he assured her.

Allen returned to Briarcliff Manor, still with the engagement ring firmly tied to a chain around his neck. Betty's mind was heavy with thoughts of Allen and of the Ludden kids. She had accumulated a small collection of letters from David, Martha, and Sarah. They were mostly friendly letters, telling Betty what they were up to lately and wondering what was going on in her life. But their letters had a blatant ulterior motive.

"We just want you around."

"We need you."

"Dad is wonderful. It would be wonderful if you lived with us."

Allen called more and more frequently. He was now calling nightly to ask "Will you marry me?"

"Not yet," Betty would answer, still trying to process this. She had given Allen every excuse that crossed her mind, every reservation and every worry. Allen shrugged off every one of them, unfazed. Whatever excuse she had, another "Will you marry me?" was just around the corner, after the jangle of the telephone, every single night.

On Easter Sunday, April 14 that year, Betty was in California and a package from Allen arrived: a stuffed white bunny rabbit, and a pair of earrings.

The note attached to the earrings read: *These won't fit on a chain. Please say yes.*

Betty later wrote, "In retrospect, the one [choice] I agonized over the most should have been the simplest."

Betty thought about her options: give up life in California and take a calculated risk by moving across the country to be with Allen, or spend the rest of her life watching every one of Allen's TV shows, like she knew she would, wondering what her life could have been. She finally realized which option seemed less appealing.

The phone rang later that night. Betty, who already knew, skipped "Hello" and answered the phone by emphatically saying "YES!"

Because of the three-hour time zone difference, Allen had called Betty late in the evening on his end. He put the phone down, so full of adrenaline that he realized he wasn't going to be able to calm himself, and that the news couldn't wait until morning.

Allen ran upstairs and knocked on his housekeeper's bedroom door. Lessie cracked the door open, and Allen, with a mix of enthusiasm and just a light hint of concern, announced, "Betty said yes! She'll marry me! But you will stay on with us, won't you?"

Lessie smiled, promised Allen that she'd stay with the family, and went back to bed.

Betty, now preparing for marriage, couldn't help reflecting on the past year and realizing how slick Allen had been about it. Getting two dogs, inviting Betty to celebrate his kids' birthdays...even the summer stock show that Allen just happened to pick seemed to be a part of the plan. She and Allen spent the summer seeing the countryside of New England.

As Betty put it later, "Allen is one hell of a salesman."

Word of the impending nuptials spread to the press. The reaction was somewhat amusing because various headline writers couldn't seem to agree on which one of the happy couple was more famous than the other. One headline read "Betty White to Wed TV Host." Another headline said "Allen Ludden to Marry Actress."

Tom Kennedy says, "The engagement didn't surprise me at all. Those were two people who were destined to be together. They were cut from the same cloth. They were very talented and very down to earth. Usually, a person with that much talent has quirks, or an ego, or personal issues. Neither one of them was like that. They were both very normal, very kind people, who happened to be extremely talented."

Allen had used up all of his contractually-permitted vacation time from *Password*, which meant that he could only get married during a weekend. At the time, forty-nine states in the union required a three-day waiting period for the results of a blood test before a marriage ceremony could take place. Nevada was the exception. Since work precluded Allen from a long wait, they got married in Las Vegas.

The plan was for Allen to tape three episodes of *Password* on Thursday, go straight to the airport, and fly to California, where he would meet up with the bride and her parents. Then they'd all head to Vegas for dinner and a show, and then the morning after, a wedding.

Allen got caught in a full-blown New York City traffic jam on the way to the airport and missed the flight. He had barely made it to the airport in time, where an employee checked his luggage and then sent Allen to the wrong gate.

Allen, in the middle of the crowded airport, fought back tears and screamed "My wedding suit is on the way to California...AND I'M NOT!"

A woman walked up, patted him on the shoulder, and quietly said, "There, there, Mr. Ludden."

Allen called Betty and explained that he wasn't on his way…not yet, anyway. The bride, getting a bit antsy on her way to the big day, blurted out, "Why don't you just stay there!"

Allen made it onto the next plane and eventually everything was back on track. And then they went to Las Vegas to check in at the Sands Hotel. After checking in at the front desk, the hotel staff put them in a jitney and sent them to a tower a quarter-mile away. Horace and Tess were in a double room. Betty was checked into the massive wedding suite, and, since the wedding wasn't until the next day, Allen was put in a tiny room at the end of the hall.

And that's when Allen realized he left a briefcase full of gifts in the lobby.

Betty asked, "What's the matter, honey? Don't you feel good?"

Allen, without telling her what was wrong, said, "I'll be right back."

And he took off running.

Betty later said, "He got so excited at the cashiers, he left my wedding present and my wedding ring. He left it right out. Right outside the cashier, out in front of all these gamblers who are walking by…in the velvet jewelry case. And he just turned, literally, the shade of paper. His color just went ZAP."

Allen ran the full quarter-mile back to the lobby of the Sands, where the briefcase was sitting exactly where he had left it. He returned and, between heavy breaths, explained that the briefcase contained presents for all of the Whites. Horace received gold cuff links. Tess got a jade and pearl bracelet with a gold tag bearing the inscription *Thank you, Doll*. Betty got a diamond bracelet to match the wedding ring that Allen had been wearing on his chain.

The next morning, June 14, 1963, they got married in the living room of the wedding suite. It was just the bride and groom, the bride's parents, the bellhop, some photographers hired by the hotel, and the same judge who had married Grant Tinker and Mary Tyler Moore. Allen and Betty exchanged their "I do's." The judge left immediately, the bellhop was on the clock, and the photographers went straight to the press to spread the photos of the celebrity wedding.

That Allen Ludden and Betty White were getting married had slipped past many people's radars; not everybody had caught the story in the newspapers. But the not-widely-known nature of the nuptials did lead to some awkwardness for the rest of the day.

Betty White later told the story to McLean Stevenson on *The Tonight Show*. "Allen had the reputation of being Mr. Clean, and I was sort of the girl next door. And I ran into about eighteen people in Vegas the day we were married…And he went over to check out and stuff, and get the airplane tickets taken care of, and I was sitting at the twenty-one table, and about nine people that I knew came by and said 'Hey Betty, what are you doing here?'

Their first photo as husband and wife, snapped in the hotel suite immediately after they said "I do." FRED WOSTBROCK COLLECTION

"And I said, 'Well, I just got married.' And they'd sort of look around and I'm all by myself, sitting there at the blackjack table."

Allen and Betty honeymooned in Laguna Beach for what was left of the weekend, where they walked past a newsstand and saw their wedding photos all over the front pages of the newspapers. They went back to New York on Tuesday, the day when *Password* taped its weekly nighttime episode. Allen had cut it so close with the airplane reservations that when the plane landed, they went straight from the airport to the studio to tape a nighttime *Password*. The scheduled celebrity guests that night were Jack Paar and Betty White.

Jack Paar famously felt uncomfortable with his own skills — or lack thereof — for game shows. He had once been booked as a panelist for *What's My Line?* and agreed to show up a few hours early and play practice games to get accustomed. After only a few minutes, Jack determined that *What's My Line?* wasn't his forte and bowed out, only after producer Gil Fates assured him that they had a substitute panelist they could call in on short notice. But when he learned that his old favorite Betty White was marrying Allen Ludden, he reached out to Betty and said that he wanted to play *Password* against her after the nuptials. He said it would be his wedding present.

Allen had always greeted the celebrities and bantered briefly with them about the upcoming projects. On this night, his chat with Betty was humorously awkward, as both of them seemed to realize right at that moment how comically fake their conversation now looked to all of America. Allen was greeting his own wife as if he had just seen her that moment, and was asking questions that he certainly already knew the answers to.

ALLEN: Hello, Betty.

BETTY: Hello, Allen.

ALLEN: What are your plans for the summer, Betty?

BETTY: Well, I'm gonna do some...*(laugh)*...what did you have in mind, Allen? I'm gonna do some summer theater with my husband, Allen.

ALLEN: Where, Betty?

BETTY: Allen and I are going to do...uh, Allen LUDDEN, that is, on *Password*...are going to do *Brigadoon* in Patterson, New Jersey, and then we're going to have a big fight and I'm going to go to St. Louis to do *The King and I*, then we make up and Allen and I are going to get back together in *Janus*.

ALLEN: It's very nice to see you, Betty.

JACK PARR: What kind of honeymoon did you have?

Mike Gargiulo says, "It never crossed our minds that it might come off improper to some viewers to have the host's wife playing the game. And to my knowledge, we never got any mail about that. I think what helped was that, even though he didn't club you over the head with it, you could tell from the way Allen looked at the passwords and the way he reacted to them sometimes that he was seeing the words for the first time. So a viewer could see that Allen couldn't have given Betty any help in advance. The other thing that helped is that she was already the best player we had. Betty was just a rock on our show and every viewer knew it. When we were booking celebrity guests and we discussed who the opponent would be the next time that Betty played, we would say 'I wouldn't give that spot to a dry cleaner.' Every time Betty was on the show, the other celebrity was exactly that: the other celebrity.

"And thinking back on it, there was one other reason that their marriage didn't affect the show too much, and it goes back to what I've said about Allen knowing his role and Betty knowing hers. They didn't typically conduct themselves as husband and wife when they appeared on *Password* together. If they were together on any other show, they absolutely acted like husband and wife. But whenever Betty played *Password*, Allen conducted himself as the host and Betty conducted herself as a guest."

The staff subjected Allen to some light teasing that they had built into that night's game. The passwords for that show included SORRY, TRIANGLE, CLUMSY, ROMANCE — a contestant caught Betty off-guard by giving the clue "Affair" — and the capper, HENPECKED. For that one, Jack tilted his head in Allen's direction and gave the clue "Later."

They reached the end of the evening, when Allen traditionally wrapped up the program by giving "the password of the day," which was usually followed by a pithy quote, a plug, or a public service statement. ("The password for today is SAFETY. Think of your family's safety; go to your neighborhood mechanic and install seatbelts in your car.") For the end of their honeymoon game of *Password*, Betty and Allen delivered the password together.

ALLEN: This is Allen Ludden saying the password tonight is…

BETTY: "HOME." Will you take me home, please, Mr. Ludden?

ALLEN: I certainly will, Mrs. Ludden.

That night, Allen and Betty arrived at Briarcliff Manor, with signs posted outside reading "CHECK!" Betty walked in, taking in the sight of her new home. The first thing that caught her eye was the opulent garden outside. Allen's letters and phone calls throughout the winter had all mentioned the tulip bulbs that he was planting. Betty always thought

The Ludden family. Clockwise from top, Allen, Martha, Betty (with Willie and Emma in her lap), Sarah, and David. FRED WOSTBROCK COLLECTION

Allen was kidding about being interested in gardening, right up to the moment that she saw the array of tulips decorating her new front yard.

They entered a house filled with party decorations and homemade posters welcoming them home. And wherever Allen, Betty, David, Martha, and Sarah were, that was, undoubtedly, home.

The Luddens were also greeted by a huge pile of mail, about nine thousand letters by Allen's count, from fans all over the country. His fans and hers, though Allen asserted it was mostly hers. The letters contained proclamations of "I knew it!" from fans who insisted they saw something special in Betty and Allen long before their romance had been made public. Many were congratulatory, although a few letters were less than complimentary. Jack Paar's fans had loved hearing Betty's stories over the years about dating Phil, and the realization that she didn't wind up marrying Phil didn't sit quite right with them.

The next stop on the public portion of the honeymoon was an appearance on *What's My Line?* as the mystery guests trying to stump the blindfolded panel. They "entered and signed in" on the show's signature chalkboard as Allen Ludden and Betty White, but the graphic identifying them for home viewers called them "Mr. and Mrs. Allen Ludden." Allen, whom television viewers had never seen or heard as anybody but Allen Ludden, stunned the audience with the wildly misleading voice he used to answer the panel's questions, sounding exactly like a stuffy old matron who had flown in from London.

Arlene Francis was the one who unlocked the mystery, asking the question, "Is the password MARRIAGE?"

Away from the cameras, Allen's parents flew in from Corpus Christi to visit. Betty wanted to make a good impression, naturally, but there was one shortcoming she knew she was going to have to deal with. She wasn't much of a chef. Betty bought a large ham; it was really the only thing she knew how to cook.

As she explained later, "I cooked the ham, and I started praying."

And for their entire visit with their son and their new daughter-in-law, all Homer and Leila got for dinner, every single night, was ham.

Early on, there was some confusion from the press about what to call Betty. Was she going to be the Betty White that they always knew or was it time to get used to Betty Ludden? Betty announced to the press that she was keeping the name White, and for an admirable reason. It was a show of respect for Margaret.

"I'm proud of my new name, but I'm not really Mrs. Ludden," she said. "There once was a wonderful woman with that name."

For much the same reason, the Ludden kids always called her Betty. She would never ask them to call her anything else.

There was never any question that Allen and Betty were in this for love. It was deep and it was strong. But the marriage also proved to be quite good for business. The press attention made their summer stock bookings that summer extremely profitable. They filled the houses for *Brigadoon* before returning to where in all began, the Cape Playhouse in Dennis, Massachusetts, where their production of *Janus* set a box office record.

The attention given to their happy union gave Allen a problem that he hadn't anticipated. Allen had exceptionally low tolerance for alcohol. For the first few months that he and Betty were married, they'd go to dinner together and some well-meaning fans would have a bottle of champagne to their table. Allen didn't want to be rude, so he'd always make it a point to make eye contact with the admirers and take a sip, but just a sip was more than he could handle. For the first two months he was married to Betty, Allen had a near-constant headache.

And "headache" didn't begin to describe some of the issues they had with fans. For Betty and Allen's one-month anniversary (Allen celebrated anniversaries by the month), they went out for dinner and a show.

Just before leaving the house, Allen politely offered, "Let me help you with your coat."

He slipped a luxurious white mink jacket around her. Although animal welfare activist Betty cringed at the memory years later, in 1963, a fur coat was the wearable status symbol above all others. Together, they ventured out into New York City and onto the sidewalk for a lovely evening.

Betty told Merv Griffin what happened next. "I was feeling so spritzy. And [Allen] was going to take me out on the town. We got out and signed some autographs, and he finally hailed a cab. He had one foot in the cab door and this woman grabbed me. You know that death grip they get on you sometimes? There's just nothing you can do.

"She says, 'Oh you've just GOT to sign my book. I'm from out of town! You just gotta sign it!' I said 'All right.' By now, traffic is beginning to kind of back up a little bit. So Allen said 'Come on honey, hurry!' And the woman pulls out her pen and she opens it up, and I felt something on my face…There was ink all over my face, on the jacket. I didn't care about the face. The face, I could wash! But it's not a drip-dry mink jacket, you know? I said, 'Oh, oh, what will I do?' The woman said 'Sign my book, that's what you can do!'"

Allen tried to fix the damage himself, but gave up and took it to a cleaner. It was mostly salvageable, except for a visible yellow streak that never went away. Betty was able to laugh off the incident in later years, saying it served her right for wearing fur.

It was easy to laugh off some of those "problems" in the first few months, but the reality was that the newly formed Ludden family did have a lot of adjustments to make. Allen and Margaret had planned on

Betty and Allen greet Carol Channing outside the theatre at opening night of *Hello, Dolly!* on Broadway. Betty is sporting a fur coat that was nearly ruined the night Allen gave it to her; she would later say the incident "served her right" for wearing a fur coat. FRED WOSTBROCK COLLECTION

remodeling the Briarcliff Manor house when they moved in and by this point, everything had been done except the kitchen, because that's where they had left off when Margaret went to the hospital for the last time. But suddenly, a hundred-year-old farmhouse on a five-and-a-half acre lot had become available in nearby Chappaqua. Betty had just moved into Briarcliff Manor and all of a sudden, it was time to move *again*. And whether it was Briarcliff Manor or Chappaqua, it wasn't California. As Allen contended with the champagne headaches, Betty was coping with serious attacks of homesickness.

Allen helped Betty through that storm with laughter. When Betty was still adjusting to New York, the newlyweds would have playful arguments about which part of the world is better.

Allen once said, "Nobody in California knows how to converse. They're all inarticulate."

Betty answered, "If you say nobody is articulate out there, how come you married a California girl?"

Allen and Betty at home in Briarcliff Manor. It took a little adjusting for Betty, but she knew that her new family had been worth making the biggest move of her life. FRED WOSTBROCK COLLECTION

Allen answered, "Who wants an articulate wife?"

Betty admitted that just about the only one totally happy with the adjustment to the East Coast was the man in charge of finding work for her. "My agent is happier about this marriage than anybody. He's been wanting me to move here for years."

And then, there were indeed the adjustments that came with becoming stepmother to Allen's children. Betty, dropped into her new family, approached her new role with the example that had been set for her. As much fun as her parents had been during childhood, they always made it clear that their word was law. No exceptions. So, Betty, as stepmother, handed down her orders the same way. No bending, no breaking. The problem was that Allen was very prone to negotiating, bowing and giving in. The kids were now dealing with two very different approaches to parenting and it was frustrating for everybody. All five of them realized this was going to take some adjusting.

Betty tried to do fun things, but went wrong with one terribly misguided attempt at making the house festive. In October, she got a pumpkin and carved a jack-o-lantern. She was surprised at how coolly the kids reacted to it. Allen was the one who explained the problem to Betty. Two years ago, their mother had died the day before Halloween.

Betty, who had lived on her own terms for nearly her entire life before marrying Allen Ludden, remembered later, "It was a difficult adjustment to go from independent single life to a household with three teenagers from Allen's former marriage. Once in a while, I got to thinking I had made a mistake, but that always passed."

Whatever problems they had, Betty and Allen could weather it no matter if it was adjusting to a new family, adjusting to a new city, or being thrust into competition with each other. For Thanksgiving Day, 1963, Betty agreed to host NBC's coverage of Macy's Thanksgiving Day Parade...and then CBS turned right around and signed Allen to host their coverage, along with Bud Collyer and Captain Kangaroo.

"May the best spouse win the highest Nielsen," quipped writer Cynthia Lowry.

The better rating ultimately went to Betty, to which Allen responded, "Her parade may get a better rating, but at least I'm working."

But they worked together, too. Betty joined Allen to co-host the Miss Teenage America pageant in Dallas. It was an interesting time in America to host a beauty pageant because 1963 was the year of the publication of *The Feminine Mystique*, Betty Friedan's groundbreaking book credited with inspiring the feminist movement. More than just a few sets of eyes were probably seeing beauty pageants — particularly ones with such young contestants — in a different light. Shortly before the broadcast, the pageant released a mission statement, a justification of sorts. Miss Teenage America pledged not to be strictly a contest of beauty, that the girls would not wear bathing suits, that the pageant was not intended to be a gateway into a show business career, that education counted (the

Allen, along with Bess Myerson, Fran Allison, and "Captain Kangaroo" Bob Keeshan, on CBS' *1963 Thanksgiving Jubilee.* FRED WOSTBROCK COLLECTION

contestants' grades in school figured into the judging), and that a separate award would be given to the winner of the talent portion, regardless of if she won the overall contest. With the amount of care and concern Allen had given his public image, it probably also unintentionally served as a reminder for why Allen was willing to have his name and faced attached to such a show.

Funnily enough, though, despite the pageant's official stance of ada-mancy that they weren't there to provide an "in" for show business, that was precisely what happened. The separate award for the talent portion was awarded to sixteen-year-old Karen Valentine, who became a star in the following decade as a cast member on *Room 222* and a semi-regular panelist on *The Hollywood Squares.*

Allen's own views on gender roles were rather interesting. He admitted that, although it was increasingly considered old-fashioned, he believed that man was meant to be breadwinner and woman was meant to be homemaker, even if his own marriage didn't fit that description (Allen was fond of saying that Betty was basically a homemaker who came and went whenever she pleased). He did, however, believe that marriage was an equal partnership; if a man wanted to be considered the head of his household, he had to work to earn that title. The husband was, for example, as much on the hook for household chores as the wife. He didn't believe that a woman should have a group of friends at the house while her husband was home, but at the same time, he also didn't believe that a man should have "guy's night out." He believed that a husband and wife should conduct themselves as, in his words, a "committee of two."

Allen and Betty with Miss Teenage America, Jeanine Zavrel. FRED WOSTBROCK COLLECTION

On November 1, Horace and Tess came to New York to visit. When they made their way to the airport to return to California, Horace was showing a few signs that he was coming down with a cold. When he made it back to California, he saw a doctor. The doctor became concerned and sent Horace to a hospital. Horace recovered and got discharged a few days later on a Saturday morning, November 16. Later that afternoon, his heart stopped.

Horace White loved his job. He had worked at a lighting company for most of his life and made his way to an executive position. The company had a mandatory retirement age of sixty-five, and Horace, whose friends and family all called him "Horace the Hummingbird" because of his energy and his work ethic, had told people that he didn't know what he was going to do with himself when his sixty-fifth birthday arrived and he would be out of a job. Betty couldn't help thinking it was a little odd that Horace had died six months before his mandatory retirement. She would always carry a theory that Horace so dreaded the idea of getting out of bed and not having anything to do, that the fear killed him.

Betty flew straight to California on the first flight out. Allen followed on the second. Allen stayed for the funeral, but he had his commitment to *Password* and Allen was nothing if not a professional. He left California immediately after the funeral but told Betty she should make this an extended stay to be with her mother. It also dawned on Allen how drastically Tess' life changed in only one year. At the beginning of 1963, she shared a house with her husband, her daughter, and three dogs. By November, all three dogs had died of old age, her husband was gone, and her daughter had moved across the country. Allen suggested to Betty that when she was ready to come back to New York, she should bring Tess with her so she could live with the Luddens for a while to offset her new loneliness.

On a Friday morning, Tess was packing while Betty called the *Los Angeles Times* to stop her mother's subscription. The employee who answered told her that the paper just got word that President Kennedy had been shot in Dallas. Betty and Tess arrived in New York and did exactly what the rest of America did during that long, dreadful weekend. They stayed glued to the television, watching the interviews, watching the updates, watching the archival clips of the president and his family in happier times, and watching the coverage of the funeral.

And as Betty watched television that weekend, she began recapping the awful events of the past few weeks in her own life. Allen was grief-stricken when Horace died. Allen had been there to help Betty cope. He was there to help Tess cope. He opened his home to Tess so they wouldn't have to be far apart while they adjusted to life without Horace. And Betty came to realize that she and Allen were living a singular life together. She had never felt that with Dick Barker. They had lived two separate lives. She had never felt that with Lane Allan. They were separate lives, too. Betty realized that together, she and Allen were a single entity. Betty, fiercely independent for her entire life, now had what she never had before. She had a partner.

FRED WOSTBROCK COLLECTION

CHAPTER TWELVE

"SUBSTANCE"

At the end of 1963, *Password* was still the king of the daytime television mountain. NBC gave up on *The Merv Griffin Show*…And then *Ben Jerrod*…And then *People Will Talk*. ABC finally called it quits with *Day in Court* and shoved reruns of *Father Knows Best* into the 2:00 p.m. time slot, more or less conceding defeat to *Password*. Nighttime *Password* was still chugging along, and to Allen's delight, CBS moved it to another timeslot, Thursday at 7:30, which meant that once again, children could watch it.

Password's audience had grown bigger during 1963. After a somewhat slow beginning, the Canadian Broadcasting Corporation (CBC) expanded its broadcasting day to include more daytime programming. The vast majority of the new programs were produced by the CBC, but also squeezing onto the schedule was American *Password* with Allen Ludden.

Demand for the *Password* home game was so strong that Milton Bradley was churning out multiple printings at a time. For fans who had completely exhausted the material in the 1962 home game, the company released the *Password* 2nd Edition home game, retail value of $2.50. For fans with a little more disposable income, Milton Bradley also released the six-dollar *Password* Fine Edition, which came with gold or wood-grain game pieces, a brass sand timer, and a special deck of cards for playing the Lightning Round. For fans with a lot of extra money, they released the *Password* Collector's Edition, which didn't come in a cardboard box like most board games. It came in a small leatherette briefcase. And for teachers and families with young children, there was Educational *Password*, designed to build vocabulary skills, and offering game cards divided into levels of difficulty to accommodate the child's current level of ability.

Allen, in response to the popularity of the *Password* home games, explained that it was because anybody could play it…"Anybody, that is, who has substance."

"Substance" was a common word when Allen discussed the stars who appeared on *Password*, and those who didn't. At the time, Allen had a theory — and whether he was right or wrong in the long run could be debated for hours — was that the emergence of television was going to cause a wave of change in how celebrities survived. There would always be the stars who got breaks because they had the right look or because they did things that grabbed attention, but Allen had a theory that in the television age, the stars who lasted — the ones that you were going to see year after year and decade after decade — would be the ones who could back it up with brains. People of all kinds could be on television, but only the smart would survive.

Allen said, "There is a whole new breed of star performers — people who are famous because they are the sort of people they are. Never before in history has it been necessary to be a person of substance to be a star… The superficial person just can't get through the tube somehow. Even Hollywood is no longer the land of cardboard characters and stars discovered at soda fountains that it was."

Substance wouldn't be enough to carry some people. Allen himself got tripped up when he played *Password*. Richard Boone was scheduled to be a guest for a week of programs, but a car accident required him to bow out. Necessity being the mother of invention, the staff decided that the sudden opening for a male guest star was a perfect opening for a fun alternative. Allen opened the show by explaining what had happened, and then took his seat at the players' desk as announcer Jack Clark came onstage and took over at the host's position. The viewers were getting a chance to see how well Allen played *Password*. Call it ironic, call it karma, or just call it funny, but Dr. Reason A. Goodwin had to zap his buzzer twice because of illegal clues from Allen. He used a hand gesture on one password, and the next time around, he used a two-word clue.

It was good fortune that after more than two years on the air with *Password*, the iron was still hot, and Allen kept looking for ways to strike it. He decided to get his name out there as a singer. He made his national singing debut on New Year's Eve for Guy Lombardo's annual special on CBS, live from the main concourse in New York's Grand Central Station. The performance was so well received that Allen got a recording contract out of it. Eight short months later, he released an album, *Allen Ludden Sings His Favorite Songs*. The most ardent fans of *Password* were probably at least a little surprised by what they were hearing: a smooth, confident voice that carried the tunes effortlessly. Allen Ludden really could sing!

And it was one of the few opportunities that he had to do so. As Allen continued seeking summer stock employment for 1964 and beyond, he and Betty did both plays and musicals, but made it clear that they were more interested in plays. Allen was only allowed so much time off from *Password*, and musicals took more preparation.

Although theatre engagements proved to be a rewarding pursuit for

Betty came about the title "Mrs. *Password*" in two ways, not just by marriage, but by how darn good she was at it. Today, she competes against "Mrs. *What's My Line?*," Arlene Francis. FRED WOSTBROCK COLLECTION

both of them, Allen and Betty were of a mind about what they preferred about theater. Neither of them was ever interested in a role in a Broadway show, which could last for months or even years and potentially keep an actor tied down. Allen and Betty, both trained in the immediate and temporary nature of performing in television, strongly preferred summer stock. They found acting far more enjoyable when they went into it knowing exactly when the job was coming to an end.

Betty recalled that Allen was fond of saying, "I'm an actor, but only a one-week actor."

Goodson-Todman was working hard to reap more rewards from the show's success. Goodson-Todman had long held an interesting policy of ripping off its own properties, in an attempt to keep competing producers from catching up to them. The success of *What's My Line?* had compelled them to release one panel show after another in the 1950s. Now, in the 1960s, *Password* instituted "word game played with stars" as the new template for them to work on.

The first one they introduced was *The Match Game*, hosted by Gene Rayburn. Two three-member teams, each captained by a celebrity,

Even at home, the Luddens couldn't get away from games. If somebody whipped out a deck of cards, the preferred pastime was gin rummy.
AUTHOR'S COLLECTION

competed against each other. Gene would read a question with a variety of answers, like "Name a trick that you teach a dog." The players would secretly write answers, trying to match their partners.

Goodson-Todman had now developed another game that fused *Password* and *The Match Game*. Their new game was called *Get the Message*. Again, three-player teams would compete against each other. Two members of a team would see a secret message, like ALFRED HITCHCOCK or PLEDGE OF ALLEGIANCE. Those two team members would then write one-word clues to the correct answer for their partner. The catch was that the two writers had to do their writing with small boxes surrounding their cards, so they couldn't collaborate what they were writing. They might end up wasting a turn by writing the same word, or, if they had good instincts, they might end up writing both halves of a perfect two-word clue.

Mark Goodson felt, at the beginning of 1964, that it was time to do something different for TV game shows. He thought it was time to have a woman hosting a game show. And since *Get the Message* and taken a few pages from the book of *Password*, what better woman to host than Betty White?

ABC loved *Get the Message* and bought it from Goodson-Todman on the spot…provided that they hire a man to host it. Nothing personal against Betty, they insisted. But the conviction remained among the top brass of TV networks that game show audiences couldn't get comfortable with a show unless a man was running things. Instead they hired Frank Buxton, a comedian and writer, to host the program.

Buxton says, "At the time, I was hosting a show on ABC called *Discovery*. It was a young people's show and it aired five days a week. ABC was building a new daytime line-up and they had struck a deal with Goodson-Todman to do a ninety-minute block of game shows in the morning: *The Price is Right* with Bill Cullen, *Missing Links* with Dick Clark, and *Get the Message*. My manager was Jack Rollins, who would later represent Woody Allen and David Letterman, and he called me in and I had a fairly typical audition. I had no idea who my competition was for the job, but I thought the audition went well and they hired me.

"After that, they brought me in and played the game with me until I got comfortable with it. The players were all office workers who came in just to help me. I saw Mark Goodson more than Bill Todman because Mark was, I suppose, the 'show man' and Bill handled the business end. Ultimately, it was an easier job than I expected, just because of all the help that the Goodson-Todman staff gave me. They played the game until I was completely broken in and accustomed to it, and then the series began and I just walked out onstage; all of the information that I needed was jotted down on cards in front of me. We'd tape a whole week in two days; three episodes on Tuesday and two on Wednesday, and then I'd fly back to my home in New Hampshire and I'd be back in time for supper. Nice gig.

"I got replaced because *Discovery* had been on hiatus and it was going back into production, and the show required that I couldn't do the Tuesday tapings anymore. I got replaced by Robert Q. Lewis, because they said he had 'a big profile with housewives.'"

Betty quietly accepted the rejection and settled for just being an occasional guest player on *Get the Message*, which she quite naturally mastered like every other game she played. In her finest moment as a *Get the Message* player, Betty was one of the clue writers for the message BOY SCOUTS. The clue that Betty wrote was *"Be."* She anticipated — correctly so — that the other clue writer had scribbled down *"Prepared."*

Betty was quickly becoming identified for her work as a game show guest. It was a distinction that would have bothered a more insecure performer. But Betty was proud of her ubiquitous presence on TV games. She wrote an essay about it that got widely syndicated in newspapers during 1964:

GAME SHOWS ARE A REFRESHING CHANGE OF PACE
by Betty White

For the past several years, I have been the victim of a frightening, recurring dream. In this nightmare, I am thrown into jail for stealing money.

"No — no," I cry, as the great steel door slams shut. "Not just me! There were others in the gang. What about Kitty Carlisle, Bess Myerson, and Henry Morgan?"

I awaken in a cold sweat and it takes me a while to face myself in the mirror because, of course, stealing is exactly what I have been doing for years. Playing games on television with nice people for a half-hour and then taking money for it is tantamount to grand larceny. Heaven forbid that Goodson-Todman should ever discover this fact.

However, let me try to defend myself. Granted it is a delight to make one's living playing games like *To Tell the Truth*, *The Match Game*, *Password*, and *Get the Message*, but I always bristle a little when people get that supercilious tone when they mention "game shows."

It would be interesting to measure how much mental exercise, vocabulary improvement, and general information is derived from watching a half-hour of *Truth* or *Password*.

Certainly, they are a refreshing change of pace after a string of westerns, dramas, and comedies with their predictable jokes and plots you can almost write yourself.

On the other hand, it is impossible to watch a game show without participating to some degree.

From a performer's standpoint, a game show is a challenge. It is a terribly revealing exercise with no script behind which to hide and no time to put on a special image. You sink or swim as yourself before millions of people.

And good luck with some of the answers you hear yourself giving. Like the day on *Password* when the word was "TINKLE" and I automatically said "puppy."

Since I married Allen Ludden, it is only natural that word games are popular at our house. But you'd be surprised how often the dictionary comes out to prove a point. That alone is worth the price of admission.

Betty didn't totally view being on game shows with rose-colored buzzers. She did acknowledge there was a downside to it; one completely out of the shows' control. "Actors love to play television games. Mostly because, if they are good at it, games reveal the performer as a person, which has never happened before. But game-playing can also be a problem — typecasting. If you are an actress by trade and have played games a lot on television, lots of luck on your career. That is one reason I'm delighted to play stock: so they remember."

Betty didn't have to worry about finding work when she uprooted and moved to the East Coast. She was in demand for television commercials just as she had been in California. She also secured a regular job hosting a CBS radio show, *Dimension*, in which listeners mailed in literally any question they had on any subject and Betty (with the aid of a research staff) would devote the program to answering the question. For example, one listener wrote in asking why little girls' shoes are called Mary Janes, and Betty gave a brief history of little girls' shoes in response.

And Betty and Allen were still in plenty of demand for summer stock, too. *Critic's Choice* had been a well-received box office hit when Betty and Allen were merely courting. Since then, it had been adapted into a film (Allen and Betty's roles were played by Bob Hope and Lucille Ball) and

Allen and Betty as a married unit had attracted a lot of press attention. So they dusted off their scripts and did several more weeks of *Critic's Choice* in new cities.

They followed that up with a rare musical venture, *Mr. President*, in which Allen covered the final days in office, and first days as a private citizen, for President Stephen Decatur Henderson and his wife. At the

Allen, content to let the game be the star, symbolically stands in the background while Betty White and Jim Backus contend with the passwords. Although Betty was a gift to any game show that had her as a player, some wrongheaded ideas about female performers kept her from breaking through as a host. FRED WOSTBROCK COLLECTION

Starlight Theater, an outdoor theater in Kansas City, Allen and Betty starred in a lavish production so spectacular that it arguably more elaborate than the Broadway production. Betty rode a live elephant to start Act II, and the show ended with a military band and dozens of servicemen. The theater's location also provided for one special effect that was never planned. For a scene in the Broadway production, a miniature

Together or separately, Betty and Allen worked more than ever during the 1960s. FRED WOSTBROCK COLLECTION

airplane flew across the stage to represent President Henderson's frequent travels. It turned out that Starlight Theater was relatively close to the airport and a regularly scheduled flight arrived every night at 10:00 p.m. At each performance, an actual airplane happened to soar over the theater at exactly the right moment in the story. Allen and Betty fell just $1,850 short of setting the box office record for any play in the history of the theater. They probably would have claimed the record if a night's performance hadn't been called off due to a thunderstorm.

Though Allen never really wanted to pursue politics, there was something about portraying a commander-in-chief that he found enticing. Betty later joked, "After *Mr. President*, it took three weeks for me to get Allen to stop waving when he sat in the convertible."

Betty and Allen also repeated their previous year's autumn workload of being together and then being in direct competition. They went to

Dallas and co-hosted the Miss Teenage America Pageant again and competed against each other with parades on NBC and CBS. Betty covered Macy's Thanksgiving Day Parade, and Allen was on duty for Gimbel's Thanksgiving Day Parade.

The Miss Teenage America Pageant that year proved to be a memorable one because of a slight catastrophe that disrupted the pageant. The "poise" portion was once again judged using the brief improvised skits that had proven popular with viewers in previous years. For one skit involving caring for a St. Bernard, Allen and Betty played a contestant's parents. The St. Bernard was played by a living, breathing, 275-pound St. Bernard. And when the skit wrapped and it was time to move on to the next contestant, the dog wouldn't budge. Allen tried pushing him, Betty tried pushing him, they tried pushing him together, and with the microphones turned on and the cameras fixed squarely on Betty and Allen, they began brainstorming different ideas with a national audience listening in. And then, a slight 130-pound stage manager, who saw a more direct solution than Betty and Allen were seeing, walked onstage,

Allen with Miss Teenage America, Carolyn Mignini, who would later perform on Broadway with Bea Arthur, who would later perform with Betty White. Small world. FRED WOSTBROCK COLLECTION

picked up the St. Bernard, and carried him away. By the end of the night, a winner had emerged. Betty helped crown young Carolyn Mignini, a soprano who said she hoped to perform on Broadway someday. She got her wish, playing the role of Sima in the Broadway cast of *Fiddler on the Roof.*

Get the Message was canceled on Christmas Day 1964, after only nine months. Betty felt no sense of justice about it. No "Shows THEM for not hiring me!" attitude. Rather, she was relieved. Game show hosts, who generally aren't actually involved in the development of the games they host, often take some of the blame when the show fails. Betty quickly realized that she would have taken a bullet if she had been viewed as the host of a game that only lasted nine months.

But Betty was viewed as the hostess of something far more successful. She was returning to California to provide commentary for the Tournament

Strange things can happen to spouses when they both work as television performers. *Left:* On New Year's Day, Betty was in Pasadena with Lorne Greene for NBC. *Right:* Allen was at the Cotton Bowl with Marilyn Van Derbur on behalf of CBS. FRED WOSTBROCK COLLECTION

of Roses Parade in Pasadena. It was a gig that had more meaning for Betty because she got a chance to visit her mother. Betty would ring in the new year with dinner and a nice long conversation in the middle of the night with Mom, until an NBC crewman came knocking on the door to pick Betty up so they could get to Pasadena by 3 a.m. Meanwhile, one time zone over, Allen was in Texas to provide commentary for the 1965 Cotton Bowl Parade.

Betty was asked if it bothered Allen that they never spent their New Year's Eves together. Betty answered that she was glad she already had the Tournament of Roses gig before she married Allen, because it meant that, to him, it came with the territory.

They had plenty of time to see each other. They both wrote in their spare time. They made the most of their free time at home. Betty redecorated, Allen built cabinets and gardened. Together, they played gin rummy. They kept a cumulative score throughout their marriage, and by their second anniversary, Betty had a 6,000-point lead. The whole family played *Password* over dinner. They also liked chess, checkers, bridge, and cribbage.

Their second anniversary would also mark the fourth summer that they did summer stock together. Mr. and Mrs. Ludden's choice to work together did create some dramas that had to be resolved quickly.

For example, Betty was a stickler for timing in comedy. She believed that comedies had rhythm, just like music, and would sometimes pause for one or two beats in her head before delivering a funny line. Allen didn't do that. Betty stopped rehearsing and explained that to Allen. Allen, who could have a short fuse if he saw or heard something that he didn't like, took the criticism so poorly that Betty never mentioned it again.

But for every one fault that Betty had to contend with in Allen, there were a hundred redeeming qualities that made her smile. For one thing, he put an extraordinary level of thought into the gifts he bought. There were little ones; Betty was reminiscing about childhood once and casually mentioned having a Raggedy Ann doll. Allen quietly filed that away for the future, and for Christmas that year, he gave her a Raggedy Ann doll.

For their second anniversary, Allen bought her a light-colored sapphire necklace. Conventional knowledge about jewelry states that darker sapphires are better, but Allen reasoned that his wife appeared frequently on television and a dark sapphire hanging around her neck would make it look like she had a hole in her throat, so for his wife, a light sapphire was better. He also knew how much Betty liked cats, but since they already had dogs in the house, she was concerned about how they would co-exist, so she just resigned herself to never having one. Allen gave her a hand-carved pendant in the likeness of a cat's face.

And Allen could even handle constructive criticism if a gift wasn't exactly right. Allen was constantly buying dresses for Betty; he strategically got his haircut at a specific barbershop that was located near a dress shop, and perpetually concluded his errand runs with a haircut and a new dress for his wife. Ninety-nine times out of one hundred, the dress was just perfect. But if there was some reason it didn't work, Betty would try it on and show him specifically what she didn't like about it. Allen would always take it to heart, and Betty would never again see another dress with whatever flaw she had pointed out.

One of Allen's finest traits was his intense dislike of seeing talent going undiscovered or unappreciated. If he ever saw a performer who was talented beyond the amount of attention that they were getting, Allen was happy to draw attention to them.

Betty's favorite example of this trait came in the summer of 1965. Allen and Betty were in Dennis, Massachusetts, and Warren, Ohio, starring in

Allen and Betty with one of their fully grown poodles; Allen bought the dogs to win Betty's heart, and three years later, the poodles were still getting that job done. FRED WOSTBROCK COLLECTION

Bell, Book, and Candle. Based on a 1958 Jimmy Stewart/Kim Novak film, *Bell, Book, and Candle* starred Betty as Gillian, a lonely witch living in modern-day Greenwich Village, New York. She meets and falls in love with handsome, successful publishing magnate, Shep, played by Allen. Because witches lose their powers if they fall in love with non-witches, Gillian is forced to choose between being a witch and being with the man of her dreams. It had been popular as a film and as a play, and it also proved to be a source of inspiration. Sol Saks, who created the sitcom *Bewitched*, freely admitted that he had been influenced in part by *Bell, Book, and Candle*.

Allen and Betty became fond of a small restaurant near the theater in Dennis and made a habit of going there nightly after the show for drinks and steamed clams. A blind pianist, a Harvard student named Tom Sullivan, performed live music every night. He got to know the Luddens and got to know their favorite songs. Before long, Tom had become accustomed to the sound of their voices and would begin playing their favorite tunes as soon as he was aware that they were in the restaurant.

Allen did two favors for Tom, one right away and one later. He immediately drew Tom's attention to a woman named Patty who frequently came to the restaurant to hear him play and fixed them up before the end of *Bell, Book, and Candle*.

Sullivan later told the story of how he avoided Patty for some time, too shy to talk to her. One night, Tom had performed the song "By the Time I Get to Phoenix" at the request of another woman. She curiously asked how Sullivan lost his sight, and Sullivan spun a tall-tale of how he lost his vision in a Vietnamese prison after his plane had been shot down.

Allen and Betty got so frustrated listening to him that Betty marched over and told him, "Tom, you're full of crap, and you're missing something wonderful. There's a girl who comes in here every night and sits alone at a front table. If you could see her eyes as she listens to you sing...I don't think you'd be dating anyone else."

Betty dragged Tom by the arm and introduced him to Patty. And when Allen and Betty returned to New York from the *Bell, Book, and Candle* engagement, Allen contacted Mike Douglas and talked him into booking Tom as a guest on his show. Tom became an overnight star. He released an album, toured all over the country, and spread his wings quite a bit. In addition to being an accomplished musician, he was also a correspondent for five years on ABC's *Good Morning America*, the author of five books, and for a time, he was go-to actor when prime-time dramas and sitcoms had written an episode involving a blind character. He appeared on *M*A*S*H*, *WKRP in Cincinnati*, *Mork & Mindy*, *Knight Rider*, and *Highway to Heaven*, to name just a few. And when he wasn't doing any of that, he was marrying Patty and raising two children with her.

Back in New York, *Password* was still humming along, still the top-rated daytime show with record-setting audiences. In a three-channel universe, it got ratings in daytime that would make a prime-time show today a smash hit. And it maintained its success despite a state of flux behind the scenes.

In 1964, *Password* producer Bob Stewart, who had refined the format into perfection, departed from Goodson-Todman Productions in what was quite an ugly divorce. Stewart was frustrated by the way that Mark Goodson ran his company — mandatory "creative" meetings where everybody sat around daydreaming and trying to invent new games just off the tops of their heads, micromanaging whenever he was inside a studio, wrongly taking credit for being the creator of most of his company's shows, and (Stewart felt) not giving enough control to the man who had created three of the most successful shows in the company's history. Bob Stewart, creator of *The Price is Right*, *To Tell the Truth*, and *Password*, had had enough.

In a conversation that's become a famous part of game show history, Goodson, in the midst of begging Bob Stewart not to quit, said, "Bob, I've made you a prince!"

Stewart responded, "Mark, I want to be the king."

Stewart left the company, hung up his own shingle, and formed Bob Stewart Productions in a small office on the other side of town. Another trusted associate, Frank Wayne — whose most famous duty in the company had been conceiving the stunts on *Beat the Clock* — took over the reins on *Password*. Wayne affectionately had his own title for the show. He didn't call it *Password*. He referred to it as "Schmucksay." He named it that in honor of viewers all over the country who were talking to their TVs: "The password is FISH? Schmuck, say 'Trout'!"

The producer switch wasn't a particularly drastic change at *Password*; the format was so smooth that the show could run on auto-pilot. But in the long run, Stewart did some damage to Goodson-Todman; he came up with new ideas and new formats, and got many shows on the air, with all the credit and all the money going straight to him. Not to mention that his shows would be taking up time slots that could have gone to Goodson-Todman. Goodson-Todman survived, but Stewart's departure ultimately cost the company millions of dollars in lost opportunities.

The following year, 1965, CBS canceled the nighttime *Password*. It was the next step in a process that had been noticeable since the quiz show scandals. Game shows had been just as much a part of prime-time television as any other genre. After the scandals, there were still game shows on the air, but they were slowly vanishing and not getting replaced by other game shows. And many games were merely used as

Allen — down there at the bottom, in the middle — joins the farewell party for *Password* producer Bob Stewart (top row, wearing the lei). Frank Wayne (top row, right) became the new producer upon Stewart's departure. FRED WOSTBROCK COLLECTION

mid-season replacements, plugging holes as needed but gone by the time a new series was ready.

A tragedy beyond anybody's control seemed to unofficially bring an era to a close in television. On November 8, 1965, gossip columnist Dorothy Kilgallen died suddenly. From the premiere of *What's My Line?* in February 1950, she had been a regular panelist on the venerable guessing game. In a span of fifteen years, *Line* had gone beyond merely being a hit show; it was an institution. Times changed, but *What's My Line?* would always be on CBS, live every Sunday night at 10:30 p.m. And now, Kilgallen, who had been so engrained into that show's identity that her shadow had practically etched itself into the floor, was gone. Allen and

Betty attended the funeral, and shortly afterward, Betty sat in on the panel. The idea of having to replace Dorothy made the Goodson-Todman staff so squeamish that for the first few months after her death, Dorothy's seat was filled by women like Kitty Carlisle and Betty, who appeared as guests on game shows so often that nobody would ever see them on *What's My Line?* and think that they were intended to be a replacement for anybody.

Allen chats with Carol Burnett and Orson Bean at the top of the show. Although *Password* only afforded Allen a minute or so to talk to the stars, he enjoyed the conversations so much that he hoped one day to do a show that would let him chat a little more. FRED WOSTBROCK COLLECTION

Only twenty-two months after Kilgallen's death, *What's My Line?* was off the air, and producer Gil Fates recalled in his memoirs that he didn't consider that a coincidence. Five months earlier, the final *I've Got a Secret* had aired. Six months before that, the primetime *To Tell the Truth* ended. Dorothy Kilgallen died and seemingly took nighttime network game shows with her.

Though the daytime *Password* was still number one, the end of the nighttime version did make Allen admit that he was thinking about his future. Unlike the Allen of 1960, he absolutely wanted to remain as an on-air talent. But now, Allen wanted to host his own creations.

During the peak of *Password*, Allen was asked what kind of program he'd like to do. "A *Tonight Show*, but daytime. I'd like a good, honest, naked conversation show. Oh, I know how Jack Paar carries on, but I don't think I'd have to be all that naked. And I'd want it daytime because I think this area of programming is opening up. Soon, it will really be the workshop for good evening television. It has, I'll admit, a long way to go. But I'd like to be in there doing the pushing."

Allen had one other idea. As much as he had been the strongest defender of television's potential, he wanted to create a show that dealt with what he felt was television's biggest shortcoming: every idea had to fit into the same basic package. Every sitcom had to be a thirty-minute show, despite having premises that were too thin to stretch over thirty minutes. He had seen a few sitcoms that weren't terrible, but didn't need to be stretched into thirty minutes, a ten or fifteen-minute episode each week would have been fine. It was an idea sort of akin to Betty's logic about the structure for *Life with Elizabeth*.

And the frustrating part, as Allen saw it, was that the problem couldn't really be fixed because the "second life" of a TV series was so valuable. Reruns of shows had to fit neatly into thirty minutes so they could be sold to station managers and easily inserted into their schedules.

Allen wanted to form a show called *Almanac*. It would be a ninety-minute weekly show with many different short programs within the larger program. Each ninety-minute *Almanac* would include a ten-minute sitcom episode, a ten-minute biting satire of that week's news (Allen liked *That Was The Week That Was*, but felt that thirty minutes was too much of it), and other elements. Although he was a fan of his own idea, he admitted that he would probably never get it on the air. Local stations didn't want to air reruns of a ninety-minute show, which meant the networks would never want to air the new episodes to begin with.

And the local stations' desire to air reruns was about to have a pleasant effect on Allen's life.

"If I only had a brain!" Ray Bolger might be thinking to himself after a tough round of *Password.* His opponent is June Lockhart. FRED WOSTBROCK COLLECTION

FRED WOSTBROCK COLLECTION

CHAPTER THIRTEEN

"COLOR"

Although primetime *Password* was gone, the daytime *Password* wasn't going anywhere. Early in 1966, CBS decided to forgo the standard thirteen-week or twenty-six-week renewal contracts that daytime shows of that era generally dealt with. They renewed *Password* for a full year.

And the "workload" for that job occupied a whopping two days a week of Allen's schedule. For the other days each week, he went on the lecture circuit, speaking on the subjects of education ("The Unsung Bargain"), television ("The TV Set: On and Off"), and dealing with today's youth ("The Cry for Excellence"). And he seemingly always had time for worthy causes, hosting fundraisers for mentally disabled children and a Corpus Christi, Texas, festival benefitting naval relief efforts.

And as usual, he saw to it that he and Betty were all booked up for summer, co-starring in *Bells Are Ringing* at the Kansas City Starlight Theater, where they wanted to take one more crack at breaking the box office record that they just barely missed the last time that they were in town. Betty would play the role of telephone operator Ella Peterson, who fell in love with lonely struggling playwright Jeff Moss, played by Allen.

The real drama happened off-stage, though. In a nightmare like the one he had right before his wedding, Allen got separated from his luggage during the trip. The baggage was mistakenly claimed by a pro baseball player for the Kansas City A's. That was resolved, and it looked to be smooth sailing from there.

But there was more. The storms that had cost Betty and Allen a box office record on their last visit had returned for an encore performance. One night, Betty got sprinkled while singing "The Party's Over." The rule in outdoor theater had always been to continue with the show until the orchestra quit. When it was a hazard to the instruments, that was the end. The problem was that the rain kept starting and stopping. Betty would sing a few lines, the orchestra would stop, and then the rain would stop, and the orchestra would play the song from the beginning. This repeated several times until Betty, totally soaked and disheveled, finally finished the whole song. For the rest of their lives together, whenever Betty looked even slightly haggard, Allen would hum a few notes of "The Party's Over."

Bells Are Ringing headed to the St. Louis Muni Opera next, where they had a very unwelcome guest in the audience for every show: a very large skunk that just kept showing up near the exit night after night after night. It was apparently a frequent problem at the Muni Opera because they had an usher on "skunk duty," who would very carefully make his way over and get the skunk to leave. It didn't take much cajoling. The skunk would wobble away without incident…and then return the following night. Betty laughingly said later that she was glad that no critics noticed the skunk; otherwise, writing the review would have been an easy task.

> Certainly, no one is going to claim that Allen Ludden or Betty White should be opera singers, but they make the songs sound good. Ludden, as a matter of fact, has a pretty good voice. He performed his part with gusto and good stage presence. — Robert C. Shaub, *The Edwardsville Intelligencer*

After the summer, Allen would do more traveling. In the years since *Password* first premiered, there had been a very slow westward trickle in the television industry. The business was gradually moving from New York to Los Angeles. *Password*, for most of the run, had made annual visits to Los Angeles, usually taping three weeks' worth of the daytime show and handful of nighttime games. The problem the show was running into was that it was still immensely popular and that there were still stars who were clamoring to play it; it's just that they couldn't.

"I'd love to, but my schedule won't allow it!" became a commonly heard lament for the talent coordinators at the show. Taking a day for the cross-country flight, taping the show, and taking a day to fly back was more than some stars' film and television schedules would allow. So in the fall of 1966, plans were made for everyone to take another trip to California, and this time, they would unpack their bags and stay for a while. They would tape four weeks while they were out there, including one special week, promoting the new CBS fall schedule, featuring ten celebrity guests from the network's prime-time line-up.

But overseas conflict and an upstart producer gave everybody an unpleasant surprise just before they all went out of town.

In 1965, Charles H. Barris, an ABC daytime executive was so under-whelmed by the proposals he had been hearing for new shows that he resigned to found a production company, Chuck Barris Productions, and try to put his own ideas on the air. Late in that year, he sold ABC a titil-lating game in which a single woman flirted with three men and chose the one that she wanted to go on a date with. *The Dating Game* was a hit, and ABC wanted more.

The network had purchased an idea from two other producers and gave it to Chuck Barris to develop it further. The basic idea was one in which newlywed couples were asked questions, and each member of a couple tried

A look just slightly behind the scenes. Near Allen, but angled so that it wasn't visible on camera, was a chute through which a stagehand would send the next password. FRED WOSTBROCK COLLECTION

to match answers for each question. Los Angeles disc jockey and concert promoter Bob Eubanks was hired to host a demonstration game for ABC executives. The plan was that if the executives liked the demonstration, they would pay Barris to produce a full-blown pilot for consideration.

The demonstration had two totally unexpected strokes of good luck. The show had rounded up four Los Angeles-area newlywed couples to

Joan Collins duels with Anthony Newley as Allen looks on. FRED WOSTBROCK COLLECTION

act as contestants for the demonstration. One of the contestants was an unemployed actor named Dom DeLuise, who was a short time away from getting his big break. His answers cracked everybody up and Eubanks took such a shine to him that they kept having extended, and very funny, conversations. The other stroke of good luck was a totally unexpected answer to what seemed like a completely innocuous question.

"What nickname do you usually call your husband?" Eubanks asked one of the wives.

"Numbnuts," she answered.

The ABC network executives in attendance loved the run-through so much that they skipped the pilot and bought the show on the spot. The *Newlywed Game* was scheduled to premiere on July 11, 1966, in the

2:00 p.m. Eastern timeslot. It would be the eighth show to occupy that slot on ABC since *Password* debuted five years earlier.

In 1966, America was mired in the Vietnam conflict. At the time, many Americans still supported the war, with a poll showing that sixty-two percent of Americans supported the bombing raids in Hanoi as part of Operation Rolling Thunder. On July 11, Secretary of Defense Robert S. McNamara held a news conference to update the country on what was happening in Vietnam.

NBC pre-empted their daytime programming to air the news conference. CBS pre-empted their daytime programming, so *Password* wasn't seen that day. ABC, on the other hand, went ahead and aired *The Newlywed Game*. What everyone in television discovered that day was that, while a majority of Americans at that time may have supported the war, they didn't support it enough to watch a news conference. The premiere of *The Newlywed Game* was seen by a massive audience. And many of them stayed with it the next day instead of going back to their normal viewing habits.

The sexual revolution was in full swing in the 1960s, and this naughty little game with husbands and wives freely sharing colorful, none-of-your-business stories from their private lives was the right show at the right time.

By no means did that represent the beginning of the end for *Password*. Once they were back on the air, they still had healthy audiences. They regularly won their timeslot. But *The Newlywed Game* had siphoned away enough viewers to knock *Password* off its perch. *Password* was no longer the number-one game show; that honor went to CBS' *To Tell the Truth*, while *Password* slipped to second place. And that was a big enough dent that CBS panicked. Suddenly, the itinerary for September had changed. *Password* wouldn't be taping four weeks in Los Angeles. They would tape for seven weeks. And before long, it was bumped up to fourteen weeks. CBS was hoping that the extended stay in Los Angeles would give the show a shot in the arm.

As *Password* made its way to California, newspaper columnist Hal Humphrey penned a column about newsreader Jack Lescoulie's dismissal from NBC's *Today* after thirteen years. Lescoulie was born into show business but Humphrey observed that "tucked away in an old box of Lescoulie mementos must be his Eagle Scout badge and a blue ribbon or two from the 4-H Club." Meanwhile, low-key broadcaster Durward Kirby had been eased out of his role co-hosting *Candid Camera* in favor of glamorous Bess Myerson.

Lescoulie and Kirby were part of a breed of television broadcasters that Humphrey called "Jaspers." The golden age of television was filled with broadcasters who were pleasantly bland and exuded some under-stated enthusiasm for whatever subject matter they were tackling. Dave Garroway had been a perfect example of a Jasper. Art Linkletter was another good one. So was Hugh Downs.

Downs himself wrote of his reputation and image as a "Jasper" in a piece he penned for *Look* Magazine. "Our heroes today come out of the ranks. Primitive people made images, then worshipped them. That also happens in TV. I am paid more for acclaim than merit. I am not in the least haunted by conscience or impelled to give the money back. This is the age of the lionization of the common man."

But the dismissals of Lescoulie and Kirby seemed to put the future of Jaspers in danger. Humphrey was concerned that the bland substance-over-style breed of broadcasters was rapidly becoming a thing of the past. Television wanted pretty faces and a high charisma factor. Among the colorless Jasper broadcasters in peril specifically mentioned by Humphrey: Allen Ludden.

And so, Allen Ludden, who had been a television star for barely a decade, went to Los Angeles with dented ratings and with at least one writer dismissing him as finished.

Juliet Prowse and Tom Poston put on their game faces for *Password,*
while Allen, as usual, is all business. FRED WOSTBROCK COLLECTION

FRED WOSTBROCK COLLECTION

CHAPTER FOURTEEN

"ESTABLISH"

Betty felt a little strange. She was back home in Southern California, but this wasn't quite what she was accustomed to. She was unpacking her luggage for a six-week stay in the Beverly Hills Hotel, courtesy of CBS. She and Allen, as usual, would make the most of it. Allen would tape *Password* episodes during the day, and then at night, they would go to nearby West Covina and star in the Carousel Theater's production of *Bells are Ringing*. As a bonus, a staffer from the ABC series *Batman* found out that Allen and *Password* were in town, and Allen wound up with a guest-starring role as a news reporter covering a brawl between the Dynamic Duo and the Penguin's henchmen.

It was actually a much busier schedule than it sounds. Staying at the hotel in Beverly Hills, Allen would have to drive to Hollywood to tape two or three episodes of *Password*, then hop in the car and make the twenty-four-mile drive to West Covina to star in *Bells are Ringing*. On days when *Password* wasn't taping, Allen would drive thirty miles to Anaheim to rehearse *Bells are Ringing*. Allen didn't complain a bit. He liked being considered a well-rounded performer and thought that the workload was good for him.

He told a reporter, "I like to combine the ad-libbing of the television show with the discipline of a stage play…It keeps me honed. I think an actor who usually works with scripts in the theater or motion pictures could profit in the same way by doing master of ceremonies work during his vacation."

Password began its extended stay at CBS Television City in Hollywood, and the show's visit to the West Coast marked two big changes to the program; one that was easily seen by viewers and one big change that nobody noticed for the moment. *Password* was now seen in color every day. And behind the scenes, the Goodson-Todman staff was now seeing to it that the tapes weren't getting erased.

In the pre-cable era of television, nobody could have anticipated the value of reruns. Sitcoms and a few prime-time dramas got a nice second life in reruns, but not much else. Nor could many have anticipated the era of DVDs and streaming video. After episodes of TV shows aired, they were stuffed into a vault, and storage space was precious. The networks had to make some tough decisions about what was worth saving and what

Allen Ludden is the reporter on the scene as The Penguin (Burgess Meredith) hatches another dastardly scheme on ABC's *Batman.* FRED WOSTBROCK COLLECTION

could be thrown away. For the most part, daytime game shows weren't preserved (though Goodson-Todman saw to it that most of their prime-time broadcasts from that era were salvaged). Most tapes of soap operas and sports bit the dust too. But starting with the September 12, 1966, the first episode in Hollywood and the first episode on color, Goodson-Todman saw to it that absolutely every day of *Password* was preserved.

Password took full advantage of its temporary home to round up a truly A-list line-up. Jerry Lewis played the game for a week; so did Danny Kaye. Lucille Ball dropped in, as she always did when *Password* visited town. Carol Burnett, who had been a supporting player on Garry Moore's comedy series five years ago when *Password* began, was now the star of her very own prime-time comedy/variety hour.

Burnett, by this point, was not only the star of her own show, she had become a mother. Her daughter, Carrie Hamilton, had been born in 1963. By the time she was four, Carrie had never seen her mommy on television (the things Carol did were usually on television after Carrie's bedtime). But she had seen Allen Ludden in the daytime. Burnett invited the Luddens over to her house, and Carrie's reaction became one of her favorite stories.

As Burnett recalled in an interview, "[Allen] and Betty came to our house, and Carrie met them. When she went up to bed, I went up to tuck her in, and she said, 'Mamma, can I ask you something about Mr. Ludden?'

"I said, 'Of course you can.'

"'Well then…is he live or on tape?'"

The Los Angeles weeks and the big stars it attracted revitalized the show and reminded everyone of its alluring reputation: *Password* was truly the game that the stars played. And the Hollywood weeks went so well that CBS gave the show a Christmas present. Effective December 25, *Password* would bounce back up to six episodes a week, with a Sunday game airing at 5:00 p.m. each week.

The renewed interest in the series brought up some talk of statistics in the press, and the show cheerfully passed some along. Among celebrity guests, Alan King had the most appearances under his belt, with twelve. King also had the undesirable record of being the only celebrity to go five consecutive episodes without winning a single game. This led to another record, the celebrity who brought in the most mail; hundreds of viewers had sent Alan King sympathy cards. Peter Lawford was the champion player of the Lightning Round, successfully playing a full five words in only twelve seconds.

But despite the game show and the acting gigs that filled every square on his calendar, Allen still had the same priorities that he had years earlier. Allen appreciated the fan mail about how much people enjoyed watching the show, but what really touched him was a letter from a group of soldiers in Vietnam who said they were using *Password* as a tool to establish friendly relations with the locals, playing games in English to teach the locals their language, and then playing the game in Vietnamese to learn the native tongue. And he concluded the first color *Password* broadcast by imploring viewers to take an active interest in their local school systems and do what they could to improve them.

In Allen's lecture about education, "The Unsung Bargain," he spoke of the negative effects of parents' behavior on their children's pursuit of education. He said that children tended to learn at an early age that public lives and private lives were two separate things, and that the behavior of parents tended to establish that. He also said that too much emphasis was placed on specialized fields, saying that it was harmful to teach children to focus on one specific goal and strive for perfection in it. That emphasis, he said, caused a "search for meaning and a quest for identity," as young people felt the need to find that one specific thing that they could be perfect in. Allen further emphasized the importance of enthusiasm, more so than perfection, and encouraged young people to seek out role models who had succeeded in part because of the enthusiasm they had for their fields.

Teenagers were getting a particularly bad rap in the public eye during the late 1960s. If you looked for teenagers on television, you would have seen an endless supply of punks, beatniks, hippies, beach bums, and the occasional criminal.

Allen didn't care for those types either. One of Allen's lectures, "The Cry for Excellence," lashed out at "the tyranny of the IN." Allen detested beatniks and the concept of the beat generation, complaining that the lifestyle glamorized ignorance and laziness, and compelled young people to settle for less. But there was another reason Allen despised them. He felt that for such a tiny segment of the population, they got too much attention, that they were spoiling the reputation of the majority.

Allen said, "I believe that we pay too much attention to the beatniks, juvenile delinquents and misfits, possibly because they are publicized so prominently in the nation's press. But it's the other ninety percent, the good kids who have an excellent awareness of the complexity of the era into which they are moving, who are the real future backbone of this nation. We, the adults, should help and encourage them at every opportunity."

It was a point he expounded on during an interview with *TV-Radio Mirror*. "I think it's preposterous that [beatniks] have taken to themselves the word 'hip.' They're not hip at all. They're square. They contribute nothing. I think the time has come when we should stop belaboring the idea that they typify today's young people. I'm tired of seeing us celebrate the negative. This nation was built on constructive ideals and ideas, and there's more need for such work and attitudes than ever."

With the ever-present horn-rimmed glasses, silvering hair, and neatly pressed suit, nobody looked more like a representative of "the establishment" than Allen Ludden. But the reality was, the American teenager never had a greater supporter.

Allen said, "Kids appreciate, maybe more than we do, that they will need knowledge and skills surpassing those of their elders. In my opinion, one of the country's most valuable resources is yet to be fully developed: the potential power of its bright young minds. I believe that it is essential to the future of our way of life to give every qualified young person in this country, no matter what the social-economic circumstances, an opportunity to go to college to develop the full potential of his or her talents."

Peter Lawford in his element, giving the clues in the Lightning Round. Carol Burnett looks on. FRED WOSTBROCK COLLECTION

In another interview, he elaborated, "I feel most young people today are seeking excellence…Young people have much too much energy to exist in that beat world, which is really a lazy world. No awake, energetic young person can survive just doing nothing."

Allen remained fixated about education. He told an interviewer that he had enthusiastic dialogues with his son, who felt that course requirements

Two top CBS stars, Amanda Blake of *Gunsmoke* and Bob Denver of *Gilligan's Island*, joined Allen for *Password* during its extended stay in Tinseltown. FRED WOSTBROCK COLLECTION

and structured education were outmoded concepts. Allen himself was against requiring a foreign language and felt that social science courses should have been mandatory.

He elaborated, "I took French for four years, and I couldn't speak it when I got through. For the most part, students today don't choose a diversified enough curriculum for themselves. Oh, the terminologies that are thrown at you! It seems they are going at conclusions before the reasons."

Allen cared about America's youth and was much more in tune with what they were thinking than many of their authority figures may have been. And the allure of a big paycheck, a flight, and a nice hotel in Dallas for one week each year couldn't make him turn a blind eye toward their thoughts and feelings. In November, Allen got geared up for another annual turn at hosting the Miss Teenage America Pageant. 1966 was the year before the Women's Liberation movement began and there seemed to be no shortage of beauty contests on the airwaves. In addition to Allen's Miss Teenage America show, viewers in 1966 watched Miss America, Miss USA, Miss Universe, America's Junior Miss, and Miss Teenage International.

Reporter Cynthia Lowry asked Allen about his thoughts regarding the pageant he hosted, and Allen was refreshingly honest in his mixed feelings about it. "I think that it could be a horrendous experience for some girls. But for those girls who get to the finals, I am certain that it is, as they keep saying, a beautiful, exciting thing they remember all their lives…[I'm] not especially defending the principle, but I am defending the magic of the pageant. From their arrival for the finals until they leave, they have a marvelous time. They are treated with great respect and there has never been any vulgarity."

But as willing as Allen was to defend the magic, the father of two teenage girls concluded with one thought: "Happily, neither of my own girls is interested in that sort of thing."

When 1967 rolled around, Allen may very well have felt as if he had won a pageant himself. The Texas Press Association named him Texan of the Year. In their official statement to the media, TPA president Jim Barnhill said, "What better choice could our committee make than to pick a man who has spent the formative years of his life in our capital city and who, both in person and on the air, frequently and proudly refers to Texas as his home state? He has given the Lone Star State millions of dollars in publicity, and it's all good."

For the ceremony in San Antonio, Betty joined him, and so did Homer and Leila, who beamed proudly as their son accepted his bronze plaque and posed for photos. And thirty-three years after he finished high school, Allen admitted that the award purged the lingering insecurity and self-doubt that had always remained after being rejected for The Congress Society.

Allen always thought of himself as a "dual citizen" when it came to his past. He revered Mineral Point, Wisconsin, the town where he was born and spent the summers with his grandmother Clara. He visited the town frequently when he reached adulthood, to get caught up with family or to enjoy all the honors and benefits that came with being the local boy who made good. He served as master of ceremonies for the Fourth of July festivities and delivered a speech for the Sesquicentennial celebration.

He said on that occasion, "In this lovely garden spot of the world you have a sense of culture, sense of beauty, and a great sense of fun. So, I'm proud to be part of it — to have my roots here. And I urge you to hold it all dear."

More fun from Hollywood, with guests Barbara Rush and Gene Kelly.
FRED WOSTBROCK COLLECTION

Allen sometimes spoke of buying a home there after his television career wound down. While Allen would never live there again, his name would. A man-made lake at the west edge of Mineral Point is named Ludden Lake in his honor.

The good news kept coming. CBS, happy with the results of Sunday afternoon *Password*, moved the sixth episode to prime-time once again. As of March, it would close out the CBS Monday night lineup at 10:30 p.m. And Allen, who was worried that departing *G.E. College Bowl* and hosting *Password* would hurt his reputation, had a full line-up of lectures booked for the month of April.

And as usual, Allen and Betty spent their spring seeing to it that their summer would be full. Their summer stock production in Dennis, Massachusetts, that year would be *Any Wednesday*, a play about a married businessman who spends his Wednesday nights with his mistress. While Allen and Betty were used to establishing box office records and soaking in the adoration from audiences, *Any Wednesday* surprised him. Audience reaction to the show was surprisingly cool. Some investigation and conversations with theater-goers led them to the explanation: audiences loved Allen and Betty so much that, despite knowing it was all just a play, they couldn't stomach the idea that Allen would ever cheat on Betty. Allen and Betty's courtship the first time they performed in Dennis was a pretty well-known story among the folks that came there to see the shows, and seeing them pretending to split up was too unpleasant to fathom.

Things went better at their next booking. Allen took a rare chance on booking a musical that summer, performing in *Guys and Dolls* in Atlanta. Allen played notorious gambler Sky Masterson and Betty played Sgt. Sarah Brown from the Save-A-Soul Mission.

They got warmer receptions this time, particularly one reaction that happened with every audience that Betty found rather funny. The show opened with a stage filled with sharp-dressed gamblers holding newspapers. Allen was onstage, in plain sight, among them, but uncharacteristically barefaced. And every night, at the start of the show, the star didn't get any reaction. And then, right before his first line of dialogue, Allen would reach into his pocket, pull out his glasses, and put them on. And the audience would instantly erupt with cheering, as if Allen had just magically appeared in front of them.

And it was a summer when Allen needed to hear some cheering. CBS made the announcement that the nighttime version of *Password* wouldn't be on the schedule for the 1967-68 season. That was a disappointment for everyone, to be sure, but it didn't quite blindside them. It was the unfortunate direction that game shows' fates were taking, and CBS had done a total game show purge from their nighttime schedules that year. But CBS' next announcement left Allen, Betty, and everyone at Goodson-Todman at a loss for words.

The daytime *Password* was canceled, too.

FRED WOSTBROCK COLLECTION

CHAPTER FIFTEEN
"WEST"

Four weeks after *Password* premiered in 1961, it was the number-one show on daytime television. Further examination of the ratings revealed that there were more television sets in use at 2:00 pm each day than there had been before the show premiered, which meant that people who hadn't been watching television at that time of day before were now tuning in specifically to see *Password*. For four consecutive years, the show maintained an average of a 55 share according to the Nielsen ratings, meaning for four years, fifty-five percent of all the televisions in use at 2 pm were tuned to *Password*.

In the months after *The Newlywed Game* premiered, *Password*'s share slipped down to the mid-40s. In 1967, when CBS decided to bring *Password* to an end, the show was still getting a fairly respectable 35.

CBS daytime head Fred Silverman openly favored soap operas to game shows and needed a spot for a pet project of his, *Love is a Many Splendored Thing*, a soap opera adapted from a 1955 film. The show would be marred by controversy. The original series was about a woman from Hong Kong who moved to San Francisco to study medicine, and was carrying on love affairs with two men. CBS censors balked at the interracial romance storyline, causing the show's creator to quit and leading to a total overhaul of the series, now focusing on two families and the emerging love triangle that caused problems for them. The show averaged about a 28 share in the timeslot; respectable, but not the same results that the network had been getting with *Password*.

On September 15, 1967, Allen Ludden hosted the 1,555th and final daytime episode of *Password* on CBS, with Frank Gifford competing against Betty White. He took a moment early in the program to ask Betty her personal thoughts about appearing on so many game shows.

She answered, "I love games and I love game shows. I think it's good mental exercise. I think it keeps everybody alert and kind of on [their] toes.

You can't watch a game show without participating, and I think that's good mental exercise for everybody; I don't care how old or how young you are."

"It keeps the mind active," Allen chimed in.

Betty replied, "And you meet a lot of husbands."

Allen cheerfully delivered his final "password of the day" nearly drowned out by the thunderous applause of the studio audience. With

Betty and Allen close out *Password* after six fun years on CBS. Betty's opponent for the final week was Frank Gifford. FRED WOSTBROCK COLLECTION

Betty — the woman he married as a result of hosting the show — at his side, Allen flashed the brightest smile of his career at the camera and told home viewers, "I'll see you SOON, I hope!"

Allen had reason to smile on that final episode. When he agreed to host *Password*, he signed contracts with Goodson-Todman and with CBS as a performer. With *Password* canceled, CBS was done with Allen, but the contract was iron-clad, so CBS paid him a nice chunk of money on his way out the door to settle it.

Password was a memory now. But not just a memory. Though the show was gone, Milton Bradley wasn't ready to give up on it. The company continued producing new editions of the *Password* home game and they continued to be big sellers.

Password had been such an enormous success that it compelled Goodson-Todman to think outside the game box. The company sold several months' worth of *Password* tapes to a single station in Southern California just to see what would happen. For viewers in California, the demise of *Password* was followed immediately by *Password* reruns. And, to many people's surprise, viewers tuned in. By December, Goodson-Todman was

spreading the word to local TV stations nationwide: they had 200 color episodes of *Password* on tape, ready to be sold for reruns. Game show reruns weren't completely unheard of. *You Bet Your Life* starring Groucho Marx had been, and would continue to be, an enormous success in its second life, but *You Bet Your Life* had always been seen more as a comedy show than a pure game show.

Password defied many expectations by drawing audiences with games that had already been watched and winners who had already spent their money. But after six years in the 2:00 p.m. Eastern timeslot, the stations

"What's next?" Allen pondered his next move as *Password* came to a close.

FRED WOSTBROCK COLLECTION

airing *Password* helped make another interesting discovery. On stations that aired the reruns in late afternoon and early evening, the reruns were getting massive audiences among the in-school demographics. Young people loved *Password*. The game, which some station managers probably plugged into the schedule as an afterthought because it was so cheap, was regularly winning its time slot in many cities.

Allen had reason to celebrate the popularity of the reruns, because Goodson-Todman went above and beyond their contractual obligations. Since game show reruns were such an unexplored concept in television, there were no considerations made about residual payments when contracts were drawn up for the hosts. Goodson-Todman was so appreciative toward Allen for his role in the success of the show that they continued paying him his full salary for hosting throughout the entire time that *Password* reruns were circulating, even though Allen wasn't hosting any new episodes of it or any other show for the company.

In 1968, Goodson-Todman made another attempt to salvage *Password*...not the show, but the actual game itself. In April 1967, the company had introduced a new game show on NBC called *Snap Judgment*, a so-so spin on *Password* hosted by Ed McMahon, in which the contestants were shown the correct answers in advance and then wrote the clues they wanted to use before the show began. Once onstage, they were fully committed to the clues they had already written and tried to prompt their celebrity partners to guess the words. The game was never wildly successful but managed to hang on for over a year. Beginning on December 23, 1968, the show's format was totally thrown out and the contestants and celebrities played *Password* instead. The format change wasn't even disguised or finessed. The press releases from NBC and Goodson-Todman literally stated that from now on, *Snap Judgment* would be played like *Password*. The show was already running out of steam when the change was made, and the intended repair didn't do anything to change those fortunes. *Snap Judgment* ended three months later.

Elsewhere in 1968, Allen, now officially out of a job, began exploring his career options, and realized how shockingly different that exploration was now than it would have been six years ago. Six years ago, if Allen had walked away from his executive position at CBS, he could have become an executive at another network, or at a local television or radio station. He probably could have gone back to teaching, maybe become a college professor. He could have written more books.

But the Allen Ludden of 1968 was a bona fide star, and he was a star on television, playing the role of himself. And if he chose to pursue that, he had very little to worry about. His show had been such a hit that it made him a household name. If he stayed with performing on television, he could find work virtually at will. The problem was, he would probably have to move across the country to do it.

The cross-country shift of the television business from New York to Los Angeles was gaining momentum. Allen could probably stay in New York if he really wanted to, but his options were going to be limited, and limited further the longer he chose to stay. And when Allen looked at his family, the timing felt right. David was at Yale, where he had just qualified for a study program that would send him to India for one year. Martha had started college the same fall that *Password* aired its final episode.

Sarah was in her sophomore year of high school, which meant that if the family moved now, it wouldn't disrupt the all-important junior and senior years. Having considered every option, and having decided what move made the most sense and what would be best for himself, Allen called a family meeting to give everybody else a say in the decision. The votes were cast, and everyone prepared for a move to the West Coast.

A local Los Angeles advertisement for Allen's next TV gig; the show would be a successful enticement to draw customers to their local supermarkets.

FRED WOSTBROCK COLLECTION

Early in 1968, Allen and Betty paid a two-week visit to Los Angeles. Betty would go house-hunting and Allen would go right to work, having already secured two jobs that would keep him occupied for nearly the entire visit. He hosted a pilot for Monty Hall, the man who had first suggested a word association game to Goodson-Todman years earlier. *Talking Pictures* pitted two contestants against each other; they faced a massive wall with ten doors and had identify, from memory, which of ten celebrities was sitting behind the door. The show had star power — Ann Miller, Peter Lawford, Angela Cartwright, Lorne Greene, Jan Sterling, Stubby Kaye, Agnes Moorhead, Tom Smothers, Carol Burnett, and

Paul Winchell — as well as a bona fide star performer as host, and a successful production company (Stefan Hatos and Monty Hall, the minds behind *Let's Make a Deal*) backing it. But the problem was the pilot was being screened for CBS, and as long as Fred Silverman was in charge, game shows didn't have much of a chance. The other problem was that it bore a strong resemblance to an NBC game, *Eye Guess* hosted by Bill Cullen; at least one CBS executive was probably a little wary of a lawsuit.

Allen had also signed a deal to host a game show for Bing Crosby Productions. The previous year, Walter Schwimmer, Inc., a division of the company, had put together a game show called *Let's Go to the Races* for television station KTLA in Los Angeles. The show's gimmick was that home viewers could win a share of the cash and prizes up for grabs by getting sweepstakes entry forms from Vons Supermarkets in the viewing area. Vons monitored its business closely during the run of *Let's Go to the Races* and determined that they had gained 300,000 regular customers per week because of the show. It worked so well that Bing Crosby Productions and the Schwimmer division put together a national game show, with the intention that the local stations that bought the show would then pitch it themselves to local supermarkets that would distribute similar sweepstakes entries. The company secured the rights to a game show format originally titled *What's the Name of This Song?* It had premiered on KTLA Channel 5 in Los Angeles in 1949 and enjoyed an impressive fifteen-year run before NBC picked it up for the network's daytime line-up in 1964, re-titling it *What's This Song?* It lasted on the network for about one year.

Bing Crosby Productions renamed the format *Win with the Stars*. As added incentive, the show could be produced at very little expense. It would be a weekly series, not daily, and would not air year-round, which meant the production company only needed to produce twenty-six episodes. And since, by 1968, taping five episodes in a single day had become the industry standard for TV game shows, that meant that the entire series could be shot in one week. Allen could get the entire season taped before he and Betty flew back.

Allen served as host for *Win with the Stars*, a game that pitted two celebrity/contestant teams against each other (sound familiar?). The teams took turns trying to identify popular songs being played by the live band joining them onstage. The team earned money for successfully naming a song, and could then win additional money by singing the song themselves, with bucks awarded for each individual word that the team correctly sang; the payout ended as soon as they said one wrong word. Joining Allen and the contestants would be an impressive roster of guests, including Roddy McDowall, Dorothy Lamour, Cliff Robertson, Michael Landon, Mel Tormé, Steve Allen, Ruta Lee, Della Reese, Regis Philbin, and Rose Marie.

Meanwhile, Betty searched for houses, and although Allen trusted his wife, he did lay down one rule for what houses he'd be willing to consider with her. Allen later remembered, "My only stipulation…was, I wasn't going to pay a fortune in Beverly Hills for the same kind of house I used to have for $62,500."

Betty steered clear of Beverly Hills altogether, focusing her energies on Brentwood, the area where she had grown up. She visited a total of twenty-six possible new homes for the Ludden clan. But her mind was made up immediately. The moment she walked through the door of the first house, she blurted out, "I want it!"

She explained a few years later, "It was the garden that sold me on the

Betty competed against Stubby Kaye on *Win with the Stars*. Allen taped the full season in a matter of weeks while Betty searched for a new home. FRED WOSTBROCK COLLECTION

house. The minute I walked in, I could see through the living room into the oriental garden. I fell in love with it."

It was a big sprawling Cape Cod-style house with a feeling of familiarity after years in the Chappaqua farm house. Betty told a reporter, "The house I found in Brentwood...was not so different in feeling from the farm house. It was the first house I looked at. The minute I opened the door I said, 'I want this house!' The real estate woman said, 'Cool it, cool it!' The owner had been hesitant about selling. We looked at twenty-five more houses, but I wanted the first one so badly."

Betty worried that maybe there were flaws in the Brentwood house that she wasn't seeing, and she was worried that if she insisted on it, she'd have to take the blame for any later problems. So, she kept house-hunting and found a few that she thought Allen might like, too. And when Allen finally had a day off, they explored all the houses together while Betty desperately tried not to let on about which one she liked the best.

To her delight, his favorite house was the one that was secretly her favorite house too. The house was perfect in every way except for the smashed lock on the bedroom door. The real problem turned out to be the previous owner, who was reluctant to move out after Betty and Allen had closed the deal. She delayed her move-out date twice, but when Allen put his foot down, she promised that she would be out before August.

Allen and Betty spent their final summer on the East Coast packing everything up and then traveling New England for four weeks of summer stock engagements. This year, they were starring in *Once More with Feeling*, in which Allen played an egotistical orchestra conductor and Betty played the harpist who put up with being married to him. The bookings lasted through the entire month of July, and then on exactly August 1, Allen and Betty moved to California.

After making their way all across the country, never to return (Betty said she would "never pass the Rockies again without a plane ticket") and arrived at their new Brentwood, California home…which still contained the previous owner as well as all of her belongings.

Allen's temper could be hard to measure sometimes. There was the night when they went out for dinner and a woman shrieked, "It's Allen Ludden and Betty White!" She hollered excitedly…she hollered non-stop…she kept hollering after the entrée arrived and after the waiter walked away, the woman sat down in the booth and tried to carry on a conversation with them.

Allen, calmly but sternly, said, "Ma'am, your dinner must be getting cold. I know ours is. I suggest you go back to your table now."

On the other hand, Allen himself was the first to admit that he had buttons that could be pushed. In his lecture series, he would share stories from his private life and acknowledged that one particular button for him was the expression "Cool it." By his own account, any time he heard the words "Cool it," the result would always be exactly the opposite.

Seeing his new home still occupied, still filled with the woman's belongings, made Allen so angry that he took the matter into his own hands, literally. Allen marched into the house, gathered the woman's personal effects, and loaded them into her car himself.

Betty later admitted to feeling sorry for the woman right up until the moment when she nostalgically bawled, "I've had two divorces in this house!"

Betty stopped feeling sorry for her immediately. It did explain the smashed lock on the bedroom door, though.

With the previous owner firmly booted from the house, Allen and Betty began turning it into their home. Allen, a self-described "marigold freak," got some paint and redid the black trim, black doors, and black shutters in an antique-looking gold tint. Allen and Betty bought furniture to match, and bright yellow, orange, and gold could be found in every room of the house, along with floral arrangements that were freshly cut and replaced on a regular basis.

Betty explained in 1969, "He plants the flowers. I pick and arrange them. He's absolutely wiggy about marigolds. We have a big Rouviere painting of marigolds and the den and living room are geared toward that painting. Our garden, too, is full of marigolds."

Allen took readers on a tour of the house in an article for *Daytime TV* Magazine. "It's a three-story, four-bedroom white frame house. Looks like a Connecticut frame house, and we can see the hills behind. It has stucco and fieldstone facing, but when you go inside, it looks like a California house in that all rooms in the back are glassed in and open into the terrace and, beyond, the beautiful swimming pool. There's a great covered barbeque pit near the kitchen, and there's a garden and fruit trees. The inside of the house is paneled in wood, I have a second-floor office…why, it's the most convenient house I've ever lived in!"

The shelves were decorated with all sorts of personal treasures: the pewter tea service that they bought shortly after they got married, a hand-signed letter from U.S. Treasurer John Connally, along with one of the first dollar bills printed with Connally's signature, and Allen's collection of mementos from the career of John Steinbeck. Allen had met Steinbeck through a college friend, they hit it off extraordinarily well and maintained a long friendship. The first time Allen introduced Betty to his friend John Steinbeck, they had entered his home right as he was in the middle of typing his Nobel Prize acceptance speech. Steinbeck re-wrote the speech, but autographed the first draft and gave it to Allen and Betty. Allen also had an autographed first edition of nearly every one of Steinbeck's books, as well as a wooden ice bucket on which Steinbeck engraved a short poem:

"Ludden's House. Take Ludden's Way, Be Kind — Be Tolerant, Be Gay."

The Luddens were still unpacking when they heard their doorbell ring for the first time. Actor Pat O'Brien surprised Betty with a cup of sugar, symbolic of their new relationship; Betty had no idea that he was going to be their new neighbor. Predictably, Betty made friends with a wide variety of other neighbors. A blue jay flew into the yard every day for peanuts, and a family of raccoons spent quite a bit of time in the yard. Betty took a little census of all the animals that were visiting regularly and figured out that it came to about twenty-five.

Betty joked that it took only "thirteen minutes" for her to get used to her new home. It was only two miles from the home where she spent her adolescent years, and once she was unpacked, it seemed like she never left.

Allen and Betty both disclosed that after years in New York and Connecticut, he adapted to his new surroundings almost instantly. He became, in Betty's words, an "instant Californian." Allen had loved gardening and quickly realized that he was now in a climate that would allow him to do it year-round. He had absolutely no interest in sports and never indulged in tennis or golf the way that seemingly everybody else in West Coast show business did, so virtually all of his outdoor energy went into the garden. It sprawled, and flowers were so plentiful that Allen usually managed to have seven or eight fresh-cut bouquets throughout the house at any given time. In the expansive yard, Allen grew marigolds for six months of the year, and daffodils year-round. He also raised orchids and had an Oriental garden.

Win with the Stars grew quickly. It initially only aired on fifteen stations, which had arranged deals with local supermarket chains for sponsorships. The show and the stations asked the supermarkets to keep them posted on how many sweepstakes entry forms they were distributing, and to the delight of the show, the stations, and certainly the supermarkets, the local stores in those fifteen television markets were giving out an average of a combined 4 million entry forms each week. Twenty-five more local stations signed up after only a few weeks.

Win with the Stars gave Allen the best of both worlds; he had a show that was keeping his name and face out there, but the show required so little of his time — he had already taped the entire season and was only needed occasionally to shoot commercials for some of the local grocery stores that were sponsoring the program — that he was free to pursue other work.

He agreed to host a series of pilots for producer Jack Barry, the producer/ host whose games *Twenty One* and *Tic Tac Dough* had been implicated in the late 1950s quiz show scandals. Barry had since attempted to break back into television by accepting a position with his former competitors, Mark Goodson and Bill Todman. The arrangement was never a good fit; Barry resigned after getting into a clash with co-workers over a pilot he was helping them develop.

Barry, once he was gone, fleshed out an idea that he had conjured up at Goodson-Todman but had never gone very far with, a question-and-answer game in which a three-wheeled slot machine chose the categories. He called the game *The Joker's Wild.* Two contestants would take turns spinning the slot machine. A category's value was determined by how many times it appeared on the wheels, one point, two points, or three points. Jokers

Guest Peter Marshall and his contestant partner try to sing the right lyrics on *Win with the Stars.* FRED WOSTBROCK COLLECTION

were wild and could be used to play any category. The pilots that Allen hosted were a bit odd because Jack Barry couldn't decide if he wanted the show to have celebrity guests. Allen hosted a pilot in which a panel of guests read the questions, while Allen merely served as a traffic cop, and another which left out the celebrities and Allen read the questions himself. CBS passed on the pilots, although Jack Barry would continue reworking and retooling the format for another three years while Allen moved on to other projects.

Allen hosted a roundtable discussion program for the local NBC affiliate in Los Angeles. Each Sunday on *Youth and the Police*, Allen would talk to Los Angeles police officers and a group of teenagers about subjects ranging from police involvement in education to the legality of hitchhiking. On some programs, Allen would open the floor to questions and let the kids ask the cops questions about whatever was on their mind. And Allen veered way out of his comfort zone briefly by trying to market his own line of soft drinks, called Cold Soul.

Despite the cross-country move, Betty was still able to host her radio program, *Dimension*, for CBS. CBS tinkered with the title, sometimes

Allen and Betty at the mic for the CBS radio show *Dimension*. FRED WOSTBROCK COLLECTION

calling it *Dimension Feature* or *Dimension at Home*, and gave Betty a co-host: Allen. Together, they discussed common domestic issues and addressed listener questions.

After fifteen years of covering the Rose Parade for NBC every New Year's Day, the higher-ups at the network did something nice for Betty. In the past, she had to be out the door at 3:00 a.m. to get to Pasadena and get ready for the broadcast.

She jokingly explained the experience of covering a New Year's Day parade early in the morning: "I pass people who are still celebrating when I'm on my way to work. How do I feel? Sober…superior…but jealous."

For the 1969 Rose Parade, NBC told Betty to stay home and sleep in just a little. They sent a limousine to pick her up at 5 a.m. For the first time since they got married, Betty and Allen got to spend New Year's Eve together and enjoy it.

Betty loved the Rose Parade. Year after year, no matter how dreadful the early call time, Betty eagerly walked around the starting point of the parade, watching the workers making repairs, adjusting the flower buds, and talking to the people on the floats to get information that wouldn't be readily apparent so she could share some facts with the home viewers.

Betty jokingly called the Rose Parade her TV series that aired one episode a year. And when Allen wasn't working on any series of his own, he was excitedly working on a new idea that he was looking to get off the ground. It was his favorite idea that he ever had.

FRED WOSTBROCK COLLECTION

CHAPTER SIXTEEN

"GALLERY"

When *Password* was in the prime of its life, Allen had been asked what kind of TV show he'd really like to do. He wanted to do a talk show, he said. And he went further. He had that idea he called *Almanac*, the ninety-minute TV show that could contain many different shows within it. And in 1969, Allen would finally get to do both.

Allen and Betty created a production company so they could pursue any projects of personal interest. They called it Albets, fusing Allen's first name with Tess' nickname for her daughter. Allen found some office space next door to MTM, Mary Tyler Moore and Grant Tinker's production complex. Since they were now working in such close proximity, old friends Allen and Grant Tinker also formed a unit called Elltee Productions (Ludden + Tinker = Elltee) that would specialize in game shows. Under the Albets umbrella, Allen pitched his idea to networks and syndicates around Los Angeles. He had ditched the title *Almanac* and come up with one that more accurately captured his idea of many shows within one: *Ludden Unlimited*.

As Allen was cobbling together the elements that would make up *Ludden Unlimited*, he came up, quite logically, with having a mini-talk show in each ninety-minute episode. But Allen was going to take a very different approach to the talk show format. Instead of talking to famous people, Allen's talk show would be talking about famous people.

Introducing a talk show in 1969 was a risky proposition because, as one writer very correctly put it, it was a genre that was becoming "swollen" on television. Every night at 11:30 p.m., the networks battled it out with Johnny Carson on NBC, Joey Bishop on ABC, and Merv Griffin leaving syndication for a new, similar show on CBS. During the day, David Frost, Mike Douglas, and Steve Allen were filling time slots in many cities, fellow game show host Tom Kennedy was getting ready to mount a talk show of his own, and the war for ratings dominance had a few casualties. Woody Woodbury and Donald O'Connor had just seen their talk shows run off the air.

Allen emphasized that his show was different, because his wasn't the tiresome form of a talk show that he was seeing elsewhere on television. He said to one interviewer, "Jack Paar started it…and people were amused and entertained by the guests who told about the funny things that happened to them on the way to the studio."

As talk shows began growing more widespread on television, more of them were copying the Paar mold of interviewing guests with more of an emphasis on lighthearted storytelling within the interview. The result, according to Allen, was a breed of professional talk show guests who "make the rounds of four or five shows with one or two stories, and then get a couple of new stories and start out all over again."

Allen still wanted to try a talk show of his own, but

Allen felt that his *Ludden Unlimited* concept had unlimited potential.
AUTHOR'S COLLECTION

didn't really see a reason to just unleash another talk show into a crowded marketplace until he had figured out how to make his different from all the rest. The inspiration came when he finally saw something different happening on a talk show.

As he told it, "I started thinking about all that self-serving chit-chat that revealed nothing about the guests one night when Truman Capote appeared on the Johnny Carson show. He started talking about some of the people he encountered when getting material for *In Cold Blood*. Even Carson shut up — it was the first time I'd ever seen Carson really listening…When you can get one person to talk about another person with objectivity and enthusiasm, you find out more about the one who is doing the talking than in any other way."

Allen was so taken by the Truman Capote interview that he developed a format for the *Ludden Unlimited* talk show segment that he would call "Allen Ludden's Gallery." Each day, he would present a profile (or, in keeping with the theme, a portrait) of a famous person and then interview a few people who had written books or magazine articles about that famous person, and they could compare and contrast their insights about major events in the famous person's life.

Allen got a lot of interest in *Ludden Unlimited* from Metromedia, a distributor for television syndication. The only change they requested initially is that they preferred the talk show name to Allen's preferred name for the whole show. *Ludden Unlimited* was retitled *Allen Ludden's Gallery*.

A gaudy advertisement, resembling an old vaudeville poster, appeared in *Broadcasting* Magazine in the spring of 1969, announcing Metromedia's new offering for TV stations in search of ninety-minute programs. The two-page ad laid out the contents of each episode:

"The Opening": The show's house orchestra would present an arrangement of a few popular tunes. They would be joined each day by "a songster or songstress" who would be introduced with a detailed introduction by Allen. The ad in Broadcasting stressed that the show would heavily emphasize and showcase new talent for this portion.

"The First Portrait," in which a published biographer would discuss their famous subject matter.

"The Kids": A mini-concert performed by a band with a big following among the younger viewers.

"Comedy": Allen would be joined by a popular comic,

OR

"Sensational Feature": Sometimes instead of the comedy segment, the show would do something of a grab-bag segment that could be any one of a number of features.

"Return of the Vocalist": The songster or songstress from The Opening would come back for another performance. Sometimes, Allen himself would perform.

"Guest Celebrity": Allen promised to be a no-holds-barred, revealing interviewer with his guest each day.

"The Second Portrait": A conversation with another biographer.

"The Kids Encore"

"The Grand Finale": Members of the audience would be selected to come onstage for a mini-game show, with cash and prizes up for grabs.

Allen was committed to the mini-shows concept in every step of the presentation. The ad stressed that each segment of the show would have a distinctive opening and closing. Set design had been a major consideration. At Allen's insistence, there was no proscenium arch or any similar framework, so that the set could be altered for every segment to look unique and distinctive.

Allen's baby, though, was the "Portrait" segment, and Allen sought out biographers who were able to discuss a broad variety of famous names. There were portraits of Ingrid Bergman, Frank Sinatra, John Lennon, Fidel Castro, Joe Namath, Barbra Streisand, Mickey Cohen, Vanessa Redgrave, J. Paul Getty, Albert Schweitzer, Eldridge Cleaver, Wilt Chamberlain, and Mickey Mouse.

Allen felt that his approach to a talk show would work. He vowed that he wasn't going to waste time or people. He said, "When a guest has something to say, he'll be on camera. When he doesn't, then he's off-camera...I'm eliminating the chit-chat [and] the funny-thing-happened-to-me-on-the-way-to-the-studio routines. And I'm not going to waste time telling people how they look."

He emphasized that he wouldn't sit at a desk, and the guests wouldn't have a comfy sofa to relax on when their segment was up. Allen and his guest would sit in a very basic set of chairs, and when their time was up, that was the end of it.

And he felt there was one other reason his talk show would work. "I noticed on other talk shows that the level of audience attention picked up when guests began talking about someone else...It amounted to gossip. Gossip and people hold the audience's attention."

Gossip was right. The critic for *Variety* gave the show a favorable but very surprised review, nothing that the Portrait segment featured "along with the puff...an almost equal measure of the more intimate background that press agents are usually paid to keep under the rug."

Allen also had a ready reply for anybody who said that it would just make more sense to invite the famous people themselves instead of inviting writers who would talk about them. Allen explained, "They are more objective than the subjects themselves."

Nevertheless, Allen did have a designated segment for the stars to talk about themselves each day, and he would deliver a wide array of guests:

Allen offered an occasional tune for viewers who tuned in to *Allen Ludden's Gallery*. FRED WOSTBROCK COLLECTION

Leonard Nimoy, Nichelle Nichols, and William Shatner all appeared on the program (Allen himself was mystified by *Star Trek* but Betty was a big fan). Allen's reliable friend from *Password* Carol Burnett appeared too, and so did her co-star Harvey Korman. Grant Tinker's wife, Mary Tyler Moore, was on the show. Allen's next door neighbor, actor Pat O'Brien (Allen and Pat would usually talk while tending to their gardens on opposite sides of the fence) was a guest. James Brolin, Gypsy Rose Lee, Ed Begley (the actor was a former co-worker of Allen's from WTIC), Redd Foxx, Andy Griffith, Jack Palance, and many more paid Allen a visit.

And Allen wasn't kidding about the intent to showcase new talent. Former Smothers Brothers writer and musician Mason Williams appeared on the program; so did sarcastic comic Scoey Mitchlll. One of the acts featured on his show was a dance trio called Hines, Hines, and Dad. It was one of the earliest television appearances of young tap dancer Gregory Hines, who would have an accomplished career in musical the-ater (*Eubie!, Jelly's Last Jam*) and films (*History of the World Part I* (1981), *Running Scared* (1986), *Waiting to Exhale* (1995)).

Joining Allen regularly on the show to lead the orchestra was H.B. Barnum, best known as the pianist for doo-wop group The Coasters ("Yakkity Yak," "Charlie Brown") before later striking out on his own and, under the pseudonym Jack B. Nimble, recording the origi-nal version of the Christmas rock hit "Nut Rocker."

Barnum's presence on the program raised a few eye-brows, and Allen was quick to justify his presence if any-body dared to question the reasons. Allen told one inter-viewer, "He's not on this show as a token Negro. He's here because we have the right chemistry and he's talented and a good friend."

Allen Ludden's Gallery taped a single week of episodes as something of a preview, to

Johnny had Doc. Dave had Paul. And Allen Ludden had H.B. Barnum. FRED WOSTBROCK COLLECTION

positive reviews ("The premiere was a success and certainly no one looked as if he were straining. It was mostly nice clean fun....") But it was going to have an uphill battle to get good time slots in major markets. Merv Griffin's departure from syndication opened a ninety-minute gap and *Variety* said that for most station managers, it would be a fifty-fifty deci-sion between Allen or David Frost. Many went with David Frost.

Allen Ludden's Gallery taped at the studios of KTTV, an independent station in Los Angeles (now the city's Fox affiliate). This opened an opportunity for Betty. Producer Ralph Andrews, who had worked with Betty when she appeared on his NBC game *You Don't Say!*, had mounted a new game for the station, in hopes that it would eventually be seen nationwide. It would involve a celebrity panel, and Ralph Andrews asked Betty if she would be a regular panelist. Betty said yes.

Liars Club boiled down to a multiple-choice quiz, but one that was presented very elaborately. Each day, the panelists and contestants were shown a series of odd-looking, esoteric objects. Each of the panelist told a brief story or gave a demonstration explaining what the object

Allen, along with H.B. Barnum and his band, on *Allen Ludden's Gallery.* Allen's ambitious effort was part of a crowded field for syndication during its one-season run, and just couldn't catch a break. FRED WOSTBROCK COLLECTION

did. The contestants had to guess which one was giving the truthful explanation.

Perhaps the most noteworthy thing about *Liars Club* was its unlikely host, Rod Serling, creator and host of *The Twilight Zone* and screenwriter of *Planet of the Apes* (1968) (the film that gave Maurice Evans film immortality as Dr. Zaius). Even if the game was good — and *Liars Club* was — it seemed, to many, a baffling career move.

Director John Frankenheimer once described Serling's mindset by explaining, "He was such a dichotomy. He was an enigma. He wanted success. He wanted money. He wanted celebrity status. He wanted to be a star. And yet underneath it was this terribly honest, very gifted artist. I don't think he could ever reconcile the two driving forces of his psyche."

Rod Serling perhaps saw *Liars Club* as an opportunity to be thought of as a star, not just the man in the black suit who introduced each week's chilling tale. But as a regular panelist on *Liars Club*, Betty spotted a problem. At heart, Rod Serling was a writer and producer, not a natural television performer and certainly not one who was comfortable performing without a script. Serling would wither any time that he was told to stretch and ad-lib. On one episode, Betty and the other panelists tried to loosen him up with a prank. Rod was told to ad-lib and he attempted to make a little conversation with the panelists to fill time. But then nobody would talk. They stared at him in total silence. Serling laughed so hard that eventually, he wasn't talking either. He was laughing so hard that he couldn't say goodbye.

Deep down, though, Rod Serling was never a good fit as a game show host, and for the moment, *Liars Club* wasn't catching on with any national distributors. *Liars Club* expired after only one season on KTTV.

Down the halls at the studio complex, Allen was enthusiastic, and an enthusiastic Allen Ludden was a force to be reckoned with. Within weeks of the spring premiere *of Allen Ludden's Gallery*, Allen was pitching more new formats to Metromedia. By fall, he had produced a pilot for *The Gathering*, a talk/variety show aimed at kids, and a game show of his own creation, *Catch a Star*. The results were mixed; *The Gathering* would get a brief run in 1970, while *Catch a Star* couldn't catch a break.

And neither, unfortunately, could *Allen Ludden's Gallery*. After only one season, it was canceled in 1970. The familiar faces in talk shows — Mike Douglas, Merv Griffin, and the rest had held on, but for the most part, the newbies didn't catch a break. Tom Kennedy's talk show, the other new entry of 1969, was canceled after its first season too. But the big surprise of the year was that yet another new talk show premiered in midseason and caught on surprisingly quickly. In January 1970, a local talk show in Dayton, Ohio went into national syndication and its host, Phil Donahue, would quickly redefine the genre of daytime talk.

Allen licked his wounds and moved on, later telling interviewer Edward L. Blank, "I did a fast sixty shows for Metromedia until they ran out of money...But it was my adventure. Every game show emcee has to have an adventure to try to become a talk show host, and that was my try at it. I don't like to think of it as a failure, but it didn't work."

That Allen used that term, game show host, to refer to himself, was somewhat telling. A number of men who had done that job on television found themselves typecast and pigeonholed into it. Fearful of not being able to find more work, many game show hosts over the years steered clear of the term. Gene Rayburn of *The Match Game* always referred to himself as an actor. A few other emcees clung to the more general term "broadcaster" or, if they dared use the term "host," they'd keep it a little broad by saying "television host."

Owing to the tremendous success that his two games had, and owing in part to the tremendous personal pride that Allen felt for both programs, he never felt any reservation about calling himself "game show host."

Beyond *Allen Ludden's Gallery*, there was another television show that met its demise in 1970. On June 14, *G.E. College Bowl* with Robert Earle came to an end after eleven years on television. The end of the venerable series triggered an unusually edgy response from Allen, who let some hard feelings come to the surface during an interview with Edward L. Blank.

He had harsh words for G.E.'s role in his departure: "The sponsor of *College Bowl* got edgy, to my surprise. They'd been used to being my sole owner, and they hadn't liked my *Password* activities anyway."

For the first time, he publicly took full credit for the show: "Ah, that game was my baby…I made it up in my backyard at Hartford. I did it on radio, I did it as a TV pilot…later we sold it to a sponsor."

And while he respected Robert Earle's talents as an emcee, Allen was skeptical of how he got hired to begin with. When asked if Earle had been hired because he looked like Allen, Allen replied, "It sounds immodest, but yes. He was in Syracuse, and at parties he used to do an imitation of me. He's a very nice guy, but it was a great mistake, I think, on their part, to have him wear my style of glasses. Even as recently as last season I would be stopped by people on the street, and they'd comment about how I treated their school on the previous Sunday's show. It shows how close some people pay attention. Anyway, they changed his style of glasses to mine. He literally went to my optician and got the same frames. It was a bad mistake."

Allen was disappointed by the demise of *Allen Ludden's Gallery*, but moved forward and gave Betty a turn. 1969 had been the year that Allen devoted to his pet project. For 1970, Albets Productions would focus its energies on a pet project for Betty. And Betty, being Betty, it was literally a pet project.

Betty White adored animals. "Animal lover" almost isn't strong enough. Betty White is a woman who saw a large spider near her front door one day, named him George, and then exited the house through the back door every day for two months until George finally went away. And Allen knew from experience that any time Betty disappeared, he knew exactly where to find her. "At parties, she'll disappear and be found with the dog or cat or pet of the house."

And Allen had a ready answer when he was invariably asked if he liked animals as much as the woman he married liked them. He always said, "I'm an animal lover; I just didn't know it until I met Betty."

Early in Betty's television career, during her *Hollywood on Television* days, she had proposed a series starring herself and her dog, called *The Bandit and Me*, but the station wasn't interested. In 1970, Betty got the idea for a daily five-minute radio show where she would talk about pets and pet care. That was all the idea was supposed to be.

But in Betty's words, "I got carried away."

The idea grew more and more ambitious. Allen had watched the glut of talk shows on television, saw what they lacked, and had been driven to develop *Allen Ludden's Gallery* to fill that void. Likewise, Betty was watching television, naturally any program involving animals, and figured out what was missing from her favorite shows.

Three animal lovers, Betty (with a friend in her arms), Allen, and Mary Tyler Moore; all would be involved in Betty's new talk show, *The Pet Set*. FRED WOSTBROCK COLLECTION

She said, "Wild animal shows were popular, but I didn't see a pet show on the boards and I wondered why."

By the middle of the year, Allen Ludden had assembled a proposal for local TV stations around the country, offering them a new syndicated TV series, titled *The Pet Set*.

Betty White would be the hostess and each day, she'd interview celebrity guests…and their pets. The conversations would be entirely about the animals in the stars' lives. In addition to the celebrities, Betty would also interview people whose lines of work revolved around animals. And each day's feature attraction was "The Wild Spot," a segment in which Ralph Helfer, the operator of a wildlife preserve called Africa USA, would bring some of the exotic creatures. Seeing the animals in a peaceful environment, she hoped, would turn people away from thinking of wild creatures as curious, vicious beasts who were meant to be trophies.

She told a reporter, "The idea that someday, we might be able to see wild animals only on film from the past just terrifies me. [The biggest problem is] the shrinking natural habitat for all the animals — the chee-tahs, the gorillas…we have to work out a way to co-exist with animals."

And before long, they were in business. To entice potential sponsors that it was going to be a low-cost venture, Betty and Allen agreed that Betty herself would only have to be paid scale, the AFTRA-set minimum wage for a television performance by a union member.

"The *Pet Set* show is a labor of love for me," she pledged.

A sponsor, Carnation, agreed to fully support the entire series as a means of promoting their line of pet foods. Carnation's advertising agency selected a New York-based television distributor to pitch the series to local stations, and they orchestrated a very cushy offer for the stations. They didn't have to pay a penny for *The Pet Set*; the stations would receive the show totally free. Commercials for Carnation would already be inserted into the episodes that the station received, and the station was welcome to fill all of the remaining commercial time to local advertisers and keep all the cash for itself. More than fifty stations signed up for the new series. With low production costs for the once-a-week series, that was enough to ensure that Betty and Allen would make a tidy profit from *The Pet Set*. But interest kept growing. In a matter of weeks, the show's outreach had grown to 110 stations, and then 125.

For the show's first episode, James Brolin brought along his Harlequin Great Dane, a breed often mistaken for Dalmatians because the Harlequin Great Dane likewise has a white coat with black spots. To Betty's delight, Brolin owned Appaloosa horses that were also spotted. Because Betty rea-soned that that Great Danes were so big that there weren't very many wild animals that could top them, Betty asked Ralph Helfer to bring an elephant.

The elephant kept poking Betty with his trunk until Betty took his trunk and handed it to Brolin, saying, "It's for you."

Mary Tyler Moore, a proud owner of two poodles, came to the show bringing…one poodle. The other, she explained, was middle aged and somehow hadn't been housebroken yet. Betty introduced her other guest that day, a dog psychologist who explained that dogs of any age could be housebroken, and he elaborated, to Allen's delight, that dogs can be taught manners.

Mary's pet problem was somewhat amusing but opened the door for a logical second guest who could chat with her and describe some solutions. And that's exactly what Betty wanted *The Pet Set* to be: a subliminal education. Her thought about television, much like Allen's thought about television, was that people could learn more when information was sugarcoated just enough that they didn't realize they were being taught something. Lorne Greene brought his German shepherd so Betty could also bring out a lupine expert who brought a wolf to demonstrate the differences and similarities between dogs and wolves. Mike Connors brought a Labrador for a discussion of guide dogs and the 4-H Club members who raise them.

Some critics discerned what Betty was doing, and they loved her for it. Sue Cameron of *The Hollywood Reporter* wrote, "This new show starring Betty White will do for the pet owner what *Galloping Gourmet* has done for the cook. This is not just a 'celebrity-bring-your-pet-and-woof-into-the-camera' show. It is warm, funny, and it clicks. Within each show is an ecology message, take care of our animals, etc. Upon hearing about this show, one could think it is a corny, throwaway gimmick just to get celebrity guests, but it is not. It will prove to be an unusually fascinating and enjoyable half hour."

Betty also wanted to use the show to put a spotlight and some unsung heroes. She spotlighted the people who oversaw the rescue efforts for animals affected by natural disasters in Southern California. When raccoons had a population explosion and were becoming a problem for residential areas in Los Angeles, a team of district rangers worked out a way to have many of the raccoons airlifted and sent to areas where the raccoon population was sparser, bringing the population under control without having to kill any raccoons. Betty welcomed the rangers who discussed how they organized the efforts.

It was fascinating and enjoyable for the hostess as well as the viewers. For some more elaborate segments, Betty and a camera crew would leave the studio and film animals on location. Doris Day, who rarely appeared on television aside from her own programs, agreed to a special interview on location when Betty and *The Pet Set* covered Day's dedication of a Fund for Animals booth at the Lion Country Safari.

But the remote excursion that stood out for Betty was the one that took her away from land and onto the water. For one broadcast, they rented a boat and went to the Santa Barbara channel island, which had become a popular breeding area for seals. After they got their footage film, the boat's journey was disrupted by a school of whales migrating south, and the camera crew hastily got all of their equipment back out and filmed it. Amazed by the luck they had, Betty and the crew began discussing how to assemble the whale footage and make use of it for a future show. Betty and one cameraman checked the water once, looking for any whales that may have been lagging. They didn't see whales...they saw dolphins. Lots of them. They had the boat totally surrounded and playfully leapt out of the water as if they were greeting the visitors. And they kept popping up. Betty studied the water closely found that for every dolphin coming to the surface, there looked to be at least ten underneath. The cameramen kept rolling the forage, amazed by the sheer number that they were seeing. When they finally had a chance to review the footage and make an attempt at getting a better estimate, they figured that there had been at least two thousand in the channel.

Betty was so committed to the show that she served as her own research department and began more and more frequently contacting a group called the Morris Animal Foundation to do fact-checking for some segments. She got to know the foundation well, and before long, she became a member and a trustee. Betty's love of animals also led the American Humane Society to appoint her National Kindness Chairman for its annual Be Kind to Animals Week.

Allen was the show's executive producer, and to reduce production costs, he also served as announcer. But as executive producer, he experienced some stressful days that most other Hollywood producers would never endure. When a guest was booked and the taping date was confirmed, Betty and Allen would ask them to come to the Albets offices for a pre-interview. One guest opened the backseat of a Lincoln Town Car and out walked a twenty-six-inch tall horse. Not a pony — just a very tiny horse. But Allen's least favorite day on the job was a day that a five-hundred-pound Bengal tiger walked down the hallway, straight into his office. The tiger was so big that he jumped up on his hind legs at one point and touched the ceiling, then hopped up on Allen's desk and sat down.

As much as Betty loved animals, one of the treats of the series was seeing how much they loved her back. A buffalo stayed completely still while Betty climbed on top, and then took her for a little ride around the study. Lions, tigers, and that 500-pound Bengal were all reduced to pussycats when they sat with Betty, cuddling against her as she wrapped her arms around each of them.

For one *Pet Set* program, Betty received a visitor named Major, a 600-pound lion. The lion sprawled across her lap, pinning her down. Betty was trapped. Fear didn't even occur to her. She began laughing because of how cute the lion looked. Major sensed that Betty was happy, and more importantly, sensed that his own behavior was making this little human laugh. So he hammed it up, stretching out his paws, rolling over, and trapping Betty even further, which only made her laugh harder.

Animal affection for Betty wasn't a new sight for Allen. For a time, he and Betty belonged to a country club. The drive there was rather scenic, and among other sites, they would pass a large farm owned by the Rockefeller family, with a large number of cattle grazing through the vast pastures.

On the drive to the country club one day, Betty abruptly said, "You never let me talk to these cattle."

Allen thought she was kidding and kept driving. The next time they passed by, Betty said, "You still never let me talk to these cattle."

Allen pulled over and stopped the car. Betty got out of the car and walked up to the fence. The nearest cow was about fifty feet away, but Betty began talking to it. After about ten minutes, Betty had an audience of 200 Black Angus cattle standing at the fence, hanging onto her every word.

But Allen was always eager to show Betty that humans loved her too. For Betty's 49th birthday, Allen casually suggested a night at an upscale restaurant, with just the two of them plus Betty's mother. Allen bought Betty a nice new dress to wear for the evening. Allen coaxed Betty up to the second floor of the restaurant, and from seemingly every corner of the room emerged Betty's friends: Mary Tyler Moore, Grant Tinker, Lorne and Nancy Greene, Michael and Marjorie Landon, Eve Arden, Brooks West, Ross and Olavee Martin, and Jim and Henny Backus.

Allen had put together the bash for her 49th birthday because he knew she was expecting something big for her 50th birthday and wouldn't be expecting anything for the 49th. And he bought her the dress so she'd have something that she wouldn't mind being surprised in.

Betty had a lot of human friends, and as Allen found when he was trying to get his *Gallery* off the ground, many of them were perfectly happy to drop by and lend support for a new endeavor. Many personal friends and many former *Password* opponents came to *The Pet Set* with the creatures in their lives. Carol Burnett brought her dog. Barbara Feldon brought her Siamese cat. Peter Lawford brought Blackie, the dog given to him by President Kennedy. Lorne Greene brought his Labrador. Jimmy and Gloria Stewart came with the Irish setter whose death a decade later would inspire Jimmy to write an unforgettable poem that he recited on *The Tonight Show*, bringing Johnny Carson to tears. Paul Lynde brought Harry McAfee, the pampered dog that he had named after his own character in *Bye Bye Birdie*. Rod Serling from *The Liars Club* brought his Irish setter. Amanda Blake brought her three falcons and two poodles

Allen and Betty could never get too far away from game shows. Here they play the syndicated game *It's Your Bet*. Allen is hearing a trivia question on the telephone and has to predict if Betty will know the correct answer. FRED WOSTBROCK COLLECTION

and explained how they coexisted. Shirley Jones brought a menagerie: two rabbits, two turtles, a lizard, and a miniature schnauzer.

The lizard and the falcons were as exotic as it got. Hollywood has had its fair share of celebrities who kept wild animals as pets, but Betty made it clear that, while her show would have wild animals from Africa USA, and it would have pets, she would never showcase wild animals kept as pets. She found it offensive.

She said, "I'm against anyone keeping exotic or wild animals in their home under the pretext of having pets. They just want to draw attention to themselves."

And the show certainly didn't miss anything by not showcasing animals who were being treated as status symbols. If the pets weren't always colorful, the conversations would be. Such was the case when Nancy Kulp brought her dog on the show and suddenly had doubts about how to talk about her.

> NANCY KULP: She's a greyhound bitch. Can I use that word on this show?
> BETTY: Yes. "Greyhound" is a perfectly acceptable word.

By early 1971, there were big plans coming together among Allen's ex-bosses. Mark Goodson and Bill Todman had lean years after the end of *Password* in 1967. For a spell in 1968, they only had two shows in production, *The Match Game* and *Snap Judgment*. But Goodson-Todman turned things around by exploring first-run syndication for the first time. They mounted a new production of *What's My Line?* to air five days a week, and it saved the company. Goodson-Todman, always on the lookout for new ideas, began looking at the shows that had already come and gone as a possible source of new fortunes. The following year, they introduced three more game shows for first-run syndication: revivals of *To Tell the Truth* and *Beat the Clock*, plus *He Said, She Said*, a new game played by celebrity couples (and of course, Allen and Betty flew back to New York to appear as guests).

And by 1971, Goodson-Todman, a company staffed largely by employees who were New Yorkers down to the bone, finally went bi-coastal, setting up a second office complex on Sunset Boulevard in Hollywood. And it was the right move at the right time because ABC was looking for a new series.

The network had introduced a wildly successful soap opera, *Dark Shadows*, in 1966, which tackled totally new subject matter for soap operas. It was a rare science fiction soap opera with gothic overtones. Its characters included vampires, zombies, werewolves, and monsters. The show reached its peak in 1969 with a series of storylines based on 19th century literature but was never able to top it in terms of creativity or popularity. ABC was ready to cancel *Dark Shadows* in 1971, a decision wildly protested by viewers but surprisingly fully supported by the show's own creator, who felt like the idea well had run dry.

In February 1971, rumors were rumbling in the press that ABC was considering replacing it with a game show. One executive determined that there was a fairly obvious answer for "Which game show?"

For the past several years, ABC had a process of screening pilots for game shows that they were considering adding to their schedule. They would show the pilot to a focus group and then give members of the group a questionnaire about how they felt about what they watched.

One of the questions was "How does it stand up to *Password*?" And when the subject of a new game show was brought up in meetings, that same executive made a fairly reasonable point. If the network had determined what game show, above all others, was the gold standard, why not air the gold standard instead of trying something else?

By the end of the month, it had been confirmed: *Password* was going back into production. After more than three years, the reruns of *Password* were still delivering good results. In many cities, the reruns scored higher ratings in direct competition with newer programming. And Milton Bradley sales figures suggested that the interest for a *Password* game was still out there. A few months earlier, the company released its *Password 9th Edition* home game, churning them out year after year because there was no reason to stop. Sales figures in the toy industry showed that the *Password* home game was America's second best-selling board game. No shame being in second place when number one was Monopoly. As game shows go, the data was there to prove that viewers loved the game and the show. ABC closed the deal with Goodson-Todman.

ABC was an interesting home for *Password* because of the company it would keep by being on the daytime line-up. They would now be joining *The Newlywed Game*, the very show that had triggered the demise of *Password*. It would also be sharing a network with *Let's Make a Deal*, hosted by Monty Hall, the man who would always maintain that he was *Password*'s true creator. And who would be hosting this new version of *Password*?

Who else?

FRED WOSTBROCK COLLECTION

CHAPTER SEVENTEEN

"NEW"

"From Hollywood…the word game of the stars: PASSWORD!*"*

What viewers saw on Monday, April 5, 1971, was so familiar, yet so different. The low-frills, cozy set of the 1960s had been replaced by a decidedly more "game show-y" stage. Strings of lights framed various pieces of a colossal arrangement of hexagons, with orange, red, yellow, beige, and a splash of pink giving the set color. The celebrity guests entered from two massive swinging doors that hugged the set. The name *Password* was spelled out twice: A sign made of light bulbs hung behind the desk, and then a much larger, darker "PASSWORD" loomed over the entire set, almost literally casting a shadow over the proceedings. The swingin' brass band tune that audiences had heard year in and year out was replaced by a finger-popping synthesizer piece.

Any viewer who saw the first few seconds of the ABC version of *Password* could be forgiven for initially sighing and saying, "Oh, this is going to be very different from the show that I used to like."

And then those giant swinging doors opened one time, and out walked the same well-pressed jacket and pants with the razor sharp crease, the head of white hair contrasting the thick black horn-rimmed frames, and the warm, familiar smile and "favorite teacher" demeanor, and those same viewers instantly knew that there was no reason to worry. *Password* was back, and so was Allen Ludden.

Allen laid down only one condition for coming aboard to host the new version, one that Goodson-Todman cheerfully obliged. They had to pull the syndicated reruns of the CBS version immediately. He admitted to several interviewers that in truth, it was a matter of vanity. Men's hairstyles had changed in the past few years, and Allen admitted that it was now a little embarrassing to see himself with the brush cut that he had sported on CBS. Having secured Goodson-Todman's word that the reruns were going away, Allen agreed to be the show's host once again.

The word "host" was an important distinction there. If he had been introduced as "the star of *Password*" at the top of the program, no viewer would bat an eye. He was, wasn't he?

Allen didn't think so. At his own insistence, he was always introduced as "the host of *Password*," never the star. He told a reporter, "We don't say '*Password* starring Allen Ludden.' It's not *The Allen Ludden Show*. I'm just

Feels like old times. Allen is back at the helm of *Password*, with old friend Peter Lawford and new friend Burt Reynolds. FRED WOSTBROCK COLLECTION

the host, the servant to the game. The camera belongs to the contestants. I get few close-ups and that's the way it should be."

To a viewer today, the idea that an old favorite is coming back for a new run can be exciting, but it's certainly not unheard of. To put this in perspective, Goodson-Todman's previous revivals to this point had been syndicated properties, the efforts of salesmen pitching their wares to local stations convincing them for a spot on the schedule. And game shows in the past had been revived again and again. *Mike Stokey's Pantomime Quiz*, for example, had been a perennial hole-filler for the major networks, sitting on the sidelines every year and brought back on the air any time a network needed a replacement for whatever had just been canceled. But it was almost never treated as anything more than a stopgap.

But, Allen explained, "It so happens that *Password* is something special, the Tiffany's in game shows."

The revival of *Password* on ABC was a different case. A major network was giving its full support to a game show, with the full expectation that it would be an enduring hit. *Password* wasn't coming back to fill a gap. It was coming back because ABC believed it was the best programming

The other queen of *Password*, Elizabeth Montgomery. AUTHOR'S
COLLECTION

they could ask for. And in 1971, that was unheard-of for a network daytime game show.

Allen told a reporter, "I'm sure the show has at least another ten years to run. It wears well, and that's half the battle. After the show left the air in first-runs, I did eighteen pilots for other game shows, but none measured up to *Password*. I love the show, and it likes me. We'll always be a pair."

The funny thing is, for a man who had originally set his sights on spending life in the theater, Allen explained that he liked *Password* for the reason that it was so real. He said, "Except for Archie Bunker looking you in the eye Saturday nights, the game shows are the only thing that don't try to get to you through the restrictions of the old proscenium arch."

And as much as he once had worried about what hosting a game show would do for his image, he was proud of the image that *Password* had given him. *Password* was an intelligent show. There was one other reason he liked it: the home game sold well. Allen actually didn't see a penny of the revenue from the *Password* home game; he admitted in one interview that he wished Milton Bradley would put his picture on the box, but it didn't bother him enough that he felt compelled to actually do anything about it. But he liked that the home game sold well to families. Kids were left out when adults played trivia games or games with complex strategies, but when parents, teenagers, and grade school-age kids sat down at the table to play *Password*, they were on even footing.

From a practical standpoint, the job still made perfect sense for him. Allen had spread his wings as a programming developer and producer in recent years, and with *Password* taping five episodes every Saturday, he had amazing flexibility in the rest of his life. He was free to develop, produce, and pitch other products, or give himself a few days off.

Kicking off the series with Allen were two of ABC's brightest stars, Bill Bixby (*The Courtship of Eddie's Father*) and Elizabeth Montgomery (*Bewitched*). Despite Betty being inarguably the star most associated with *Password*, Elizabeth Montgomery was such a strong player that it earned her a moniker of respect from the host.

Television historian Monika Cotrill told author Herbie J. Pilato, "Liz may not have always applied herself in school, but her sharp wit, clever mind, and competitive spirit are all clearly evident in her game show appearances. *Password* seemed to have a special place in her heart, as she appeared as a contestant many times…She seemed to have a special rapport with host Allen Ludden, who referred to her as the 'Queen of *Password*' on more than one occasion. When she is giving clues or receiving them, Liz gives her all. She seems at ease with the others on the panel, famous and non-famous alike, but when the game starts, she steels herself as if she is ready to assume a runner's starting position. She [delivers] the one-word clues in rapid-fire succession, and is the first to laugh at herself if she makes a mistake. Her sense of humor is firmly intact."

Game show historian Fred Wostbrock added for Pilato, "She did very few other game shows, but she was a fan of *Password*. *Password* was not an easy game. No script. No acting. No stunts. It required pure brain power… She took the game seriously; very seriously…She was real. That's what made her a great *Password* player."

Bixby and Montgomery dueled through the entire week as Allen walked them through a game that was nearly the same as the show that audiences had loved in the 1960s. Goodson-Todman had, however, added what Allen called "subtle extensions."

The program had a new announcer, John Harlan. Reason A. Goodwin remained in New York, and the show hired a new judge, Dr. Robert Stockwell, UCLA Professor of Linguistics whose services were provided by Funk & Wagnall's Standard College Dictionary.

The value of the password still started at ten points, with one point disappearing for every wrong guess. On ABC's *Password*, they no longer let the value dwindle down to nothing. If the word wasn't guessed at the five-point mark after six clues, the word was thrown out.

The show found a way to infuse strategy. On each password, the player who had the right to give the first clue was now given an option to "pass or play." If they chose to pass, the opposing team went first for ten points. If a clue-giver saw a difficult password, they could pass; it would mean sacrificing the shot at ten points, but now that player could give the second clue in hopes that it would be enough information to win nine points.

The Lightning Round was still played for fifty dollars a word for up to five words, but was now followed by a new feature, the Betting Word. The contestant was shown a single word and had fifteen seconds to convey that word to the celebrity partner. Before the clock started ticking, the contestant had to wager all or part of the money won in the Lightning Round.

And on the old *Password*, contestants played two games, one with each of the celebrity guests. On the new *Password*, a winner stayed and kept playing and playing and playing, as many games as possible, through a maximum of ten episodes. The game moved so quickly that most episodes had at least two complete games and some crammed in three or four, which meant that even with the same modest stakes up for grabs as the original show, a contestant on ABC's *Password* could amass a small fortune.

And a new director, Stuart W. Phelps, turned the show into a more elaborate production. Throughout the run of the 1960s version, Allen and the show's staff had talked about the way that the game put its celebrity guests through the emotional ringer: the pressure of thinking of the perfect clue, the pained confusion of trying to decipher a clue that didn't make enough sense, the joyful release when the password was

All bets are on Betty as she battles with the new Betting Word feature on *Password.* FRED WOSTBROCK COLLECTION

guessed correctly. Phelps maneuvered the cameras to different angles, using zooms and close-ups to capture those high-pressure moments.

Allen himself looked a bit newer on ABC's version of *Password.* Years ago, in *Plain Talk for Men Under 21*, he laid out basic rules for suits: stick with traditional styles and don't give into fads; don't buy a suit with out of the ordinary characteristics; only wear a white button-down shirt with a suit; and always wear a tie, either solid color or a tasteful stripe.

But in the 1970s on *Password,* Allen's wardrobe became more of a pallet. He wore beige or blue button-down shirts. Sometimes, he didn't bother with a tie, leaving the collar unbuttoned and wearing a decorative gold chain around his neck. He wore leisure suits, sometimes with a butterfly collar and sometimes with a turtleneck. He would wear denim jackets or sometimes, a traditional tie, shirt, and slacks, but with a distinctive safari-style bush jacket. Allen had never engaged in the common television practice of having a clothier supply a full wardrobe in exchange for a mention in the closing credits. He always selected and purchased his own outfits, and he suddenly felt very experimental.

Allen would forgo the necktie quite often on the new *Password*, sporting the 70s-trendy ascot. The guests this week are Sheila MacRae and Adam West. FRED WOSTBROCK COLLECTION

ABC put the show in a late afternoon slot, 4:00 p.m., and after the first few weeks of *Password*'s new run, it was very apparent that it had instantly become an after-school ritual for kids. The game was easy to follow, it moved rather quickly, and Stuart Phelps gave the show a dramatic flavor that didn't overshadow the natural humor that the game often created.

Allen said, "Now they say young people don't watch game shows… the truth is that young people don't watch TV regularly — but the challenge, the learning process with words in *Password* is something they do respond to."

In another interview, he elaborated, "The young people like the suspense of the game, they enjoy competing along with the players, and although they may not like to admit it, the program does increase their knowledge of vocabulary."

And after a decade of the CBS series and the syndicated reruns, *Password* was such an institution that it managed to lasso in more and more big stars. Playing *Password* well was a badge of honor in Hollywood, and stars like Henry Fonda, Burt Reynolds, Carol Burnett, Mary Tyler

...And sometimes Allen didn't even bother with the ascot either. Here, he does the unthinkable, hosting a game show with an open collar, with guests Pat Carroll and Mel Tormé. FRED WOSTBROCK COLLECTION

Moore, Johnny Mathis, Carl Reiner, Adam West, John Forsythe, Rod Serling, and many more wanted their turn at showing off.

Didn't anybody ever say no? Of course, Allen said. "The only ones who don't want to play *Password* are the papier-mâché people, the stars put together by the press agency…they can't say 'hello' without a script."

Despite the young audience the show had attracted, ABC moved *Password* after only six months, switching it to 12:30 p.m. and then moving it again to noon, where it aired in direct competition with the original *Jeopardy!* starring Art Fleming.

The *Jeopardy!* time slot switch was the first time that Allen seemed concerned about the future of the program. One reporter noted that when the impending switch to the noon slot was brought up during an interview, Allen became visibly edgy. Putting it against *Jeopardy!* was not a particularly ideal move because both shows had very similar fan bases; both were game shows with large followings among people who didn't typically like game shows. To entice viewers to follow the show to its new slot, *Password* held a tournament of champions, with two top stars who were also top game players: Elizabeth Montgomery and Carol Burnett. They were joined by the eight top money winners of *Password*'s first year on ABC, with the winner of the tournament collecting a $5,000 grand prize.

Password survived in the noon time slot, but not as well as they had hoped. The audiences for *Password* and *Jeopardy!* had a big overlap; viewers were split and both shows suffered in the ratings when they aired against each other. But ABC stuck to their decision and *Password* remained firmly in place at noon.

Allen and Betty suffered some professional setbacks. Carnation had re-evaluated their advertising budget for the upcoming year and decided only to advertise on television through the purchase of individual spots, and no longer provide full sponsorship and backing for programs. Since Carnation had totally overseen the production and distribution of *The Pet Set*, this decision doomed the series, and Betty's dream project ended after only one season.

Allen, meanwhile, had developed a game show format that he called *Look Who's Talking*. A pilot was shot that didn't air, but found its way into gossip columns because of the unexpectedly heated turn that the game took. It was a celebrity game like *Password*, and for the pilot, Allen booked Burt Reynolds and former game show model Joanne Carson. Joanne had recently filed for divorce from Johnny Carson and Reynolds, a friend of Johnny, took several opportunities to bring up the divorce during the game, with the conversation turning so ugly that Joanne nearly walked off the set.

David, Martha, and Sarah had all grown up and moved out — David was at University of Pennsylvania working on his master's degree; he would remain at the university and ultimately become a tenured professor; he later became Professor Emeritus of History at New York University. Martha got married, eventually got a law degree, and worked with the handicapped. Sarah became a martial arts instructor, moved to Chicago,

Allen gets extra casual with a denim and turtleneck combo. After years of advocating for conventional, conservative styles of men's wear, Allen's wardrobe on the ABC version of *Password* became a daily experiment. FRED WOSTBROCK COLLECTION

and helped her partner (ultimately, her wife) open a self-defense training center for women and children.

Although the three kids were gone, the Ludden house was hardly an empty nest. Willie and Emma, the poodles Allen got to grab Betty's attention, were still there, along with a parakeet and two other dogs, another poodle plus a waif that Betty took in when she saw it being dumped out of a van on Sunset Boulevard. (They named the waif Sooner because Betty said she'd sooner bring him home than leave him out there.) Indoors, Allen and Betty played parlor games.

Betty, in her free time, continued working as an advocate for animals, serving as honorary chairman for National Dog Week and giving numerous interviews about dog rearing. Like her husband's approach to teenagers, Betty the dog lover believed in plain talk.

She said, "I don't believe in darling dog talk. Dogs understand if you explain things to them. Even a young puppy catches on to a firm 'no' and a happy 'Come here' if you are consistent."

1971 proved to be an interesting year for game shows, for reasons besides the return of *Password*. The FCC, in the wake of some impressive lobbying from Goodson-Todman Productions Executive Vice President Jerry Chester, imposed a ruling that the major television networks could no longer start their prime-time line-ups at 7:30 p.m. Eastern. They had to wait until 8:00 p.m. and give that extra half-hour back to local stations, theoretically for local programming. Since most local stations didn't have the resources to produce prime-time caliber programs, most stations instead looked toward syndicated programming to fill those gaps. As a result, once-a-week game shows were suddenly back in prime-time. Almost overnight, the 7:30 p.m. (or 6:30) time slot in stations across the country were suddenly filled with shows like *Beat the Clock*, *To Tell the Truth*, *What's My Line?* and *Truth or Consequences*. Many new titles came onto the scene, too. *Celebrity Bowling*, *Sports Challenge*, *All About Faces*, *Anything You Can Do*, and nighttime versions of the daytime staples *Let's Make a Deal* and *The Hollywood Squares* all emerged in 1971.

The genre was suddenly "in" again, and the timing was perfect, because in 1972, CBS programming executive Bud Grant decided his network's daytime line-up needed a facelift. The network drifted through daytime with reruns of the prime-time shows, and Grant thought it was time to revive the schedule with a block of game shows. On September 4, 1972, CBS unveiled three new game shows. One was *Gambit*, with host Wink Martindale. Another was *The Joker's Wild*, which Jack Barry not only managed to finally sell after four years, but CBS reluctantly allowed him to host, ending his exile from television once and for all. The third was *The New Price is Right* with Bob Barker. Like they had done with *Password*, Goodson-Todman took a previous property, moved it to Hollywood and gave it a glitzy, faster-paced and more exciting makeover.

Password was still in business over at ABC as part of that network's own blockbuster line-up of five VERY different games, along with *Split Second*, *Let's Make a Deal*, *The Dating Game* and *The Newlywed Game*. Allen and *Password* continued to thrive thanks to a simple game (game show history reveals a noticeable inverse relationship between complexity and popularity) that presented a deceptively strong level of challenge and thought, as well as flat-out entertainment. As usual, the game seemed to bring out a competitive streak among its celebrity guests. But it was one particularly fierce week of competitive spirits that wound up securing *Password*'s spot in pop culture history.

For the week of August 28-September 1, 1972, *Password* welcomed Betty White and Tony Randall. Randall, who had never been one to hold

Allen with friend Tom Kennedy. Their respective ABC shows, *Password* and *Split Second*, were part of one of the strongest game show line-ups ever on daytime TV. FRED WOSTBROCK COLLECTION

back hubris, had a conversation with Allen in his dressing room before the taping and made a bold proclamation.

"Allen, I am I superb *Password* player," Randall declared. "No one can beat me."

Allen laughed at him and said, "Betty is the best player we've ever used; you'll have to be perfect to top her."

Tony reacted with what Allen described as a condescending smile, and walked out of the dressing room headed for the stage. And then Betty absolutely wiped the floor with him for five straight episodes.

Rather than having his pride wounded, Randall found quite a bit of humor in his own arrogance and how soundly he was defeated. Randall's character on *The Odd Couple*, fussy Felix Unger, was not so far removed from his true personality, so he went to the producers of *The Odd Couple* and suggested an episode based on his experience.

The Odd Couple revolved around Tony's character, Felix Unger, a fastidious photographer prone to being too smart for his own good; and Jack Klugman's character Oscar Madison, a slobby, street-smart sportswriter. After both men are divorced, they share an apartment in New York and have to co-exist despite having almost no common ground. To put those two into a game of word association was a natural clash of styles, which is why the episode works so well. Two men who are never on the same wavelength played *Password*, a game that required them to think alike. The writer who penned the episode: Frank Buxton, former host of *Get the Message*.

Buxton explains, "I had done *The Bill Cosby Radio Program*, which nobody has ever heard of, but it lasted for two years and it was a nice gig. Then I did *Children's Letters to God* with Gene Kelly, and through that, I got to know Lee Mendelson, who was known for the Charlie Brown specials, and we collaborated on *Hot Dog*, a children's show that was co-hosted by Jonathan Winters, Woody Allen, and Jo Anne Worley. It was a show where we demonstrated how people do things, or how certain objects were made. *Hot Dog* wrapped up after one season and my agents, Jack Rollins and Charlie Joffee were managing Ted Bessell, an actor who had just been hired to star in a series called *Me and the Chimp*. Funny thing — that show was supposed to be called *The Chimp and I*, but Ted said he would only do it if the title got changed to *Me and the Chimp*. Now, *Me and the Chimp* didn't last long, but I impressed Garry Marshall, who had created the program. He said of me, and this is a very Garry thing to say, 'He is not without talent.'

"I did story editing for *Love, American Style* for a little while, and then there was some sort of personnel upheaval at *The Odd Couple*, which was not uncommon for that show, and Garry Marshall brought me aboard as 'executive story editor,' or some other stupid no-meaning job title. But I was pretty much a producer."

As the episode begins, Felix and Oscar are on a double date when Allen and Betty walk into a restaurant. Allen promptly recognizes Oscar ("my favorite sportswriter") and explains that *Password* is looking for celebrity guests to join them for a special New York week. Oscar declines, to the dismay of Felix, who is obsessed with *Password* but didn't get picked when he tried out to be a contestant.

"I gave a powerful audition!" Felix laments.

Felix talks Oscar into appearing on the show after Oscar learns that the celebrity guests are paid $750 for an appearance. Felix sets up a practice game for Oscar, which proves to be a disaster; Oscar's girlfriend gives terrible clues because she doesn't know the difference between "Aquarium" and "Aquarius."

Buxton says, "It wasn't just the story that was based on Tony's real

Allen tries to extend an invitation to Oscar Madison to join *Password* as a celebrity guest, but he's forced to deal with Felix Unger, in this scene from the ABC sitcom *The Odd Couple,* with Jack Klugman and Tony Randall. AUTHOR'S COLLECTION

experience with *Password.* The attitudes of the characters were very much drawn from real life. Tony and Jack both did game shows. Tony loved doing game shows. Jack always felt uncomfortable and nervous about them. And so we reflected that with the way that Felix and Oscar reacted to the offer to be on *Password.*"

The day of taping rolls around and the roommates — reluctant Oscar and eager Felix — take to the stage to square off against Betty White and her partner.

Buxton says, "Allen and Betty were both great. We didn't want to waste the effort of writing the episode if they weren't interested; there was no way to do a *Password*-centric episode without them, obviously, and we were very grateful. They agreed to do the episode before we had written the script. Betty White, I had worked with once before. I lived in Australia for a little while, playing Dick Van Dyke's role in the Australian production of *Bye Bye Birdie*. And while I was there, I was booked to be a celebrity guest on a game show down there. I remember nothing about it except that Betty was also on the program — I have no idea why she was even in Australia — and at one point, I misspoke, and Betty says 'The only time Frank opens his mouth is to put his foot in it.' I thought that was a great line!

"Allen and Betty were both total pros. They walked in on day one with their lines already memorized. They were playing themselves so preparing for the show hadn't been a big process, exactly for them, but I think Allen liked stepping out of the game show host mold and being able to act just a little bit."

Not just Allen. Betty hadn't been on a sitcom set since *Date with the Angels* was canceled. And when she arrived for the script read-through on the first day of rehearsals for *The Odd Couple*, Allen immediately sensed a change in his wife.

That night, Allen told her, "When you walked into the studio, it was like coming to work with an old fire horse. All of a sudden, your ears perked up, you smelled the smoke, and it was like you were back home."

ALLEN: Thank you and welcome back. We have some new players who are going to challenge our winning team of Betty White and Millicent Thomas. First, our good friend from the New York Herald, sportswriter Oscar Madison.

(Applause. Oscar enters and sits to Allen's left.)

ALLEN *(cont'd):* You nervous?

OSCAR: No. Hi, Betty White! *(As he waves, he knocks over the microphone)*

ALLEN: Welcome to *Password*, Oscar.

OSCAR: Thank you. It's nice to be here. I think.

ALLEN: As you know, for this special series of *Password* games, we've allowed the celebrity guests to pick their own partners. Who is your partner going to be?

OSCAR: My partner is Felix Unger.

(Applause. Felix enters and sits to Oscar's left.)

FELIX *(Sotto to Oscar):* That wasn't much of an introduction.

OSCAR *(Sotto):* What do you want, a testimonial?

Allen Ludden as Himself, on *The Odd Couple*. AUTHOR'S COLLECTION

ALLEN: Welcome to *Password*, Felix. Tell us a little about yourself.

FELIX: Thank you, Allen — Well, Allen…I'm a commercial photographer, portraits a specialty. I was married but I'm not now, although I wish I were. I have two wonderful children; Edna and Leonard.

OSCAR: A little about yourself.

FELIX *(Goes on):* I'm an excellent cook and they tell me I'm a lot of fun at parties, Allen…

ALLEN *(Interrupting):* Sounds like you lead a full rich life. Let's play *Password*. Ready? I give the password to Oscar Madison and Betty White — as they look at it, we want you to see it at home…

ANNOUNCER *(Sotto):* The password is "Gravy."

Frank Buxton says, "That's me playing the announcer in the episode, by the way. I had my Screen Actors' Guild membership and we needed somebody to play the announcer, so why not me?"

ALLEN: Betty, you have the option. Pass or play.

BETTY: I'll play. "Sauce."

MILLICENT: "Mayonnaise."

ALLEN: Nine points. Oscar?

OSCAR: "Meat."

FELIX: "Lincoln."

ALLEN: Eight points. Betty?

BETTY: "Covering."

MILLICENT: "Gravy."

(Applause.)

ALLEN: Eight points. Very good.

OSCAR *(Sotto to Felix):* Lincoln?

FELIX: It's a historical fact that Lincoln loved mayonnaise.

OSCAR: Felix!

ALLEN: Here's the next password. This time it goes to Felix and to Millicent and as they look at it we want you to see it at home.

ANNOUNCER *(Sotto):* The password is "Bird."

ALLEN: Felix, you have the option.

FELIX: I'll play. "Aristophanes."

OSCAR: Aristophanes? Uh…"Greek"?

ALLEN: Nine points. Millicent?

MILLICENT: "Canary."

BETTY: "Bird."

(Applause.)

ALLEN: Nine points. Very good. We'll have our next password in a minute, after these messages. *(Turns to Felix)* Aristophanes?

FELIX: That was a perfect clue. Aristophanes wrote a play called "The Birds." Everybody knows that.

OSCAR: Everybody but me. Felix, try to be a little less perfect, will you? It's embarrassing. I'd like to win a little here.

FELIX: Me, too, fella. Why do you think I'm giving these great clues?

OSCAR: Great clues? If Charlie Chan got clues like this, he'd be running a laundry. We're losing seventeen to nothing.

FELIX: It's okay, it's okay. I always win when I play at home.

OSCAR: Felix, this is the real thing. The big time. You're not playing at home now. We're here in front of millions of people and I want to look good. Give me something to work with. Let's go!

FELIX: That's the spirit! I knew you could do it.

OSCAR: No more Greek clues. Aristophanes is ridiculous!

ANNOUNCER: Stand by!

ALLEN: And here we are back at *Password* with the score seventeen to nothing. Betty's team could win on this password. I will give it to Oscar and to Betty.

ANNOUNCER *(Sotto):* The password is "Ridiculous."

"Aristophanes?!" AUTHOR'S COLLECTION

ALLEN: Oscar, it's your option this time.

OSCAR: I'll play. *(Sotto)* Come on, Felix. *(Aloud)* "Aristophanes."

FELIX: "Ridiculous."

(Applause.)

ALLEN *(Puzzled):* Aristophanes again?

FELIX *(Excited):* Yeah. It's our all-purpose clue.

OSCAR *(Excited):* Atta babe! Now we're cooking.

Frank Buxton says, "I'm pretty proud of the Aristophanes joke. I think stuff like that is better than a 'Why, you, I oughta…' joke. The follow-up gag about 'Ridiculous' actually came from a reaction from one of the other writers when they read the script the first time. A writer blurted out 'Aristophanes? That's ridiculous!' And we made that the next password."

ALLEN: So it's seventeen points for Betty and Millicent and ten points for Oscar and Felix. Here's the next password. To Felix and Millicent.

ANNOUNCER *(Sotto):* The password is "servant."

ALLEN: Felix, you have the option. Pass or play.

FELIX: I pass, Allen.

ALLEN: Millicent…

MILLICENT: "Waiter."

(Oscar reacts.)

BETTY: "Waitress."

ALLEN: Nine points. Felix?

FELIX *(Sotto):* Think, Oscar, think. *(Aloud)* "Household."

OSCAR: "Servant."

(Applause.)

FELIX: Good, Oscar!

OSCAR: Great clue, buddy!

ALLEN: Okay. The score is nineteen to seventeen. Oscar and Felix ahead. This password could win the game.

ANNOUNCER *(Sotto):* The password is "Pencil."

ALLEN: Betty, you're behind. It's your option. Pass or play.

BETTY: Pass.

ALLEN: Oscar?

OSCAR: I'll play. *(Sotto)* This is it. *(Aloud)* "Lead."

FELIX: "Graphite."

OSCAR: That wasn't it.

ALLEN: Nine points…and possibility of winning. Betty?

BETTY: "Writing."

MILLICENT: "Pencil."

(Applause.)

ALLEN: And you win the game!

Frank Buxton says, "It was important for them to lose the game. If they had won, it's a feel-good moment but it isn't funny. Felix's reaction to losing is one of the best parts of that episode."

ALLEN: And we say goodbye to Felix Unger with many thanks for playing our game.

FELIX: Why?

ALLEN: Because you lost.

FELIX: Wait! My clue was perfect. I can prove it.

ALLEN: Sorry, but we're going to have to go to our next player. Of course, you get a copy of our home game.

FELIX: I already have two home games. I've got one in my car. I'm a sensational player. I don't understand this.

OSCAR: There's nothing to understand. You lost.

FELIX: But I should win. It's not fair. Oscar's clues are misleading. He should lose.

ALLEN *(Going right on):* Thanks for being a terrific sport, Felix Unger. And here to take your place is our next contestant, Julie Robbins.

(Applause. Felix hasn't budged from his seat. Julie Robbins comes in and stands next to Felix's chair.)

FELIX: You can't do this. My lifelong dream is to play *Password* and I'm not leaving.

OSCAR: Felix, get off the stage.

ALLEN: Thanks again, Felix Unger. Now if you'll just relinquish your chair...

FELIX: "Chair!" Uh...seat!

OSCAR: We're not playing anymore, Felix. Get off the stage.

FELIX: Please. Just one more chance. Please. Oh, what a gyp!

The scene ends with a final line from Allen, not found in the actual script for the episode: "And for all of you playing with us at home...I'm terribly sorry."

Buxton says, "We actually worked pretty hard on that episode. I still have, on my book shelf, every form of the script, from the first draft to the re-writes to the final. The only things from the first draft that made it through all the way to the final form were the actual game of *Password* and a scene in the living room with Myrna and Murray playing *Password*...we were building up Penny Marshall, who played Myrna, because we liked what we saw in her, so we knew we had to have her involved, and Al Molinaro, who played Murray, always delivered gold.

"No episode of *The Odd Couple* was easy to write. We fine-tuned the episode constantly. We had a staff of writers — Lowell Ganz was one of them — who would come in after Wednesday night rehearsal and go line-by-line through the script looking for improvements. Tony and Jack would not sit still for anything less than perfection, and we loved them for that. We appreciated that."

Back in the world of real games, Allen and Betty were both presented in 1973 with offers to host new game shows. *The Joker's Wild* had caught on so quickly that Jack Barry was able to pitch another game show to CBS, an idea that he called *Hollywood's Talking*. The premise was that celebrities would give pre-recorded interviews in which they were asked to talk about a variety of subjects. In the studio, contestants would watch spliced-together clips of those interviews and try to guess what subject the celebrities were discussing. To the surprise of quite a few people in CBS management, Jack Barry wanted Betty White to host the show.

Barry personally called her and asked if she would be interested. Betty told Barry the story of what had happened nearly with *Make the Connection* and *Get the Message*, and Barry brushed it aside and said that television was changing. It was time to try a female game show emcee again. Times hadn't changed quite enough, though. CBS agreed to give Betty a chance, but Jack Barry had to produce two pilots; one with Betty hosting, and one with a man, Al Lohman hosting. CBS screened the pilots for focus groups and Betty's got much more favorable reactions from the viewers, but the network said that in the long run, "it wouldn't work." Funnily enough, though, Al Lohman didn't get the job either. The nod went to Los Angeles disc jockey Geoff Edwards, who had made a name for himself hosting a local game show called *Lucky Pair* and filling in for Monty Hall on *Let's Make a Deal*.

Hollywood's Talking premiered on CBS on March 26, 1973. It was one of two game shows that premiered that day. *Hollywood's Talking* expired after only thirteen weeks. Again, Betty was disappointed by missing out on the job, and then relieved when she was able to avoid blame for the failure. But the other game show that premiered that day proved to have a little more staying power: *The $10,000 Pyramid*. CBS picked the show up to replace

Joining Allen this week are Carol Burnett and the man who would always maintain that he was the true creator of *Password*, Monty Hall. Hall would even guest-host this version of *Password* occasionally while Allen acted as a celebrity guest. AUTHOR'S COLLECTION

the canceled *Love is a Many Splendored Thing*, Fred Silverman's pet project, which, at its peak, never got ratings as strong as a 34 share, which was the lowest performance that *Password* ever delivered on CBS.

In 1964, Bob Stewart had pitched a game show format to Mark Goodson in which one member of a team would give a list of items ("Money...a driver's license...social security card....") and the partner would guess the category that the items all fit ("Things Kept in a Wallet"). Goodson told him that not only did he not like the idea, but he warned Stewart that if he tried to pitch it on the company's behalf, Goodson would tell network executives that he disliked the idea. This caused Stewart to reach his breaking point and give his notice to Goodson-Todman Productions. By 1973, he refined it into *The $10,000 Pyramid*, played on a lavish set with a massive gilded pyramid at center stage. To earn the right to go for $10,000, the celebrity-contestant teams played a word association game with almost no restrictions on the types of permissible clues, with the object being to convey as many words as possible within thirty seconds. Compared to *Password*, which could sometimes devote two or three minutes to conveying a single word, it looked as though Stewart was attempting to out-do the game that he had developed and refine himself twelve years earlier.

Network game shows suddenly felt the need to keep up with the Joneses, or in this case, the Stewarts, by infusing already-existing formats with more cash. *Password* itself obliged by holding a series of tournaments. Every thirteen weeks, the four top-money winners of that time period would return for a small tournament, with the winner receiving $5,000. That winner would then face the winner of the previous tournament for $10,000.

So Betty missed out on *Hollywood's Talking*, but Allen was given an opportunity to pursue the most perfect gig that anybody could offer him: an educational game show. WITF, the public television station in Hershey, Pennsylvania, was putting together a limited-run ten-episode game show as part of an experiment with a very interesting mission: WITF wanted to determine whether or not game shows were a viable form of educating and informing an audience. Allen was asked to host.

The game, called *You Owe It to Yourself*, was a consumer education quiz. The National Association of Life Underwriters provided funding for the series, which was "designed to help consumers learn the basics of managing family finances." The underwriters actually went all out when it came to the production end of *You Owe It to Yourself*. One might think that a public television game show might hold back a little; maybe a quiet game on a barebones set, but no. Since the specific goal was to determine if a game show was an effective learning tool, the underwriters made darn sure that *You Owe It to Yourself* was a full-blown game show: bright colors, flashing lights, bells, buzzers, automated scoreboards, and a jazzy theme song (composed and performed by Joe "Handyman" Negri of *Mister Rogers' Neighborhood* fame). The only area where any restraint was shown was in the game's prize budget. The contestants were competing for clocks and calculators — though to be fair, they were nice calculators, with a retail value of $150 each. Allen traveled to Hershey to tape the ten episodes of the game over four days in June.

It even occurred to them to give Allen a tagline. Allen opened each episode by welcoming viewers to "the serious game show that doesn't take itself too seriously."

You Owe It to Yourself was designed with a curriculum of sorts, with each of the ten episodes of the series revolving around a specific topic:

> *Budgeting and Buying*
> *Health Insurance*
> *Using Credit*
> *Property and Liability Insurance*
> *Housing*
> *Banking and Savings Institutions*
> *Social Security*
> *Investment Programs*
> *Life Insurance*
> *Estate Planning*

Behind the scenes, putting together the content for the game was an exhaustive process. Employees from insurance agencies and financial institutions were recruited to help write the material. With experience from years of reading *College Bowl* questions, Allen himself took the rare step of helping edit the material to make it more engaging. The show hired two nationally recognized economics professors — Dr. Elsie Fetterman of the University of Connecticut and Dr. Larry Coleman of Indiana State University — to join Allen onstage for every program to serve as the game's judges and provide clarification and context after ruling certain answers right or wrong.

As part of the study, a group of educators in Connecticut assembled supplemental materials based on the game show. A series of screenings of *You Owe It to Yourself* was organized, with groups of area residents assembled and shown tapes of the game. Before watching the tapes, they had to take a written test called "What You Know." After watching the tapes, the viewers were given another written test, called "What You Know NOW."

Dr. Fetterman was thoroughly impressed by what she had seen, both in content and in presentation, during the production of *You Owe It to Yourself*, and personally lobbied the United States Department of Agriculture for federal funding to carry out the study further. She personally obtained permission from WITF to copy the master tapes of the show onto cost-effective 16mm film and ship the films to 200 other public television stations in forty states and asked to pass along any viewer feedback.

In a letter to the WITF general manager, Fetterman wrote, "This has been about the best way I know to teach money management to all income levels…and the proof of the pudding is that there is a gain in knowledge from exposure to the series."

The screening and testing method conducted in the Connecticut studies was done again for audiences in Arizona, North Dakota, Georgia, and Pennsylvania, and this time, the further step was taken of carefully selecting and categorizing the audience members who watched. Pennsylvania worked with young single adults, young families, and families experiencing financial difficulties. Arizona used senior citizens, minorities, and children from the local 4-H chapters for their screenings. Georgia brought in families with limited resources and participants in a wage earner bankruptcy plan. North Dakota oversaw testing with independent farmers.

When all the testing was completed and more than 4,500 people had attended the screenings and taken the "What You Know" and "What You Know NOW" tests, the results were in.

Straight from a report on the *You Owe It to Yourself* project: "Evidence and figures are abundant to show that the participants did indeed learn… The participants and leaders found it agreeable and effective. Inspection of the pre- and post-tests show a range from about eighteen percent to thirty percent increase in knowledge from exposure to these consumer education programs. Testimonials are numerous in the reports. Many indicated they would recommend the program to their friends. Some asked when more of the programs would be available. College students who saw the programs as part of a financial management course preferred this method of teaching over the traditional lecture method. An Indian girl who helps other Indians adjust to city life found the program on the subject of credit most beneficial. After seeing the film, she felt more confident about explaining installment contracts and familiarizing the Indians with their credit bureau. Some leaders were amazed at how much they themselves had learned about the topic…Positive comments from leaders and participants, along with the increase in knowledge as shown by pre-test and post-test scores indicate that this approach to teaching is effective."

Critics could keep sneering and holding their noses over game shows all they want. The research was done and the results were on paper. When Allen Ludden said that TV game shows could be educational, he now had concrete proof from a scholarly report. The 14,000 fan letters Allen had tallied from teachers who wrote to say that they used *Password* in their classrooms was pretty solid evidence, too. And so were the handful of cab drivers who proudly told Allen that *Password* had taught them some of the colorations of the English language.

Although, Allen worried, "I just hope they didn't learn all of their colorations from us."

Allen and Betty attend a benefit with, among other guests, Ruta Lee, Rev. Billy Graham, and Rose Marie. FRED WOSTBROCK COLLECTION

FRED WOSTBROCK COLLECTION

CHAPTER EIGHTEEN

"TROPHY"

Allen and Betty celebrated a decade of marriage in 1973, and because they were well into their forties when they tied the knot, they very much had the look and lifestyle of a couple who had been together for their whole lives. The nest was empty, they spent all of their free time together, and they were facing the reality of — gulp — growing old together.

Allen's light brown hair had faded to blonde and then to white, and his lenses were necessarily getting a little bit thicker. Betty's hair was turning, too. She thought white hair was a good look, but when Betty realized that her hair was instead becoming a "mousey" shade of gray, she colored it blonde and kept it that way.

In a realm where marriages could sometimes be measured in weeks or months, Allen attributed their longevity to how darn busy they both were. "We enjoy the business and talk about it together. We're very lucky. Sometimes I think that marriages fail when one of the couple doesn't have enough to do."

Betty agreed. Both of them loved their work so much that the best news either of them could imagine was knowing that the other had some-place to go tomorrow. She said, "He's as interested in my work as I am in his, so there's never any conflict of 'Gee, you working again?' Our sched-ules work out just fine. We manage to steal time to get away together."

If one or both of them worked that day, they had a routine for the end of the workday not so different from many other couples. Allen came home and made a cocktail for himself, and Betty would get out her needlepoint and work on a project. It became such a habit that the movements were reflexive. Allen would pull out his glass and Betty would instinctively grab her sewing kit. Her proudest creation was a rug depict-ing a number of birds and nests. Allen liked it so much that instead of putting it on the floor, he picked out a bare wall in the house and hung it up. Most of the time, her projects were less ambitious, but after a decade

301

of married life, they began piling up. One night, as Allen sipped on his cocktail, he looked around the room and realized how many doilies and samples surrounded him.

He remarked, "God, I must drink a lot."

If they had a day off together, they spent a quiet afternoon playing Scrabble together while munching on liverwurst sandwiches. If they were

Allen, Betty, and Morris at the PATSY Awards. FRED WOSTBROCK COLLECTION

able to round up several days in a row of free time, they'd make the drive up to Carmel and enjoy some time in a rented cottage.

One example of how they always found enough to do was the work that enveloped their anniversary that year. Allen and Betty kicked off their summer in 1973 by hosting a unique awards show: the 23rd Annual Performing Animal Top Star of the Year (PATSY) Awards. Sponsored by the American Humane Society, the ceremony, under the guise of presenting awards to animals who had delivered outstanding performances in movies and TV shows, was actually a way of spotlighting Hollywood productions that had been conspicuously humane in their treatment of the animals that they used. Ben the rat was a big winner that night. So was Morris the finicky cat from the 9 Lives commercials. A newcomer, Farouk the dog, won an award for his performance on an episode of *Ironside*. The press wound up having a field day with a charming photo of the ceremony. The famously cranky Morris warmed right up to Betty and contentedly cuddled against her. Allen himself was more captivated by the scene of the rat and the cat peacefully lying side-by-side on the stage at one point.

Behind the scenes, Allen and Betty were working harder than many people realized. The American Humane Society had nearly called off the event after the previous year's broadcast because a low number of stations signed on, which made it difficult to offset the costs of producing the broadcasts. That was when Allen went above and Betty went beyond the call of duty. They stepped forward and offered to host the next PATSY Awards television broadcast if the AHA decided to go through with it. Not only would they work for free, but Allen, through Albets Productions, would oversee the distribution end of the endeavor, getting the broadcast sold to local stations across the country. With Allen and Betty running the show, the number of stations increased fifty percent.

Allen and Betty had such a good time that they gladly agreed to return the following year, with Allen glibly explaining why an animal awards show was so much better than the ones held for humans. "All our nominees show up and they all behave beautifully too."

The truth is, the PATSY Awards were for humans. Staging such a lavish presentation involving animal performers required the presence of the trainers. The hope of the American Humane Society was that people would continue being kind to animals if those who did so were paraded out onstage to bask in the spotlight every year.

"This is not all cutesy," Allen emphasized in a statement. "It is very urgent that the proper and humane treatment of animals be stressed. So much cruelty to animals has crept into films. It is not necessary; for instance, in no picture in which John Wayne appeared has there been cruelty to animals."

It had been years since the Luddens had won any awards for their own work. Summer stock didn't have an awards show, the Emmys ignored game shows, and Betty hadn't won an award since her surprise win in the Best Actress category in 1950. But for all they had given to the performing arts by this point, it was clear they weren't in it for the awards. That was about to change, though.

For now, though, Allen and Betty enjoyed some of the other perks that came with show business careers, like the chance to forge friendships with people that they revered, and the once-in-a-lifetime opportunities that arose because of those relationships. Allen loved cocktail parties — holding them and attending them. Betty didn't really care for large gatherings herself, but since Allen tolerated her devotion to animals, Betty let him indulge in cocktail parties, seeing it as her form of compromise. And during summer months, it wasn't just cocktail parties. Allen had everybody over for barbecues. He had mastered outdoor cooking. Betty, by her own count, could cook about four things (her strong suit, according to Allen, was sewing), but Allen was so proficient that he often "ad-libbed" recipes when it was his turn to make dinner. His specialty was something that Betty had affectionately named Chicken a la Ludden — rotisserie chicken that was brushed with melted butter that had been spiked with Angostura bitters. Whenever they had a barbecue, Allen would make that, while Betty served one of the few things she was comfortable cooking: Baked beans. Her recipe included crushed pineapple, barbecue sauce, dry mustard, molasses, Worcestershire sauce, molasses, Tabasco sauce, and crumbled bacon.

And believe it or not, Allen didn't leave work at work. He admitted to one reporter that yes, he actually did bring friends over to the house to play *Password* at the parties. (Although he and Betty had the home game, they preferred to make their own sets of words.) Through one gathering, they met the daughter of Fred Astaire, who said her father was obsessed with *Password*. The Luddens were invited to dinner with the Astaires, and *Password* was virtually the only thing that the legendary dancer wanted to discuss. That fascination continued well after dinner. Weeks later, Fred called Allen at home because he wanted to know why a certain clue had been deemed illegal on that day's episode of *Password*.

Allen was surprised to find himself becoming a confidant to Fred. He had become enamored with a woman named Robyn and contacted Allen for advice. Betty told author Peter Levinson, "One night around dinner time, he called Allen and said, 'I have to talk to you. I am just going crazy.

I am so nuts about this woman. My family doesn't like her. I was not that particularly fond of Robyn myself, but she was a big animal person, so that is where we connected.

"Allen dropped everything and went over to see Fred. When he came back, he said, '[Fred] wants to marry this woman.' Allen had told him to go ahead if he was feeling it was that important to him. Allen was such a

Betty wasn't as comfortable in the kitchen as Allen was, but as long as she could handle coffee or baked beans, they were all set. FRED WOSTBROCK COLLECTION

romantic. He said that it was amazing, Fred just poured it all out. Allen was not involved with the rest of the family. He could level with Fred. Fred knew that Allen had fallen in love with [me] and wouldn't take no for an answer. I think he wanted to get some of that from Allen."

Apparently, he got plenty of it, because he did wind up marrying Robyn. The marriage lasted the rest of Fred's life.

Tom Kennedy remembers, "Usually, when my wife and I socialized with Betty and Allen, it was a small dinner party. I remember showing up one night, and there's Fred Astaire! Damn near wet my pants. He was the most impressive person I had ever met. I found out that the reason for this get-together was because Fred Astaire had mentioned to Allen that he was a big fan of *Split Second*, the show I was hosting at the time. And Allen said, 'You know, Betty and I are friends with Tom Kennedy, would you like to meet him?' You can't beat that! I tried to control myself. I didn't want Fred Astaire to feel like he had to spend the whole party answering questions about himself. But I had to tell him about when I was a child in Louisville and I told him about taking tap dancing lessons at the public park because I wanted to be Fred Astaire. And now, here I am having dinner with him because he wanted to meet me. That's a keeper memory for me, and Allen made it happen. And so was meeting Lucille Ball the next time we went to their house.

"Allen had a very wide circle of friends, understand. He never threw big blow-outs. He would have small parties, with different groups of friends invited over each time. That was actually why it was a treat to be invited. When you got invited, you knew you'd meet some friend of Allen and Betty's that you had never met before. They were very popular people because they lived a very normal, happy, out-of-show business life. People in the industry liked being around them because you didn't have to think about work or your image or networking when you came over there. You just came over to enjoy their company and that was all they wanted you to do."

Allen and Betty admitted that they weren't really gregarious people. Allen liked parties more than Betty, but Betty had taught him an appreciation for solitude that he never had before. When they had parties, though, they tended to have a lengthy guest list.

He explained, "You really are stuck in that kind of situation with your dinner partner. Unless the invitation comes from very dear friends, we just don't go."

Allen and Betty would usually invite about twenty people and set up a buffet for the guests. A typical guest list included Grant Tinker and

Mary Tyler Moore (Allen called Grant "my next best friend after Betty"); Burt Reynolds and Dinah Shore; Carol Burnett and Joe Hamilton; and Fred Astaire brought along his sister Adele. Together, everybody played *Password*. (According to Allen, any time that Fred Astaire came to the house, they HAD to play *Password*.) When Adele, who had married into royalty, learned at one gathering that the Luddens were planning a summer vacation in Europe, she invited them to spend a few nights in her hundred-room castle in Ireland.

In 1970, Mary Tyler Moore was rebuilding her career. *The Dick Van Dyke Show*, on which she had made a name as Laura Petrie, the ground-breaking role of a housewife who was treated very much as her husband's equal, had ended in 1966, and Moore's career hit a nasty slump; nothing seemed to suit her as well as that role had, and nobody in show business seemed to know what to do with her. A one-night-only reunion with Van Dyke, on a primetime special called *Dick Van Dyke and the Other Woman*, was so overwhelmingly well-received that in a matter of months, CBS had signed Moore to star in her own prime-time sitcom, inking the deal before a premise had been figured out.

In time, the premise was settled. Moore would play Mary Richards, a thirty-year-old single woman wounded by a broken engagement who moved to Minneapolis and landed a job producing the news for WJM-TV. CBS had buyer's remorse about the premise (the network spent months fighting and compromising with Moore and Tinker, who wanted Mary Richards to be a divorcee) and early expectations were low. *Time* Magazine predicted that the show would be a disaster.

But when *The Mary Tyler Moore Show* went into production in the fall of 1970, Moore received a gentle but elaborate reminder that she did have people in her corner who believed in her. On the night of the show's first taping, Allen sent Moore a lavish floral arrangement in the shape of the number 1. Allen, who had a soft spot in his heart for traditions, followed that gesture a year later, when *The Mary Tyler Moore Show* began its second season, with a big floral 2. And in 1972, he sent #3.

Allen and Betty's support went further. Week after week, when it was time to film the episode in front of the live studio audience, they were always there in the bleachers with the rest of the audience, laughing at every joke, oooh-ing every plot turn, and applauding the happy conclusion.

Allen and Betty became familiar faces to the show's staff. As a nod to the support they had always shown, Allen's name was worked into a joke in one episode — Mary's boss, Mr. Grant (Ed Asner), receives a chain letter and insists that its warnings of death and bad fortune must be legitimate because the letter mentions Allen Ludden was a recipient. Early publicity for the show namedropped Betty, who was used as a frame of reference as the writers explained that Mary Richards had struggled so much in life because she was too nice, and now she was trying to be more assertive.

"Niceness is for Betty White," the character write-up said.

Mary Tyler Moore, Grant Tinker, Allen and Betty. Best friends Mary and Betty were about to become co-workers. FRED WOSTBROCK COLLECTION

But as the Luddens continued showing up to support their friend, the staff discovered that there was more to Betty than niceness. She could actually have a rather wicked sense of humor sometimes.

In 1973, to kick off season four (and yes, Allen made sure that he sent a 4 that year), the writers had penned a fantastic episode called "The Lars Affair," in which Mary's landlady, Phyllis (Cloris Leachman), learns that her husband, Lars, is having an affair with a WJM on-air personality named Sue Ann Nivens, the hostess of *The Happy Homemaker*. In their script, writers Ed. Weinberger and Stan Daniels called the character "a Betty White type," a sugary sweet woman so pleasant that she was almost too good to be true. In fact, she was too good to be true. Underneath the all-smiles exterior, wrote Weinberger and Daniels, Sue Ann Nivens would be "as vicious as a barracuda."

Despite the inspiration, the writers were actually adamant that the role shouldn't be played by Betty White. The Luddens had been so conspicuously supportive that the staff realized what a deep friendship they had with the star of the show. Merely considering Betty was mixing friendship with business, and the writers were dreading the worst-case scenario. For whatever reason, Betty might prove to be wrong for the role, and that could torpedo the friendship.

The new problem that this reluctant attitude caused was that nobody else would make a good Sue Ann. The casting directors looked at ten actresses and they were all wrong. The writers had followed the character's inspiration with such precision that it was obvious that nobody else would work in the role. It had to be Betty White. Series co-creator Allan Burns finally made the reluctant phone call to Moore, explaining why everyone was dreading the idea of bringing Betty White in for the part.

Moore responded, "I think she'd rather be asked than not given the chance because it might go badly."

What they didn't realize was that Betty was as scared as they were. She loved the show so much, and got to know the people behind it so well, that she felt as if the expectations for her performance were extraordinarily high.

Betty took the part, her nerves calmed to some extent after Moore jokingly objected to the casting and told Betty, "I have veto power!" Dinah Shore also lent her support. After learning that Betty had been cast as a TV hostess who did cooking demonstrations on her show, who projected a sunny image on camera but was truly nasty off-camera, the Tennessee-born Shore called Betty and politely asked her, please, don't play the part with a southern accent. On September 15, 1973, viewers of *The Mary Tyler Moore Show* first met Sue Ann Nivens, WJM's *Happy Homemaker*.

Looking back, Betty and the staff agreed there were two seemingly minor details that made Sue Ann work as a character as well as she did. The first was a bit in the episode where an oven door is left open, leaving a distracting black hole in the middle of the shot. The writers couldn't figure out a logical way to close it — Sue Ann has her arms full with a ruined soufflé — but Betty got the biggest laugh of the episode by raising her knee up high and gracelessly kicking the oven shut. The other detail was the way that Mary Richards was clearly entertained by the mean, self-centered Sue Ann. She was such an unlikeable character, but since Mary laughed off her worst traits, the audience felt free to laugh, too.

After the taping wrapped, series co-creators Allan Burns and James L. Brooks told Betty that they felt they had struck upon something special. The following morning, Grant and Mary showed up at the Luddens' house with the soufflé dish that had been used in the key scene. They had filled it with flowers and surprised Betty with the news that the writers were already preparing additional scripts for episodes

Betty joined *The Mary Tyler Moore Show* a few seasons in, but it felt like she had been there all along. Clockwise from bottom, Mary Tyler Moore, Betty White, Gavin MacLeod, Ed Asner, Ted Knight, and Georgia Engel. AUTHOR'S COLLECTION

with Sue Ann. After nearly thirty years in radio and television, Betty had revealed a new side of herself, and the audiences adored it. Truth is, she did too.

"Playing Sue Ann is so much fun," Betty told a reporter. "The character was patterned on Betty White, I'm afraid. She's really so bitchy. At least that's what Allen says...Mary and Grant are good friends of mine...they know what a dirty old broad I am."

She wasn't just bitchy, she was promiscuous. In one episode, she excitedly tells Mary, "Last night while I was lying in bed, I had an idea, so I raced right home and wrote it down!"

She slept in a heart-shaped bed, with a button that activated magic fingers and another button that played swelling classical music. Though *The Mary Tyler Moore Show* was set in a newsroom, the Happy Homemaker found her way to scenes because a running gag was that she was trying to sleep with Mr. Grant.

In another interview, Betty delved further into the character she was playing. "I don't know how I got a goody-goody reputation. But playing Sue Ann as a girl who likes sex and makes no bones about it isn't all that difficult for me. Maybe I can lose some of my own inhibitions playing a character like that. She lives life to the fullest. She has no hang-ups about right and wrong. She is the center of her own universe. How Sue Ann keeps from being arrested I don't know."

Betty, as Sue Ann, delivered such a strong performance that it's easy to forget that she was never a regular cast member. Over the remaining four seasons of *The Mary Tyler Moore Show*, ninety-six more episodes would be produced, and Betty would only appear in forty-six of them. But despite her status as a perpetual guest star, she was absolutely regarded as one of the family. Whenever the "full cast" was needed for any sort of publicity, the full cast always included Betty White.

What was gratifying for Betty was that Allen was as happy for her success as she was. He celebrated it, he joked about it. Betty was always tickled by Allen's ready answer when fans saw them in public and approached them.

"How close is Sue Ann to Betty?" the fan would ask Allen.

Allen would answer, "They're really the same character, except Betty can't cook."

Allen would always tweak Betty about her inability to cook. It never bothered her because she noticed that cooking never seemed to be particularly important to her husband. Allen was a very light eater; breakfast was a protein shake, and he usually skipped lunch, sustaining himself with coffee throughout the day. Dinner was usually the only meal of the day, and Allen had no compunction about cooking for himself on a night when they weren't going out to a restaurant. So Betty always happily joined in the joshing whenever Allen gleefully revealed that the Happy Homemaker didn't know her way around the kitchen.

Betty's lack of prowess in the kitchen had always been something of a running joke in her life outside of the studio. Burt Reynolds and Dinah

Shore frequently came to the Luddens' place for dinner and it was always either Allen or Dinah that did the cooking.

"Dinah really is a great cook and she loves to cook," Allen once explained. "Betty really isn't and really doesn't."

When Sue Ann Nivens became popular, Dinah invited Betty to be a guest on her talk show for a cooking segment. Betty thought it would be a good opportunity to poke fun at her own image. There was a dog food company that was manufacturing a meat loaf for dogs, and Betty called a representative of the company, explained who she was and why she wanted their recipe. Not only did the company give Betty their recipe, they shipped her all the necessary ingredients divided into individual bowls so she could easily mix everything on the air. Betty made the meatloaf and Dinah brought a dog to the stage. The dog sniffed the meatloaf… then walked away without touching it.

The most gratifying part of *The Mary Tyler Moore Show* for Betty was that people had suddenly remembered that she was an actress. It was the career that she had originally been pursuing when she decided to give show business a shot, but she went down a rabbit hole of sorts, becoming a television hostess, a talk show raconteur, a game show player, a commercial spokeswoman….

As Betty explained to interviewer Jerry Bick, "Once you get into the talk routine, producers don't want to trust you as an actress. They forget you started out as an actress. Sue Ann was the best thing that ever happened to me. It revived my acting career."

The Luddens' friendship with Moore and Tinker grew stronger, even as Moore and Tinker began to grow apart. One night, the Luddens got a crushing phone call from their friends, letting them know that they were getting separated and that Tinker was moving into a new house. They made it clear that they weren't expecting their friends to choose one or the other. Allen and Betty continued to involve Mary in their lives, and involve Grant in their lives. They were just going to involve one at a time.

When Tinker's next birthday rolled around, Allen and Betty decided to treat him to dinner at Chasen's, an upscale eatery in West Hollywood popular among the A-list. Jack Benny and Mary Livingstone were dining there that night, as was Frank Sinatra. Allen and Betty nervously walked in. Tinker had called them earlier in the day to ask them a question that weighed heavily on them.

"Can I bring someone?"

Allen and Betty agreed, determined to be as fair to their friend as he had been to them. And then Grant Tinker walked in, arm-in-arm with

Mary Tyler Moore. They had patched things up. The funny thing that night was that they told ONLY Allen and Betty. The separation was well-known in the press by that point, leaving a baffled gossip columnist to try to explain what she had seen in the restaurant that night:

"Since their announced separation, Mary Tyler Moore seems to be dating no one but her husband. The other night in Chasen's no one would

Cooking with Dinah Shore always seemed to end in catastrophe for the Luddens. The dog wouldn't touch Betty's meatloaf...and Allen's cooking segment went considerably worse. FRED WOSTBROCK COLLECTION

have suspected an estrangement between Mary and Grant Tinker, that's how much merriment was coming from the booth they were sharing with Betty White and Allen Ludden."

A few months later, Betty wrapped up her first year of *The Mary Tyler Moore Show*. Allen and Betty decided to spend their summer break on vacation in Tahiti, totally void of television, radio, or newspapers. They stayed in a cottage built on top of a lagoon, with a window in the floor so they could watch the sea life swimming by directly beneath them, and a deck for watching the sunset. Allen brought along a stack of books, Betty brought along her needlepoint, and that's how they spent their time in Tahiti between snorkeling expeditions. As it happened, *All in the Family* producer Norman Lear was vacationing there too, and at night, he got together with the Luddens to watch native musicians and dancers perform. Betty and Norman entertained themselves by "translating" some of the lyrics with their own interpretations, much to Allen's irritation.

Betty and Allen got back to California and got right back to work. Grant and Allen were still trying to get some game show formats off the ground through EllTee Productions. They mounted a pilot called *The Gossip Game*, hosted by columnist Rona Barrett.

The Gossip Game was envisioned by Allen as being a very different presentation of a game show. The idea for the show had struck him instantly one night, and like *College Bowl*, he had put the idea to paper within minutes. Allen insisted the show needed a female host, and with a title like *The Gossip Game*, who better than the foremost gossip columnist of the era, Miss Rona? Allen actually consulted with Barrett about the way she did her hair and eye make-up for the taping of the pilot, giving her a "softened" look to blend with the show's set, which resembled a country home — Allen and Betty stressed that not every game show needed a "carnival set."

EllTee developed another game show pilot based on an idea that Burt Reynolds suggested. Neither Reynolds' idea nor *The Gossip Game* ever got off the ground, but Allen took it in stride. Networks paid producers for the pilots they screened, so though his ideas for formats weren't selling, it had still been a profitable enterprise for him, and that made him happy.

When a reporter asked him about EllTee Productions, Allen said, "I consider this my prime job. *Password* is that game they let me play on weekends."

Allen truly loved game shows and wanted to put as big a stamp on them as he could. Author Marie Winn called TV "the plug-in drug," and the term "couch potato" had, admittedly, quite accurately described those who were content to stare at the screen all day. What Allen liked about game shows was that they forced a viewer to participate, and sometimes inch forward to the edge of the seat.

Allen said, "The reason game shows are a TV staple is that the medium has gotten to the point where all prime-time entertainment puts the

After all these years, *Password* still loved Lucy. FRED WOSTBROCK
COLLECTION

viewer in a third person position. The viewer has to look at most shows through a proscenium arch, just like in a theater. Outside of Johnny Carson and the news, the game shows are the only thing on television in which the viewer can become a participant."

Saturday, March 9, 1974, was a true sign of the times worldwide. The early 1970s were the peak of the streaking craze, and for some reason, major incidents happened around the world on that single day. Three men streaked through a Women's Lib demonstration in London. A streaker ran back and forth through the aisles of a 747 jumbo jet flying over the Atlantic and then calmly returned to his seat. In Austin, Texas, a streaker disrupted Walter Cronkite's interview with Ladybird Johnson. In Dallas, yet another streaker ran through the stadium, disrupting the Cowboys' rookie training session.

And in Hollywood, a streaker ran across the stage and disrupted a game of *Password*, leaving Allen, guests Dick Gautier and Pat Harrington Jr., the contestants, and the 300 members of the studio audience stunned speechless. The show aired on April 5, and to the surprise of many viewers, the show elected not to remove the incident from the tape. The streaking aired exactly as it had happened a month earlier. Ever since videotape had become the norm and live TV had gone out of favor, game show producers by and large had preferred to maintain the suspense and excitement of live TV by doing as little editing as possible. Fluffs and gaffs were left intact, the hosts would vamp while technicians would repair broken microphones while the tape kept rolling, and in moments of confusion, viewers would see the host having a conversation with a producer who couldn't be seen or heard. For better or worse, the streaking incident helped preserve the "live" illusion, and besides, in a strange way, it helped cement *Password*'s status as a culturally relevant program. After

Finally, a little recognition! Allen accepts the Emmy for *Password*. FRED WOSTBROCK COLLECTION

all, why would a streaker go to the effort of disrupting and ruining an unimportant or unpopular show?

And looking important and relevant could only be good for *Password*, because in 1974, the show was approaching its thirteenth birthday, and because of that three-year patch of reruns, its run for those thirteen years was virtually uninterrupted. They were still playing a quiet, cerebral game while the TV landscape was otherwise populated by Gene Rayburn and the panel swapping double entendres on *Match Game*, Paul Lynde firing off zingers on *The Hollywood Squares*, and giant bananas screaming and jumping into the arms of Monty Hall on *Let's Make a Deal*. More importantly, after a year at CBS, *The $10,000 Pyramid* was doling out money by the truckload to big winners on Bob Stewart's faster-paced, glitzier word association game. The thirteen-year-old *Password* looked... well, old.

On May 28, 1974, however, everyone got a nice reminder that they hadn't made it to thirteen years by accident. The Academy of Television Arts and Sciences had finally set up a separate ceremony and group of

Hard to be humble when you're great. Allen shows off the modified *Password* set after the 1st Daytime Emmy Awards. FRED WOSTBROCK COLLECTION

award categories for acknowledging daytime television, a field that had never received any significant recognition. Soap operas and talk shows would finally get their due, and so once again would game shows. The Primetime Emmys, as they would now be known, hadn't had any awards for game shows since 1963 (irritating Mark Goodson so much that he resigned from his membership in the academy).

At the 1st Annual Daytime Emmy Awards, the nominees for Outstanding Game Show were *Let's Make a Deal*, *The Hollywood Squares*, and *Password*. And the big winner was *Password*; the Academy had spoken, and they declared that oldest wines were still the best. It was Goodson-Todman's first Emmy Award. It was Allen's first Emmy, too. Later that night, at the Primetime Emmys, *The Mary Tyler Moore Show* pocketed five Emmy awards, including an award for Cloris Leachman for "The Lars Affair," Betty's first episode.

Password would be conspicuously immodest about the big victory at the Daytime Emmys, immediately making a modification to the set. A massive plywood replica of the Emmy statuette now adorned the wall directly behind Allen's lectern.

But there remained a feeling that *Password* needed some new life breathed into it. *Jeopardy!* had moved out of the noon timeslot, to the shock of many viewers, and NBC had plugged in a new game, *Jackpot*. Created by Bob Stewart (the man who brought *Password* to life) and hosted by Geoff Edwards (the surprise winner of the *Hollywood's Talking* gig over Betty), *Jackpot* was arguably the most jarringly different game show that the genre had seen so far in the 1970s. A whopping fifteen contestants sat at a gallery while one stood at a pulpit, attempting to solve riddles and feed money into a growing jackpot; as a side task, the contestants were hoping to feed exactly the right amount of money needed for the jackpot to match a predetermined target number; doing so enabled them to answer a much harder riddle for a bonus that could be worth as much as $50,000. The thirteen-year-old *Password* was already showing signs of wear and tear, but against *Jackpot*, the orange and pink set of *Password* began to look mighty gray.

There was one other problem that *Password* was running into. Look at any dictionary. No matter how thick it is, that was how much usable material for *Password* existed. And even then, you had to figure that the show was never going to use a word like "Ameliorate" for a password. The show, at one point, had a list of 3,000 words that were deemed usable for the purposes of the game. And after thirteen years of games and Milton-Bradley's home versions, the problem for the game that everybody could play was that seemingly everybody had played it, and mastered it by now.

Producer Robert Sherman later gave author Jefferson Graham an example, pointing out that the word CHOPSTICKS didn't provide challenge to players after a certain point because everybody had figured out a perfect single clue for it: "Utensils," spoken with an Oriental accent.

The ratings for *Password* were measurably dented, and as a small indicator that things might not get better, *Jackpot* host Geoff Edwards was enthusiastically greeted on an airplane by fellow passenger Fred Astaire, who walked right up to him and shouted, "JACKPOT!"

During the summer of 1974, *Password* would get some of its best ratings of its ABC years with a series of all-celebrity episodes. Monty Hall served as guest host for ten straight episodes while Allen Ludden competed against Elizabeth Montgomery, with new celebrity guests coming in for every game to act as partners. Allen was paired up with Lucille Ball, Dick Gautier, Mary Tyler Moore, Harvey Korman, Kate Jackson, and Betty. Elizabeth joined forces with Greg Morris, James Hampton, Tom Kennedy, Robert Reed, Robert Foxworth, and Lew Retrum, the contestant who had won the previous year's tournament of champions and was held in high regard as possibly the best *Password* player that the show had ever seen. The ten-day series was followed by Allen returning to the host's position to oversee a week of games pitting Elizabeth Montgomery and Robert Foxworth against Dyan Cannon and Carl Reiner.

ABC demanded more all-star weeks, and *Password* delivered all they could. There was a Celebrity Husbands and Wives Week; Monty Hall returned to host Allen vs. Betty Week; producers and writers emerged from behind the scenes of hit prime-time shows for a special week of charity games.

Allen did his best to keep the network happy, occasionally traveling to ABC stations for local publicity boosts. He ventured to Indiana during a week in August, visiting Evansville and Indianapolis. While in Indianapolis, he agreed to give an interview at WNTS-AM, a talk radio station. He met the host, a shaggy twenty-seven-year-old with a toothy grin who moonlighted at WLWI-TV, the local ABC affiliate, as the weatherman on the evening newscast. Allen didn't realize it at the time, but he was talking to a broadcaster who was quickly developing a reputation for rather unpredictable comments that cracked up some and annoyed others. During a weather report, he offered his most sincere congratulations to a tropical storm for its recent upgrade to hurricane. On his radio show one day, he had expressed outrage that WISH-TV was making anchorwoman Jane Pauley come into work even though today was her wedding day, triggering so many angry phone calls to WISH that Pauley was forced to go on the air that night and assure viewers that she hadn't gotten married that day. And now, that broadcaster was interviewing Allen Ludden. David Letterman was interviewing Allen Ludden.

Letterman surprised Allen with how funny he was…and how smart he was. Allen gleaned that he was well-read and extremely knowledgeable about broadcasting, and combined with the razor sharp wit, Letterman was something rare — a smart aleck who really was smart. Allen soon developed the same stirring he had when he first listened to Tom Sullivan play the piano. He realized he was in the presence of an extraordinary talent that nobody knew about yet.

Off the air, Allen asked Letterman about his plans for the future, and Letterman told him that he had been hemming and hawing about leaving Indianapolis and trying to mount a comedy career in Hollywood. Allen wrote down some contact information and pointedly told Letterman to call him if he ever did find his way to Hollywood.

Allen himself returned to Hollywood, where the need to breathe new life into *Password*, and viewers' positive reaction to the celebrity specials from the summer convinced the network that all-star games were the perfect new direction for the show. The network apparently hadn't learned anything from what happened the previous year to *Baffle*, a game on NBC that re-invented itself as *All-Star Baffle* and disintegrated almost immediately. Part of the appeal of game shows was watching a common person like you winning the big money, and while it was fun to break loose every now and then and watch an occasional all-celebrity game, but all-celebrity games were akin to a steak dinner or an ice cream sundae. If you have a steak and an ice cream sundae for every meal, you'll get tired of it. ABC wanted more stars, and *Password*, had no choice but to deliver.

On November 15, 1974, *Password* disappeared. On Monday, November 18, announcer John Harlan introduced Loretta Swit, Greg Morris, Linda Kaye Henning, Martin Milner, Elaine Joyce, Don Galloway, and host Allen Ludden for the debut of *Password All-Stars*.

The mere sight of the first few seconds was a sign that this game was going to be something different. The cozy orange set was gone, replaced by a colossal arena decorated in an ultra-patriotic red, white, and blue motif. The stage was divided in sections. The lectern and giant desk was still there, but Allen walked right past them and headed a second lectern and desk, facing a cluster of four podiums. The finger-snapping synthesizer piece was gone. The show had a new theme, composed by Score Productions; a bombastic arrangement of horns, woodwinds, and a banjo, titled "Bicentennial Funk." *Password All-Stars* was reinventing the wheel, the axle, and the entire engine block.

Here's how the new game was played. Pay attention. To start Monday's episode, two stars were randomly selected to be the clue-givers, while the other four stars sat across the stage from them, all equipped with lockout buttons, ringing in to guess the passwords from the clues. The first two celebrities to guess two passwords each would then pair up with the clue-givers for a traditional game of *Password*, while the two losing celebrities waited in the wings to act as the clue-givers for the next game.

The four remaining celebrities played *Password*, with a new wrinkle added to the options that started each password. Instead of asking, "Pass or play?" Allen now asked, "Pass, play, or double?" If the star chose "double," the partner had a single chance to guess the word for twenty points. If they failed, the opposing team got a single chance worth twenty points, and if they failed, the word would be thrown out — so you only wanted to declare "double" if you were <u>positive</u> you had a perfect clue.

Allen, in front of a wall of lights on the massive new set of *Password All-Stars.* FRED WOSTBROCK COLLECTION

The first side to score twenty-five points or more won the game. All the points scored during the game were added to the celebrities' cumulative scores, which would accumulate throughout the week as more games were played. The winning team played a bonus round called 20/20 Password. Each teammate tried to convey a password to the other in less than twenty seconds. If both passwords were successfully guessed, each star got twenty points added to the cumulative scores.

This continued until the end of Thursday's show, when the two stars with the lowest scores were eliminated. On Friday's episode, the cumulative scores were reset to zero. The four remaining stars would play as many traditional games and 20/20 bonuses as time would allow, switching partners for every game, and the high-scoring player at the end of the half-hour received $5,000 for his or her favorite charity.

After six weeks, the six weekly champions returned for a Grandmasters Tournament. The winner of the Grandmasters Tournament won a golden award platter and an additional $25,000 for the charity.

Password All-Stars flopped and flopped badly. Viewers continued to trickle away, but some remained faithful though even the loyal viewers wrote letters to the show saying that they didn't like the new version. After fourteen weeks, Allen wrapped up the second and final Grandmasters Tournament by announcing that there would be no more *Password All-Stars*, and he was giving all the credit to the home viewers.

"Thanks to you and your requests, we begin a new version of *Password* next week…it should be a very interesting new format, and it's all because that's the way you wanted it."

The night of the final *Password All-Stars*, Allen co-starred in one of the more peculiar productions of his career. ABC's late night time slot by this time was occupied by *Wide World of Entertainment*, an anthology series that presented concerts, stand-up performances, documentaries, and whodunit stories. For the February 21, 1975 broadcast, the program presented a two-hour made-for-TV adaptation of the musical *It's a Bird, It's a Plane, It's Superman!*

The musical was an extremely campy adaptation of the Superman mythos, revolving around the evil Dr. Abner Sedgwick's efforts to destroy the Man of Steel, with the aid of conniving gossip columnist Max Mencken. It had originally debuted on Broadway in 1966, where it lasted less than three months. The 1975 production was just as campy — the set was designed to resemble a massive comic book landscape. Announcer Gary Owens provided highly melodramatic narration ("Will Lois Lane forget Superman and surrender her virtue to the conniving Max Mencken?")

while the cast, including Loretta Swit and Lesley Ann Warren, gleefully
chewed all the scenery in sight. Playing the role of Perry White, editor
of *The Daily Planet*, was Allen Ludden.

With teeth clenched and fists bunched, Allen as Perry passionately
tells a young reporter, "I want all the news that's fit to print! And I want
it now! Get me that story!"

Allen gets the last word of the show, emphatically telling his reporters
that a massive tidal wave is heading right for Metropolis...as reporter
Clark Kent's empty desk chair spins.

Password hadn't had its last word. The following Monday, *Password* got
reinvented a little more, as ABC and Goodson-Todman were trying to
search for the magic fix that would keep the program alive.

The new version, reverting back to the name *Password* (although fans
have been known to call it *Password '75*), was scaled back to two celebrities
but now with four contestants, in a format that seemed to be designed to
justify all the new set pieces that had been created for *Password All-Stars*.

The two celebrities gave clues while the four contestants rang in to
make their guesses. The first two contestants to guess three words each
played regular *Password* with the celebrities, still with the "pass, play, or
double" option, but now with a goal of fifty points.

The winning team played the new Big Money Lightning Round. The
game was played in three levels. For Level One, the celebrity tried to
convey three passwords in thirty seconds or less. The payoff was twenty-
five dollars per word plus five dollars for every second remaining on the
clock. So, if all three words were guessed (for seventy-five dollars) and
there were still nine seconds on the clock (forty-five dollars), that would
be a total of $120. In Level Two, each password was worth the total Level
One payoff ($120 in this example) plus $10 for every second remaining.
So if all three passwords were guessed (for $360) and there were five sec-
onds remaining, that would be $410. For the third and final level, guessing
all three passwords was worth ten times that payoff ($4,100 here).

Bill Granger of *The Chicago Sun-Times* wrote a review of the new
Password. Critics have never had particularly kind words for game shows,
but again, *Password* had always been an unusual critical darling. Granger
even led off by assuring readers that he had been a fan of *Password*, or at
least what it used to be.

And this is what a *Password* fan thought when he took a look at the
new version on ABC: "It has changed. It has been infected by greed...We
are not talking about hundreds of dollars anymore...*Password* has passed
from a mildly amusing show to a big-money program. The fun has gone

out of it. Now the *Password* set looks like a Las Vegas idea of heaven: All sparkling lights and the lusty promise of wealth…*Password* hasn't changed in game structure. Despite the sleazy set, the game show is still mildly and intellectually stimulating. But it is not fun to watch folks work that hard for money that really means something to them. Something nice that was in the program is not there anymore."

Allen and Betty hand out the PATSY Awards once more. FRED WOSTBROCK COLLECTION

To put it candidly, the game show that attracted people who didn't like game shows had repelled its audience by turning into a game show.

As *Password* continued to apparently fade away, Allen soothed whatever bad feelings he had about the fate of his signature show with more awards shows. His calendar for May included another turn with Betty at co-hosting the PATSY Awards — 1975's big winner was Tonto, the cat that co-starred with Art Carney in *Harry & Tonto* — and, while Allen and *Password* were both left out of contention for the 2nd Annual Daytime Emmys, Allen did have the honor of nudging Betty out of her seat when she was too shocked to stand up after her name was announced as the winner of Best Supporting Actress in a Comedy Series. Twenty-three years ago, Betty walked into the ceremony thinking that Zsa Zsa Gábor was a sure win in her category and being stunned when her own name was announced instead. In a spell of déjà vu, Betty looked at her competition: Julie Kavner from *Rhoda*, Nancy Walker from *Rhoda*, and Loretta Swit from *M*A*S*H*. Betty had taken one look at the ballot and deduced that the *Rhoda* fans in the Academy would split their votes and that made Loretta Swit a lock to win. And once again, Betty couldn't believe it was her. Betty ended up going onto the stage one more time that night, this time with her cast mates, when *The Mary Tyler Moore Show* won for Best Comedy Series.

The sight of Betty and all of her friends — their friends — sharing a moment of triumph was enough of an award for Allen. She shared his success and he would always share hers. And it provided a comforting salve for the hard news that hit Allen that same month: ABC was cancelling *Password*.

In an unusual deal, Goodson-Todman had signed with ABC to produce the show that would replace *Password*, a new charades-based game called *Showoffs*. Goodson-Todman was no doubt sorry to see *Password* come to an end, but fourteen years of first-runs and reruns had been a good ride, and the concession was that the show had reached its expiration date.

The final episode of *Password* saw an almost-teary Allen (he paused for a deep breath at one point and said, "I may not get through this") hosting a brief game between members of the Goodson-Todman staff before Mark Goodson himself walked onstage to pay tribute to the show and to the host. Having noticed Allen enviously eyeing his Cartier Tank watch in recent months, Goodson presented Allen with his own Tank watch and succinctly told him, "You are Mr. Password."

At the end of the program, Betty sat by Allen's side, as she had done on the final CBS *Password* eight years earlier. Allen, straight from the heart, told the viewers, "I met this lady on this game fourteen years ago. I've loved every minute of it. I've worked for the best. It'll be a tough game to replace. Someday, maybe, somewhere there's another game show worthy of this kind of interest and love, but this is the best game show you can be associated with and I'm darn grateful that I had fourteen lovely years with it. Thank you for supporting it."

Allen did everything he could to stay busy. He filmed his one and only movie role, playing a game show host, naturally, in the sci-fi film *Futureworld*. He appeared as a guest panelist on other game shows, took part in charity fundraisers, hosted telethons, and helped raise money for Jimmy Carter's presidential campaign.

Allen considered himself a liberal, though he was quick to tell people that he maintained a friendship with John Connally even when Connally switched parties — political philosophies weren't that important. When asked about his contribution to Carter, Allen prognosticated, "I think he will be one of our greatest presidents…He has a remarkable intellect and is one of the brightest and best informed men I've ever met."

As for Betty, she was actually conservative when she and Allen first met, later telling one interviewer that Watergate left her disillusioned. Allen, seeing his wife's stance altered, smirked, "I always knew he was a crook."

For a few months, Allen commuted to Massachusetts once a week to host *The Big Money Game*, a game show run by the state lottery. He talked to CBS about reviving *Allen Ludden's Gallery*. Allen and Betty took another vacation to Tahiti, this time bringing Grant and Mary along to stay in the cottage next door.

Betty, who took pride in being able to blend in with a crowd whenever she really wanted to, regaled a newspaper columnist with a story from the trip. "I'm pretty unrecognizable. To let you know how unrecognizable, we got talking to some Australians about television and they told us they liked situation comedies. They proceeded to explain to us just what a situation comedy was. They cited as an example a show called *Maude*. Two days later, having apparently figured there was something familiar about me, they told us how very much they like my show too."

Betty rang in 1976 with a bittersweet milestone, her final Rose Bowl parade. When Sue Ann Nivens became popular, NBC suddenly became a little embarrassed about Betty, now considered "a CBS star," hosting their Rose Parade and dumped her before the 1975 festivities.

She told *People* Magazine, "On New Year's Day, I just sat home feeling wretched, watching someone else do my parade."

CBS saw an opportunity to make their competition look small by recruiting Betty to host their coverage of the 1976 Rose Parade. Betty took the offer, mainly because 1976 would mark her twentieth anniversary hosting the event, but the unpleasantness with NBC had left such a bad taste that she never hosted another Rose Parade.

May rolled around and once again it was Emmy time. Despite the demise of *Password* nearly a year ago, part of its run had been within the window of opportunity for it to be nominated in 1976. And in a wonderful consolation prize after seeing the show come to an end, Allen Ludden won the award for Outstanding Game Show Host. The victory got sweeter at the Primetime Emmys the following week. Betty once again won Best Supporting Actress for her role as Sue Ann Nivens.

Allen and Betty, with other volunteers at a Pet Assistant Foundation event. When they didn't have commitments in show business, they stayed committed to animal welfare. FRED WOSTBROCK COLLECTION

FRED WOSTBROCK COLLECTION

CHAPTER NINETEEN

"FIND"

After once again hosting the PATSY Awards — this time, Fred the cockatoo from *Baretta* took top honors — Allen decided to spend the summer of 1976 going back into the theater, and with a familiar show. He starred in another production of *Critic's Choice*. The only problem was Betty wouldn't join him this time, so now he had to make sure he got the timing of the kiss correct.

In early July, Allen arrived at Cherry County Playhouse in Traverse City, Michigan, to begin rehearsals with the cast and crew, and a dirty little cat. With a dingy layer covering what would have normally been a white coat, the cat drifted into the rehearsal hall, stayed for a while, and got to know the actors. She was a friendly kitty, but not friendly enough to stay. She wandered off, but returned the next day and the day after that.

This continued for a while before Allen, after apparently asking himself, "What would Betty do?" treated the cat with some extra affection and convinced her to stay for a while. Once he was sure he had earned the cat's trust, he immediately took her to a local veterinarian, paid out of his own pocket, got her all the treatments that she needed, cleaned her up, and gave her a name: Password.

When the local newspaper showed up to get a story about the TV star who had come to town to star in a summer play, Allen was far more interested in getting Password a home. He told the reporter that she was an outdoor cat, so the ideal home for her would be someplace where she could roam, and he gave a phone number that readers could call if they wanted to adopt her. The cat was finally adopted by a farmer who thought that Password would enjoy the company of all the cats he already owned.

Spending so much time apart from Betty wasn't really anything new for Allen. He missed New York, but approached his homesickness rather rationally, feeling that he could get it out of his system if he just took an extended trip every year. He'd stay for about five weeks, visit as many old friends as he could, do some guest spots on New York-based TV shows, and head back. Once in a while, he would wind up getting a job offer for a show in New York, entailing that he commute by air every few weeks to tape the program. It wasn't an unheard-of idea — Gene Rayburn flew

Allen's 1976 game show *Stumpers!*, with guests Bill Bixby, Dick Gautier, and their contestant partners. FRED WOSTBROCK COLLECTION

from Massachusetts to California to tape *Match Game*. But the experience of *The Big Money Game* had soured Allen on commuting for life. He found it too stressful.

Luckily, Allen could find work, or work could find him, just as easily in Los Angeles. The kind of work wasn't in question. Allen had what another performer might have considered a problem. *Password* had been so successful that it virtually dictated his career options for whatever time he still had in his career. Whereas Allen Ludden twenty years ago could probably have found plenty of opportunities for a stage actor, lecturer, commentator, columnist, or reporter, Allen of 1976 was almost certainly going to be a game show host exclusively.

Did he mind? "Not at all. I love it and wouldn't want to do anything else in the few more years I've got left…I've been luckier than most. I've had good shows. But I guess I have the ability to communicate through the screen. And you know, Mark Goodson, the producer, once said, 'A good game show host is an on-the-air producer. He knows how to run the game, the show, and at the same time make people like him.'"

Allen, with feet firmly planted in California, got a new show for the fall of 1976. Thirteen years after leaving *G.E. College Bowl*, Allen returned to NBC with a new game show, a daytime offering called *Stumpers!*

Stumpers! had an interesting pedigree. It was developed by Lin Bolen, NBC's vice president of daytime programs. She had taken the position with the goal of attracting a younger audience to the network's daytime line-up. She had been the one who moved the "too-old" *Jeopardy!* out of the noon time slot in favor of *Jackpot*. She also brought the ax down on NBC's longest-running game show, *Concentration*, after a fourteen-year run. She had also introduced a new crop of younger, hipper, handsome game show hosts, like Jim McKrell of *Celebrity Sweepstakes* and Alex Trebek of *The Wizard of Odds*. In an infamous interview, she referred to her hosts as "young studs."

In 1976, she resigned to assemble her own production company, and after building a reputation by giving game shows a major facelift, *Stumpers!* raised a lot of eyebrows. For a host, she handpicked white-haired, bespectacled Allen Ludden. And the game she developed looked quite a bit like good old *Password*.

Bolen raved to *People* Magazine, "He's the perfect host. You can't write lines as good as the ones he keeps coming up with spontaneously."

Premiering on October 4, 1976, *Stumpers!* pitted two celebrity/contestant teams against each other. The object was somewhat similar to Bob Stewart's original vision of *Password*: players were giving clues to their opponents. Without actually being told the answer, a team saw a list of three word-association clues for a person, place or thing. The player tried to pick the least helpful clue and give it to the opponents. If the opponents actually managed to guess the answer on that first clue, it was worth fifteen points. If a second clue was needed, the opponent could score ten points. Needing all three clues brought the value down to five points. If the opponent was stumped, the clue-givers could score fifteen points by declaring the correct answer. The high-scoring team after time was called and two final double-value puzzles were played advanced to Super Stumpers, a bonus round, played basically the same way but now against the clock, for $10,000. If a contestant won two straight games, Super Stumpers paid $20,000.

Unfortunately, *Stumpers!* never really caught the attention of viewers and it vanished in only thirteen weeks. The failure left Allen somewhat jaded. One of the things that made him especially proud of *G.E. College Bowl* and *Password* was that both games rewarded knowledge and skill; the winners of each game were truly the best players. Allen now saw a game show landscape populated by dice and goodies hidden behind boxes and found it a bit off-putting.

He fumed to *People* Magazine, "It's the first time I've been cancelled

Betty lends Allen some moral support for one of the final tapings of *Stumpers!*, along with guests Santa Claus, Dick Gautier, Joanna Barnes, and Peter Bonerz. FRED WOSTBROCK COLLECTION

like this. I'd waited a long time rather than just take anything, and *Stumpers!* was the best game show that came along. We've reached a nadir in game shows now. Nobody ever does anything anymore — they spin a wheel and they win or they don't."

Bolen, who hired Allen partly because of his high Q-rating (a method in the television business of assessing and scoring a performer's likeability among viewers), told the magazine, "The network's really going to be sorry when the women find out Allen's been cancelled."

The program aired its final episode on New Year's Eve. Allen closed out the year in a tuxedo and sipping champagne with the game's final guests, Bill Bixby and Anita Gillette. Thirteen weeks seemed like a grain of sand in an hourglass compared to the run that *Password* had enjoyed. And it stood to reason that Allen closed out *Password* with a sincere, heartfelt farewell. But viewers who tuned into the final day of *Stumpers!* on New Year's Eve were probably surprised by the grace and reverence that Allen had shown for a game that was disappearing after a short and forgettable run. Allen gave an eloquent and memorable speech in the final minutes of the series.

ALLEN: You know, I've been telling you all week that I hoped you could join us on Friday at this time because I had an important announcement. And I do have a very important announcement, and the reason I've been building it up as I have is because I hoped as many of our friends as possible could be with us today…our new friends and our old friends. In this past thirteen weeks, I've realized through your letters and through your response both in person and through the mail that we have made a lot of new friends, and we have got a lot of our old friends back, playing this game with us.

We have had a very interesting and a very happy thirteen weeks. We've been playing a game which we think has tested the imagination and tested the intelligence of the players and the viewers sometimes. We've already heard from several people that they're using this game as a teaching device in schools, so that makes us feel good.

For me personally, after fourteen years with *Password,* it was delightful to come back to a game like this and to work with the people as I have been working. Lin Bolen has assembled in this group of young people — and everybody is young, including Lin — a group of enthusiastic people who work eighteen hours a day developing and working on these clues and putting this game together. For me, it's been a pleasure to work with them, and a privilege.

Now, the point of the whole announcement is that we are going to leave you as of now, or we're going to leave NBC as of now. As of this day, when we sign off, *Stumpers!* will no longer be on NBC. It might turn up somewhere else, but it won't be here.

And I want you to know that we have appreciated your interest and appreciated your enthusiasm. It's been a pleasure. Now I want you, please, to look at the names of these people. I would like to have had them here with me, but I don't have the people. But will you now share with me a round of applause for the people who put together *Stumpers!* for thirteen good weeks.

Allen leads the audience in a round of applause as the credits roll.

Bill Bixby and Anita Gillette now join Allen on stage. They all have glasses of champagne.

ALLEN: We're back! And first of all, I want to toast you, lovely lady.

ANITA: Gee, thank you.

ALLEN: And I want to toast Bill.

BILL: To a gentleman and one of the premier hosts on television.

ANITA: Absolutely.

ALLEN: Oh, come on…we're not going to talk about that. But we've had marvelous players, you know? Everybody who has played *Stumpers!* in these thirteen weeks…it's been a game that you've had to learn.

BILL: It's a great home game, too.

ALLEN: And the kind of response we've had from all the stars in town who want to play the game, who want to get in there and play…It's really kind of tough.

ALLEN: It's exciting.

BILL: You've been very personally involved.

ALLEN: We can't talk about the reasons for the cancellation —

ANITA: *(Fake crying)* I don't understand why!

ALLEN: No, no, we're not going to cry. This is New Year's Eve! This is going to be a great new year. We've got a very exciting future in this country coming up in this year ahead of us. We've got 1977 ahead of us and it's going to be a good year. A good year for you, a good year for you…I hope it's a good year for you. If you're going to be out tonight, be careful. Drive carefully tonight. But have, by all means, from all of us, all the Lin Bolen company, from all of us on Stumpers! who really have been happy to be with you, have a very happy new year. And here's to you. You've been marvelous.

Going into 1977, Betty unfortunately had something in common with her husband. Her show was going away, too. *The Mary Tyler Moore Show* had been more than a hit TV show. It had been the foundation of an empire, MTM Productions, which oversaw two spinoffs — *Rhoda* and *Phyllis* — as well as *The Bob Newhart Show*. All of the shows produced under the MTM banner had been sophisticated, clever, realistic, and favored character-driven humor more than situational humor, the kind of humor that *M*A*S*H* and *All in the Family* were also doing so well. But going into 1977, that kind of television was falling out of favor. The

Allen and Betty look ahead to their next career moves for 1977. Both of them were in search of new shows and new opportunities. FRED WOSTBROCK COLLECTION

big hits were shows like *Happy Days*, *Laverne & Shirley*, *The Captain and Tennille*, *Donny and Marie*, and *Charlie's Angels*...bland, broadest-common-denominator humor and escapism.

The Mary Tyler Moore Show was into its seventh season at this point. Emerging complaints from conservative groups about content on prime-time shows had led to the institution of a "family hour" policy at the major networks, dictating that shows airing between 8:00-9:00 pm had to be as safe for family viewing as possible. It was a well-meaning policy, and one that Allen himself actually liked (he anticipated that requiring family programming for an hour a night would bring game shows back to network prime-time schedules, but that ultimately didn't happen), but it suddenly meant that well-known shows were being moved to later time slots, or being treated with closer scrutiny than before. Although *The Mary Tyler Moore Show* never had a reputation for crossing the line or tackling serious controversies the way that *All in the Family* and *Maude* had, the show's depiction of Mary's personal life (at least once, she was seen in the morning wearing the same clothes she had worn the previous night for a date) and the raw, unapologetic sexuality of Sue Ann Nivens looked

Saying goodbye to some good friends. Allen with Ed Asner and Mary Tyler Moore, toward the end of *The Mary Tyler Moore Show.* FRED WOSTBROCK COLLECTION

like it might cause some headaches. Besides, after seven years, everyone considered themselves darn lucky to be on a show that they could still be proud of, one that hadn't been strained for ideas or had to force gimmicks upon itself to stay fresh, but how long could that last? And among some cast members and writers, the itch to seek out a new challenge was growing a little stronger.

The decision was made, not by the network, but by Mary Tyler Moore herself, that it was time to end the series. *The Mary Tyler Moore Show* was going off the air, bringing an end to Allen's annual order for flowers, and his Friday night customs of going to a coffee shop with Betty before the filming, and sitting in the bleachers to laugh right along with the rest of the audience. The series ended with Sue Ann — and Betty, really — sharing an unforgettable group hug with her co-workers, and marching out of the WJM newsroom belting out "It's a Long Way to Tipperary."

But as fast as their careers seemed to be heading for valleys, Allen and Betty both began climbing again. Allen got a new show less than a week after the final *Stumpers!* aired. And coincidentally, it was a show that Betty already knew pretty well: *Liars Club*.

This meeting of *Liars Club* is now in session! FRED WOSTBROCK COLLECTION

Ralph Andrews had finally managed to get a national version in syndication. Rod Serling had passed away in 1975, and when the national *Liars Club* premiered in the fall of 1976, Andrews initially hired Bill Armstrong to host. Armstrong had been a producer at Merrill Heatter-Bob Quigley Productions where he oversaw *The Hollywood Squares* for several years. He departed in 1974 to serve as producer and announcer for a new NBC game from Ralph Andrews, *Celebrity Sweepstakes*. And in 1976, at the same time that *Liars Club* was starting its first national season, Armstrong was also serving as the announcer for *Stumpers!*

But on January 7, 1977, Armstrong's contract was abruptly cancelled and Allen was asked to take over *Liars Club*. Allen became the new host, while Bill Armstrong took Ralph Andrews to court, seeking a $1.7 million settlement.

Allen also hosted a pilot for NBC called *The Smart Alecks*, in which he moderated the proceedings involving a three-celebrity panel. For the pilot, the three panelists were Pat Carroll, Don Meredith, and an ex-talk radio host from Indianapolis. David Letterman had moved to Hollywood, where he was performing stand-up at the famous Comedy Store. He had found some early work acting as a stand-in for an NBC pilot, *Word Grabbers*, where he made such a strong impression on producer Ron Greenberg that Greenberg lobbied NBC to let Letterman, a near-unknown, be a panelist if the pilot sold. Letterman did pick up the phone and made use of the contact info that Allen had given him in 1974, and Allen was ready to help. Allen had just been hired by *Newlywed Game* host Bob Eubanks, who was putting up a shingle for his own production company, to emcee *The Smart Alecks*. Allen asked Eubanks to put Letterman on the panel for the pilot.

The Smart Alecks was an early form of *Shark Tank*. An entrepreneur would demonstrate an invention or small business. Allen and the panelists would interview the entrepreneur, and then each panelist would make a speech to the studio audience summing up their individual feelings about the invention and whether or not it had any merit or long-term prospects. The studio audience would then vote on how much money the entrepreneur would receive to help further their creation.

Demonstration of an anti-snoring aid:

ALLEN: You know, I have a confession to make. I snore. I snore so loud that sometimes I wake myself up. But I stop easy. Betty just nudges, I roll over, and I stop. That's a traditional way to stop snoring.

DAVID: Actually, Allen and I have the same solution. Whenever I start snoring, Betty rolls over and nudges me, too.

Allen used his spot at *Liars Club* to call in some more favors for the budding young talent. He secured a seat on the panel for Letterman on that show, too. Letterman would appear on the show dozens of times, because of all game shows, *Liars Club* was the one that probably suited his talents best. His absurd-sounding explanations of the contraptions in front of him toed the line between deadpan and biting sarcasm, to the point that the contestants could never get a good feeling for when he was kidding and when he truly meant it.

DAVID: I know exactly what this is, and it's a little silly, but it comes to us from the spirit world and I've had occasion to use one of these. It's used to record the voices of spirits that have been left behind by people who have gone on to the other world. When my cousin Herb died, my mother used one of these because we thought perhaps that Herb was the one who was stealing the garden tools.

Allen introduces David Letterman to the studio audience during a break in taping for the unaired *Smart Alecks* pilot. FRED WOSTBROCK COLLECTION

While reminiscing about *Liars Club* in 2000, Letterman said, "I loved that show! It was never as big as I thought it ought to be."

Letterman, with his incredibly dry style and uniquely mischievous Midwestern look (numerous writers covering the stand-up scene during the late 1970s would compare him to Huckleberry Finn) seemed to strike Ludden as *Liars Club*'s answer to Richard Dawson. Dawson charmed audiences with his sarcastic quips on *Match Game* and charmed female contestants with big kisses after he had helped them win the big money. Whenever a female contestant incorrectly voted for a lie from Letterman, Allen would kid her about how she probably got distracted by Letterman's eyes or his smile.

Although nothing could ever meet the success of *Password*, Allen had least had a steady gig in *Liars Club*. It attracted an audience large enough to keep it on the air, with a straightforward game that was fun to watch. In 2009, one of the show's writers, Shelley Herman, wrote this remembrance of the program for Game Show Congress 7, a game show fan convention:

THOSE GLASSES! THOSE JACKETS! THAT HAIR!
A Fond Remembrance of Liars Club
By Shelley Herman (Reprinted with permission)

In the winter of 1976, I had the opportunity to work on what is still my favorite game show of all time, *Liars Club*…I cherish the times spent huddled in the run-thru room on Riverside Drive in Toluca Lake, California, at the offices of Ralph Andrews Productions where Jim Schwab, Scott Yagemann, Mike Henry, Laurie "Bumpers" Berman, "Big" Bob Burkhart and an assortment of colorful characters all learned to invent and tell colorful stories with conviction mentored by executive producer, the heart of *Liars Club*, Larry Hovis.

Whatever came in the mail, whatever the production assistants found at flea markets or gadget stores, Larry had one edict we all had to follow: "Will the story about the item be good enough to fool Allen?" Not the players, Allen.

So while he masterfully moved the show along, Allen was flying blind, delighting in stories, playing along as each item was revealed. This presented a bit of a problem. If Allen knew what the item was, he might accidentally reveal the correct answer to the players with a glint in his eye or a self-assured smile on his face. Now, the glint in his eye might have been difficult to see with those glasses, but his smile was to our show what Pinocchio's nose was to the Blue Fairy. It was his "tell."

Whenever Allen came by the office for a visit, we'd have to quickly, in a stealth-like manner, lock the doors where the items were kept and hide scripts with all our note cards and story suggestions. Allen was one of those people who always looked like Allen Ludden. You'd never see him in casual attire. He was always dressed as we saw him on television, wearing a jacket with a bold design and never a hair out of place. Allen was always curious as to what we could possibly dream up next. But, after a quick meeting

A legend of the time meets a legend of the future. Charlton Heston says hello to David Letterman on *Liars Club*. FRED WOSTBROCK COLLECTION

over very strong coffee or packets of Carnation Hot Cocoa (which we lived on), we resumed our secret operation once we were sure Allen had left the building.

Part of the fun of *Liars Club* was having the celebrity panel and Allen handle each item. They, along with the viewers, could see if the item spun or if it had a secret compartment or if it seemed useful in any way, shape or form. Once, a viewer sent an item to the office that looked like a hand-rolled cloth cigarette covered in wax. Was it a device used to help people stop smoking? Was it part of a floral arrangement to help preserve flowers? Was it something ladies used at the turn of the century as part of their nail care regimen? Or, was it something you stick in your ear and light so you can loosen earwax, in effect wicking the wax away? If you guessed Story Number 4, you are correct. So, when the time came to demonstrate the product, Allen stuck the item in Larry's ear, flicked his Bic, and laughed uncontrollably. And, whenever the brilliant Betty White played *Liars Club*, her mother Tess would cheer on her daughter and son-in-law.

I suppose the "best" worst item was the long, black cable that resembled something that, many years later, we would use to attach our DVD players to the back of our televisions. As always, Allen handled the item, looked at it every which way, and twirled it between his fingers until he heard the announcer reveal the correct story. The item he'd been holding was Sigmoidoscope, a device used for detecting polyps in the colon. Once again, there was that smile.

Someday, *Liars Club* may be revived. But it will never be the same without the joy and playfulness Allen brought to each show.

Shelley Herman's words of kindness would have been deeply appreciated by Allen. There was always one little thing about Allen's chosen profession that wasn't sitting right with him; the occasional disrespect. All the respect in show business was reserved for the actors, the comedians, the singers…not much leftover for game show hosts. In fact, quite the opposite. Hosts were caricatured and spoofed as empty-headed shills who smiled dumbly and spoke with unnatural, phony-cheer cadence. Allen could take occasionally being teased, but he was particularly sensitive to knocks about what he did for a living.

Allen and Betty were in bed one night watching *The Tonight Show*. Johnny Carson's guest that night was Dean Martin, legendary comic actor, singer, and host of the famous *Celebrity Roast* specials in which a famous figure was on the receiving end of an hour-long parade of barbs from other stars.

As he chatted with Dean Martin, Johnny quipped, "I watched your roasts all season. You're running out of people. I mean, that last one you had, *Dean Martin's Roast of Allen Ludden's Cousin!*"

The couple that plays together. Betty sits on the panel while Allen oversees another meeting of the *Liars Club*. AUTHOR'S COLLECTION, FRED WOSTBROCK COLLECTION

Allen and Betty laughed right along with the audience.

Dean Martin said, "Well, his cousin would be better than him, I'll tell you that! I don't know how Allen Ludden got into show business. He's always saying 'Why does a bumblebee not have a tail? I'll give you the answer in a minute.' I don't know what the hell he's talking about!"

The next day, Allen and Betty went for a walk on the beach. They had been talking about everything — the kids, the garden, and anything else, and out of absolutely nowhere, Allen said, "I didn't think that was necessary."

He was talking about Dean Martin's joke. It had gnawed at him the entire night and well into the day. The quip about "roasting Allen Ludden's cousin" he could take; it was a pretty innocuous jab, obviously. But Dean

Martin deriding his job had stung badly. Allen didn't take himself seriously, but no matter what he was doing to earn a living, he always took his work seriously.

Betty assured him, "Honey, they only tease you like that because they know that you can take it."

Allen, sounding like he didn't really believe her, nodded, "Sure."

David Letterman gives another off-the-wall explanation on *Liars Club*. Allen always took Letterman's kidding remarks in good fun, but he could be rather sensitive when others targeted him for punch lines.
FRED WOSTBROCK COLLECTION

But whether Dean Martin respected the work or not, Allen went to the *Liars Club* studio and kept right on working.

Betty, meanwhile, was getting ready to begin life after *Mary*. MTM wanted to make Betty the leading lady for a new sitcom and got to work dreaming one up. The first idea, quite logically, was a spinoff starring Betty as Sue Ann Nivens. Sue Ann had been an immensely popular character, but MTM disliked the idea the more it was considered. The show had already inspired two spinoffs, *Rhoda* and *Phyllis*. *Rhoda*, after a white-hot first season, had settled into so-so territory. *Phyllis* started off so-so and never got better. *Phyllis* in particular was of concern when Betty White's new series was being considered. The character of Phyllis Lindstrom had always been depicted as flighty and self-centered as a supporting character on *The Mary Tyler Moore Show*, but since those are such undesirable traits for a central character, she was altered somewhat when she became the star of her own show. The problem, naturally, was that she was now no longer the same character that audiences had enjoyed so much. Acid-tongued nymphomaniac Sue Ann Nivens would require the same type of major rewrite, so the spinoff idea was abandoned.

She explained at the time, "We all agreed immediately she was great as a seasoning but not as a main course."

Instead, Betty suggested a show-within-a-show premise about an actress starring in a new TV series, to be directed by her ex-husband. The first idea suggested was that Betty's character be the star of a show about a nun named Sister Scholastica.

"I scotched that pretty fast," Betty said. They considered delving into Betty's past by having her character be a star of summer stock, then considered a sitcom and a variety show. Betty considered tapping into her *Star Trek* fandom and wanted her character to be the star of a sci-fi series, but Ed. Weinberger suggested that since police shows were popular on television at the moment and sci-fi shows were virtually non-existent, Betty's character should star in a police drama.

The Betty White Show premiered in the fall of 1977, starring Betty and an eight-performer ensemble cast. That, she said, proved to be the biggest problem with the show. All eight actors had signed contracts explicitly stating that they would appear in every episode. *The Mary Tyler Moore Show* had an ensemble cast, too, but not every character appeared in every episode. *The Betty White Show*, in Betty's eyes, was a little bit bloated. She felt that the show had come together well, though, and was optimistic that it would be a success.

After fourteen episodes were filmed, Allen came home one night, bringing Grant Tinker with him, and together they gently broke the news that *The Betty White Show* was canceled. Soothing the pain was a dinner a few weeks later where the president of CBS had invited a number of friends, including Allen and Betty to join him. As Betty sat and watched, two other guests, Bob Newhart and Dick Martin, bluntly told the president that he had exercised poor judgment in canceling the show, giving a point-by-point defense of *The Betty White Show* until the boss had caved and admitted that it was a mistake. By then, of course, it was too late.

In 1978, Allen and Betty celebrated their fifteenth anniversary. A writer at the time said that they were known in their Brentwood neighborhood as "the nice people who still treat each other like newlyweds."

Lin Bolen, Allen's boss on *Stumpers!*, used the newlyweds comparison too when she told *People* Magazine, "When they can't be together at work, they call each other from their dressing rooms."

Truthfully, they didn't quite feel like newlyweds anymore. Willie and Emma, the two poodles that helped Allen charm Betty, were both gone. The poodle they got together shortly after they got married was losing

Betty, Allen, and their poodles. The poodles had gone gray right along with Allen and enjoyed long, happy lives. FRED WOSTBROCK COLLECTION

his sight and his hearing and had a heart problem on top of that. Betty herself was beginning her fight against the effects of time. She had a plastic surgeon do some work around her eyes, and when her eyes themselves became a problem to deal with, Betty stubbornly resisted having to admit she needed reading glasses for quite some time until Allen finally convinced her to do something about it by leaving a note under her pillow.

Allen has some choice words for Betty on *The Dean Martin Celebrity Roast.* FRED WOSTBROCK COLLECTION

It read, "If you can't see that I love you — SQUINT."

Betty laughed, and then she finally went to an eye doctor and got some reading glasses. A short time later, Betty spoke to Johnny Carson and reflected on the successful marriage she and Allen had nurtured together.

She told Johnny, "We've had a lot of fun for fifteen years, or for most of those years…Marriage should be fun, and…it really is. We tease Allen so much and…you only tease the people who you know like to take it a little bit. And Allen takes it up to a point, and all of a sudden you see the eyes just slipping around a little bit. He's thinking, 'They're <u>kidding</u>, aren't they?'"

The two of them were always able to make each other laugh and had no problem getting laughs at each other's expense. Allen did get his chance to get back at Betty for all the playful teasing in deliciously public fashion. In the ultimate demonstration of the expression "I only kid because I love," Allen fired off a few barbs when Betty was honored as Woman of the Hour on *The Dean Martin Celebrity Roast*.

"I realize that a woman is entitled to have her own pursuits, certainly. But really, dogs have such a part in Betty's life. It's her whole life. For

Allen, along with Jesse White, Jane Wyman, and Cesar Romero, on the annual *Stop Arthritis* Telethon. Allen would play Billy Flynn in a production of *Chicago*, with Jesse White joining him as Amos Hart.
AUTHOR'S COLLECTION

instance, when I proposed to her, the first thing she said was 'Sit up and beg.' She wouldn't even accept my ring until I rolled over and played dead. And on our honeymoon, SHE rolled over and played dead. There isn't a husband in the world who doesn't spend some time in the dog house, but he should consider himself very lucky if he's married to the best in breed. And I am."

Shortly after the milestone fifteenth anniversary, Johnny Carson asked Betty if she had any advice for couples considering marriage. Betty answered, "I think what I'd tell them to do is wait, and wait until you've lived through at least one cold that you've each had."

During the summer of 1978, Allen took another summer stock engagement, this time playing slick-talking lawyer Billy Flynn in the musical *Chicago*, with Jesse White (best known as TV's lonely Maytag Repairman) in the supporting role of Amos Hart. As a child, Allen had visited Chicago and came away concluding that he'd want to be in the theater. Allen brought his career full-circle by starring in a show named for the city that first sparked his interest.

It was one of the last stage roles that Allen took, but television certainly hadn't seen the last of him. It hadn't seen the last of *Password* either.

FRED WOSTBROCK COLLECTION

CHAPTER TWENTY

"PLUS"

"PASSWORD'S BACK!" Allen exclaimed.

"PASSWORD'S BACK!" he repeated for good measure.

Allen couldn't contain his excitement. As Gene Wood announced his name, he bounded down the stairs at center stage and ran toward the camera. He stuck his arm out, palm up, whipping it back and then dashing over to the familiar desk. The fundamental difference between Allen Ludden and other hypothetical performers with fourteen years of a single role under their belts: When *Password* revved up for a new run, nobody could have been happier about it than Allen.

Although NBC's primetime fortunes were ailing in late 1978, their daytime line-up was one of the better network line-ups of the decade, and if you were a fan of game shows, it was absolutely your best bet. Their schedule toward the end of the year included *Wheel of Fortune*, *The Hollywood Squares*, *Card Sharks*, *The New High Rollers*, and *Jeopardy!*

And since game shows were one of the few things that the network was getting a good return on, they wanted more. In 1978, NBC contacted Goodson-Todman with a special request: They wanted a new version of *Password*...but they didn't exactly want *Password*.

Fourteen years of first-runs and reruns was nothing to sneeze at, but NBC couldn't help dwelling on the way that the show had withered during its final year at ABC and concluded that *Password* was a good game, but not one built for current audiences. They asked Goodson-Todman to come up with a re-invented form of *Password*.

There are those in television who would balk at reinventing the wheel, but Goodson-Todman had developed an incredible reputation for doing exactly that. Two of their former NBC games, *The Match Game* and *The Price is Right*, had been revived on CBS in forms that bore almost no resemblance to their original forms, and in both cases, the new versions were more successful than the originals. And despite the fact that they had tried to re-invent *Password* twice with dismal results — *Password All-Stars* and the so-called *Password '75* — Goodson-Todman was willing to give it one more shot.

"One more shot" finally worked. They came up with a game that, knowing it would premiere after the new year, they were going to call *Password '79*. A few weeks before the pilot taping, the title was changed

Elizabeth Montgomery and Robert Foxworth help Allen christen *Password Plus.* FRED WOSTBROCK COLLECTION

to *Password Plus.* The story that Goodson-Todman gave at the time was that when Carol Burnett heard the new concept, her reaction was, "Oh, it's *Password* PLUS!" A Goodson-Todman staffer disputed that years later, noting that the Goodson-Todman offices on Sunset Boulevard were located across the street from a record store called Music Plus.

The new game set sail on January 8, 1979, and aware that the viewers might be wary at the thought that *Password* was being tinkered with, Allen punctuated his explanation of the rules by repeatedly emphasizing, "We're playing *Password*, just the same as we always have."

No more lockout buttons, no more qualifying game. They were back to two teams, each comprised of a celebrity and a contestant. Correctly guessing the password now allowed a team the opportunity to solve the

Password Puzzle. ("You've played *Password*, now here's the *Plus*," Allen liked to say in those first few weeks.)

Each sequence of five passwords served as clues to the identity of a person, place, or thing. For example, the passwords BLONDE, WIGS, BREASTS, SONGS, and COUNTRY would serve as clues to the answer "DOLLY PARTON." Solving either of the first two puzzles paid $100, every puzzle thereafter paid $200, and $300 won the game and the chance to play a new end game, Alphabetics. Ten passwords were arranged in alphabetical order and the contestant was told and shown the first letter of each password. Each password guessed paid $100, solving all ten in sixty seconds or less paid $5,000.

Allen naturally signed on to host, although he had one complaint that had to be addressed before the show premiered. The show's director had figured out a way of shooting the game that would use five cameras. During rehearsals for the pilot, Allen noticed that he wasn't appearing on camera very much.

Allen took a certain pride in his appearance that could occasionally cross a thin line into vanity. During an appearance on *Tattletales* (a Goodson-Todman game in which celebrity couples dished about their own private lives), Allen and Betty agreed that, when they walked past anything reflective, like a window or a puddle, Allen was apt to check his reflection as he passed by. Allen always looked perfect, always dressed perfectly, and from all the words that reporters and critics had written over the years, it was clear that people noticed. And as much as Allen resisted becoming a television personality twenty years earlier, the kind words had made an impact on him. The once camera-shy Allen now loved his close-ups.

"I don't want to do the show as a voiceover!" he complained. During a break in rehearsal, a sixth camera was moved into the *Password Plus* studio, exclusively for Allen's close-ups.

After the series went to air, Allen was prone to auditing. He once called director George Choderker at home and asked, "Does the number six mean anything to you?"

Choderker didn't know what he was talking about, so Allen clarified, "That's how many close-ups I had in today's show."

The occasional flash of vanity from Allen could understandably rub some staffers the wrong way, but Howard Felsher, the veteran producer who had dealt with any number of egos in his decades-long career, was quick to invoke the names of other stars who had caused him far more headaches. "I would rather have 100 Allen Luddens," he would always conclude.

Password Plus had all sorts of other pluses, beyond the puzzles and the cash up for grabs. After so much concern in the waning years of the ABC version that the show was overusing all usable material, *Password Plus* broadened the range of possible passwords. Passwords could now be proper names ("Hitchcock"), numerical ("Forties"), hyphenated ("x-ray"), initials ("NBC"), or a common two-word term ("New York" or "ice

Marcia Wallace and Tony Randall join Allen. Instead of the superimposed graphics used by previous versions, Password Plus had a slide projector mounted inside the desk, which meant that the passwords were actually part of the set. FRED WOSTBROCK COLLECTION

cream"), although the rules for what constituted an acceptable clue were still in place. A few months into the series, *Password Plus* added an interesting challenge to the game with a new rule that opposites were no longer acceptable clues. While Allen emphasized that it made the game tougher, it also confused a number of viewers because of the semantics issues it caused ("black" and "white" weren't opposites because any two colors are part of a broad spectrum; likewise, "Adam" and "Eve" aren't opposites because members of a pair aren't necessarily opposite of each other).

Though the no-opposites rule got a mixed reception, the game overall accomplished what Goodson-Todman had previously failed to do. It revitalized *Password* without wrecking it. The set was a tasteful arrangement of red and beige, with just enough neon to remind you that you were watching a game show. Alphabetics worked infinitely better than the Big Money Lightning Round had. It gave away big cash without seeming "infected by greed." The game had new rules, but not to such a degree that the game was bogged down. And in the most amazing achievement of all,

The set of *Password Plus.* FRED WOSTBROCK COLLECTION

some of the *Password* purists out there found themselves admitting that they liked *Password Plus* better.

The only problem was it wasn't capturing the country's imagination the way that original *Password* had. It was a problem that *Password Plus* could never quite overcome. By producer Robert Sherman's account, the program would always get "good but not great" ratings on NBC, and in fact, when those thirteen-week renewals came around, there were several periods when the Goodson-Todman staff was surprised that NBC wanted to keep the show on the air. Allen himself deserved some of the credit for taking initiative with *Password Plus* the way he had with *College Quiz Bowl.* On a few occasions, as the renewal period loomed, Allen would gently ask the home audience to write to NBC to let the network know that how much they enjoyed the show.

Although, not quite everybody enjoyed *Password Plus*. Guest George Peppard disrupted the game with an uncomfortable tirade about network standards and practices for TV game shows.

With cameras rolling and Allen visibly wincing, Peppard said, "I would like to tell you Allen that this is a wonderful game and I really enjoy playing it. BUT…the forms we have to sign in order to play that game, I want to discuss with you later in the program. I want the audience to know that there are some terrible things that they make us do before we're allowed to play this game…It's about NBC executives and I want everyone to write them a letter."

Allen allowed him to elaborate, but Peppard refused and insisted that he wanted to play the game. A few minutes later though, he got fired up and said, "I want to play the game. This is not about Goodson-Todman, this is not about *Password*. It's about NBC forms."

Allen again offered Peppard a chance to get this off his chest. Peppard refused, only to look squarely into the camera and go on a full-blown tangent a few minutes later. "You should know, friends, that before we do this program…There's a form that says that you won't cheat, you won't steal, you won't kick your mother…it goes on and on and on like you were some crook. Now, it's really unnecessary in this game. I mean, everybody around this game is paranoid about the truth, they're very careful, and we even have somebody from NBC who watches us. Now, that gets into the police state mentality and I do not think it's necessary, and I personally resent it, Mr. Silverman. Would you all write him a letter?"

Allen put on a brave face, smiling at the camera even as Peppard called out the current head of NBC, Fred Silverman, the man who, you might recall, canceled *Password* twelve years earlier, with far higher ratings than *Password Plus* was enjoying.

Allen calmly responded, "This is America. Everybody has a right to his opinion. There is, though, this very important fact to remember. When you watch game shows today, you are now assured that what you see is what you get. There is no hanky-panky. There is no planning. There is no arrangement. There's no way, because all of the networks — all of the networks — very carefully supervise their games. The fact that NBC elects to have a form offends some people. But it is true that game shows are militantly supervised by the networks, and for that, all of us in the game show business are really grateful. It's true. It's straight. There's no cheating."

The segment was so uncomfortable and so awkward that, per Mark Goodson's orders, the episode never aired on NBC.

Viewers tuning in a few weeks later also saw a strange game involving celebrity guests Patty Duke Astin and Bill Cullen. As the puzzle played out, the first three passwords in the puzzle were PROSTITUTES, FAMILY, and GAMBLING. When the puzzle went unsolved, the game moved onto the fourth password. Viewers at home saw a large black bar covering the password at the bottom of the screen. Patty Duke Astin gave a clue that

Allen and guest George Peppard in less awkward times on *Liars Club.* Peppard would later commandeer an episode of *Password Plus* with a tirade that Mark Goodson felt was unairable. FRED WOSTBROCK COLLECTION

was censored. Her partner's guess was also censored. Bill Cullen gave the clue "southward." The home audience heard that, but his partner's correct guess was censored, too. The password was SICILIAN. Patty Duke Astin had given the clue "Italian." The solution to the puzzle was "MAFIA." NBC had determined after the game had already played out that the puzzle was offensive.

So, too, had a number of Italian viewers who were able to read lips and figure out what they had been missing in the moments of silence. It created enough of a backlash that a few weeks later, Allen addressed it, after a not-coincidental puzzle with the solution "Michelangelo."

Allen very soberly addressed the camera. "Michelangelo is the answer to our first puzzle. Michelangelo of course being one of the great creative geniuses of all time. He was Italian. It seems appropriate that at this time, I should point out the fact that several weeks ago, we played a Password Puzzle involving clues to the word 'MAFIA.' Now, some of our viewers were offended by the use of the word 'Sicilian' as a clue. We did not intend to make any derogatory ethnic associations between this group and the Mafia...We have the highest regard for Americans of Italian descent, of

Gardening was a two-person job at Allen and Betty's house. FRED WOSTBROCK COLLECTION

course, and we very sincerely apologize to those who took offense."

In both situations, Allen showed remarkable regard for the home audience. No tap dancing, no sugar coating the discomfort of the situation. Allen was straightforward, he was honest, and he left nothing out. Even when hosting a game show, Allen used a plain-talk approach.

Password Plus attracted enough of an audience that Milton Bradley got right to work making a *Password Plus* home game. What made that noteworthy was that, after all these years, they still hadn't stopped making home games for the original *Password*. If you went to a department store in 1979, in one stop, you could buy new copies of the *Password Plus* 1st edition and the *Password* 19th Edition.

While Allen got settled with *Password Plus* on NBC, he was making plans to follow up on a promise that he had made to Betty when he was courting her. He knew that Betty loved Carmel, California. She spoke fondly of her childhood trips up there, and Allen came to find that he liked the area as much as she did. When he was trying to get Betty to change her mind and accept the marriage proposal, he promised to build a house in Carmel.

Betty and Allen could travel to virtually any spot in the world for a vacation — and by this point, they had — but no exotic ports or bustling nightlife anywhere in the world appealed to them the way that this smaller town five hours north of Hollywood did. They rented the same cottage over and over again whenever they had time to get out of town together, but during a drive through Carmel one day they spotted a piece of property that they both became enamored with the moment that they saw the "for sale" sign.

Before long, they had hired the architect, and any spare time that they had was dedicated to making extended trips to Carmel to oversee construction and make all the little decisions that came with it — what types of doorknobs, the type of light fixtures, and the two workaholics discovered that, despite all the arguments they were expecting at the beginning of the project, both of them genuinely seemed to enjoy the adventure of creating a new home from scratch.

FRED WOSTBROCK COLLECTION

CHAPTER TWENTY-ONE

"MINUS"

At the beginning of *Password Plus* in 1979, Allen had some vague sense that there was something wrong with him. He couldn't quite figure out what. He was sixty-one by this point, and maybe those not-so-good days came with the aging process. In time, he found himself noticing some discomfort whenever he leaned over his lectern to hand the password wallets to the contestants, to the point that he spoke up about it and had a small cushion added to it to alleviate the problem. When *Password Plus* staffers became concerned, Allen casually attributed it to diverticulitis. It was possible that he actually thought that was the problem.

As 1979 wore on, between the bouts of excitement and occasional stress that came with building the Carmel dream house, Betty became troubled by some spells that Allen went through. He'd have low energy and a slight fever, but after a day or so, he'd bounce right back and feel fine. But then those spells began lasting two days, and then longer. The bad days began happening often enough that Allen realized he had to see a doctor. Two doctors and two CT scans couldn't find anything wrong, but a gallium scan found a "hot spot" in Allen's stomach, and he needed surgery immediately.

Password Plus producer Robert Sherman was attending NATPE — a convention of television producers, packagers, and local station managers — in Las Vegas when he was paged and received an emergency call notifying him that Allen Ludden had to take the week off from hosting *Password Plus*. Because of the taping schedule that the show had been maintaining, the next taping couldn't be canceled. The show taped so close to its scheduled air dates that when Sherman received the call, there were only two episodes in the can that hadn't aired yet.

Robert Sherman immediately called Bill Cullen, veteran game show host (he had been a host or regular panelist on forty shows during his career) and a frequent guest of *Password* and *Password Plus*. He was a noted quick study, which meant minimal training would be needed. He was also so well-liked by audiences that he could easily fill Allen's role without viewers feeling that something was amiss. And it was humorously appropriate to have Bill Cullen fill in for the role because at one point in their careers, Bill and Allen both sported crew cuts and horn-rimmed glasses, and Bill appeared on television with Betty somewhat often. As a result, Allen had reached a point where he didn't bother correcting any-body who shouted "Hi Bill!" at him when they saw him walking down the street. And Bill, for his part, had enjoyed a fair share of "Hi Allen!" when he was out and about.

Bill Cullen made his first appearance on *Password Plus*, with the set unintentionally accentuating the absence of the regular host. Because Allen stood directly between four seated players, the show's set design had always tried to prevent the illusion that Allen was towering over everybody by putting a small pit behind the lectern where Allen would stand. Bill, significantly shorter than Allen, peered over the lectern when he stood in that pit. Bill did optimistically tell home viewers that Allen would be back next week and that there was nothing to be concerned about. Unfortunately, that turned out not to be the case (not that Bill knew that).

Allen had held Betty and the doctor to a promise that they would tell him the whole truth when he woke up. Before Allen woke up, the doctor went to Betty and told her, "Bad news, darling."

When Allen woke up a short time later, he immediately sensed that whatever he went through was only the beginning. As soon as his eyes opened, the first word out of his mouth was, "What?"

The doctor broke the news to him: He had stomach cancer. During the surgery, the medical team had removed as much as they could, but they hadn't removed all of it. And they wouldn't be able to. Best case scenario, he said, Allen had only a few months to live. Allen stared at Betty quietly and squeezed her hand. At that moment, a thoughtless nurse asked for an autograph.

Allen spent the next few weeks at home convalescing while Bill Cullen, despite his early assurances, continued hosting *Password Plus*, with Allen's pit filled in for him. Betty helped put a brave face on things by appearing as a guest for Bill's fourth week as host to preserve the illusion of normalcy.

The following week, *Password Plus* opened with Gene Wood intro-ducing that week's guest players, Susan Richardson and Bill Cullen, who no longer stood at the host's lectern. A shadowy figure scaled the stairs at center stage as Gene Wood introduced "the star of *Password Plus*...."

After a pause for dramatic effect, the shadowy figure emerged into the bright lights of the set. "ALLEN LUDDEN!"

Allen smiled broadly and proclaimed, "I missed you!" to the home audience. He bounded over to the lectern, stepped into his pit, and called Bill Cullen "a beautiful man" as they shared an embrace.

Allen cheerfully told the audience that he was coming back because

Business as (almost) usual. Allen kept coming to the studio and hosting *Password Plus* even as he was privately battling cancer. This week was a special series of episodes, with Vicki Lawrence and Carol Burnett competing in character as Mama and Eunice. FRED WOSTBROCK COLLECTION

Bill was "having too much fun" as host and left it at that. He would, in due course, reveal to the press that he was battling cancer, but indicated that the surgery had been successful and that he was on his way to a full recovery. Tess knew the truth. So did David, Martha, and Sarah. Grant Tinker and Mary Tyler Moore knew too. But Allen obstinately maintained that he didn't want the general public to find out that he had terminal cancer. He imagined viewers watching *Password Plus* every day, carefully studying his face and his body and actively looking for signs of deterioration.

Password Plus executive producer Howard Felsher had left the show in early 1980 to focus more attention on the other game he oversaw for Goodson-Todman, *Family Feud*. *Feud* was preparing to expand its nighttime version from twice a week to five nights a week, on top of the five

ALLEN LUDDEN

daytime episodes per week for ABC. This left Robert Sherman fully in charge of *Password Plus*, but Felsher was concerned about Allen's condition and he began calling Sherman to ask for updates.

Throughout Allen's four-week absence, Sherman remained in regular contact with his host, but Allen wouldn't even elaborate on his condition, only telling him, "The doctors don't know what's wrong with me."

The staff of *Password Plus* never actually found out the true nature of Allen's condition during this period, although Robert Sherman admitted that he was getting phone calls from tabloid newspapers, looking for updates that Sherman couldn't provide.

Although Allen hid the truth from the general public, he was willing to discuss it in vague terms. He acknowledged what was already fairly obvious anyway, that he had endured an illness serious enough that he had to leave work for four weeks to get it dealt with.

And as Allen revealed to one reporter, Stacy Jenel Smith, his sickness had a profound effect on his mood. It made him far more philosophical about himself, and about life. "Illness is such an opportunity for realizing what's really important. All the good things in day-to-day life are SO good, and the bad ones are so unimportant.

"I've learned something, something that applies to everything in life from communication to work to lovemaking to relationships to trees and flowers — well, to everything. I'd always thought of myself as a positive kind of person before, but now I know I never really was."

It was a stunning declaration of self-awareness from Allen, whose temper could burn in the studio. He once chided the woman who handled cue cards on *Password Plus* so harshly that Betty got involved, forcing Allen to apologize to the young lady after the taping. Allen now took stock of those occasional flare-ups and was saddened to realize how unnecessary it all was.

He continued, "When I was ill, I started eliminating all the things that were wasteful uses of energy. For instance, have you ever stayed awake at night being angry over something, without deciding what to do about it? That kind of pointless anger is so harmful. Maybe it's an old cliché, that 'power of positive thinking' — but that power is now being recognized even by the medical profession. I've certainly discovered what it can do."

Truth be told, any signs of deterioration that viewers would have seen would have been imaginary. Allen looked as lively as ever, maintaining a full head of hair, a healthy skin tone, and a twinkle in his eye. Cancer wouldn't destroy his outward appearance.

It also didn't seem to have any effect on his work ethic. Allen didn't sit at home to relax away whatever time he had left. If anything, he viewed terminal cancer as a reason to load up his calendar. The famous Allen Ludden work ethic was magnified by the prognosis. He signed up for a final summer stock gig; fittingly, Allen brought his theater career to a close with one more run of *Critic's Choice*, the show that possibly meant more

Allen, on the mend, as a panelist on *Match Game*. FRED WOSTBROCK COLLECTION

to him personally than any other. And the engagement was in Corpus Christi, tying his life and his professional career together.

Allen and Betty returned the favor to Bill Cullen by appearing as guests on his game show, *Chain Reaction*. They sat side-by-side on the panel for a week of *Match Game*. They filmed cameos in a made-for-TV movie called *The Gossip Columnist*. Allen played for charity on a special game show hosts tournament on *Card Sharks*. He appeared in an episode of *Fantasy Island*. And he and Betty appeared together on *The Love Boat*. It was actually a slightly demanding performance for Allen; he had to learn how to ride a horse for the role. Allen admitted to being tired and occasionally unhappy during the filming of *The Love Boat* — as light-hearted as the show was, it carried a heavy workload like any other TV series — but used the experience as an example of how his illness had affected his attitude, and vice versa.

He explained to one reporter, "[*The Love Boat*] made me tired, and I got worried about being tired. I thought, 'God, I'm hurting again.' But I've found that if I can rewind negative thoughts, go back to their roots and either resolve the problem that's worrying me or put it aside, pain goes away. If there's psychosomatic illness, you'd better believe there's psychosomatic healing."

For that episode of *The Love Boat*, Allen and Betty starred in a story called "The Horse Lover," playing a bickering couple, Paul and Louise Willis. Paul surprised Louise with a cruise on the *Pacific Princess*, insisting that she deserved it. It wasn't until she boarded the ship that Louise realized that Paul had brought along his beloved racehorse; he had booked the cruise because its destination was the site of the next big race. Paul was so fixated on the big race that he didn't bat an eye when he found out Louise was seeing another passenger during the long cruise. Paul's horse won the race, but Paul was stunned to realize that Louise didn't care... and that he didn't really care either.

That night, he sold the horse to Louise's suitor, with the man's promise that he would never pursue Louise again. Paul and Louise held each other close as Paul passionately told her, "I love you...it took almost losing you for me to realize how much I love you." They shared a long kiss like they had on that stage in Massachusetts eighteen years earlier. And hearing the force in the words on that final "I love you," it was hard to figure out where Paul and Louise ended and Allen and Betty began. Real life and a surgical team's diagnosis had already dictated that there wouldn't be a blissful conclusion to this story. But this episode of *The Love Boat* ultimately proved to be one of the final times that Allen and Betty ever appeared on national television together. And viewers saw them in a "happily ever after" ending.

Allen's sixty-second birthday rolled around at the beginning of October, and he and Betty went north to celebrate. On October 7, 1980, Allen and Betty woke up in Monterey, California, about five miles north of Carmel, where they were still overseeing the extensive work going into their dream house. Allen rose out of bed and had trouble getting himself oriented, and after a very, very slow walk that didn't take him very far, he walked directly into a wall, as if he couldn't avoid it. He and Betty immediately realized that there was something wrong and called an ambulance.

At Monterey Community Hospital, the initial diagnosis was a stroke, although it would later turn out to be a severe reaction to some medication. Nevertheless, it was so severe that by afternoon, he had slipped into a coma.

The next day, NBC viewers would learn the bad news from, of all people, David Letterman. Letterman had been booked as a guest on *The Tonight Show Starring Johnny Carson* in November 1978 and got incredible returns from it, not only being asked back but getting promoted to guest host after only his third appearance. He became something of a project for NBC and Fred Silverman. Silverman, who still disliked game

The television viewing public's last image of Allen: With Betty by his side and a smile on his face. A perfect exit in imperfect circumstances.
FRED WOSTBROCK COLLECTION

shows as much as he had thirteen years earlier, wiped three of them off the schedule in the summer of 1980 to make way for a daytime talk show hosted by Letterman. The daytime show flopped — Letterman's ideal audience was not an audience that watched daytime television — and was in its final month of programs when the bad news broke. A daily feature of Letterman's daytime show was a five-minute newsbreak anchored by Edwin Newman, who typically worked a few lighter stories into each update so that he and Letterman could banter about them afterward. That morning, Newman announced that Allen Ludden was in a coma, and Letterman wrapped up the show with a sincere expression of remorse for the circumstances and offering his best wishes toward the man who had done so much for him at the very beginning of his career and before that.

Allen lingered in the coma with a prognosis so grim that the family came to say goodbye. Half-brother Frank came in from Texas, and so did all three children. Doctors didn't expect Allen to wake up from the coma, but Betty, six months after the terminal diagnosis, was sure that Allen still had some gas left in his tank. She stayed right where she was, holding Allen's hand and telling visitors, "He's not going to go."

On October 12, Allen woke up from the coma. Love's intuition proved correct, and Allen gave credit where he felt credit was due.

"The good Lord and Betty White got me out of it, and I'm going to live because of her," he told the Associated Press. "…[T]he doctors up there had said, 'Forget it,' my brother came out, my son came out, and everybody came out and expected me to die when I was in the coma, and Betty just sat there and held my hand and said, 'No he isn't, he's not going to go.'"

A doctor told reporter Dick Donovan, "He was comatose and grayish looking when he came into E.R. It didn't look too good for him at the time. Frankly, I thought he was a goner. But you never really know about these things. Less than a week later, he was talking to his nurses and was making a rather remarkable recovery."

He still had some time left, and unlike the initial diagnosis, which had inspired Allen to commit a heavy workload while he still had it in him, this time, he realized that he really would have to take it easy. He made it known that he wasn't going to host *Password Plus* anymore.

On October 14, Allen was sound asleep when Betty was called to the nurses' desk at midnight. A nurse handed her the telephone. It was Mary Tyler Moore, sobbing as she told Betty that earlier in the day, Richie, her son from her first marriage, had accidentally killed himself while handling a shotgun.

Taking stock of her own situation and her friend's situation, Mary helplessly asked, "Where did it all go wrong for us?"

They stayed on the phone together while they cried for the next ten minutes. After Betty hung up, she went back into Allen's hospital room, and experienced what she could only describe later as a "purge." In the privacy of the hospital room, she didn't have to put on a brave face, she didn't have to hide details, she didn't have to be a professional. She finally let loose all of her pent up emotions from the most difficult year she had ever endured.

Password Plus would continue without Allen, although he was so syn-onymous with the show — fans and the press alike would often refer to him as "Mr. Password," as Mark Goodson had — that the show's staff wanted his input about who should host the show. Bill Cullen was hosting a new game show for Goodson-Todman himself, called *Blockbusters*, and a few staffers had heard rumors that the powers-that-be felt that Bill hadn't moved *Password Plus* quickly enough during his time as guest host. Either way, Bill Cullen was out of contention.

At Allen's suggestion, the show hired Tom Kennedy, host of *Name That Tune* and formerly Betty's announcer on *Date with the Angels*.

Tom remembers, "Jerry Chester, the executive vice president of Goodson-Todman, called me one day and said, 'Well, I guess you know Allen is under the weather.' I was floored! I hadn't heard anything about it. He said, 'We have tapings coming up. Would you consider hosting?' I said I understood the plight they were in, but I held Allen and *Password* in very high regard. I told Jerry that I would only host it if Allen signed off on it. Jerry said, 'Well, Allen was the one who told me to call you, so there you go.'"

Less than twenty-four hours later, Tom was at the Goodson-Todman offices. "The Goodson-Todman staff was all over me as soon as I walked in. They were one of the most professional groups in television history. I was surrounded when I walked through the door. They sat me down and went through every rule and every nuance, all the details, they answered all of my questions, and then a handful of them stayed late and we spent a few hours playing game after game after game. It only took me one day and I felt totally prepared and comfortable with the show.

"The only problem was that I had a mindset for classic *Password* and not so much for *Password Plus*. For the first few weeks, I kept forgetting and forgetting to give them chances to guess the puzzle. And Betty, who was a trooper, came in to play the game while she was tending to Allen, and she did everything she could to put me at ease. She was just terrific. She treated me like a brother; she cuddled me on that show and took good care of me. There was a day when she and Dick Martin played, and I bungled explaining a rule, and kept bungling it and bungling it, and Dick Martin kept butting in and interrupting me and breaking me up. She looked into the camera and said, 'Don't worry, Allen, everything's fine.' I loved that."

Allen's final taped episode of *Password Plus* aired on Monday, October 27, 1980. In a truly strange coincidence, one of the puzzles in that episode was "FAMOUS KENNEDYS," and one of the passwords used in the round was "TOM." The following day, Tom Kennedy opened the program with a dedication to Allen Ludden, and then strolled onstage to take over as the host of *Password Plus*.

Three weeks into Allen's hospitalization, Grant Tinker arranged for a private jet to transfer Allen to Good Samaritan Hospital in Los Angeles, where Allen's own familiar team of doctors could look after him. In time, Allen was walking and talking comfortably again. After a few more weeks, Allen had made such significant improvement that he was discharged and sent home. Doctors warned him that his medication was causing a calcium build-up in his body, so he was instructed to avoid all dairy products indefinitely. Beyond those orders, Allen was basically being left by his doctors to live however he wanted, and Allen decided that this time, he wouldn't hurry back to work.

At home, he was greeted by cards and a few flowers from friends, but more amazing to him was the avalanche of fan mail that awaited him. Over the years, Allen had believed in the power of the mail, possibly more than any other performer on television. He had seen it save *College Quiz Bowl*. He had seen it save *Password*, and then save *Password Plus*. And now, the mail was saving his own spirit.

"I just can't believe it," he told Betty over and over again.

In one of his last interviews, Allen mused, "I've been on television for about twenty years, and I just did my job. But the mail that I have had, the prayers I've had said — I start to cry every time I talk about it. You just don't realize how many people can relate to you and care about you."

Allen mostly stayed out of show business. When he felt up to it, he appeared on a couple of talk shows with Betty to discuss his battle, and he took one gig, recording a series of radio and TV commercials for Southern California Gas Company. He kept the secret of the terminal diagnosis from the public as long as he could. He was willing to acknowledge battling cancer and suffering an apparent stroke, but in his final interviews with newspaper writers (one of whom said that "Allen looked good but sounded tired"), Allen continued to keep up the illusion that he was merely battling an illness that was going to take a little longer to shake off, but that he was going to recover.

It was under the guise of being on the mend and planning a comeback that Allen gave Tom Kennedy an impressive seal of approval, telling interviewers that he planned on returning to television full-time down the road, but he didn't plan on ever returning to *Password Plus* because Tom Kennedy was doing such a great job hosting the show.

Tom modestly replies, "Oh, please. No. I appreciate Allen giving me a compliment like that, but if he had ever recovered, I would never have stayed. I wouldn't allow it. That show belonged to him."

Betty agreed with Allen's assessment, though, noting in her autobiography that "Tom Kennedy took good care of *Password*."

One reporter asked Allen what his plans for the future were if he didn't plan on returning to his beloved game show. Allen answered, "I'm going back to college…I want to become a licensed landscape gardener and start a landscaping company."

Tom Kennedy agreed to become host of *Password Plus*, but only after receiving Allen's personal thumbs up. FRED WOSTBROCK COLLECTION, AUTHOR'S COLLECTION

Tom Kennedy says, "Allen kept up that illusion for all of his friends. I had no idea. I'd call him on the phone and ask how he was doing, and he'd reply, 'I'm great! I went for a walk today! I walked for — *how long, Betty, was it twenty?* Yeah, I walked for twenty minutes today! I'm building my strength up and feeling better every day.' He didn't want anyone to worry about him."

Allen also felt that, if he didn't want his friends worrying about him, then it was important for Betty to continue with her life outside the house. She wanted to stay at home and take care of her husband. Allen practically pushed her out the door, encouraging her to accept bookings for the next game show taping or appear in a comedy sketch with Johnny Carson. Anything to get her out of the house; Allen knew he had married a workaholic, and he didn't want to get in the way.

Betty told reporter Bob Thomas, "Allen would drive me out of the house to go to work. He thought that was the best thing for me, and he was right."

By February of 1981, the long process of building the house in Carmel finally ended. The furnishings were added, and in March, Allen got the go-ahead from his doctors to leave Los Angeles for a few days

One of Allen and Betty's last public photos, a shot used in conjunction with their work for Southern California Gas Company. AUTHOR'S COLLECTION

to visit the house. He enjoyed two days and two nights in the house before heading back to Los Angeles with Betty. Betty was able to find the best in a bad situation. Allen wouldn't live long enough to really enjoy the house he had been bringing to life for the past year and a half. But as far as Betty was concerned, those forty-eight hours were enough time that she felt comfortable and honest referring to it as "our house."

A short time later, Allen went back into the hospital, and Betty went back to work, at Allen's and their family doctor's urging. Allen couldn't help noticing parallels between Margaret's demise and his own, and he told Betty so. Allen and Margaret had both been stricken by cancer, both endured a slow deterioration, and in both cases, the one who was suffering recognized that their spouse needed to work for a sense of normalcy. Betty agreed. She signed on to play the role of Ellen Jackson, a role that she had played multiple times in the recurring "Family" skits on *The Carol Burnett Show*, for a made-for-TV movie featuring the characters, called *Eunice* (1982). The timing and the subject matter made Betty squeamish — the movie was set at a funeral — but from a more objective standpoint, she recognized that the script was hilarious, so she agreed to it. Betty had signed on to do another episode of *The Love Boat*, but by that point, Allen had taken such a bad turn that she initially tried to back out of her commitment.

Allen's doctor told her, "You have to do it for yourself, and for Allen."

Betty spent several days in an exhausting relay from the on-location filming aboard an actual cruise ship, back to the mainland, and back to Los Angeles to be with Allen in the hospital. She would never forget the date that filming on that episode wrapped: Saturday, June 6, 1981.

Carol Channing, who appeared in the episode with her, told a gossip columnist, "Work is the best therapy for her. She comes in completely knocked out, but as I'm working with her, I can feel it when the blood starts coursing through her veins."

Betty didn't have to worry about Allen being left alone in the hospital while she worked. Every day during that final stay in the hospital, without fail, Grant Tinker dropped by. The hospital was in downtown Los Angeles, while Tinker's office was a twenty-minute drive away in Burbank. Allen was surprised to see his friend so often, and Tinker would always justify it by saying, "I was in the neighborhood."

On June 8, 1981, at 1:25 a.m., Allen Ellsworth Ludden, husband, father, accidental radio and television institution, died at age sixty-three, five days shy of his eighteenth wedding anniversary.

A television lover in Los Angeles remembered reading the news that day. He remembers, "Allen and Betty were always together. You almost never saw a photo of one or the other in the paper. It was a photo of some party they were attending together, or some ceremony that they were attending together, or a photo from a television show that they had just taped. And when I saw Allen Ludden's name in the obituaries, I remember, my first thought was, 'What's Betty White going to do?'"

FRED WOSTBROCK COLLECTION

AUTHOR'S COLLECTION

CHAPTER TWENTY-TWO
"LEGACY"

Very early in the morning, Betty called Grant Tinker and told him that the battle was over. Betty asked if Grant would speak at the memorial service, and Tinker calmly told her he would "produce" the whole thing, making all the phone calls and assembling all of Allen's closest friends to say a few words. Betty, he promised, wouldn't have to deal with it. Later that afternoon, Grant came to Betty and Allen's house in Brentwood and spent some time with her, helping her get through her grief, focusing totally on her. As Betty recalled, he showed no signs of distraction or preoccupation. His attention was entirely on his grieving friend and the loss they were both suffering.

It wasn't until weeks later, when Betty read the newspaper, that she discovered what Grant Tinker himself had gone through that day. NBC had been in bad shape in recent years, with far more shows that were misses than hits. (Gene Rayburn cheekily referred to the network as "the late NBC.") The network had signed Fred Silverman to turn things around and ultimately the network was in worse shape by the time his disastrous tenure ended. On June 8, 1981, hours after learning that Allen had died, Grant Tinker attended a luncheon in Burbank in which he was offered the grueling task of trying to right the ship. Tinker accepted and had become Chairman of the Board for NBC. He had never said a word about it, instead quietly focusing on Betty and getting her through her crisis. As Betty would put it later, the final thing that she ever learned about Allen Ludden was he had done an outstanding job of picking a best friend.

But before Grant Tinker would do anything for NBC, he prepared a wonderful send-off for Allen Ludden, organizing a memorial service at Church of the Hills in Hollywood's Forest Lawn Memorial Park. It was attended by 250 guests, mostly film and television stars, including Jack Klugman, George Peppard, Earl Holliman, Dom DeLuise, Angie Dickinson, Ruta Lee, Ross Martin, Don Fedderson, Delbert Mann,

Garry Marshall, Ross Hunter, Eve Arden, Frank De Vol, Ed Reimer, and Carl Reiner. From the fraternity of TV game shows, Monty Hall, Peter Marshall, Jack Barry, Bob Barker, Alex Trebek, and Gene Wood were present. A series of eulogies was given by Tinker, Burt Reynolds, Dick Martin, Mark Goodson, Gene Rayburn, Bert Convy, and Tom Kennedy. At the front of the church was Allen, in a casket covered completely in marigolds.

Tinker called the service "a well-cast party, because it is a celebration."

Reynolds said in his speech, "Allen was a child, boy and man, and you never knew which was going to be there when you met him. In a town full of cynicism, I'll miss the marriage based on love and laughter that he and Betty had. He loved this town, he loved this business, and he loved us."

Tinker added, "What we have here is a good friend, a good husband, and a good father. He touched all our lives. Saying goodbye is always a bad business. But Betty told me the other day Allen dearly loved a party and people. He liked nothing better than a well-cast party, which is what we have here, to celebrate a good man. We are glad he came our way and touched our lives."

Tom Kennedy said, "When you're fortunate enough to acquire the friendship of Allen Ludden, you've hit the jackpot."

Gene Rayburn's voice cracked as he struggled to keep his emotions under control. He said, "Many of us take pride in saying he was a good friend. He was generous and he was kind…Allen Ludden was a good man." After another crack of his voice and a pause to regain his composure, Gene hastily wrapped up with, "He will be missed."

Rev. Robert S. Spicer-Smith, a classmate of Allen's at the University of Texas, eulogized him with the last sentence of their alma mater's school song: "The eyes of Texas are upon you until Gabriel blows his horn."

Afterward, in accordance with Allen's final wishes, his body was flown to Mineral Point, Wisconsin, where only Betty and the children attended the funeral. He was interred in a family plot that his grandfather had purchased. Betty returned home to Carmel, where she was overcome by the sight of her dogs lying on Allen's robe.

She told *People* Magazine, "I just fell apart, and we sat there together on the floor."

A few weeks later, Betty was contacted by the Los Angeles Zoo. She was informed that the zoo had received a sizable amount of money from an anonymous donor, with the provision that the koala preserve at the zoo was to be renamed Allen Ludden Plaza. Thinking about those daily hospital visits, the visit at home after the NBC luncheon, and the superbly produced memorial service, Betty didn't have to do much detective work figuring out who the anonymous donor was.

In those difficult first few months after losing Allen, Betty got by with a little help from her mother, who had been down this road herself and could offer the wisdom that came with experience. She also got support from

Back to work. Betty appeared on *The Tonight Show Starring Johnny Carson* only two months after Allen's death. After the sketch, she chatted with Johnny and announced the Los Angeles Zoo had received a donation to re-name the koala preserve "Allen Ludden Plaza." AUTHOR'S COLLECTION

friends like Lucille Ball, who came over to the house one day and taught Betty how to play backgammon. She gave Betty such an unwieldy, confusing explanation that Betty was reduced to fits of laughter throughout the game, which Lucy won handily. As usual, her pets — two dogs at this point, Sooner and Timmy — gave her comfort too, although Betty noticed a profound change in their behavior after Allen died. Allen and Betty had long enjoyed a pleasant little routine of sitting in the living room every evening to discuss what they had done that day. Timmy would lie on the couch while Allen scratched his tummy, and Sooner would lie on the floor next to Betty's feet. After losing Allen, Timmy never lied on the couch again. He would always lie on Betty's lap, while Sooner sprawled completely across Betty's feet.

In time, Betty's life went back to whatever "normal" could possibly be. She spent a lot of time in Carmel, which amazed friends who had advised her to sell the house because they worried that the emotional toll of living there made be too much for her. To the contrary, she remained there because it was precisely what Allen wanted. In his final weeks, he held Betty to a promise that she would never sell it.

She threw herself into as much work as possible to keep herself focused and busy. She signed on for commercials, she hosted a charity benefit in Hawaii, she taped a guest-starring role on the sitcom *Love, Sidney*. She played *Match Game*. In her spare time, she wrote a screenplay for which she had no plans. She merely wrote it to keep herself busy. She made her way back to *Password Plus* in September.

Familiar territory, guest-starring on a sitcom with Tony Randall. Betty appears on *Love, Sidney*. AUTHOR'S COLLECTION

The idea that Betty was able to get back to *Password Plus* so quickly came as a surprise to fans. Surely the experience would be difficult for her. But Betty rationalized it while talking to the press. Returning to the show immediately, at least for her, was part of the grieving process, as well as part of the recovery. "[*Password*] is like family to me, and I figured if I left, it would be too painful for me to go back."

Betty was more blunt about the experience talking to *People* Magazine. She soldiered on because she felt there was no reason not to, and she admitted she was growing a bit tired of being commended for not staying cooped up in her house all day. "…[I]f one more person said, 'Oh, you're so strong,' I would have decked them."

Tom Kennedy says, "Betty faces reality. She's really good about seeing things through even if she's worried about them. So there was never a doubt in my mind that she'd be back. And she came with a smile on her face. She was never dour. The thing that we all had in common was that we were doing the best we could, and she was doing the best she could."

That taping of *Password Plus* proved to be a special day. Goodson-Todman Productions had ordered special jackets for the crew of *Password Plus*, as a token of appreciation for the effort they put into the program. They were snazzy blue jackets with a gold rendering of the *Password Plus* logo across the back. It was reversible too; when it was turned inside-out, it became a gold jacket with a blue *Password Plus* logo across the back.

On the air, Tom Kennedy explained to viewers that there had been a shipping error when the jackets were ordered and that, for the time being, not enough were made for everybody to have one. Behind the scenes, the show was going to have to deal with figuring out the silly little problem of which staffers got to have jackets first while their co-workers waited. But, Tom said, the entire crew agreed that one very special person in particular couldn't be left out. After announcing that none of the jackets had been distributed yet, Tom gave the first one to Betty White. It was a touching symbol of the way that the general public regarded the game and regarded Betty. In the beginning, Betty was a guest of the show and nothing more. She and Allen didn't have a stake in the program. But her husband had always been "Mr. Password." And now that Allen was gone, people regarded *Password* and all the variants that followed as "Betty's show."

"Betty's show" came to an end on March 26, 1982. For the final broadcast of *Password Plus*, Tom Kennedy took a moment to pay tribute to his predecessor: "This is the last in our series of *Password Plus*, and even though our dear friend Allen Ludden isn't with us at this particular moment, as you well know, he hosted this show as only he could do for something like eighteen years…and so, I was very proud to have the last year and a half at the helm."

Tom looks back now and says, "When I showed up for the first time, I thought I was coming in as a temporary solution. I was a substitute. And even as the weeks turned into months and Allen didn't come back, I still viewed myself as temporary. And then we lost Allen and honestly, that was still how I viewed myself. I never saw myself as the host of *Password Plus*, and when I look back now, I don't consider myself the host of that show. I always saw it as Allen Ludden's show. When I close my eyes and picture *Password*, I picture him, not me. *Password* was Allen Ludden and Allen Ludden was *Password*. He had this indelible personality and style, and it had rubbed off on the show. It always carried this certain atmosphere that he had helped give it."

The cancelation was part of a movement by NBC to get out of the game show business and build a daytime line-up with other forms of programming. Late in the year, it was apparent that the strategy wasn't working, and the network went in search of new game shows to revitalize the fizzling daytime schedule.

And that's when Betty got a phone call from a producer named Rick Rosner, saying that he was putting together a new game for NBC, and he thought it would be a fun twist to have a woman host the game. Betty agreed to a meeting, but sort of laughed off the notion that anything might come of it. After all, in the 1950s, she had been burned by *Make the Connection*; in the 1960s, by *Get the Message*, and in the 1970s, by *Hollywood's Talking*. By the end of the meeting, Betty had agreed to host some run-throughs of the game. Again, she had extraordinarily low hopes, because even if she got this far, the network had to approve having a female master of ceremonies, and that wasn't going to happen.

NBC executives, including President of Entertainment Brandon Tartikoff, watched the run-through. To Betty's shock, not only did they like it, but Tartikoff himself said that he thought casting a woman to host the game had been a stroke of genius.

On January 3, 1983, NBC unleashed its revamped daytime line-up with three new game shows: *Sale of the Century* starring Jim Perry, *Hit Man* starring Peter Tomarken, and *Just Men!* starring Betty White.

Betty's game tested contestants' intuition and their ability to judge human nature. Two contestants — always women, no men allowed — faced a panel of seven celebrities — always men, no women allowed. The men were asked a yes-or-no question, and the contestants had to predict how the majority answered. Every correct answer earned a key. At the end of the program, the winner took one of the keys earned and used it to try to start the new car sitting onstage. A fantastically eclectic group of celebrities sat on the panel for the game, including David Hasselhoff, Jerry Seinfeld, George Brett, Tommy Lasorda, Garry Marshall, Pat Sajak, Gene

Three decades of rejection flushed away in an instant. Betty was finally hired to host a game show, *Just Men!* AUTHOR'S COLLECTION

Rayburn, Mr. T, Byron Allen, Fred Willard, Hervé Villechaize, Bubba Smith, composer Mike Post, and old friend Tom Sullivan.

The program was canceled after only thirteen weeks — Betty was actually amused to admit that part of the reason for the show's early demise was because NBC Chairman Grant Tinker didn't really like the

Betty joins George Fenneman, Ralph Edwards, and Carl Reiner for the 1984 NBC special *Those Wonderful TV Game Shows*. During the special, Betty fought back tears as Reiner narrated a photo and video tribute to his old army captain, Allen Ludden. AUTHOR'S COLLECTION

show — but two months after its final broadcast, Betty was at the tenth annual Daytime Emmy Awards, in contention for the Outstanding Game Show Host category against Dick Clark and Richard Dawson. And one more time, faced with two candidates that she considered more likely winners, Betty came out on top. It was the first time a woman had ever won in the category.

A year later, NBC paid tribute to Allen as part of a prime-time retrospective called *Those Wonderful TV Game Shows*, in which Betty joined Carl Reiner as they looked at clips of *G.E. College Bowl*, *Liars Club*, and *Stumpers*. Later in 1984, *Password* came back, now titled *Super Password* with host Bert Convy. Early in the run, Convy paid sincere tribute to Allen, assuring viewers that he wasn't trying to replace the original host and that, despite his new job, whenever he thought of *Password*, he would always think of Allen Ludden.

In 1985, sixty-three-year-old Betty had no reason to expect that the greatest success of her career was on the horizon, but that was exactly what happened. Betty was cast as the darling but dense Rose Nylund on *The Golden Girls*. She'd spend seven years in the role, plus an additional year reprising it for a spin-off, *The Golden Palace*. Her spot as a pop culture icon was secure.

Five years later, on March 24, 1989, *Super Password* aired for the final time, with Convy joined by guests Christopher Hewitt and Betty White. Convy wrapped up by saying how much it meant to him that Betty was there for the final program, insisting that, "this is really her show."

Betty, choking back a tear or two, replied, "Not my show. It was a fellow who started the show that I liked a lot."

Before things got too emotional, she happily pointed out that it was the fifth time that she had appeared on the final episode of *Password*, and she promised viewers that it was a sure thing the phoenix would rise again.

It took a while, but Betty did eventually make her way back to a set to play *Password* one more time, with CBS introducing a mega-money version, *Million Dollar Password*, hosted by Regis Philbin, in 2008. As a nod to the show's legacy, when Betty appeared on the program, the show ended with a sign-off from Allen Ludden of forty-five years earlier.

Not everything was warm fuzzy memories. Loss is loss — Betty did have her moments of sadness and sorrow. Once, while walking through a department store in Beverly Hills, she passed a display of televisions. As it happened, the TVs were tuned to a station airing a rerun of *The Love*

Boat. And to Betty's shock, there was Allen, on screen, in a close-up shot, as if talking directly to her. She froze in place and stared at the TV for so long that she lost all sense of time. She stood there, gazing at the screen, too shocked to move.

And Betty looked back at her life and found herself dwelling often on a choice that she had made in 1962 and could never quite forgive herself for. As she admitted to Oprah Winfrey, "I spent a whole year, wasted a whole year that Allen and I could have had together, saying, 'No, I wouldn't marry him. No, I won't. No, I won't leave California. No, I won't move to New York…I wasted a whole year we could have had together."

Sometimes, the thought of Allen affected her on the job. For an episode of *The Golden Girls*, Betty, as Rose Nylund, had to say the line, "Why did you have to leave me all alone, Charlie?" She had to concentrate extra-hard throughout the rehearsals and taping of that episode, because she kept almost-blurting out, "Why did you have to leave me all alone, Allen?"

A second-season episode of *The Golden Girls*, titled "A Piece of Cake," shows the four roommates reminiscing about their most memorable birthdays. Betty's key scene in the episode shows Rose's last birthday in her hometown of St. Olaf, a few months after her husband Charlie's death, throwing a surprise party for herself by lighting the candles on her cake, walking out of the room, and walking back in to be "surprised" by her cake.

Rose silently makes her wish, blows out the candles, looks around the room, and wistfully says out loud that she knew it wouldn't really come true. In the week leading up to the taping, the scene was rehearsed only twice. The production staff recognized how much trouble Betty was having getting herself through it.

In a rare dramatic turn, she co-starred in a made-for-TV movie called *The Lost Valentine* (2011). For one of the only times in her career, she had a crying scene, and it was a scene in which her character bends over to kiss a flag-draped casket. The day after the movie aired, she got a call from a friend who had been haunted by the sight of the hard, heavy crying that Betty had done in that scene, explaining to her, "I could tell who you were thinking about when you filmed that."

Betty could be grateful, though, that other people were thinking about Allen, too. At the height of *The Golden Girls'* popularity, Betty was doing a photo shoot with her cast mates when the session was interrupted by legendary producer/host Ralph Edwards, who told her, "Betty White, solid gold Golden Girl…*This is Your Life!*"

In an emotional evening, with a coast-to-coast audience looking in, Betty was surprised by her high school drama teacher, Bob Whitney, and her high school *Pride and Prejudice* co-star Larry Rose; Jack Paar was there too. And so was Mark Goodson. Ed Asner, Cloris Leachman, Georgia Engel, Valerie Harper, and Gavin McLeod from *The Mary Tyler Moore Show* were there, with Mary, who was performing on Broadway, joining the reunion via satellite. Grant Tinker appeared, pledging that he would go anywhere that people expressed love for Betty White.

But the biggest surprise of the night came from the honorary mayor of Hollywood, Johnny Grant, who strolled onstage to announce the address, "6747 Hollywood Boulevard." That was the spot on the famous Hollywood Walk of Fame where Betty's star was located. And with Betty struggling to keep her composure, Johnny Grant announced that another star was being placed directly next to Betty. Allen Ludden was getting a star.

In time, Allen Ludden would return to the public eye, along with Bill Cullen, Jack Barry, Garry Moore, John Daly, Bud Collyer, and other stars of game shows past. Game Show Network signed on in 1994, with Allen Ludden's *Password* and *Password Plus* among the shows on the schedule. BUZZR, a digital channel from FremantleMedia, the company that eventually took ownership of the Goodson-Todman library, went on the air in 2015, and there was Allen Ludden yet again.

The *Password* home game went back into production. Milton Bradley had ceased producing them in 1986, after cranking out an admirable twenty-four regular editions, two Educational Editions, the Fine Edition, the Collectors' Edition, and three *Password Plus* Editions. A new company, Endless Games, picked up the mantle, releasing more and more *Password* games, including, in 2011, a 50th Anniversary Edition, with photos of Allen and Betty adorning the cover, just like Allen always wanted. It took fifty years, but he finally got his wish.

Betty had her house in Carmel. At dawn each day, she passed a photo of a familiar silver-haired bespectacled face and said, "Good morning." And after all these years, she still called it "our house." Not only because it was the house that she and Allen helped build and design, but because the house was filled with mementos that came from their unique lives, those that they lived separately and those that they shared. Lots of houses had his and hers towels, and some have his and hers cars, but there's only one house in the world, somewhere in Carmel, California, with his and hers Emmy Awards for Outstanding Game Show Hosts.

FRED WOSTBROCK COLLECTION

FRED WOSTBROCK COLLECTION

ALLEN LUDDEN'S RESUME

(Dates included refer specifically to Allen's involvement and not necessarily the premiere or end of a series)

GAME SHOWS

College Quiz Bowl — Host (October 10, 1953-1956, NBC Radio)

G.E. College Bowl — Host (January 4, 1959- June 17, 1962, CBS-TV)

What in the World? — Guest Host (February 21, 1961, CBS-TV)

Password — Host (October 2, 1961-September 15, 1967, CBS-TV)

What's My Line — Guest (1962-70, eighteen episodes, CBS and SYNDICATION)

You Don't Say! — Guest player (October 30-November 3, 1967, NBC-TV)

Talking Pictures (Unsold pilot) — Host (February 25, 1968, CBS-TV)

Win with the Stars — Host (c. March 1968-c. September 1969, SYNDICATION)

The Joker's Wild — Host for unaired pilots (December 1968-January 1969, CBS-TV)

Catch a Star (Unsold pilot) — Producer (1969)

It Takes Two — Guest player (July 28-August 2, 1969, NBC-TV)

He Said, She Said — Guest player (Ten episodes, 1969-70, SYNDICATION)

Lucky Pair — Guest player (Six episodes, March 1970, KCBS-TV Los Angeles)

Perception (Unsold pilot) — Host (c. 1970)

Password — Host (April 4, 1971-November 15, 1974, ABC-TV)

Beat the Clock — Guest player (1971)

Look Who's Talking (Unsold pilot) — Host (November 1971)

I've Got a Secret — Special guest (1972, SYNDICATION)

You Owe It to Yourself — Host (Ten-episode series taped June 26-29, 1973; aired on various public television stations throughout the next four years)

The Gossip Game (Unsold pilot) — Producer (Taped May 1974)

Password All-Stars — Host (November 18, 1974-February 17, 1975, ABC-TV)

Password — Host (February 20-June 27, 1975, ABC-TV)

Showoffs — Guest player (August 18-22, 1975, ABC-TV)

The Big Money Game — Host (September 14, 1975, syndicated in New England by the Massachusetts State Lottery)

The Cross-Wits — Guest player (1976, 1977, 1978, SYNDICATION)

FRED WOSTBROCK COLLECTION

The Gong Show–Judge (1976-77, NBC-TV and SYNDICATION)

Stumpers! — Host (October 4-December 31, 1976, NBC-TV)

The Smart Alecks (Unsold pilot) — Host (1977)

Liars Club — Host (January 1977-1979, SYNDICATION)

Password Plus — Host (January 8, 1979-October 27, 1980, NBC-TV)

Chain Reaction — Guest player (1980, NBC-TV)

Card Sharks — Guest player (September 8-12, 1980)

Match Game — Panelist (Five episodes, 1980

TELEVISION — ACTING

Batman — Episode "Dizzoner the Penguin," as David Dooley (November 3, 1966, ABC-TV)

O'Hara: U.S. Treasury — Episode "Operation: Lady Luck," as Undercover Agent (January 14, 1972, CBS-TV)

The Odd Couple — Episode "Password" as Himself (December 1, 1972, ABC-TV)

Banacek — Episode "Horse of a Slightly Different Color," as Interviewer (January 22, 1974)

It's a Bird, It's a Plane, It's Superman! — Made-for-TV movie, as Perry White (February 17, 1975, ABC-TV)

The Love Boat — Episode "The Big Deal," as Martin Scott (October 14, 1978, ABC-TV)

Fantasy Island — Episode "Skater's Edge," as Judge Meyer (November 8, 1980, ABC-TV)

The Love Boat — Episode "The Horse Lover," as Paul Willis (November 22, 1980, ABC-TV)

THEATER — PERFORMER *(Partial list)*

Hell Bent for Heaven (1935)

Drums of Death (1936)

Romeo and Juliet — Romeo (1937)

Bury the Dead — Private Webster (1937)

Idiot's Delight — Donald Navadel (1937)

Fashion — Colonel Howard (1938)

Critic's Choice — Parker Ballantine (1961, 1964, 1976, 1977, 1980)

Brigadoon — Tommy Albright (1962)

Janus — Denny (1962)

Mister President — Stephen Decatur Henderson (1964)

Bell, Book, and Candle — Shep Henderson (1965)

Bells Are Ringing — Jeff Moss (1966)

Any Wednesday — John Cleves (1967)

Guys and Dolls — Sky Masterson (1967)

Once More with Feeling — Victor Fabian (1968)

The Girl with the Freudian Slip — (1970)

Chicago — Billy Flynn (1978)

THEATER — DIRECTOR *(Partial list)*

May Blossom (c. 1939) for University of Texas Curtain Club

Resident director for Austin's Little Theater

Resident director for United States Army, Special Services (1942-46)

Goodbye Again (1946)

FILM

Futureworld — Game Show Host (1976)

The Gossip Columnist — Himself (1980)

RADIO

KEYS-AM, Austin, TX: Announcer (1941-42)

WTIC-AM, Hartford, CT: Announcer/Continuity director/Program executive (1947-53)

Backstage — Host/Producer (1947, WTIC-AM)

Mind Your Manners — Host/Writer (1947-1956, WTIC-AM; March 15, 1948-c. 1954, NBC RADIO)

FRED WOSTBROCK COLLECTION

Inside Our Schools — Producer (Spring 1952, WNBC-AM)

New Talent USA — Host (June 13-September 12, 1953, NBC RADIO)

NBC Radio — Program Sales Coordinator (August-November, 1956);
  Manager of Program Planning and Development (November 1956-
  May 1957)

Weekend — Co-host/Producer (October 4, 1953-June 5, 1955,
  NBC RADIO)

Monitor — Producer (June 12-October 1955)

Weekday — Supervising Producer; also hosted "Teenage Forum" and
  "Family Forum" segments (November 7, 1955-1957, NBC RADIO)

Pocketbook News — Producer (March 3, 1957-April 1957, NBC RADIO)

WCBS-AM — Program director (May 1957-June 26, 1959)

CBS — Director of program services for network owned and operated
  stations (June 29, 1959-March 1961)

Plain Talk — 36 episode limited-run series produced by USMC
  (SYNDICATION, July 1962)

Arthur Godfrey Time — Guest host (CBS Radio, July 24, 1962)

Arthur Godfrey's 30th Anniversary All-Night Program — Guest
  (CBS RADIO, January 25, 1964)

Dimension At Home — Co-host (December 30, 1968-c. 1970,
  CBS RADIO)

Meet the Cook — Host (June 1978-1979, SYNDICATION)

OTHER TELEVISION WORK

Mind Your Manners — Host (June 24, 1951-March 2, 1952, NBC-TV)

Inside Our Schools — Producer and panel moderator (Spring 1952,
  WNBT-TV)

On the Carousel — Host (December 5, 1953-May 29, 1954, WCBS-TV)

Good Morning — Host (July 5-August 27, 1954, WABC-TV)

Dance Time — Host (July 5, 1954-April 8, 1955, WPIX-TV)

Sentimental You — Host (August 30, 1954-February 25, 1955, WNBT/WRCA-TV)

CBS — News division: Creative services consultant (April-September, 1961)

The Tonight Show — Guest (July 20, 1962 and August 1, 1963, NBC-TV)

The Miss Teenage America Coronation — Co-Host (October 26, 1962, CBS-TV)

Miss Teenage America 1964 — Co-Host (November 1, 1963, CBS-TV)

1963 Thanksgiving Jubilee — Co-Host (November 28, 1963, CBS-TV)

New Year's Eve with Guy Lombardo — Guest performer (December 31, 1963, CBS-TV)

The United Cerebral Palsy Telethon — Guest (May 10, 1964)

Art Linkletter's House Party — Guest (May 22, 1964; October 18, 1966, CBS-TV)

Mike Douglas and Marilyn Van Derbur help Allen crown Miss Teenage America. Pictured here is big winner Collette Daiute. FRED WOSTBROCK COLLECTION

The Steve Allen Playhouse — Guest (October 8, 1964)

The 1965 Miss Teenage America Pageant — Co-Host (November 13, 1964, CBS-TV)

The 1964 Thanksgiving Day Parade Jubilee –Co-Host (November 26, 1964, CBS-TV)

The 1965 Cotton Bowl Parade — Host (January 1, 1965, CBS-TV)

That Regis Philbin Show — Guest (January 20, 1965)

The Merv Griffin Show — Guest (August 4, 1965; October 4, 1965; April 26, 1966)

The 1966 Miss Teenage America Pageant — Co-Host (October 22, 1965, CBS-TV)

The 1966 Cotton Bowl Parade — Host (January 1, 1966, CBS-TV)

The 1967 Miss Teenage America Pageant — Co-host (November 5, 1966, CBS-TV)

The Milton Berle Show — Guest star, performed in two sketches (November 18, 1966, NBC-TV)

The 1966 Thanksgiving Day Parade Jubilee — Co-host (November 24, 1966, CBS-TV)

The 1967 Mummers Parade — Co-host (January 1, 1967, CBS-TV)

The Mike Douglas Show — Guest Co-host (October 9-13, 1967, SYNDICATION)

Youth and the Police — Host (c. 1969-1970, KNBC-TV Los Angeles)

The Donald O'Connor Show — Guest (March 5, 1969, SYNDICATION)

Agriculture USA — Guest (1969, SYNDICATION)

Allen Ludden's Gallery — Executive producer/Host (Spring 1969-1970, SYNDICATION)

The Gathering (Unsold pilot) — Producer (1969)

The Virginia Graham Show — Guest (1970, SYNDICATION)

The Real Tom Kennedy Show — Guest (1970, SYNDICATION)

The Pet Set — Executive producer/announcer (1970-71, SYNDICATION)

The Steve Allen Show — Guest (1971)

Dinah's Place — Guest (March 2, 1973; January 9, 1974, NBC-TV)

Easter Seals Telethon — Co-host (April 7 and 8, 1973)

The 23rd Annual PATSY Awards–Co-host (June 13, 1973, CBS-TV)

The 19th Annual Stop Arthritis Telethon — Guest (February 3, 1974)

The 24th Annual PATSY Awards — Co-host (May 1974, SYNDICATED)

Inside the Los Angeles Zoo (Special) — Co-Executive producer (Fall 1974, syndicated)

The 20th Annual Stop Arthritis Telethon — Co-host (January 31, 1975)

The 25th Annual PATSY Awards — Co-host (May 1975, syndicated)

Dinah! — Guest (August 1974, October 1976, March 1977, January 1978, May 1978, June 1978, August 1978, November 1978, February 1979, May 1979, June 1979, August 1980)

Mitzi and a Hundred Guys (Special) — Guest star (March 24, 1975, ABC-TV)

FRED WOSTBROCK COLLECTION

Phyllis Diller's 102nd Birthday Party (Special) — Guest star (August 6, 1975, ABC-TV)

The Merv Griffin Show — Guest (August 1975, February 1978, SYNDICATION)

The 21st Annual Stop Arthritis Telethon — Co-host (January 31, 1976)

Take My Advice — Guest (February 3, 1976)

Georgia Loves Jimmy Carter — Guest (February 14, 1976, SYNDICATED in Georgia)

The 26th Annual PATSY Awards — Co-host (June 1976, syndicated)

The Peter Marshall Variety Show — Guest (October 1976)

The 22nd Annual Stop Arthritis Telethon — Co-host (February 6, 1977)

Arthritis Foundation Auction Special — Host (1977, SYNDICATED)

The 27th Annual PATSY Awards — Co-host (June 1977, SYNDICATED)

What Would You Pay for Yesterday? (Special) — Host (December 1977, SYNDICATED)

The 23rd Annual Stop Arthritis Telethon — Co-host (January 28, 1978)

The 1978 Iris Awards — Presenter (March 4, 1978)

A Special Evening with Carol Burnett (final episode of *The Carol Burnett Show*) — Guest (March 29, 1978, CBS-TV)

Tomorrow with Tom Snyder — Guest (April 28, 1978, NBC-TV)

The Dean Martin Celebrity Roast — Guest speaker for the roast of Betty White (May 31, 1978, NBC-TV)

Yesterday II (Special) — Host (August 1978, SYNDICATED)

The 24th Annual Stop Arthritis Telethon — Host (January 28, 1979)

Yesterday III (Special) — Host (November 1979, SYNDICATED)

The 25th Annual Stop Arthritis Telethon — Host (January 26, 1980)

Hour Magazine — Guest (January 30, 1981)

Toni Tennille — Guest (February 1981)

RECORDING

Allen Ludden Sings His Favorite Songs (LP) — RCA-Victor, 1964

A Pet is a Special Friend (LP) — Pet Food Institute, 1973

WRITER

Fashion and Fiction magazine — Advice Columnist

Varsity magazine — Advice Columnist

Compact magazine — Advice Columnist

Senior Prom magazine — Advice Columnist

Movie Stars Parade magazine — Columnist

Plain Talk for Men Under 21! — Author

Plain Talk for Women Under 21! — Author

Plain Talk About College — Author

Plain Talk for Young Marrieds — Author)

MILITARY SERVICE

United States Army (1941-46)

Officer-in-Charge of the Entertainment Section of the Pacific Ocean
    Areas

Bronze Star recipient

OTHER WORK

Jack Bonner Co. — Office supply sales (1934)

Lichtenstein's Department Store — Clothing sales (1935)

Perkins Brothers Department Store — Clothing sales (1936)

Business manager for Maurice Evans (1945-47)

Press agent, Summer Theatre, Ivoryton, CT (1947)

Master of ceremonies, Miss DePauw Pageant (April 27, 1963)

Master of ceremonies, Little Miss America Pageant (1969)

Bonus Detergent — Television spokesman (1970)

Bank AmeriCard — Television spokesman (1972)

Petiquette — Filmstrip narration (1973)

King Tut: Tomb of Treasure (Home video release) — Narrator (1978)

Gloria Marshall Figure Salons — Print advertising spokesman
   (1978-79)

Southern California Gas Company — Radio spokesman (1981)

ALLEN LUDDEN'S NEWSPAPER COLUMNS AND ESSAYS

Note: Allen Ludden never had a regular job as a newspaper columnist, but sometimes took opportunities to submit single essays or fill in for a vacationing columnist. This is a selection of those writings.

INFORMATION PROGRAMS CAN ENTERTAIN
August 22, 1962

Back in the days when I studied such things, I seem to remember philosophical lectures about the true nature of "entertainment."

Investigating the history and growth of the theater, my professors made great point of the fact that the human being needs a "divertissement" that will take his mind off of himself, transport him into another environment — in short, entertain him.

All this has come to mind because I've been disturbed by the fact that people insist on dividing television programs into two kinds: (1) Those that entertain and (2) those that inform.

I don't think these two kinds need be so separate. I believe that there is entertainment inherent in information.

If you take the broad, basic definition of entertainment as something that diverts your attention from yourself, then certainly a program that provides information can answer the qualifications for entertainment.

It can, that is, if your attention is so held that you think about the information and are not self-conscious about learning. Producers and writers too often accept as a fact of life the old concept that entertainment shows get audiences and the do-good informational programs don't.

Traditionally, if you're producing an "entertainment" show, you concern yourself with all the "show business" devices to hold your audience. But, if you're producing an informational show, the tendency is to look askance at such tricks, feeling that they are beneath the level of your subject matter or your high-minded motivation.

Not always, but too often, a producer of an informational program becomes so concerned with getting information into the program and satisfying the intellectual demands that he and his staff put on the content that he forgets the essential equation. To impart information is the first half of the equation. To have it understood is the second half.

FRED WOSTBROCK COLLECTION

It is just as important for the producer-writer of an informational program to have a consistent, easy-to-follow storyline, to have devices to renew attention and to build an element of excitement and vitality as it is for the producers of *Gunsmoke* or *The Garry Moore Show*. These past few years, we've seen more concern for the entertainment inherent in information, as witness *David Brinkley's Journal*, and, of course, *CBS Reports*.

This coming season, we'll see more. And before long, I hope the programmers and the audience will discard the ridiculous old idea that just because a program is informational, it is not entertainment. I believe it must entertain to hold attention. If you hold attention, you entertain. If you don't hold attention, why bother? You're talking to yourself.

OUR FUTURE HOPE: TEENAGERS
November 2, 1963

In my opinion, one of this country's most valuable natural resources is yet to be fully developed: the potential power of its bright young minds.

I don't mean to say that we adults ignore the youth of the United States. We pay a lot of attention to beatniks, juvenile delinquents, and misfits. But what about the other ninety percent?

In the six years I conducted a radio program called *Mind Your Manners*, I received more than a million letters from teenagers all over the nation. When you have read that many letters, you cannot help getting an insight into the personalities of this segment of the country's population. And I gained a great respect for the teenager. I believe it essential to the future of our way of life that we give every qualified young person in this country, no matter what the socio-economic circumstances, an opportunity to go on to college to develop the full potential of his or her talents.

We also need to glamorize the teaching profession. We need to attract more teachers with the right qualifications who are now heading for more remunerative positions with attendant prestige. I don't subscribe to that old saw, "Those who can, do. Those who can't, teach." It simply is not true.

ALIAS: MR. BETTY WHITE
July 22, 1966

Among the many notable things that have happened to me since the advent of a little television game called *Password* has been the fact that I am called so many different things. You may take that any way you wish, but what I mean is that people call me different names.

Because they see me on the tube in the afternoon, they associate me with my electronic neighbor Linkletter and I'm hailed as "Art." So, I answer. Because I emcee a game show, they call me "Bud," as in Collyer. Because I wear glasses and I belong to that venerable group known as television hosts, I get "Bill" for Bill Cullen, I guess.[1]

But the one I enjoy the most is, "Hey, there's the guy who married Betty White!"

It's been three years now since Betty and I married and I've become something of an authority on Betty White fans.

Let me make it clear at the outset that I have nothing but the heartiest respect for these people. Obviously I respect their taste. I married the girl! Most of them look upon me as a Johnny-Come-Lately. They've known her much longer than I have.

There is a very large group who remember Betty from the "Al Jarvis Days." She was doing a 5 1/2-hour daily local show in Los Angeles. There weren't many television sets to begin with (I kid Betty about being a star of the silent TV) and it was a local show. Yet these people turn up all over the country. When we married we had 9,000 cards and at least 6,000 of them mentioned Al Jarvis.

They usually went on to mention *Life with Elizabeth*, too, because all of her Al Jarvis friends followed on to the series. They were joined by armies of new and vigilantly faithful followers. A lot of them must have been about ten at the time, but they loved *Life with Elizabeth*. I've read some of the scripts just lately, and the reason those shows were so popular is that they were very, very funny. Betty is constantly amazed to have teenagers today come up to tell her that her's was their favorite show when they were kids.

Then there are the hardcore fans, or, even better, friends, who have known Betty through *Life with Elizabeth*, *Date with the Angels*, and *The Betty White Show*, which was her daytime NBC network show.

These are the people from all over the country who know about her love of animals, her jokes, her favorite songs, her wise streak of sentimentality, her curiosity. They follow Betty's every move. They write regularly. Their generosity is embarrassing. But their affection is so genuine and their intentions are so right, one could only be touched by their gestures.

I think I can safely say that most of the hardcore fans are glad that Betty and I married. At the time of our marriage in fact, many wrote to say that

1. This is actually a cute bit of wordplay from Allen. At the time he wrote this essay, Bill Cullen was hosting a game show called *Eye Guess*.

they had picked me out for her. That was not true of them all. There was another group that came in later, a nighttime group, the "Jack Paar" group. Not all of them were Ludden-oriented. As a matter of fact, it got a bit sticky on several occasions, but time has a way of taking care of those things.

Now, when I hear somebody yell, "Hey, there's the guy who married Betty White!" I just smile, keep moving, and don't even think about ducking.

AUTHOR'S COLLECTION

HOW IT FEELS WHEN YOUR SHOW DIES
July 7, 1967

How does it feel to leave a show you've done five days a week for six years? I'm sad to leave *Password*. It's a great game. It's an original. I can honestly say that I have never once been bored playing it. Each day is a fresh challenge.

The men who produced it are thorough professionals and they've taught me a lot. And of course, it was great fun to be part of an instant hit. Within four weeks of its start, *Password* became the most popular show in its time period. Not only that, the sets in use at the time it was shown increased, proving that people who had never even had their sets on at that time turned them on just to watch our show. That has to make you feel good.

So — how does it feel? Strange! I think a lot of people will join me in missing it. But that is the business I find myself in these days. The ratings have dictated the demise of the show and now I've got to look ahead. Certainly, things look different than they did six years ago. When *Password* started, I was so tentative about a full-time job as a performer that I asked for a six month leave from my CBS executive job. I'd been

FRED WOSTBROCK COLLECTION

working weekends on *College Bowl*, but it had been many years since I had on camera work as a full-time occupation. Six months later, I was hooked. I still am.

I like working in front of the camera. And I like working with daytime television audiences. I have no idea whether my next show will be a game show. But I'll make book that it will be a daytime show with some kind of audience participation. There is no more challenging job as far as I am concerned. I believe that the eye-to-eye daytime shows can and do raise the level of television programming.

How? Through a simple but logical process. The better of the daytime games and talk shows actually educate the audience. The viewer is asked to participate, to think, to question, and the result is that the viewer learns. The overall sophistication of the viewer is increased. And the only thing that will improve television programming is the increase in viewer sophistication, viewer discrimination. When the audience asks more of its programs, it will get more. Since daytime programming involves them in good games or interesting conversation, that's for me.

TELEVISION IN REVIEW
July 22, 1968

My mother has had a problem all year: She can't explain where I'm working.

Password was taken off the CBS network, yet friends from all over the country write her to tell her they still see it every day. She reads that I had a new, once-a-week musical quiz called *Win with the Stars*, yet none of the stations in Corpus Christi were carrying it. (It helped when one of her local stations started carrying it.)

Since Mother and her friends are confused by the mysteries of syndication, I thought I might state the case for what I believe to be a great source of television programming. Within the next five years, I believe, network programming will be reduced. As quality syndicated programs in a wide variety of styles and shapes become available, those stations are going to use more of them to suit the tastes of their local audiences. There will be a whole new look to the national television picture.

So, what exactly is this syndication? Quite simply it is the production of a program on video tape which a local station can buy and broadcast. The money the station gets from the sale of commercial spots within the show is likely to get it a fatter profit than does the network shows they carry. One instance of syndication is the success of *Password* which in syndicated reruns is in many markets outrating first-run network shows.

Suddenly the whole field of syndication — new shows and reruns — has started to look like a gold mine and many are rushing in to stake claims. This is both encouraging and dangerous. Dangerous, because some producers will try to fob off a second-rate product. Encouraging, because others see a chance to produce programs of network quality often overlooked these days by movie-oriented networks.

As the networks become more and more locked into large blocks of movies and movie-type serials, local stations are discovering this bonanza of quality programs, designed better to suit their local audiences.

And that, Mother, is what syndication is all about. And I'm for it.

WHY OUR MARRIAGE WORKS
By Betty White and Allen Ludden
May 21, 1976

BETTY: Our marriage is improved by the little war between us. Although we have our work in common, there are marked differences in our tastes and interests. For example: In public, no matter how I feel, I'm all sweetness; but at home, I can be a tiger. Allen is Allen anywhere, but he is more apt to be harmonious at home. Also, I am a fighter, ready to do battle at the drop of an emotion. Allen is cool, logical, and rational.

Despite our differences — or maybe because of them, we have wonderful communication. A successful marriage needs two people who are willing to bounce off each other in ideas, interests, competition, anger, and love. Both of us are unafraid to express what we feel.

Lastly, Allen is my best friend as well as my husband. And if that's not enough, I think he's kind of cute.

ALLEN: Betty White is the most stimulating person I know. She is involved with everything around her. Although I would rather be with Betty than with any other friend, we are not always together. We thrive on our individual pursuits. I like the idea of Betty wanting a life of her own, of making it on her own terms. Although this does separate us, it nourishes the relationship. When we get together, there's so much to talk about!

Our marriage works because it's a constant discovery. I am always learning about Betty from her far-flung interests. Imagine, twelve years of "togetherness" and I've never been bored! The fact that we are opposites in many ways helps. Since we are often on different wavelengths, we have had to "fight" that much more to stay tuned into each other.

FRED WOSTBROCK COLLECTION

FRED WOSTBROCK COLLECTION

PASSWORD EPISODE GUIDE

Provided by Brendan McLaughlin.
★ *Denotes a prime-time episode.*

1961

OCT. 2-6	Kitty Carlisle and Tom Poston
OCT. 9-13	Arlene Francis and Chuck Connors
OCT. 16-20	Betty White and Don Ameche
OCT. 23-27	Jayne Meadows and Bennett Cerf
OCT. 30 - NOV. 3	Edie Adams and Peter Lind Hayes
NOV. 6-10	Vivian Vance and Abe Burrows; *guest host Jack Clark*
NOV. 13-17	Dorothy Kilgallen and Darren McGavin
NOV. 20-24	Carol Burnett and Garry Moore
NOV. 27 - DEC. 1	Kitty Carlisle and Pat Harrington
DEC. 4-8	Betsy Palmer and Zachary Scott
DEC. 11-15	Pat Carroll and Jean-Pierre Aumont
DEC. 18-22	Dorothy Collins and David Wayne
DEC. 25-29	Joan Bennett and Mike Nichols

1962

JAN. 1-5	Mary Healy and Peter Lind Hayes
JAN. 2 ★	Carol Burnett and Garry Moore
JAN. 8-12	Peggy Cass and Ben Gazzara
JAN. 9 ★	Betsy Palmer and Dick Van Dyke
JAN. 15-19	Abbe Lane and Tom Poston
JAN. 16 ★	Jayne Meadows and Jackie Cooper
JAN. 22-26	Elaine Stritch and Robert Morse
JAN. 23 ★	Pat Carroll and Johnny Carson
JAN. 29 - FEB. 2	Betty White and Barry Nelson
JAN. 30 ★	Dorothy Collins and Bill Cullen
FEB. 5-9	Pat Suzuki and Orson Bean

FEB. 12-16	Jayne Meadows and Darren McGavin
FEB. 13 ★	Arlene Francis and Shelley Berman
FEB. 19-23	Celeste Holm and Martin Gabel
FEB. 20 ★	Dina Merrill and Abe Burrows
FEB. 26 - MAR. 2	Betsy Palmer and Durward Kirby
FEB. 27 ★	Peggy Cass and Tom Poston
MAR. 5-9	Mimi Benzell and William Marshall
MAR. 6 ★	Ginger Rogers and Orson Bean
MAR. 12-16	Betty Furness and Jack Carter
MAR. 13 ★	Carol Burnett and Darren McGavin
MAR. 19-23	Dorothy Loudon and Sam Levenson
MAR. 20 ★	Betsy Palmer and Peter Lind Hayes
MAR. 26-30	Carmel Quinn and Mel Tormé
MAR. 27 ★	Jane Fonda and James Mason
APR. 2-6	Sally Ann Howes and Douglas Fairbanks Jr.
APR. 3 ★	Ann Sothern and Alan King
APR. 9-13	Viveca Lindfors and Fred Gwynne
APR. 10 ★	Susan Strasberg and Van Johnson
APR. 16-20	Bess Myerson and John Ireland
APR. 17 ★	Kitty Carlisle and Jack Carter

FRED WOSTBROCK COLLECTION

APR. 23-27	Fran Allison and Alan King
APR. 24 ★	Carroll Baker and Bennett Cerf
APR. 30 – MAY 4	Nancy Walker and Tom Poston
MAY 1 ★	Sally Ann Howes and Joe Montgomery
MAY 7-11	Ruby Dee and Orson Bean
MAY 8 ★	Bess Myerson and Hugh O'Brian
MAY 14-18	Audrey Meadows and Barry Nelson
MAY 15 ★	Olivia de Havilland and Douglas Fairbanks Jr.
MAY 21-25	Ann Sothern and Lee Marvin
MAY 22 ★	Edie Adams and Dennis Weaver
MAY 28 – JUN. 1	Jane Wyatt and Mickey Rooney
MAY 29 ★	Joan Benny and Jack Benny; *taped at CBS Television City in Hollywood*
JUN. 4-8	Cara Williams and Alan Young
JUN. 5 ★	Eve Arden and Chuck Connors
JUN. 11-15	Arlene Dahl and Darren McGavin
JUN. 12 ★	Audrey Meadows and Sam Levenson
JUN. 18-22	Phyllis Newman and Hugh O'Brian
JUN. 19 ★	Carol Burnett and Garry Moore
JUN. 25-29	Pat Carroll and Dan Duryea
JUN. 26 ★	Carol Channing and James Mason
JUL. 2-6	Carol Haney and Robert Morse
JUL. 3 ★	Arlene Francis and Merv Griffin
JUL. 9-13	Kaye Ballard and Orson Bean
JUL. 10 ★	Anne Bancroft and Robert Goulet
JUL. 16-20	Lillian Roth and Richard Hayes
JUL. 17 ★	Betsy Palmer and Barry Sullivan
JUL. 23-27	Betty White and Jim Backus
JUL. 24 ★	Bess Myerson and Tom Poston
JUL. 30 – AUG. 3	Jayne Meadows and Abe Burrows
JUL. 31 ★	Florence Henderson and Buddy Hackett
AUG. 6-10	Monique Van Vooren and Forrest Tucker
AUG. 7 ★	Carol Lawrence and Barry Nelson; *guest host Jack Clark*
AUG. 13-17	Agnes Moorehead and Hal March; *guest host Jack Clark*
AUG. 14 ★	Dina Merrill and Darren McGavin; *guest host Jack Clark*
AUG. 20-24	Betsy Palmer and Tom Poston
AUG. 21 ★	Rita Moreno and Bill Cullen

AUG. 27 - AUG. 31   Peggy Cass and Bennett Cerf
AUG. 28 ★   Carol Haney and E.G. Marshall
SEP. 3-7   Carol Lawrence and Chester Morris
SEP. 4 ★   Joan Fontaine and Jack Carter
SEP. 10-14   Arlene Francis and Jack E. Leonard
SEP. 16 ★   Marjorie Lord and Danny Thomas; *taped at CBS Television City in Hollywood; first Sunday night episode*
SEP. 17-21   Polly Bergen and Barry Sullivan
SEP. 23 ★   Abby Dalton and Joey Bishop; *taped at CBS Television City in Hollywood*
SEP. 24-28   Rhonda Fleming and William Bendix
SEP. 30 ★   Polly Bergen and Raymond Burr; *taped at CBS Television City in Hollywood*
OCT. 1-5   Rita Moreno and Louis Nye
OCT. 7 ★   Peggy Cass and Tony Perkins
OCT. 8-12   Sheila MacRae and Gordon MacRae
OCT. 14 ★   Carol Burnett and Mitch Miller
OCT. 15-19   Florence Henderson and Skitch Henderson
OCT. 21 ★   Betsy Palmer and George Maharis
OCT. 22-26   Ann Sothern and Peter Lind Hayes
OCT. 28 ★   Jane Powell and Red Buttons
OCT. 29 - NOV. 2   Kitty Carlisle and Sam Levenson
NOV. 4 ★   Connie Francis and Darren McGavin
NOV. 5-9   Joan Fontaine and Sam Levene
NOV. 12-16   Beatrice Lillie and Tom Poston
NOV. 18 ★   Carol Lawrence and Robert Goulet
NOV. 19-23   Phyllis McGuire and Douglas Fairbanks Jr.
NOV. 25 ★   Peggy Cass and Jack Paar
NOV. 26-30   Betty White and Henry Morgan
DEC. 2 ★   Phyllis Newman and Jack Carter
DEC. 3-7   Rita Moreno and Jackie Mason
DEC. 10-14   Florence Henderson and Skitch Henderson
DEC. 16 ★   Joan Crawford and Barry Nelson
DEC. 17-21   Teresa Brewer and Darren McGavin
DEC. 23 ★   *All-star special:* Kitty Carlisle, Peter Lind Hayes, Tom Poston, Mary Healy
DEC. 24-28   Betsy Palmer and Barry Sullivan
DEC. 30 ★   Carol Burnett and Orson Bean
DEC. 31   Carol Channing and Fred Gwynne

1963

JAN. 1-4	Carol Channing and Fred Gwynne
JAN. 6 ★	Rosemary Clooney and Bobby Darin
JAN. 7-11	Shelley Winters and Chester Morris
JAN. 13 ★	Ann Sothern and Sam Levenson
JAN. 14-18	Audrey Meadows and Joseph Cotten
JAN. 20 ★	Dina Merrill and Tony Perkins
JAN. 21-25	Bess Myerson and Cliff Robertson
JAN. 27 ★	Lena Horne and Mitch Miller
JAN. 28 - FEB. 1	Dorothy Collins and George Grizzard
FEB. 3 ★	Dorothy Loudon and Garry Moore
FEB. 4-8	Peggy Cass and Eli Wallach
FEB. 10 ★	Betsy Palmer and Buddy Palmer
FEB. 11-15	Eve Arden and Henry Morgan
FEB. 17 ★	Betty White and Shelley Berman
FEB. 18-22	Maureen O'Sullivan and Sam Levenson
FEB. 24. ★	Nanette Fabray and Douglas Fairbanks Jr.
FEB. 25 - MAR. 1	Gypsy Rose Lee and Peter Cook
MAR. 3 ★	Florence Henderson and Steve Lawrence
MAR. 4-8	Tammy Grimes and Artie Shaw

AUTHOR'S COLLECTION

MAR. 10 ★	Jane Fonda and Bill Cullen
MAR. 11-15	Kitty Carlisle and Tom Poston
MAR. 17 ★	Diahann Carroll and E.G. Marshall
MAR. 18-22	*Special week: Mon:* Peggy Cass. *Tues:* Phyllis Newman. *Wed:* Arlene Francis. *Thurs:* Sally Ann Howes. *Fri:* Dina Merrill. *All Week:* Allen Ludden. *Guest host Jack Clark*
MAR. 25 ★	Janet Leigh and Peter Lawford; *first Monday night episode*
MAR. 25-29	Rita Moreno and Ray Bolger
APR. 1 ★	Marjorie Lord and Danny Thomas
APR. 1-5	Jane Wyatt and Keenan Wynn
APR. 8 ★	Jeanne Crain and Richard Boone
APR. 8-12	Janis Page and Max Baer
APR. 15 ★	Eydie Gormé and Alan King
APR. 15-19	Susan Strasberg and Orson Bean
APR. 22 ★	Dina Merrill and Paul Anka
APR. 22-26	Carroll Baker and Peter Lind Hayes
APR. 29 ★	Rosemary Clooney and Arthur Godfrey
APR. 29 - MAY 3	Sandy Stewart and Jack Carter
MAY 6	Nanette Fabray and Buddy Hackett
MAY 6-10	Susan Kohner and Skitch Henderson
MAY 13 ★	Olivia de Havilland and Anthony Perkins
MAY 13-17	Marjorie Lord and Alan King
MAY 20 ★	Dorothy Loudon and Donald O'Connor
MAY 20-24	Pat Carroll and Artie Shaw
MAY 27 ★	Carol Channing and Hugh O'Brian
MAY 27-31	Marty Allen and Steve Rossi
JAN. 3 ★	Carol Burnett and Douglas Fairbanks Jr.
JUN. 3-7	Bess Myerson and William Bendix
JUN. 10 ★	Lena Horne and Abe Burrows
JUN. 10-14	Anne Jackson and Eli Wallach
JUN. 17 ★	Florence Henderson and Tony Randall
JUN. 17-21	Peggy Cass and Paul Anka
JUN. 24 ★	Betty White and Jack Paar
JUN. 24-28	Lisa Kirk and Jack E. Leonard
JUL. 1 ★	Jane Wyatt and Richard Boone
JUL. 1-5	Barbara Cook and Sydney Chaplin
JUL. 8 ★	Susan Strasberg and Bill Cullen
JUL. 8-13	Georgia Brown and Ray Oliver

JUL. 15 ★	Betsy Palmer and E.G. Marshall
JUL. 15-19	Kitty Carlisle and Robert Reed
JUL. 22 ★	Eydie Gormé and Hugh O'Brian
JUL. 22-26	Dorothy Collins and George Grizzard
JUL. 29 ★	Phyllis Newman and Buddy Hackett
JUL. 29 – AUG. 2	Marilyn Maxwell and Ty Hardin
AUG. 5 ★	Gretchen Wyler and Arthur Godfrey
AUG. 5-9	Shelley Winters and Jack Cassidy
AUG. 12 ★	Nanette Fabray and Robert Stack
AUG. 12-16	Florence Henderson and Peter Lawford
AUG. 19 ★	Carl Channing and Ray Bolger
AUG. 19-23	Carol Haney and Peter Cook
AUG. 26 ★	Carol Burnett and Peter Lawford
AUG. 26-30	Marty Allen and Steve Rossi
SEP. 2 ★	Dorothy Loudon and Alan King
SEP. 2-6	Kaye Ballard and Chester Morris
SEP. 9 ★	Gisele MacKenzie and Paul Anka
SEP. 9-13	Nanette Fabray and Peter Lind Hayes
SEP. 16 ★	Carol Burnett and Anthony Perkins
SEP.16-20	Carol Channing and Robert Reed
SEP.23-27	Rita Moreno and Orson Bean
SEP. 26 ★	Lucille Ball and Gary Morton; *special Thursday night broadcast*
SEP. 30 – OCT. 4	Elizabeth Montgomery and Peter Lawford
OCT. 2 ★	Edie Adams and Robert Stack; *first Wednesday night episode*
OCT. 7-11	Barbara Rush and Barry Sullivan
OCT. 9 ★	*All-star special:* Janet Leigh, Polly Bergen, Peter Lawford, Sammy Davis Jr.
OCT. 14-18	*All-star special:* Betty White, Allen Ludden, Jane Wyatt, Richard Boone; *guest host Jack Clark*
OCT. 16 ★	Carol Lawrence and Steve Lawrence
OCT. 21-25	Marjorie Lord and Sydney Chaplin
OCT. 23 ★	Barbara Rush and Hugh O'Brian
OCT. 28 – NOV. 1	Betty White and Milt Kamen
OCT. 30 ★	Eydie Gormé and Alan King
NOV. 4-8	Janis Page and Sam Levenson
NOV. 6 ★	Vivian Vance and Douglas Fairbanks Jr.
NOV. 11-15	Kitty Carlisle and Ray Bolger
NOV. 13 ★	Phyllis Newman and Tony Randall

NOV. 18-22	Lena Horne and Douglas Fairbanks Jr.; *Friday's episode did not air due to assassination of John F. Kennedy*
NOV. 20 ★	Rosemary Clooney and Shelley Berman
NOV. 25-29	Julia Meade and Frank Fontaine
NOV. 27 ★	Gloria and Jimmy Stewart
DEC. 2-6	Eva Gabor and Darren McGavin
DEC. 5 ★	Dorothy Loudon and Garry Moore; *first Thursday night episode*
DEC. 9-13	Betsy Palmer and George Grizzard
DEC. 12 ★	Dorothy Collins and Steve Lawrence
DEC. 16-20	Elizabeth Ashley and George Peppard
DEC. 19 ★	Eydie Gormé and Jose Ferrer
DEC. 23-27	Marty Allen and Steve Rossi
DEC. 26 ★	Lucille Ball and Gary Morton
DEC. 30-31	Betty White and Allen Ludden; *guest host Jack Clark*

1964

JAN. 1-3	Betty White and Allen Ludden; *guest host Jack Clark*
JAN. 2 ★	Betsy Palmer and Frank Gifford
JAN. 6-10	Peggy Cass and Roddy McDowall
JAN. 9 ★	Carol Burnett and Robert Preston
JAN. 13-17	Audrey Meadows and Robert Q. Lewis
JAN. 16 ★	Eva Gabor and Paul Anka
JAN. 20-24	Phyllis Diller and Peter Lind Hayes
JAN. 23 ★	Carol Channing and Alan King
JAN. 27-31	Georgia Brown and Jack Jones
JAN. 30 ★	Florence Henderson and Peter Lawford
FEB. 3-7	June Havoc and Orson Bean
FEB. 6 ★	Georgia Brown and Jack Carter
FEB. 10-14	Peggy Cass and Frank Gifford
FEB. 13 ★	Audrey Meadows and Sam Levenson
FEB. 17-21	Carol Burnett and Douglas Fairbanks Jr.
FEB. 20 ★	Elizabeth Ashley and Buddy Hackett
FEB. 24-28	Arlene Francis and Paul Anka
FEB. 27 ★	Phyllis Newman and Hugh O'Brian
MAR. 2-6	Carolyn Jones and Chester Morris
MAR. 5 ★	Paula Prentiss and Tony Perkins

MAR. 9–13	Jane Harvey and Jack Carter
MAR. 12 ★	Rosemary Clooney and José Ferrer
MAR. 16–20	Juliet Prowse and Tom Poston
MAR. 19 ★	Betsy Palmer and Frank Gifford
MAR. 23–27	Elizabeth Ashley and Skitch Henderson
MAR. 26 ★	Carol Burnett and Alan King
MAR. 30 – APR. 3	Lauren Bacall and Frank Gifford
APR. 2 ★	Georgia Brown and Alan King
APR. 6–10	Jane Wyatt and Dick Shawn
APR. 9 ★	Carol Channing and Sidney Chaplain
APR. 13–17	Chita Rivera and Peter Fonda
APR. 16 ★	Lauren Bacall and Douglas Fairbanks Jr.
APR. 20–24	Marty Allen and Steve Rossi
APR. 23 ★	Nanette Fabray and Orson Bean
APR. 27 – MAY 1	Pat Carroll and Peter Lind Hayes
APR. 30 ★	Carol Lynley and Jack Jones; *taped at CBS Television City in Hollywood*
MAY 4–8	Carolyn Jones and Peter Lawford
MAY 7 ★	*Special game:* Lucille Ball and Lucie Arnaz vs. Gary Morton and Desi Arnaz Jr.; *taped at CBS Television City in Hollywood*
MAY 11–15	June Lockhart and Ray Bolger

AUTHOR'S COLLECTION

MAY 14 ★	Gloria and Jimmy Stewart; *taped at CBS Television City in Hollywood*
MAY 18-22	Marjorie Lord and Mickey Rooney
MAY 21 ★	Barbara Rush and Peter Lawford; *taped at CBS Television City in Hollywood*
MAY 25-29	Georgia Brown and Alan Young
MAY 28 ★	Betty White and Paul Anka
JUN. 1-5	Barbara Rush and Robert Merrill
JUN. 4 ★	Georgia Brown and Laurence Harvey
JUN. 8-12	Zsa Zsa Gabor and Bobby Rydell
JUN. 11 ★	Florence Henderson and Hugh O'Brian
JUN. 15-19	Phyllis Kirk and Peter Lawford
JUN. 18 ★	Carol Lawrence and Roddy McDowall
JUN. 22-26	Gloria Swanson and Chester Morris
JUN. 25 ★	Carol Channing and Steve Lawrence
JUN. 29 - JUL. 3	Penny Fuller and Barry Nelson
JUL. 2 ★	*All-star special:* Eydie Gormé, Peggy Cass, Peter Lawford, Sammy Davis Jr.
JUL. 6-10	Carol Lawrence and Tom Poston
JUL. 9 ★	Marjorie Lord and Paul Anka
JUL. 13-17	Virginia Graham and Frank Gifford
JUL. 20-24	Kitty Carlisle and Skitch Henderson
JUL. 23 ★	Carol Burnett and Alan King
JUL. 27-31	Marty Allen and Steve Rossi
JUL. 30 ★	Betsy Palmer and Peter Fonda
AUG. 3-7	Eydie Gormé and Peter Lawford
AUG. 10-14	Rita Moreno and Darren McGavin
AUG. 13 ★	Carol Lawrence and Tony Randall
AUG. 17-21	Carol Burnett and Dick Patterson
AUG. 20 ★	Eydie Gormé and Bob Newhart
AUG. 24-28	Betty White and Robert Reed
AUG. 31 - SEP. 4	Florence Henderson and Robert Walker
SEP. 3 ★	Marty Allen and Steve Rossi
SEP. 7-11	Piper Laurie and Marty Ingels
SEP. 10 ★	Sally Ann Howes and Steve Lawrence
SEP. 14-18	Dorothy Loudon and Wally Cox
SEP. 17 ★	Phyllis Newman and Alan King
SEP. 21-25	Phyllis Kirk and Peter Lawford
SEP. 24 ★	*All-star special:* Lucille Ball, Gary Morton, Vivian Vance, Peter Lawford

SEP. 28 – OCT. 2	Jan Sterling and José Ferrer
OCT. 1 ★	Gloria and Jimmy Stewart; The Stewarts' daughters, Judy and Kelly, played with their parents
OCT. 5–9	Peggy Cass and Dick Patterson
OCT. 8 ★	*All-star special:* Angie Dickinson, Peter Lawford, Pat Carroll, Otto Preminger
OCT. 12–16	June Lockhart and Ray Bolger
OCT. 19–23	Rose Marie and Jack Jones
OCT. 22 ★	Betsy Palmer and Douglas Fairbanks Jr.
OCT. 26–30	Jane Wyman and Peter Lind Hayes
OCT. 29 ★	Eydie Gormé and Tony Randall
NOV. 2–6	Georgia Brown and Alan King
NOV. 5 ★	Carol Channing and Peter Lawford
NOV. 9–13	Jessica Tandy and Hume Cronyn
NOV. 12 ★	Lucille Ball and Gary Morton
NOV. 16–20	Lauren Bacall and Sydney Chaplin
NOV. 19 ★	Jayne Meadows and Steve Allen
NOV. 23–27	Florence and Skitch Henderson
NOV. 26 ★	Rosemary Clooney and Alan King
NOV. 30 – DEC. 4	Betty White and Roddy McDowall
DEC. 3 ★	Sally Ann Howes and Jack Jones
DEC. 7–11	Martha Wright and Barry Sullivan
DEC. 10 ★	Rita Moreno and Paul Anka
DEC. 14–18	Anne Jackson and Eli Wallach
DEC. 17 ★	Carol Channing and Mitch Miller
DEC. 21–25	Dorothy Loudon and Tom Ewell
DEC. 24 ★	Monique Van Vooren and Arthur Godfrey
DEC. 28–31	Jayne Mansfield and Orson Bean
DEC. 31 ★	*All-star special:* Angie Dickinson, Peter Lawford, Pat Carroll, Otto Preminger

1965

JAN. 1	Jayne Mansfield and Orson Bean
JAN. 4–8	Arlene Francis and Peter Lawford
JAN. 7 ★	Lucille Ball and Gary Morton; *from CBS Television City in Hollywood*
JAN. 11–15	Marjorie Lord and Peter Fonda; *from CBS Television City in Hollywood*
JAN. 14 ★	Barbara Rush and Gene Kelly; *from CBS Television City in Hollywood*

JAN. 18-22	Amanda Blake and Bob Denver; *from CBS Television City in Hollywood*
JAN. 21 ★	Juliet Prowse and Hugh O'Brian; *guest host Jack Clark*
JAN. 25-29	Jane Wyman and Ray Bolger; *from CBS Television City in Hollywood*
JAN. 28 ★	Angie Dickinson and Efrem Zimbalist Jr.
FEB. 1-5	Peggy Cass and George Grizzard
FEB. 4 ★	Elizabeth Ashley and Roddy McDowall
FEB. 8-12	Peter Lawford and Sammy Davis Jr.
FEB. 11 ★	Lauren Bacall and Jack Palance
FEB. 15-19	Florence Henderson and Jack Carter
FEB. 18 ★	Eydie Gormé and Frank Sinatra
FEB. 22-26	Betty White and Tom Poston
FEB. 25 ★	Martha Raye and Barry Nelson
MAR. 1-5	Audrey Meadows and Allan Sherman
MAR. 4 ★	Carol Channing and Tony Randall
MAR. 8-12	Anne Jackson and Eli Wallach
MAR. 11 ★	Gloria and Jimmy Stewart
MAR. 15-19	Sally Ann Howes and Douglas Fairbanks Jr.
MAR. 18 ★	Inga Swenson and James Mason

FRED WOSTBROCK COLLECTION

MAR. 22–26	Marty Allen and Steve Rossi
MAR. 25 ★	Martha Raye and Barry Nelson
MAR. 29 – APR. 2	Penny Fuller and Frank Sinatra Jr.
APR. 1 ★	Monique Van Vooren and Arthur Godfrey
APR. 5–9	Rita Moreno and Peter Lind Hayes
APR. 8 ★	Dorothy Collins and Wally Cox
APR. 12–16	Kitty Carlisle and James Mason
APR. 15 ★	Eydie Gormé and Alan King
APR. 19–23	Jane Wyatt and Frank Gifford
APR. 22 ★	Angie Dickinson and Peter Lawford
APR. 26–30	Shari Lewis and Chester Morris
APR. 29 ★	Nanette Fabray and Sidney Chaplain
MAY 3–7	Juliet Prowse and George Hamilton
MAY 6 ★	Rosemary Clooney and Sammy Davis Jr.
MAY 10–14	Sheila MacRae and Skitch Henderson
MAY 13 ★	Elizabeth Ashley and Darren McGavin
MAY 17–21	Joan Fontaine and George Grizzard
MAY 20 ★	*All-star special:* Betty White, Arlene Francis, Al Capp, Alfred Andriola, Mort Walker, Leonard Starr, Allen Saunders, Lee Falk
MAY 24–28	Dorothy Loudon and Orson Bean
MAY 27 ★	Audrey Meadows and Tony Randall
MAY 31 – JUN. 4	Nancy Ames and Orson Bean
JUN. 3 ★	June Lockhart and Barry Sullivan
JUN. 7–11	Elizabeth Allen and Tom Poston
JUN. 10 ★	Carol Lawrence and Arthur Godfrey
JUN. 14–18	Gisele MacKenzie and Jack Cassidy
JUN. 17 ★	Rosemary Clooney and Sammy Davis Jr.
JUN. 21–25	Virginia Graham and Milt Kamen
JUN. 24 ★	Olivia de Havilland and George Hamilton
JUN. 28 – JUL. 2	Anita Gillette and Frank Gifford
JUL. 1 ★	Vivian Vance and Jim Backus
JUL. 5–9	Anne Jeffreys and Alan Young
JUL. 8 ★	Nancy Sinatra and Woody Allen
JUL. 12–16	Shirl Conway and Peter Lind Hayes
JUL. 15 ★	Jayne Meadows and Steve Allen
JUL. 19–23	Dina Merrill and Cliff Robertson
JUL. 22 ★	Carol Burnett and Alan King
JUL. 26–30	Betty White and Wally Cox
JUL. 29 ★	Carol Channing and Eli Wallach

AUG. 2-6	Bess Myerson and Sam Levenson
AUG. 5 ★	Joan Collins and Anthony Newley
AUG. 9-13	Marty Allen and Steve Rossi
AUG. 12 ★	Phyllis Newman and Tony Randall
AUG. 16-20	Florence Henderson and Dick Patterson
AUG. 19 ★	Sally Ann Howes and Alan Young
AUG. 23-27	June Lockhart and Ross Martin
AUG. 26 ★	Lucille Ball and Gary Morton
AUG. 30 – SEP. 3	Amanda Blake and Eddie Albert
SEP. 2 ★	Natalie Schafer and Jim Backus
SEP. 6-10	Rose Marie and Peter Lawford
SEP. 9 ★	*All-star special:* Barbara Rush, Bob Denver, Bea Benaderet, Richard Crenna
SEP.13-17	Nancy Kulp and Alan Hale
SEP. 20-24	Betsy Palmer and Douglas Fairbanks Jr.
SEP. 27 – OCT. 1	Carol Burnett and Barry Nelson
OCT. 4-8	Lena Horne and Peter Lind Hayes
OCT. 11-15	Jane Wyatt and Roddy McDowall
OCT. 18-22	Sheila MacRae and Jack Jones
OCT. 25-29	Betty White and Frank Gifford

AUTHOR'S COLLECTION

NOV. 1-5	Florence Henderson and Bill Cullen
NOV. 8-12	Joan Fontaine and Pernell Roberts
NOV. 15-19	Arlene Francis and Elliot Reid
NOV. 22-26	Sally Ann Howes and Ray Bolger
NOV. 29 - DEC. 3	Joanna Barnes and Peter Falk
DEC. 6-10	Virginia Graham and Chester Morris
DEC. 13-17	Monique Van Vooren and Arthur Godfrey
DEC. 20-24	Audrey Meadows and Douglas Fairbanks Jr.
DEC. 27-31	Angie Dickinson and Peter Lawford

1966

JAN. 3-7	Betty White and Frank Gifford
JAN. 10-14	Lucille Ball and Gary Morton
JAN. 17-21	Rose Marie and Bob Denver
JAN. 24-28	Elizabeth Ashley and Danny Kaye
JAN. 31 - FEB. 4	June Lockhart and Ross Martin
FEB. 7-11	Carol Burnett and Barry Nelson
FEB. 14-18	Sheila MacRae and Nipsey Russell
FEB. 21-25	Betsy Palmer and Darren McGavin
FEB. 28 - MAR. 4	Angie Dickinson and Peter Lind Hayes
MAR. 7-11	Florence Henderson and Lloyd Bridges
MAR. 14-18	Lee Remick and Ray Bolger
MAR. 21-25	Betty White and Frank Gifford
MAR. 28 - APR. 1	Phyllis Newman and Alan King
APR. 4-8	Jane Morgan and Larry Blyden
APR. 11-15	Barbara Feldon and Jerry Vale
APR. 18-22	Arlene Francis and Ross Martin
APR. 25-29	Carol Burnett and Soupy Sales
MAY 2-6	Irene Ryan and Douglas Fairbanks Jr.
MAY 9-13	Bea Benaderet and Ray Walston
MAY 16-20	June Lockhart and Bob Crane
MAY 23-27	Lee Remick and Peter Lawford
MAY 30 - JUN. 3	Betty White and Roddy McDowall
JUN. 6-10	Nancy Ames and Jack Cassidy
JUN. 13-17	Arlene Francis and Alan Young
JUN. 20-24	Marty Allen and Steve Rossi
JUN. 27 - JUL. 1	Florence Henderson and Paul Anka
JUL. 4-8	Elizabeth Ashley and Soupy Sales
JUL. 11-15	Tippi Hedren and Brian Keith; *Monday's episode did not air due to Vietnam news conference*

JUL. 18-22   Dorothy Loudon and Arthur Godfrey
JUL. 25-29   Jane Wyatt and Robert Young
AUG. 1-5   Betty White and Barry Nelson
AUG. 8-12   Phyllis Kirk and Peter Lawford
AUG. 15-19   Joan Fontaine and Sam Levenson
AUG. 22-26   Lee Remick and Jack Cassidy
AUG. 29 - SEP. 2 Florence Henderson and Frank Gifford
SEP. 5-9   Carol Lawrence and Darren McGavin
SEP. 12-16   *Special week. Mon:* Barbara Bain and Brian Keith.
                  Tues: Bea Benaderet and Eddie Albert. *Wed:*
                  Nancy Kulp and Frank Sutton. *Thurs:* Donna
                  Douglas and Steve Hill. *Fri:* Carol Wells and Bob
                  Denver. *Taped at CBS Television City in Hollywood;*
                  beginning with this week, the show aired in color.
SEP. 19-23   Lucille Ball and Gary Morton; *Taped at CBS*
                  Television City in Hollywood
SEP. 26-30   June Lockhart and Danny Kaye; *Taped at CBS*
                  Television City in Hollywood
OCT. 3-7   Carol Burnett and Ross Martin; *Taped at CBS*
                  Television City in Hollywood

FRED WOSTBROCK COLLECTION

OCT. 10-14	Irene Ryan and Bob Crane; *Taped at CBS Television City in Hollywood*
OCT. 17-21	Barbara Rush and John Forsythe; *Taped at CBS Television City in Hollywood*
OCT. 24-28	Barbara Eden and Peter Lawford; *Taped at CBS Television City in Hollywood*
OCT. 31 - NOV. 4	Carolyn Jones and Barry Sullivan; *Taped at CBS Television City in Hollywood*
NOV. 7-11	Audrey Meadows and Jerry Lewis; *Taped at CBS Television City in Hollywood*
NOV. 14-18	Amanda Blake and Ray Bolger; *Taped at CBS Television City in Hollywood*
NOV. 21-23, 25	Angie Dickinson and Frank Gorshin; *Taped at CBS Television City in Hollywood*
NOV. 28 - DEC. 2	Nancy Ames and Jack Cassidy; *Taped at CBS Television City in Hollywood*
DEC. 5-9	Carol Burnett and Roger Smith; *Taped at CBS Television City in Hollywood*
DEC. 12-16	Elizabeth Montgomery and Jim Backus; *Taped at CBS Television City in Hollywood*
DEC. 19-23	Florence Henderson and Frank Gifford
DEC. 25 ★	Lee Remick and Peter Lawford
DEC. 26-30	Sheila MacRae and Soupy Sales

1967

JAN. 2-6	Dorothy Loudon and Chester Morris
JAN. 8 ★	Pamela Tiffin and Larry Blyden
JAN. 9-13	Betty White and Ross Martin
JAN. 16-20	Marty Allen and Steve Rossi
JAN. 23-27	Arlene Dahl and Gordon MacRae
JAN. 29 ★	Joan Fontaine and Jim Backus
JAN. 30 - FEB. 3	Marjorie Lord and Paul Anka
FEB. 5 ★	Shelley Winters and Barry Nelson
FEB. 6-10	Virginia Graham and Nipsey Russell
FEB. 12 ★	Betsy Palmer and Alan King
FEB. 13-17	Gretchen Wyler and George Segal
FEB. 19★	Arlene Francis and Tony Perkins
FEB. 20-24	Jill Haworth and James Mason
FEB. 26 ★	Anne Jeffreys and Darren McGavin
FEB. 27 - MAR. 3	Connie Stevens and Roddy McDowall

MAR. 5 ★	Betty White and Frank Gifford
MAR. 6-10	Leslie Uggams and Soupy Sales
MAR. 12 ★	Lynn Redgrave and Cliff Robertson
MAR. 13-17	Mimi Hines and Phil Ford
MAR. 19 ★	Polly Bergen and Tony Randall
MAR. 20-24	Joan Fontaine and Douglas Fairbanks Jr.
MAR. 27-31	Armed Forces Week, with Chris Noel and Roger Smith
APR. 3-7	Betty White and George Grizzard
APR. 10 ★	Barbara Feldon and Jim Backus
APR. 10-14	Arlene Francis and Larry Blyden
APR. 17 ★	Carol Burnett and Alan King
APR. 17-21	Connie Stevens and Dick Shawn
APR. 24 ★	Florence Henderson and Eli Wallach
APR. 24-28	Agnes Moorhead and Barry Nelson
MAY 1-5	*Tournament of Champions:* June Lockhart and Ross Martin
MAY 8 ★	Gloria and Jimmy Stewart
MAY 8-12	Audrey Meadows and Bob Crane
MAY 15 ★	Phyllis Diller and Gary Morton
MAY 15-19	Elizabeth Montgomery and Martin Landau
MAY 22 ★	Barbara Rush and Noel Harrison; *final nighttime episode*
MAY 22-26	*Tournament of Champions:* Carol Burnett and Peter Lawford
MAY 29 - JUN. 2	Donna Douglas *(Mon. and Tues.)*, Arlene Francis *(Wed.-Fri.)*, Jack Cassidy
JUN. 5-9	Eva Gabor and Hugh O'Brian
JUN. 12-16	*Tournament of Champions:* Betty White and Frank Gifford
JUN. 19-23	*Family Week:* Irene Ryan and Guy Williams
JUN. 26-30	Joan Fontaine and Jack Jones
JUL. 3-7	Phyllis Newman and Paul Anka
JUL. 10-14	Rose Marie and Alan King
JUL. 17-21	Florence Henderson and Jack Carter
JUL. 24-28	Betsy Palmer and Joel Gray
JUL. 31 - AUG. 4	Marty Allen and Steve Rossi
AUG. 7-11	Claire Bloom and Barry Nelson
AUG. 14-18	Sheila MacRae and George Grizzard
AUG. 21-25	Arlene Francis and Skitch Henderson

AUG. 28 – SEP. 1	Eve Arden and Ray Bolger
SEP. 4–8	Dorothy Loudon and Jim Backus
SEP. 11–15	Betty White and Frank Gifford; *final week on CBS*

1971

APR. 5–9	Bill Bixby and Elizabeth Montgomery; *first week on ABC*
APR. 12–16	Robert Reed and Jo Anne Worley
APR. 19–23	Carol Burnett and Merv Griffin
APR. 26–30	Peter Lawford and Burt Reynolds
MAY 3–7	Kaye Ballard and Harvey Korman
MAY 10–14	Carol Lawrence and Burt Reynolds
MAY 17–21	Mel Tormé and Pat Carroll
MAY 24–28	Jack Cassidy and Mary Tyler Moore
MAY 31 – JUN. 4	Bob Crane and Sally Ann Howes
JUN. 7–11	Elizabeth Allen and Arte Johnson
JUN. 14–18	Bill Bixby and Meredith MacRae
JUN. 21–25	Sheila MacRae and Adam West
JUN. 28 – JUL. 2	Werner Klemperer and Jo Anne Worley
JUL. 5–9	Angie Dickinson and Peter Lawford
JUL. 12–16	Florence Henderson and Bill Cullen

FRED WOSTBROCK COLLECTION

JUL. 19-23	Jack Klugman and Anne Meara
JUL. 26-30	James Brolin and Virginia Graham
AUG. 2-6	Amanda Blake and Darren McGavin
AUG. 9-13	Nancy Kulp and Darren McGavin
AUG. 16-20	Johnny Mathis and Betty White
AUG. 23-27	Juliet Mills and Marty Allen
AUG. 30 - SEP. 3	Barbara McNair and Jackie Cooper
SEP. 6-10	Jack Cassidy and Mary Tyler Moore
SEP. 13-17	Chad Everett and Elizabeth Montgomery
SEP. 20-24	Carol Burnett and Henry Fonda
SEP. 27 - OCT. 1	Nanette Fabray and Arte Johnson
OCT. 4-8	Julie Adams and Tony Randall
OCT. 11-15	Edie Adams and Carl Reiner
OCT. 18-22	Pat Carroll and John Forsythe
OCT. 25-29	Carol Burnett and Dick Martin
NOV. 1-5	Monty Hall and Brenda Vaccaro
NOV. 8-12	Art Linkletter and Denise Nicholas
NOV. 15-19	Jack Carter and Vera Miles
NOV. 22-26	Martin Milner and Abby Dalton
NOV. 29 - DEC. 3	Peter Lawford and Elizabeth Montgomery
DEC. 6-10	Brett Somers and Jack Klugman
DEC. 13-17	Bill Bixby and Anita Gillette
DEC. 20-24	James Brolin and Juliet Prowse
DEC. 27-31	Carolyn Jones and Greg Morris

1972

JAN. 3-7	Joseph Campanella and Florence Henderson
JAN. 10-14	Ross Martin and Betty White
JAN. 17-21	Lois Nettleton and Soupy Sales
JAN. 24-28	Tige Andrews and Jo Anne Worley
JAN. 31 - FEB. 4	Abby Dalton and Rod Serling
FEB. 7 - FEB. 11	Carol Burnett and Elizabeth Montgomery
FEB. 14-18	Sheila MacRae and Martin Milner
FEB. 21-25	Bill Bixby and Ruta Lee
FEB. 29	*Special week commemorating the 2000th episode of* Password; Pat Carroll and Roddy McDowall *(no program aired on the 28th due to coverage of Richard Nixon's visit to China)*
MAR. 1-3	Anne Francis and Arte Johnson
MAR. 6-10	Pat Carroll and Tom Kennedy

MAR. 13-17	Jack Cassidy and Betty Grable
MAR. 20-24	*Tournament of Champions:* Carol Burnett and Elizabeth Montgomery
MAR. 27-31	*Tournament of Champions, Week 2:* Carol Burnett and Elizabeth Montgomery
APR. 3-7	Peter Lawford and Greg Morris
APR. 10-14	Monty Hall and Peter Lawford
April 17-21	Barbara Feldon and Roddy McDowall
April 24-28	Amanda Blake and James MacArthur
MAY 1-5	Arte Johnson and Nancy Kulp
MAY 8-12	Carol Channing and Martin Milner
MAY 15-19	John Forsythe and Cloris Leachman
MAY 22-26	Darren McGavin and Dina Merrill
MAY 29 - JUN. 2	Abby Dalton and Chad Everett
JUN. 5-9	Lynda Day George and George Peppard
JUN. 12-16	Ruta Lee and Ross Martin
JUN. 19-23	Joel Gray and Barbara Rush
JUN. 26-30	Nancy Kulp and Douglas Fairbanks Jr.
JUL. 3-7	Tom Kennedy and Jo Anne Worley
JUL. 10-14	Carolyn Jones and George Peppard
JUL. 17-21	Paul Lynde and Elizabeth Montgomery
JUL. 24-28	Lucille Ball and Ross Martin
JUL. 31 - AUG. 4	Nanette Fabray and Martin Milner
AUG. 7-11	Bill Bixby and June Lockhart
AUG. 14-18	Greg Morris and Polly Bergen
AUG. 21-25	Pat Carroll and Jack Cassidy
AUG. 28 - SEP. 1	Tony Randall and Betty White
SEP. 4-8	Jack Klugman and Susan Oliver
SEP. 11-15	Paul Lynde and Elizabeth Allen
SEP. 18-22	Carol Burnett and Elizabeth Montgomery
SEP. 25-29	Martin Milner and Greg Morris
OCT. 2-6	Elizabeth Montgomery and Richard Long
OCT. 9-13	Arte Johnson and Linda Kay Henning
OCT. 16-20	Sally Struthers and Gene Rayburn
OCT. 23-27	Abby Dalton and Peter Lawford
OCT. 30 - NOV. 3	Anita Gillette and Tom Kennedy
NOV. 6-10	John Forsythe and Jo Anne Worley
NOV. 13-17	Bill Bixby and Linda Day George
NOV. 20-24	Carol Burnett and Ross Martin
NOV. 27 - DEC. 1	Nanette Fabray and Johnny Mann

DEC. 4-8   Elizabeth Montgomery and Bert Convy
DEC. 11-15   Sally Struthers and Paul Lynde
DEC. 18-22   Florence Henderson and Robert Fuller
DEC. 25-29   Martin Milner and Greg Morris

1973

JAN. 1-5   Carol Burnett and Burt Reynolds
JAN. 8-12   Jack Klugman and Tony Randall
JAN. 15-19   Betty White and Rod Serling
JAN. 22-26   Elizabeth Montgomery and Bert Convy
JAN. 29 - FEB. 2   Florence Henderson and Robert Fuller
FEB. 5-9   Pat Carroll and Robert Reed
FEB. 12-16   *No data available*
FEB. 19-23   Carolyn Jones and Dick Gautier
FEB. 26-Mar 2   Paul Lynde and Sally Struthers
MAR. 5-9   Jack Cassidy and Nancy Kulp
MAR. 12-16   Darren McGavin and June Lockhart
MAR. 19-23   John Forsythe and Anita Gillette
MAR. 26-30   Martin Milner and Greg Morris
APR. 2-6   Carol Burnett and Elizabeth Montgomery
APR. 9-13   *All-star week:* Carol Burnett, Elizabeth
                   Montgomery, Rod Serling, Betty White
APR. 16-20   Dick Gautier and Susan Oliver
APR. 23-27   Peter Lawford and Bert Convy
APR. 30 - MAY 4   Lois Nettleton and Tom Kennedy
MAY 7-11   Bill Bixby and Lucie Arnaz
MAY 14-18   George Kennedy and Pat Carroll
MAY 21-25   Helen Reddy and Larry Blyden
MAY 28 - JUN. 1   Jack Klugman and Linda Kaye Henning
JUN. 4-8   June Lockhart and Dick Sargent
JUN. 11-15   *"Celebrity Charity Week":* Elizabeth Montgomery
                   and 1973 Password grand champion Lew Retrum,
                   Jim and Henny Backus, Jack Narz and Tom
                   Kennedy, Carolyn Jones and James Shigeta, Dick
                   Gautier and George Eckstein, Betty White
                   and Wayne Rogers, Dave Madden and Jo Anne
                   Meredith
JUN. 18-22   *No data available*
JUN. 25-29   *Due to extensive coverage of the Watergate hearings,*
                   the show was pre-empted every day of this week.

JUL. 2-6	*Special week:* Carol Burnett and 1973 Password Grand Champion Lew Retrum vs. six all-star teams: Monty Hall and Joanna Gleason; Jack Klugman and Brett Somers; Jack Cassidy and Shari Lewis; Helen Reddy and Jeff Wald; Peter Lawford and Joe Hamilton; Rock Hudson and 1972 Password Grand Champion Martha Peukert
JUL. 9-13	Peggy Cass and Richard Long
JUL. 16-20	Martin Milner and Greg Morris
JUL. 23 - JUL. 27	Ruta Lee and Bill Cullen
JUL. 30 - AUG. 3	Elizabeth Montgomery and Bert Convy
AUG. 6-10	Anita Gillette and Wayne Rogers
AUG. 13-17	Bill Bixby and Richard Dawson
AUG. 20-24	Bill Bixby and Richard Dawson
AUG. 27-31	Joanna Barnes and Michael Landon
SEP. 3-7	Angie Dickinson and Richard Crenna
SEP. 10-14	Dick Gautier and Vicki Lawrence
SEP. 17-21	Sandy Duncan and Peter Lawford
SEP. 24-28	Betty White and James Shigeta
OCT. 1-5	Sandy Duncan and Peter Lawford
OCT. 8-12	Susan Oliver and Alan Alda
OCT. 15-19	Martin Milner and Greg Morris
OCT. 22-26	Jack Klugman and Brett Somers
OCT. 29 - NOV. 2	Linda Day George and Nipsey Russell
NOV. 5-9	Richard Dawson and Loretta Swit
NOV. 12-16	Helen Reddy and Bill Cullen
NOV. 19-23	Elizabeth Montgomery and Robert Foxworth
NOV. 26-30	Betty White and Greg Morris
DEC. 3-7	Lynda Kaye Henning and Michael Evans
DEC. 10-14	Florence Henderson and Dick Gautier
DEC. 17-21	Sandy Duncan and Bill Bixby
DEC. 24-28	Sandy Duncan and Bill Bixby
DEC. 31	Pat Carroll and Peter Lawford

1974

JAN. 1-4	Pat Carroll and Peter Lawford
JAN. 7-11	Carol Burnett and Elizabeth Montgomery vs. Carl Reiner and Robert Foxworth
JAN. 14-18	Martin Milner and Greg Morris

JAN. 21-25	Susan Oliver and Jack Cassidy
JAN. 28 – FEB. 1	Anita Gillette and Ed Asner
FEB. 4-8	Anne Meara and Tennessee Ernie Ford
FEB. 11-15	Juliet Mills and Jack Cassidy
FEB. 18-22	Joanna Barnes and Nipsey Russell
FEB. 25 – MAR. 2	Marcia Wallace and Robert Reed
MAR. 4-8	Lee Meriwether and George Peppard
MAR. 11-15	Betty White and Joanna Barnes
MAR. 18-22	Sandy Duncan and Tom Kennedy
MAR. 25-29	*"Celebrities, Their Children, and Their Mothers":* Helen Reddy, Jack Klugman, Florence Henderson, Jack Cassidy, Richard Dawson, Susan Oliver
APR. 1-5	Pat Harrington and Dick Gautier
APR. 8-12	Linda Kaye Henning and Ed Asner
APR. 15-19	Martin Milner and Greg Morris
APR. 22-26	Carol Burnett and Elizabeth Montgomery
APR. 29 – MAY 3	Anita Gillette and Joel Grey
MAY 6-10	Susan Oliver and Bill Cullen
MAY 13-17	Loretta Swit and Richard Dawson
MAY 20-24	Ruta Lee and Carl Reiner
MAY 27-31	Peter Lawford and Greg Morris
JUN. 3-7	Frank Gifford and Bill Bixby
JUN. 10-14	Abby Dalton and Tennessee Ernie Ford
JUN. 17-21	Sandy Duncan and Bill Bixby
JUN. 24-28	Betty White and Joanna Barnes
JUL. 1-5	Joyce Bulifant and Richard Dawson
JUL. 8-12	Linda Kaye Henning and Martin Milner
JUL. 15-19	*Special week:* Allen Ludden vs. Elizabeth Montgomery; Allen's partners were Lucille Ball, Dick Gautier, Mary Tyler Moore, Harvey Korman, and Betty White; Elizabeth's partners were Greg Morris, James Hampton, Tom Kennedy, Robert Reed, and Robert Foxworth; *guest host Monty Hall*
JUL. 22-26	*Special week:* Allen Ludden vs. Elizabeth Montgomery; Allen's partners were Mary Tyler Moore, Betty White, Robert Reed, and Kate Jackson. Elizabeth's partner was two-time Tournament of Champions winner Lew Retrum. Friday's game pitted Allen and Lew against Elizabeth and Betty; *guest host Monty Hall*

JUL. 29 – AUG. 2	*All-star week:* Elizabeth Montgomery and Robert Foxworth vs. Dyan Cannon and Carl Reiner
AUG. 5-9	Linda Kaye Henning and Martin Milner
AUG. 12-16	Elaine Joyce and Robert Fuller
AUG. 19-23	*No data available*
AUG. 26-30	Helen Reddy and Tony Randall
SEP. 2-6	Joyce Bulifant and Joseph Campanella
SEP. 9-13	*"Celebrities and Their Wives" all-star week:* Greg Morris and Leona Keyes, Ed Asner and Nancy Sykes, Don Galloway and Linda Robinson, Dick Gautier and Barbara Stuart, Bobby Van and Elaine Joyce, Bert and Anne Convy
SEP. 16-20	*All-star week:* Greg Morris and Martin Milner vs. Joanna Barnes and Betty White
SEP. 23-27	*"Allen vs. Betty" week;* Allen's partners were Arlene Francis, Kate Jackson, Vicki Lawrence, Joyce Bulifant, and Betty's mother Tess White; Betty's partners were Richard Dawson, Eddie Albert, Dick Gautier, James Hampton, and James Shigeta; *guest host Monty Hall*
SEP. 30 – OCT. 4	*Celebrity Husbands and Wives Week:* Bert and Anne Convy, Ed and Nancy Asner, John and Patty Duke Astin, Robert and Sheila Sullivan Culp, Sam and Ann Melville, Dionne Warwick and Bill Elliot, Orson and Carolyn Bean
OCT. 7-11	Joyce Bulifant and Loretta Swit
OCT. 14-18	*All-star week,* with Carol Burnett and Vicki Lawrence vs. celebrity opponents, including Rock Hudson, John Schuck, Lyle Waggoner, Nancy Walker, David Groh, Tony Randall
OCT. 21-25	Kate Jackson and Peter Lawford, featuring winners from past years
OCT. 28 – NOV. 1	Bill Bixby and Elaine Joyce, featuring winners from past years
NOV. 4-8	George Peppard and Linda Kaye Henning; all contestants during this week were television producers and writers playing for charity
NOV. 11-15	*Data indicates that no episodes were produced for this week. It is believed that ABC aired reruns of a previous all-star week.*

NOV. 18-22	*First week of Password All-Stars:* Loretta Swit, Greg Morris, Linda Kaye Henning, Martin Milner, Elaine Joyce, Don Galloway
NOV. 25-29	Ed Asner, Sandy Duncan, Patty Duke Astin, Bill Bixby, Patti Deutsch, James Shigeta
DEC. 2-6	Carol Burnett, Nancy Walker, Ross Martin, Lynda Day George, Robert Reed, Gene Rayburn
DEC. 9-13	Sandy Duncan, Mike Evans, Eddie Albert, Joyce Bulifant, Victoria Principal, Pat Harrington Jr.
DEC. 16-20	Shelley Winters, Robert Culp, Phyllis Newman, Peter Bonerz, Ruta Lee, Orson Bean
DEC. 23-27	Wilt Chamberlain, Florence Henderson, Vicki Lawrence, Dick Gautier, Susan Oliver, Richard Dawson
DEC. 30-31	*Grandmasters Tournament #1:* Nancy Walker, Peter Bonerz, Don Galloway, James Shigeta, Dick Gautier, Joyce Bulifant

1975

JAN. 1-3	*Grandmasters Tournament #1, continued:* Nancy Walker, Peter Bonerz, Don Galloway, James Shigeta, Dick Gautier, Joyce Bulifant
JAN. 6-10	Bill Bixby, Nipsey Russell, Rue McClanahan, Adrienne Barbeau, Gunilla Hutton, John Gavin
JAN. 13-17	Tennessee Ernie Ford, Dick Martin, Theresa Merritt, Paul Williams, Lee Meriwether, Sally Struthers
JAN. 20-24	Ed Asner, Vicki Lawrence, Gene Rayburn, Elaine Joyce, Richard Dawson, Juliet Mills
JAN. 27-31	Monty Hall, Betty White, Avery Schreiber, Anne Meara, Greg Morris, James Hampton
FEB. 3-7	Jack Albertson, Bill Dana, Barbara McNair, Linda Kaye Henning, Kaye Stevens, Password grand champion Lew Retrum
FEB. 10-14	Sandy Duncan, Leslie Nielsen, Elaine Joyce, Martin Milner, Hal Linden, Password grand champion Martha Peukert
FEB. 17-21	*Final week of Password All-Stars: Grandmasters Tournament #2* with Sally Struthers, Bill Bixby, Betty White, Richard Dawson, Kaye Stevens, Hal Linden

FEB. 24-28	Bill Bixby and Greg Morris
MAR. 3-7	Linda Kaye Henning and Richard Dawson
MAR. 10-14	Vicki Lawrence and Betty White
MAR. 17-21	Nipsey Russell and Elaine Joyce
MAR. 24-28	Allen Ludden and Elizabeth Montgomery; *guest host Betty White*
MAR. 31 - APR. 4	Jack Klugman and Juliet Mills
APR. 7-11	Jack Albertson and Joyce Bulifant
APR. 14-18	Gloria DeHaven and Martin Milner
APR. 21-25	Arlene Francis and Dick Martin
APR. 28 - MAY 2	Alan Young and Sally Field
MAY 5-9	Marcia Wallace and Ron Masak
MAY 12-16	Ed Asner and Anne Meara
MAY 19-23	Don Galloway and Ruta Lee
MAY 26-30	Lucille Ball and Gary Morton
JUN. 2-6	Lynn Redgrave and Richard Dawson
JUN. 9-13	Sally Struthers and Gary Crosby
JUN. 16-20	Carol Burnett and Jack Cassidy
JUN. 23-27	*Final week on ABC,* with Kate Jackson and Sam Melville; Mark Goodson and Betty White appear on the final episode

FRED WOSTBROCK COLLECTION

WIN WITH THE STARS
EPISODE GUIDE

Win with the Stars taped its first season in February 1968 and in some television markets, it began airing as early as March. The show became more widely distributed in September 1968, but all stations aired the episodes that taped in February. Because the program aired once a week in syndication, airdates varied from city to city. Solely for a frame of reference, the airdates below come from Long Beach, California broadcasts.

1968

SEP. 18	Peter Marshall and Barbara McNair
SEP. 25	Tammy Grimes and Richard Long
OCT. 2	Bob Crane and June Lockhart
OCT. 9	Greg Morris and Kaye Ballard
OCT. 16	Betty White and Stubby Kaye
OCT. 23	Mel Tormé and Jaye P. Morgan
OCT. 30	Judy Carne and Paul Lynde
NOV. 6	Rose Marie and Bill Anderson
NOV. 13	Della Reese and Andy Russell
NOV. 20	Abby Dalton and Jim Backus
DEC. 4	Ruta Lee
DEC. 11	Janet Blair
DEC. 18	Robert Clary and Helen O'Connell
DEC. 25	Jo Anne Worley and Billy Eckstine

1969

JAN. 1	Kay Starr
JAN. 8	Jonathan Harris
JAN. 15	Greg Morris and Gisele MacKenzie
JAN. 22	Arte Johnson
JAN. 29	Rosemary Clooney and Bill Bixby

FEB. 5	Ketty Lester and Richard Long
FEB. 12	Stubby Kaye and Ruta Lee
FEB. 19	George Jessel and Nancy Ames
FEB. 26	Dorothy Lamour and Peter Marshall
MAR. 5	Cliff Robertson and Roberta Sherwood
MAR. 12	Sue Raney and Marty Ingels
MAR. 19	Janet Blair and Rusty Draper
APR. 23	Janis Paige and Morey Amsterdam
APR. 30	Gisele MacKenzie and Paul Lynde
MAY 14	Roberta Sherwood and Regis Philbin
MAY 21	Shari Lewis and Peter Marshall
MAY 28	Betty White and Forrest Tucker
JUL. 2	Steve Allen and Jayne Meadows
JUL. 9	Keeley Smith and Roddy McDowall
JUL. 16	Abby Dalton and Michael Landon
JUL. 23	John Gary and Jaye P. Morgan
JUL. 30	Soupy Sales and Jack Carter
AUG. 6	Kaye Starr and Frankie Avalon
AUG. 13	Ruta Lee and Charley Weaver
OCT. 7	Greg Morris and Irene Ryan
OCT. 14	June Lockhart and Richard Deacon
OCT. 21	Judy Carne and Bill Bixby
NOV. 4	Helen O'Connell and Billy Eckstein
NOV. 11	Ann Miller and James Darren
NOV. 18	Kaye Stevens and Billy Daniels
NOV. 25	Kaye Ballard and Paul Lynde

STUMPERS EPISODE GUIDE

All episodes aired in 1976.

OCT. 4-8	Dick Gautier and Robert Reed
OCT. 11-15	Peter Bonerz and Bill Bixby
OCT. 18-22	Jamie Farr and Mike Farrell
OCT. 25-29	Betty White and John Schuck
NOV. 1-5	Rick Hurst and Don Galloway
NOV. 8-12	Lois Nettleton and Orson Bean
NOV. 15-19	Vicki Lawrence and Ross Martin
NOV. 22-26	Patty Duke Astin and Joanna Barnes
NOV. 29 - DEC. 3	Adrienne Barbeau and Jamie Farr
DEC. 6-10	Rita Moreno and Greg Morris
DEC. 13-17	Jack Cassidy and Mike Farrell
DEC. 20-24	*All-star week:* Betty White and Joanna Barnes vs. Peter Bonerz and Dick Gautier
DEC. 27-31	Bill Bixby and Anita Gillette

BIBLIOGRAPHY

"A Bird? A Plane? No, It's a Streaker." *Bucks County Courier Times.* 10 Mar. 1974.

Adams, Val. "NBC to Revise Week-End Shows." *The New York Times.* 2 Mar. 1955.

Adams, Val. "Schoenbrun Gets CBS Capital Job." *The New York Times.* 17 Nov. 1961.

"Allen Ludden." Superman Super Site. *http://www.supermansupersite.com/ludden.html*

"Allen Ludden Becomes Instant Californian." *Daytime TV* Magazine. November 1971.

"Allen Ludden Chosen by Press Group to Receive Texan of the Year Award." *The Aransas Pass Progress.* 11 Jan. 1967.

"Allen Ludden Eulogized." *Galveston Daily News.* 12 Jun. 1981.

"Allen Ludden Has Prize Role in Play at University." *Corpus Christi Times.* 10 Oct. 1938.

"Allen Ludden Heads Alpine Pioneers Club." *El Paso Herald-Post.* 4 Oct. 1937.

"Allen Ludden: He Likes Teenagers." *Pasadena Independent Star-News.* 5 Feb. 1967.

"Allen Ludden His Own Boss." *Sandusky Register.* 5 May 1969.

"Allen Ludden MC of Network Show." *Janesville Daily Gazette.* 14 May 1948.

"Allen Ludden Openly Confesses: Being Married to Betty White is Like Having An Affair!" *TV Dawn to Dusk* Magazine. September 1974.

"Allen Ludden's Gallery." *Variety.* 23 May 1969.

"Allen Ludden Says Wife Pulled Him Out of Coma." *St. Petersburg Times.* 9 Jan. 1981.

"Allen Ludden Stars Jan. 2." *San Antonio Express and News.* 2 Dec. 1961.

"Allen Ludden Wins 1962 Alger Award." *Biddeford Journal.* 12 May 1962.

"Allen Ludden Wins Horatio Alger Award." *Janesville Daily Gazette.* 5 Jun. 1962.

"American Airlines Adds Stereo Sound." *Broadcasting Magazine.* 7 Jul. 1957.

"American Unity Urged." *San Antonio Express.* 4 Jun. 1940.

Anderson, Nancy. "Betty Thrilled by Hubby's Gift." *Norco Pony Express.* 21 Feb. 1974.

Anderson, Nancy. "David Almost Answers Questions on Diahann." *Greeley Daily Tribune.* 20 Dec. 1972.

"And the Password is…Mineral Point." *Mineral Point Historical Society.* February 2014.

"Animals to Have a Chance at Their Own Emmy Awards." *Hattiesburg American.* 20 Apr. 1975.

"Another Visit to the Teahouse." *Abilene Reporter News.* 26 Oct.1962.

Averill, Marie. "Critic's Choice is Choice." *Traverse City Record Eagle.* 4 Aug. 1976.

Batelle, Phyllis. "Betty White Show May Be Season's Sleeper." *Brownsville Herald.* 15 Sep. 1977.

Beck, Andee. "Betty White Will Not Move." *Corpus Christi Times.* 20 Aug. 1976.

Beck, Marilyn. "Betty White, Carol Channing Filming Love Boat." *Santa Fe New Mexican.* 6 Jun. 1981.

Beck, Marilyn. "Hollywood Closeup." *The Milwaukee Journal.* 19 Nov. 1971.

"Be Kind to Animals Week Under Way." *Portsmouth Herald.* 3 May 1971.

"Betty White." *Intimate Portrait.* Lifetime Television. 2000.

"Betty White Answers Questions on Dimension." *Avalanche Journal.* 21 May 1967.

"Betty White Engrossed in Work Following Death of Allen Ludden." *Spartanburg Herald-Journal.* 11 Mar. 1982.

"Betty White May Be TV's First Sweetheart." *San Mateo Times.* 20 Feb. 1954.

"Betty White Ready for 15th Rose Parade." *North Adams Transcript.* 14 Dec. 1968.

"The Betty White Show." *Broadcasting Magazine.* 22 Feb. 1954.

Bick, Jerry. "Betty White: Naughty Was Nice." *Pittsburgh Post-Gazette.* 22 Oct. 1977.

"Brownsville Boys Will Perform on Program Thursday." *Brownsville Herald.* 25 Jul. 1933.

Bryars, Chris. "The Real Mary Tyler Moore." *San Antonio Light.* 30 Jan. 1977.

Buck, Jerry. "Allen Ludden Enjoys Password, Says TV Game Shows Valuable to Audience." *Lubbock Avalanche Journal.* 24 Jul. 1974.

Bundschu, Barbara. "Television Can Entertain While Education, TV Emcee Claims." *Mason City Globe Gazette.* 28 Nov. 1961.

"Career Spans the Growth of Broadcasting." *Broadcasting Magazine.* 29 Jan. 1968.

Case, Barry. "TV for 2." *Billings Gazette.* 20 Nov. 1961.

"Catty Role Helped Betty White." *Annapolis Capital.* 31 Oct. 1977.

"Celebrities Gather at Ludden Funeral." *Santa Ana Orange County Register.* 12 Jun. 1981.

Clements, Erin. "Betty White Reveals Heartbreakingly Sweet Regret About Late Husband." Retrieved 16 Jul. 2016 from *http://www.today.com/popculture/betty-white-reveals-her-greatest-regret-about-late-husband-t11866*

Coleman, Emily. "From Red Barn to Package and Tent." *The New York Times.* 19 Jul. 1964.

"College Entrance Problem Explored." *Biddeford Journal.* 25 Mar. 1961

"Corpus Christi Radio Producer Returns Home for Conference." *Corpus Christi Caller Times.* 3 Jun. 1956.

"Cragsmoore Boy, 6, Joins Play Cast." *Middletown Times Herald.* 12 Jul. 1946.

"Critic's Corner." *Independent Press Telegram.* Long Beach, CA. 17 Jan. 1971.

Crosby, Joan. "Aggie Introduction Irks UT-Ex Ludden." *Abilene Reporter News.* 26 Oct. 1962.

"Da Costa Has Lead in Goodbye Again." *Middletown Times Herald.* 8 Jul. 1946.

Danson, Tom E. "Betty White's Dimples Win Her Many TV Friends." *Long Beach Press Telegram.* 19 Nov. 1951.

Danzig, Fred. "Inspirational But Disturbing." *Santa Fe New Mexican.* 29 Nov. 1961.

Denion, Charles. "Allen Ludden Says Password Separates Creeps from the Class." *Charleston Gazette Mail.* 28 Apr. 1963.

Denis, Paul. "Allen Ludden Marries Betty White." *TV Radio Mirror* Magazine. August 1963.

Donovan, Dick. "Allen Ludden Reveals: I was Saved from Death by God and My Wife's Love." *Weekly World News.* 3 Feb. 1981.

"The Double Life of Allen Ludden." *Pulaski Southwest Times.* 2 Nov. 1966.

Drake, Chris. "You Gotta Stand Up: The Life and High Times of John Henry Faulk." Cambridge Scholars Publishing. Newcastle, United Kingdom. 2007.

"Dr. Homer Ludden, Age 85, Prominent Physician, Dies." Wisconsin State Journal. 20 Mar. 1965.

DuRoss, Martin H. "Let's Read." *Lebanon Daily News.* 23 Jan. 1955.

"Earl Carter is President." *Corpus Christi Times.* 16 Feb. 1934.

"Educational TV Circuit Group Confers." *San Antonio Express.* 10 Dec. 1959.

"The Eggheads Muscle In." *San Antonio Light.* 22 May 1960.

"Episode #1399." *Late Show with David Letterman.* CBS-TV. 8 May 2000.

"Fates and Fortunes." *Broadcasting Magazine.* 3 Apr. 1961.

Faulk, John Henry. "Fear on Trial." University of Texas Press. Austin. 1983.

Felt, Dave. "Dave Felt's Column." *Southern Illinoisan.* Carbondale, IL. 16 May 1962.

Fischler, Grace. "Betty White: Call Me Wholesome!" *TV Stage* Magazine. December 1954.

Foster, Bob. "TV-Radio: That Betty White Girl." *San Mateo Times.* 14 May 1954.

Foster, Bob. "TV-Radio: Where's Betty White?" *San Mateo Times.* 23 Aug. 1954.

"Four U of T Ex-Students to Be Honored Oct. 19." *Corpus Christi Caller Times.* 1 Oct. 1962.

Freeman, Don. "Allen Ludden Believes Password is a Classic." *Kingsport News.* 6 May 1971.

"Fugitive Seen in Many Countries." *Lubbock Avalanche-Journal.* 29 Jan. 1967.

"Game Show Based on Money Facts." *The Evening Independent.* St. Petersburg, FL. 1 Jul. 1975.

"GE, Texaco Win Two Peabody Awards." *Broadcasting Magazine.* 24 Apr. 1961.

Gehman, Nev. "Inside Our Schools." *Billboard.* 12 Apr. 1952.

"The GI Hamlet." *Life Magazine*. P. 57. 7 Jan. 1946.

Gill, Alan. "Bill Fiset…About Television." *Oakland Tribune*. 12 Mar. 1962.

Gould, Jack. "TV: Classes in French." *The New York Times*. 17 Oct. 1961.

Granger, Bill. "Old Password a Thing of the Past." *Chicago Sun-Times*. 3 May 1975.

Griffin, John David. "Females Turn Out for Robert Goulet." *San Antonio Light*. 4 Feb. 1963.

Hammer, Alexander E. "Advertising: Wurzburger Hofbrau Drive Set." *The New York Times*. 2 Jan. 1959.

Handsaker, Gene. "Stars' Pets Have Center Stage." *Oakland Tribune*. 12 Jan. 1971.

"Happy Homemaker is Happy Homewrecker." *Madison Wisconsin State Journal*. 25 Aug. 1974.

Hawk, Don. "Elyria-Born Vermilion Student Receives Honors for Heroism." *Elyria Chronicle Telegram*. 24 Mar. 1950.

Hearings Before a Subcommittee of the Committee on Interstate and Foreign Commerce House of Representatives, Eighty-Second Congress, Second Session on H. Res. 278. Jun., Sep., Dec. 1952.

Henderson, Florence, with Joel Brokaw. "Life is Not a Stage: From Broadway Baby to a Lovely Lady and Beyond." Hachette Book Group. New York. 2011.

Hughes, Jack A. "Ludden Lauds Enthusiasm In Lecture Club Address." *Terre Haute Tribune*. 23 Apr. 1967.

Humphrey, Hal. "Have the Jaspers Had It?" *The Portsmouth Times*. 19 Aug. 1966.

"Hundreds Mourn Allen Ludden." *Nashua Telegraph*. 12 Jun. 1981.

Hyatt, Wesley. "Emmy Award Winning Nighttime Television Shows, 1948-2004." McFarland. Jefferson, NC. 2006.

"In Review: Pocketbook News." *Broadcasting Magazine*. 18 Mar. 1957.

"In Review: Weekday." *Broadcasting Magazine*. 14 Nov. 1955.

"In Review: Weekend." *Broadcasting Magazine*. 12 Oct. 1953.

"Inside Our Schools in New York." *Broadcasting Magazine*. 17 Mar. 1952.

"Inventions Worth Millions." *Oshkosh Daily Northwestern*. 10 Mar. 1900.

"Just for San Benito." *Brownsville Herald*. 15 Oct. 1943.

Kalb, Bernard. "For and By Teenagers: A Panel Discusses the Age Group's Problems." *The New York Times*. 12 Aug. 1951.

"K.C. Starlight Theater Announces Show Schedule." *Joplin Globe*. 15 May 1966.

Keating, John. "College Bowl Graduate Goes Into the Word Game." *TV Guide*. 25 Aug. 1962.

Kennedy, Tom. Personal interview. 17 Nov. 2014.

Kilgallen, Dorothy. "The Voice of Broadway: Richard Burton Plans Broadway Hamlet Cast." *Phoenix Arizona Republic*. 2 Sep. 1963.

"Kiwanis Hears TV Moderator." *Newport Daily News.* 1 Mar. 1962.

"Kiwanis Plans Career Day." *Newport Daily News.* 24 Feb. 1962.

Kleiner, Dick. "Betty White Keeping Busy." *Cedar Rapids Gazette.* 20 Feb. 1982.

Kleiner, Dick. "Ludden-White Romance Bloomed in Summer Stock." *The Victoria Advocate.* 16 Jun. 1963.

Kleiner, Dick. "Mrs. Allen Ludden Still Betty White." *Lowell Sun.* 15 Jun. 1963.

Kleiner, Dick. "Stars Tough to Imitate." *The Victoria Advocate.* 1 Feb. 1976.

Kule, Mrs. Charles. "Library Corner." *Daily Herald Suburban Chicago.* 10 Feb. 1955.

Lassan, Kurt. "TV Showman Thinks Today's Youth Are Better Informed." *Zanesville Times Recorder.* 27 Feb. 1967.

Late Night with David Letterman. NBC-TV. 1 Oct. 1985.

"Lecture Club Announces Allen Ludden." *Terre Haute Tribune.* 10 Oct. 1966.

"A Lecture Series Set for Radio-TV.' *The New York Times.* 30 Jun. 1954.

"Lester is Back — For the Fun of It." *Jefferson City Post Tribune.* 23 Nov. 1962.

Lester, John. "'Inside Our Schools' Keeps Getting Better." *Long Island Star-Journal.* 3 Apr. 1952.

"Let's Go to the Races Runs Strong in Second Outing." *Broadcasting Magazine.* 20 May 1968.

Levinson, Peter J. "Puttin' On The Ritz: Fred Astaire and the Fine Art of Panache." St. Martin's Press. New York. 2009.

"Life Smiles on Betty White." *Snyder Daily News.* 27 Jul. 1975.

"Local Boy Makes Good — Business." *The Billboard.* 16 May 1953.

"Local Man Manager for Actor Evans." *Corpus Christi Times.* 14 May 1947.

Lohman, Sidney. "News of TV and Radio." *The New York Times.* 10 Jun. 1951.

Lowry, Cynthia. "Desk-and-Sofa TV Show on Increase." *Lumberton Robesonian.* 19 Apr. 1969.

Lowry, Cynthia. "Local Boy Makes Good." *Corpus Christi Caller Times.* 15 Apr. 1962.

Lowry, Cynthia. "Ludden Says TV Pageants Are Good." Luddington Daily News. 4 Nov. 1966.

Lowry, Cynthia. "Ludden to Quit College Bowl; Circle Theater at 10 Tonight." *North Adams Transcript.* 9 May 1962.

Lowry, Cynthia. "A Noble Experiment." *High Point Enterprise.* 16 Oct. 1963.

Lowry, Cynthia. "Threesome of New Programs Seen Thursday." *Biloxi Daily Herald.* 6 Oct. 1961.

Lowry, Cynthia. "TV Quietly Using Many Negroes This Season." *Corpus Christi Caller Times.* 18 Oct. 1963.

Ludden, Allen. "Allen Ludden Has Alias: Mr. Betty White." *Burlington Daily Times News.* 22 Jul. 1966.

Ludden, Allen. "Future Hope Is Teenager." *Hutchinson News.* 2 Nov. 1963.

Ludden, Allen. "Information Program Can Entertain." *Salt Lake Tribune.* 22 Aug. 1962.

Ludden, Allen. "Password Star Sad at Demise." *Tuscon Daily Citizen.* 7 Jul. 1967.

Ludden, Allen. "Television In Review." *Morris Daily Herald.* 22 Jul. 1968.

Ludden, Allen, and Betty White. "Why Our Marriage Works." *The Prescott Courier.* 21 May 1976.

"Ludden Cuts Disc." *Fairbanks Daily News Miner.* 29 Aug. 1964.

"Ludden Has 7 Weekly Shows on TV Network." *Bedford Gazette.* 1 Feb. 1962.

"Ludden is Happy to be Helping." *Hattiesburg American.* 11 Aug. 1974.

"Ludden to Direct WCBS Programs." *Broadcasting Magazine.* 6 May 1957.

"Ludden to Stage TV Quiz Show Here." *Corpus Christi Caller Times.* 26 Mar. 1961.

MacKenzie, Bob. "The Happy Homemaker." *Oakland Tribune.* 19 Jul. 1974.

"Mainly About People." *Corpus Christi Times.* 1 Mar. 1938.

Manners, Dorothy. "Comedians Special Party Guests." *San Antonio Light.* 21 Jan. 1976.

Manners, Dorothy. "Star Makes Comeback." *San Antonio Light.* 22 Jan. 1974.

"Margaret Frances McGloin is Hostess Tuesday for Affair Honoring Miss Alice Jones." *Corpus Christi Times.* 30 Dec. 1936.

"Marines Present Series on Radio." *Danville Bee.* 30 Jun. 1962.

Marshall, Peter, with Adrienne Armstrong. "Backstage with the Original Hollywood Square." Rutledge Hill Press. Nashville. 2002.

Martin, Bob. "Betty White Gets to Pet the Men on Miss Moore's Series." *Independent Press-Telegram.* Long Beach, CA. 1 Sep. 1974.

Maurice, Dick. "Coast to Coast." *Hurst Mid Cities Daily News.* 20 Jan. 1980.

McManus, Margaret. "Peaceful Home Ironical Setting." *Syracuse Post.* 20 Dec. 1964.

Mercer, Charles. "Radio, TV Highlights." *The Evening Independent.* Massillon, OH. 22 Jan. 1959.

Miller, Stephen. "Phyllis Adams, 80, Female Pioneer of Early Television." *New York Sun.* 2004 Mar. 3

"Miss Margaret McGloin to Marry Allen Ludden." *Corpus Christi Times.* 10 Oct. 1943.

"Miss Teenage America Won By California Lass." *Lubbock Avalanche Journal.* 28 Oct. 1962.

Morrow, Don. Personal interview. 17 Nov. 2014.

"Mrs. Allen Ludden." *Corpus Christi Caller Times.* 31 Oct. 1961.

"Mrs. J.S. McGloin, Teacher in Crossley Ward School, Dies." *Corpus Christi Times.* 21 Jul. 1938.

"NBC Radio Promotes Three in Programming." *Broadcasting Magazine.* 26 Nov. 1956.

"NDAC Army Men to be Featured at Park Sing." *Moorhead Daily News.* 4 Aug. 1948.

Newman, Jack. "Lucky Ludden Has Roots in S.A." *San Antonio Light.* 10 Apr. 1977.

"New Members Accepted for Le Cercle Francais." *Corpus Christi Times.* 15 Jul. 1936.

"New Year's Eve Show to Come From Station." *Huntingdon Daily News.* 27 Dec. 1963.

Nigh, Phyllis. "Corpus Christi Man Emcees NBC Show." *Corpus Christi Times.* 30 Apr. 1948.

Noble, Bob. "Talks of Television: CBC-TV on Mornings in Fall." *Winnepeg Free Press.* 13 Jul. 1963.

"North Fannin High School Student Wins Record Player." *Bonham Daily Favorite.* 11 Jan. 1951.

"NY BMI Clinic: Radio's Strength Cited." *Broadcasting Magazine.* 30 Jun. 1952.

O'Brian, Jack. "On the Air." *Sandusky Register Star News.* 11 Jul. 1955.

O'Dell, Carrie. *Women Pioneers in Television: Biographies of Fifteen Industry Leaders.* MacFarland and Company. Jefferson, North Carolina. 1997.

Oliver, Anna Cypra. "Assembling My Father: A Daughter's Detective Story." Houghton Mifflin Company. Boston. 2004.

Oliver, Wayne. "Betty Not Opposed to Marriage; She's Just Too Busy Working." *Independent Press Telegram.* Long Beach, CA. 19 Dec. 1954.

"On the Carousel." *Variety.* 9 Dec. 1953.

"Open House Held Tuesday." *Corpus Christi Times.* 1 Sep. 1937.

Pack, Harvey. "Allen Ludden Gets Wild Clues from Password Guests." *Mansfield News Journal.* 14 Jul. 1963.

Pack, Harvey. "Busy Pair Visit 'Odd Couple.'" *Charleston Gazette.* 1 Dec. 1972.

"Password: Cherry County Players' Adopted Cat Needs a Home." *Traverse City Record Eagle.* 24 Aug. 1976.

"The Password Family." *The Daily Review.* Hayward, CA. 4 Jun. 1967.

"Password Finds New Home." *Traverse City Record Eagle.* 1 Sep. 1976.

"Password Makes Nighttime Debut." *Biddeford Journal.* 30 Dec. 1961.

"Password's Allen Ludden Terms Himself a Marigold Freak." *Racine Journal Times.* 21 Apr. 1972.

"Password's Host Allen Ludden Dies After Battle with Cancer." *Lakeland Ledger.* 10 Jun. 1981.

"Paul Tripp to Do Education Series." *The New York Times.* 26 May 1954.

"People." *Broadcasting Magazine.* 1 Jun. 1953.

"People Sought for Show." *Lebanon Daily News.* 30 May 1973.

"People Stare." *Lima News.* 30 Jun. 1962.

"Phi Beta Kappa Key to Success." *TV Guide.* 23 Oct. 1954.

Phillips, H.I. "The Once Over." *The Morning Herald.* Hagerstown, MD. 16 Aug. 1954.

Pilato, Herbie J. "The Essential Elizabeth Montgomery: A Guide to Her Magical Performances." Taylor Trade Publishing. Toronto. 2013.

Purple Heart Austin War Stories–Frank C. Ludden *http://www.purpleheartaustin.org/ludden.htm*

"Radio Pioneers." *Bridgeport Telegram.* 9 Dec. 1954.

"Radio-TV Notes." *The New York Times.* 13 Aug. 1954.

"Rags to Riches." *Broadcasting Magazine.* 30 Apr. 1962.

Ramage, Margaret. "U.S. Youth Gets TV Man's Praise." *Corpus Christi Caller Times.* 24 Jul. 1960.

"Rat (4-Legged Kind) Wins Patsy Award." *Independent Press-Telegram.* Long Beach, CA. 12 Jun. 1973.

"A Rosy Situation." *The Pittsburgh Press.* 28 Dec. 1969.

Royal, Don. "Money Gone, Schultzy's Back at Work." *Appleton Post Crescent.* 7 Jul. 1963.

Royal, Don. "TV Sketch: Allen Ludden." *North Adams Transcript.* 28 Oct. 1961.

Russell, Fred H. "Airwave Topics." *Bridgeport Post.* 5 Nov. 1961.

Russell, Fred H. "Video to Cover Miss Teenage Pageant." *Bridgeport Post.* 3 Oct. 1962.

Sarmento, William E. "Betty White's Enthusiasm Good for Hangovers." *Lowell Sun.* 27 Dec. 1970.

Schaub, Robert C. "Bells Are Ringing Refreshing Fare at St. Louis Muni Opera." *Edwardsville Intelligencer.* 2 Aug. 1966.

Scheuer, Steven H. "Carole Mathews Is TV Dance Hall Girl." *Troy Record.* 19 Jan. 1959.

Schwartz, Cindy. "Password Host Ludden Buries." *Hutchinson News.* 12 Jun. 1981.

Scott, Vernon. "Betty White Hosts the TV Series The Pet Set." *Lowell Sun.* 6 Feb. 1971.

Scott, Vernon. "'Bouncing' Actress Betty White Gets Permanent Billing in Lengthy Series." *Lubbock Morning Avalanche.* 14 May 1957.

Scott, Vernon. "Password is Exciting New Panel Feature." *Weirton Daily Times.* 1 Apr. 1963.

Scott, Vernon. "Password Man to Have New Talk Show." *Phoenix Arizona Republic.* 6 May 1969.

Shanley, John P. "Exacting Quiz Show: College Bowl Requires Gifted Contestants." *The New York Times.* 24 Apr. 1960.

Sharp, Nancy. "Young Marrieds Travel the Road Side by Side." *Oakland Tribune.* 15 Mar. 1964.

Shull, Richard K. "Stroke of Genius Brought Show Back." *Ocala Star-Banner.* 4 Jun. 1971.

Simpson, Peggy. "Baltimore Girl is Top Teenager; Pittsburgh Entry Gets New Prize." *Corsicana Daily Sun.* 14 Nov. 1964.'

"Singer Natalie Cole Secretly Wed." *Santa Ana Orange County Register.* 11 Feb. 1977.

"Six Teen Semifinalists Ready for Big Day Today." *Lubbock Avalanche Journal.* 1 Nov. 1963.

Smith, Jerry E. "To Make Friends, Influence People." *Wichita Daily Times.* 14 Nov. 1954.

Smith, Stacy Jenel. "Allen Ludden Finds Health and New Life." *Madison Wisconsin State Journal.* 27 Jul. 1980.

"Stars Take Vacations." *The Sandusky Register.* 22 Aug. 1961.

Sullivan, Kay. "What's Bothering Our Teen-Agers?" *Salt Lake Tribune.* 22 Apr. 1951.

Sullivan, Tom. "As I See It: My View from the Inside Out." Howard Books. New York. 2012.

"Talking Straight to Your Dog is Best Method of Training." *Anniston Star.* 27 Sep. 1972.

"Television in Review: Wake Me Up." *The New York Times.* 28 Jul. 1954.

"Testing Ground." *Broadcasting Magazine.* 5 Jul. 1954.

Thomas, Bob. "Betty White's Smile Brings Big TV Role." *Long Beach Press Telegram.* 8 Feb. 1954.

Thomas, Bob. "Strychnine With a Smile." *Oakland Tribune.* 28 May 1975.

Thomas, Bob. "Work Saved Betty White." *The Capital Times.* Madison, WI. 8 Mar. 1982.

Thompson, Ruth H. "Allen Ludden and Betty White Co-Host the Patsy Awards." *Mt. Vernon Register News.* 3 May 1974.

Thompson, Ruth H. "Betty Produces Zoo Documentary for TV." *The Titusville Herald.* 21 Sep. 1974.

Thompson, Ruth H. "Betty White Again Describes Rose Parade." *Greenfield Recorder Gazette.* 26 Dec. 1964.

Thompson, Ruth H. "Password Leads Firsts." *Oil City Derrick.* 18 Mar. 1972.

Thompson, Ruth H. "Password Will Bat Against Mighty Casey." *Cumberland Evening Times.* 23 Mar. 1963.

The Tonight Show Starring Johnny Carson. Guest host McLean Stevenson. NBC-TV. 17 Mar. 1976.

The Tonight Show Starring Johnny Carson. NBC-TV. 9 Aug. 1978.

The Tonight Show Starring Johnny Carson. NBC-TV. 16 Aug. 1978.

The Tonight Show Starring Johnny Carson. NBC-TV. 22 Dec. 1978.

"TV Moderator Allen Ludden to Emcee DePauw Pageant." *Terre Haute Star.* 12 Mar. 1962.

"TV Personality Ludden, 63, State Native, Dies of Cancer." *Madison Wisconsin State Journal.* 10 Jun. 1981.

"TV Review." *Marshall Evening Chronicle.* 3 Oct. 1961.

"TV Scout Reports." *Abilene Reporter News.* 28 Jun. 1962.

"TV Shorts." *Titusville Herald.* 1 Jun. 1974.

"TV Show Host Remains Critical." *Gadsden Times.* 9 Oct. 1980.

"TV Takes Manners." *Bridgeport Telegram.* 15 Jun. 1951.

"Valley Places Two in Phi Beta Kappa." *Brownsville Herald.* 28 Mar. 1940.

Vernon, Terry. "Tele-Vues." *Long Beach Independent.* 14 May 1953.

Vespa, Mary. "Some Literary Skeptics Are Asking of Margaret Truman's New Mystery: 'Whodunit?'" *People.* Vol. 13. No. 24. 16 Jun. 1980.

Vils, Ursula. "Widowed Star Pens Book About Pets." *Los Angeles Times*. 21 Feb. 1984.

"WASTELAND! Quick, Give a Related Word." *TV Guide*. 19 May 1962.

"What You Won't See On Miss Teenage Coronation." *Colorado Springs Gazette Telegraph*. 26 Oct. 1963.

Whitbeck, Charles. "The Hollywood Scene." *Winnipeg Free Press*. 13 Mar. 1971.

White, Betty. "Game Shows Refreshing Change of Pace in Video." *The Evening News*. Sault Sainte Marie, MI. 21 Jul. 1964.

White, Betty. *Here We Go Again: My Life in Television*. Scribner. New York. 1995.

White, Betty. *If You Ask Me (And Of Course You Won't)*. G.P Putnam's Sons. New York. 2011.

Whyde, Kathy. "Betty is an Animal Activist." *The Indianapolis Star*. 4 Feb. 1983.

"Wide Knowledge of Young Scholars Amazes TV Host." *Oelwein Daily Register*. 16 Nov. 1961.

"William A. Jones House." Retrieved July 16, 2016, from *http://www.jonesmansion.com/history/william.htm*

Wilson, Earl. "Gals Say Men More Vain." *Zanesville Times Recorder*. 5 Aug. 1966.

Wilson, Marian, and Arland Meade. "Can a Consumer Quiz Show be Educational?" *The Journal of Business Education*. Dec. 1977.

Witbeck, Charles. "TV Emcee Plans Fight for Better Schools." *Greenfield Recorder-Gazette*. 20 Apr. 1963.

"W&L Retains Quiz Bowl Title." *Danville Bee*. 15 Mar. 1954.

"W-L Students Score Victory on Radio Show." *Kingsport News*. 15 Mar. 1954.

"WNBT Tops WBNS, WOI-TV and KTLA." *Billboard*. 21 Feb. 1953.

"A Would Be Professor." *The Alcalde*. Jan. 1972.

"WTIC AM." Hartford Radio History. *http://www.hartfordradiohistory.com/WTIC__AM_.php*

"WTIC Leads Attack." *Broadcasting Magazine*. 25 Jun. 1951.

"You're Great, Dad, But You're No Bud Collyer!" *TV-Radio Mirror* Magazine. June 1962.

http://www.hartfordradiohistory.com/WTIC__AM_.php

INDEX

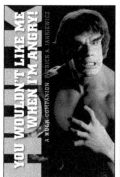
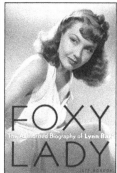

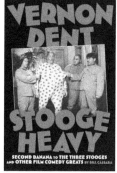